IN THE BELLY OF A LAUGHING GOD
Humour and Irony in Native Women's Poetry

In the Belly of a Laughing God

Humour and Irony in Native Women's Poetry

Jennifer Andrews

UNIVERSITY OF TORONTO PRESS
Toronto Buffalo London

© University of Toronto Press Incorporated 2011
Toronto Buffalo London
www.utppublishing.com
Printed in Canada

ISBN 978-0-8020-3567-7

Printed on acid-free, 100% post-consumer recycled paper
with vegetable-based inks.

Library and Archives Canada Cataloguing in Publication

Andrews, Jennifer Courtney Elizabeth, 1971–
In the belly of the laughing god : humour and irony in Native women's poetry
/ Jennifer Andrews.

Includes bibliographical references and index.
ISBN 978-0-8020-3567-7

1. Canadian poetry (English) – Indian authors – History and criticism.
2. American poetry – Indian authors – History and criticism.   3. Canadian
poetry (English) – Women authors – History and criticism.   4. American
poetry – Women authors – History and criticism.   5. Canadian poetry
(English) – 20th century – History and criticism.   6. American poetry –
20th century – History and criticism.   7. Humor in literature.   8. Irony in
literature.   I. Title.

PS8155.A54 2011   C811'.540917   C2011-900927-7

University of Toronto Press acknowledges the financial assistance to
its publishing program of the Canada Council for the Arts and the
Ontario Arts Council.

 Canada Council   Conseil des Arts
for the Arts   du Canada

 ONTARIO ARTS COUNCIL
CONSEIL DES ARTS DE L'ONTARIO

This book has been published with the help of a grant from the Canadian
Federation for the Humanities and Social Sciences, through the Aid to
Scholarly Publications Programme, using funds provided by the Social Sciences
and Humanities Research Council of Canada.

University of Toronto Press acknowledges the financial support for its
publishing activities of the Government of Canada through the Book
Publishing Industry Development Program (BPIDP).

For Chris, Alex, and Gillian

Contents

Acknowledgments

Writing a book is always, without a doubt, a collective endeavour. While I take full responsibility for any errors or omissions, the successes of this text are communal and warrant acknowledgment. I am grateful to the Social Sciences and Humanities Council of Canada for providing post-doctoral (1998–9) and standard research grant (2002–6) funding for this project; a Fulbright Doctoral Fellowship awarded in 1997 allowed me to begin researching the poets examined in this book. In addition, the University of New Brunswick provided monetary support and research assistance throughout this project, which was essential to ensuring its completion.

I have had a superb group of research assistants since joining the faculty at UNB, and they deserve a big round of applause for tirelessly photocopying materials, transcribing interviews, and indulging my requests: Kristel Thornell, Brecken Hancock, Erin Whitmore, and Genevieve Wesley. The support of my colleagues at UNB and elsewhere has also been invaluable; thank you to Roger Ploude, John Ball, Randall Martin, Ann Brigham, Cheryl Dueck, Linda Hutcheon, and Percy Walton, in particular.

The poets who are the focus of this book were incredibly generous, far beyond anything I ever expected. Marilyn Dumont, Diane Glancy, Louise Halfe, and Kim Blaeser deserve special thanks for their encouraging words throughout the writing process. I hope I have done their work justice. They have also given me permission to reprint family photographs and book covers without hesitation. Likewise, Nik Burton at Coteau Press enthusiastically agreed to let me reproduce the cover of Halfe's book, *Blue Marrow*, in a new way.

Many of the ideas explored in this book were first tested out at an array of conferences: MLA (1998, 2000), ACCUTE (2000), CACLALS (2003, 2005), MMLA (2003), ACLALS (2004), and the Indigenous Women and Feminism: Culture, Activism, Politics Conference (2005). Thank you to the thoughtful audiences at these conferences who offered important interventions at this formative stage. In addition, the publication of two articles, 'In the Belly of a Laughing God: Reading Humor and Irony in the Poetry of Joy Harjo' in *American Indian Quarterly* 24.2 (2000), and 'Humour and Irony, Métis Style: Reading the Poetry of Marilyn Dumont and Gregory Scofield' in *Canadian Poetry: Studies, Documents, Reviews* 50 (2002), provided another significant step towards the drafting of my manuscript; both articles have been substantially revised for inclusion here. Finally, several of the poets granted me interviews, which have subsequently been published in *American Indian Quarterly* 26.4 (2002), *Studies in Canadian Literature* 29.1 (2004), and *Studies in American Indian Literatures* 19.2 (2007). Listening to the words of these women writers has been crucial in shaping this book; I am grateful to both the poets themselves and the journal editors for their permission to draw on these published interviews.

I have been lucky enough to find a colleague and friend, Madeline Bassnett, willing to assist in the copy-editing and proofreading of this book in its early stages; her work on the manuscript has been marvelously meticulous and thoughtful. Brenna Clarke Gray was hired to assist with the final months of manuscript preparation and proved to be a superb editor, with an eagle eye and a gracious manner that kept me calm. Alison Toron was equally adept in creating a superbly detailed index in record time. Siobhan McMenemy deserves a special thank-you for pushing me towards the finish line with patience and professionalism, and I am indebted to Ryan Van Huijstee for keeping my spirits buoyant and the manuscript moving in Siobhan's absence. I was also lucky to have anonymous readers at UTP who were extremely generous with their time and provided crucial feedback during the revision process. Frances Mundy and Ken Lewis were incredibly helpful in ensuring the manuscript's seamless transition to a published book, and I am delighted that Shelley Niro granted permission to use her wonderful painting, aptly titled 'Skywoman 2,' on the cover.

Finally, I cannot express how grateful I am to my husband, Chris, for being an unwavering believer in this book, long before I ever began writing it. My children, Alex and Gillian, remind me every day of the wonders of childhood and the magic of reading literature; without the three of them, there would be no book.

IN THE BELLY OF A LAUGHING GOD
Humour and Irony in Native Women's Poetry

Introduction

Humor is widely used by Indians to deal with life. Indian gatherings are marked by laughter and jokes, many directed at the horrors of history, at the continuing impact of colonization, and at the biting knowledge that living as an exile in one's own land necessitates ... Certainly the time frame we presently inhabit has much that is shabby and tricky to offer; and much that needs to be treated with laughter and ironic humor.

> Paula Gunn Allen, 'Answering the Deer: Genocide and Continuance in the Poetry of American Indian Women'

We are in the belly of a laughing god ... I think that Indian people have one of the most developed senses of humor.

> Joy Harjo, 'A Laughter of Absolute Sanity: Interview with Angels Carabi'

As Paula Gunn Allen argues in her now famous essay on Native[1] American women's poetry, humour and irony are fundamental survival tools for many female Native writers. These two discursive strategies play important but often undervalued roles in Native North American cultures and literatures by overturning stereotypical assumptions about Native people and their tribal histories. Humour and irony are particularly effective methods of expressing the contradictions and dichotomies that shape the lives of Native populations today, as individuals and communities blend 'tribal tradition' and 'contemporary experience' (Gunn Allen 1986, 160). By combining the two, Native women writers and activists from Canada and the United States – from E. Pauline Johnson and Mourning Dove, to Joy Harjo, Kimberly Blaeser, Marilyn Dumont, and Louise Halfe – have attempted to convey both the humanity of Native peoples and the pain that they have suffered over hundreds of years due to colonization and forced assimilation and acculturation. Humour can channel anger, celebrate survival, and even unite diverse groups of readers by bringing them together through laughter. Irony, in turn, often tempers the playful elements of humour by reminding readers of the legacy of oppression that has shaped the lives of Native North Americans for centuries; it also creates space for other perspectives and voices, offering a venue for alternative articulations of selfhood and community.

Harjo's description of Native people as being 'in the belly of a laughing god' (Carabi 1996, 141) provides a vivid and powerful image from which to launch such an investigation into humour and irony. Her work, as I will suggest, offers one model for talking about Native North American women's poetry and, more specifically, their varied uses of humour and irony. The image she describes above expresses both the relief and pleasure that laughter can provide to a population that continues to fight for recognition. Yet it also represents a complex and ironic vision of post-contact Native people who have been figuratively consumed and destroyed by non-Native settlers and policy-makers, groups that have typically justified such tribal colonization with the rhetoric of Christian conversion and manifest destiny. Harjo's laughing god can be read as a reinterpretation of this legacy of colonization, a legacy that has had especially dramatic effects on Native women. Gunn Allen, for example, chronicles the impact of moving from 'gynocentric-egalitarian and ritual-based systems to phallocentric, hierarchal systems' (1986, 40); as a result, she argues that Native women have become increasingly interested in 'self-redefinition' in order to restore their former status and recognize their power both within tribal communities and in urban centres (30). The laughing god's belly may provide a much needed sanctuary for Indigenous populations from a world that has threatened their existence. The belly becomes a womb-like space of relaxation, contemplation, and even celebration where community members, like Harjo, are protected and nurtured by shared laughter. In this context, the feminine dimensions of the belly as womb and the maternalized rendering of the laughing god create a distinctly female vision of god, birth, and the power of humour, particularly when paired with irony. For it is, appropriately enough, the 'unsaid' or implied aspects of the laughing god that hold special potential for Harjo and her readers; the belly becomes a space of self-redefinition that is playful, potentially subversive, and yet also can be used to establish and reinforce normative values.

Without discounting the importance of humour and irony for Native

North Americans generally, this book narrows the field in order to attend to the interrelated specificities of race and gender as well as genre by focusing on the importance of these two discursive strategies for eight contemporary Native women poets from Canada and the United States. At the same time, I am interested in rethinking how specific political and economic borders have been used to limit definitions of Native identity, and what the women poets under consideration do to challenge such impositions. As Nira Yuval-Davis argues, 'Women ... have an ambivalent position within the collectivity' of a settler nation because 'they ... symbolize the collective unity, honour, and *raison d'être* of specific national ... projects' but 'are often excluded from the collective "we" of the body politic, and retain an object rather than a subject position' (1997, 47). In settler nations, women traditionally have fulfilled the role of passive bearers of the nation, producing and raising future generations with little or no ability to voice their own opinions; their wishes become subordinate to those of the (predominantly masculinized white) nation. Gloria Bird, however, contends in the introduction to *Reinventing the Enemy's Language: Contemporary Native Women's Writings of North America* that 'native women, in particular, who are the caregivers of the next generation, play an important role as mothers, leaders, and writers' (1997, 25); they cultivate and sustain the existence of Native nations by celebrating the use of their tribal languages and encouraging the retention of specific cultural practices and beliefs. There are numerous examples of Native women in literature who creatively reconfigure identities imposed by settler nations. In Thomas King's 'Borders,' for example, a Blackfoot woman and her son living in Alberta become caught between the Canadian/American border because the mother will not declare her citizenship in anything but tribal terms. The result is a multiple-day standoff with border guards until media attention and public pressure finally allow mother and son to take their trip to Utah, to visit an older daughter who has moved to Salt Lake City. The mother's pride and her insistence that her son recognize his distinctive heritage outside the borders of the nation-state becomes a powerful lesson in identity politics. Likewise, as Harjo argues in *Reinventing the Enemy's Language*, 'Native women in the Americas share similar concerns based on community. We also share the questions of any artist doing her work within any culture ... [Yet w]e, too, appreciate the differences between us ..., for our differences add dimension to any knowledge' (1997, 23). She also points out that Native peoples have been 'restricted by national and political boundaries that did not exist before colonization' and that remain unacknowledged by many tribal communities (26). Thus, rather than dividing the anthology on the basis of nation, she and her co-editor have strategically formulated a thematic cycle of genesis, struggle, transformation, and return to reflect the concerns of the poets under consideration.

Like Harjo,[2] I have resisted relying on national borders as the organizing principle of this text and instead have selected the following eight contemporary women poets from Canada *and* the United States as the subject of my study: Joy Harjo (Muskogee), Wendy Rose (Hopi, Miwok), Kimberly Blaeser (Anishinaabe), Jeannette Armstrong (Okanagan), Diane Glancy (Cherokee), Marie Annharte Baker (Anishinaabe), Marilyn Dumont (Métis), and Louise Halfe (Cree). That is not to say that issues of nationhood are to be ignored; rather, bringing writers from both sides of the forty-ninth parallel together raises important questions about how these poets reconfigure that political divide through their writing. The eight poets are of mixed blood. Many are affiliated with an academic institution as teachers, scholars, and/or writers-in-residence, but they also are independently responsible for their own writing careers, and several have branched out into other avenues of expression, including music and photography. The selected poets come from a variety of regions within Canada and the United States; likewise, they represent a total of eight different tribes, though over half were born and raised in urban centres and had little contact with their tribal affiliation as children. Most have travelled extensively and are highly aware of both their ties to a 'home place' and the impact of mobility on their writing. And they dialogue with writers locally, nationally, and internationally, creating communities that defy traditional borderlines as they negotiate multiple worlds.

While each poet examined in this book is distinguished by virtue of her location in and connection to a particular place or places, they all have spent much of their lives 'off the reservation.' This, Gunn Allen explains, is a loaded term in current political and military circles because it 'designates someone who doesn't conform to the limits and boundaries of officialdom, who is unpredictable and ... [thus threatens] the power structure' (1998, 6). It is this edginess and its manifestations in the poetry of these writers that is especially intriguing as these women find a way to retain their Native identities in a global society (6). Instead of simply trying to 'fit in,' the poets articulate the complexities of being mixed-blood Native North American women in contemporary society in compelling ways. Of course, humour and irony can be used to create or reinforce order; rather than presuming that these discursive strategies are always employed as methods of resistance, this study takes up Kristina

Fagan's call to view humour – and irony – in Native literature as 'moving towards both order and disorder: it at once crosses and guards borders, deconstructs and enforces categories, and incites and represses resistance' (2002, 25). Thus, I suggest that it is through the double-voiced discourse of irony and the textual surprises of humour that these women writers repeatedly challenge hegemonic renderings of themselves and their cultures, even as they enforce their own cultural norms.

My selection of poets may be perceived, particularly by literary nationalist critics (such as Jace Weaver, Craig Womack, and Robert Warrior), as a self-serving one:[3] I am a white western female academic who focuses on mixed-blood women writers, most of whom have academic affiliations and training and thus are familiar with and part of the white western institutional discourses in which I was trained. And as Kristina Fagan and Sam McKegney so eloquently point out in 'Circling the Question of Nationalism in Native Canadian Literature and Its Study,' 'We need to be ... careful about a kind of mental gate-keeping that insists that only some research goals are valid' (2008, 42). What fascinates me about the remarkably talented and prolific female poets I have chosen is their ability to articulate their complex positionings in ways that complicate and challenge white western ideas about identity, genre, history, and memory. They probe definitions of nationhood, land and homeplace, and demonstrate the creative possibilities of religious transformation as well as combining photography and text to explore representational (in)visibility for their own purposes. And while humour and irony provide a broad framework for the book, the poets' textual interests and their differing uses of these discursive strategies have fundamentally shaped the focus of each chapter. Further, in straddling the forty-ninth parallel, this book does not dismiss the importance of nationalism but uses the words of these poets and their creative work to attend to a notion of literary nationalism that questions the sanctity of the Canadian/ American border and enables specific and differing tribal contexts to shape the readings of their work, while also respecting the difficult positions of those writers who perceive themselves as potentially marginalized by tribal nationalism, such as Dumont and Rose.

In his important essay 'Splitting the Earth,' in *American Indian Literary Nationalism*, Weaver argues that literary nationalists in the field of Native North American studies do not wish to exclude non-Natives scholars from working on Native literature; they 'ask that non-Natives who study and write about Native peoples do so with respect and a sense of responsibility to Native community' (11), a responsibility that I take very seriously. Weaver goes even further:

> If one is to study and write about Native Americans and their literatures, one must be prepared to listen to and respect Native voices and, in keeping with the traditional Native ethic of reciprocity, not take without giving something back. (12)

In this book, I endeavour to let the voices of these women writers take centre stage and to treat their wonderful bodies of work with integrity and respect, creating a dialogic relationship that in many cases emerged as a result of contacting the poets to see if they would be willing to be interviewed about their work; I draw extensively not only on the interviews I conducted and the readings and papers I have heard these women deliver first-hand, but also on the informal conversations and immensely generous exchanges that have continued since I began this project in 1998. These women poets deserve much more critical attention than they have received, and this is one step, hopefully of many, meant to address this neglect.

Defining Native Humour and Irony

In a recent collection of essays on Native humour aptly titled *Me Funny*, compiled and edited by Drew Hayden Taylor, and including diverse contributions from Native scholars, creative writers, and even comedians, Cherokee writer Thomas King describes the growth of this area of inquiry in a particularly witty fashion:

> In the last five years or so, Native humour has become a minor subject of discussion – not so much on reserves or in urban centres, mind you, but within the academy, where the creation and explication of such subjects is encouraged and where it can lead to publications and promotions ... And in this regard, two things have happened. One, we've decided that Native humour exists, and two, we've come up with a general definition. Or description. Or good guess. (2005, 169–70)

King willingly takes on the task of describing humour, focusing primarily on how humour ensures survival and cultivates community. But when pressed to provide a definition, he is much less enthusiastic, stating, 'While I'm certainly a member in good standing in the academy, I'm not sure that a valid definition of Native humour exists' (171). He notes, too, that if such a definition rests 'and change[s] with performance,' then to try to fix a singular definition is to violate its flexibility and usefulness (171). King prudently sidesteps a difficult set of questions,[4] foregrounding the impossibility of fully articulating the multiplicity of Native humour.

His discussion of how to define (or not define) Native humour provides a helpful road map, and King's refusal to embrace any one approach to Native humour is a constant and necessary corrective to my urge to try to articulate what it is and how it works.

King's comments on humour signal the need to attend to the importance of both speech and silence in Native cultures. As Cheryl Glenn explains in *Unspoken: A Rhetoric of Silence*, 'the common perception of silent Indians permeates popular as well as scholarly work,' yet the source of this stereotype is directly connected to Euro-American colonialism; with the introduction of 'English-only policies coupled with other anti-Indian government policies,' Native populations were directly silenced 'in both their indigenous languages as well as English' (2004, 113). Jeannette Armstrong elaborates on this struggle in her poem 'Threads of Old Memory,' in which her first-person narrator employs memory as a tool for refashioning history, turning to 'the origination place / a pure place / silent / wordless / from where thoughts I choose / silently transform into words / I speak and / powerfully becomes actions' (1991, 59). Armstrong gives equal weight to speech and silence; she also stresses the need to understand both as important forms of action. Her poem expresses what Molly McGlennen, drawing on Glenn, argues is critical for comprehending the value of silence: the need to recognize that silence is not only 'a form of respect, but more pressingly is a strategy for learning. It is also the component that balances talking, thus essential to the rhetoric of expression' (2006, 13). In other words, 'it reminds one to speak mindfully' (13). And poetry, by its very nature, emphasizes the value of words and 'has built into it the space for silence' (13). Thus part of my task is to listen closely and carefully and to attend to the individual and differing uses of humour and irony, by drawing not only on texts themselves but also acknowledging the variety of contexts, both Native and non-Native, that are part of my readings of these works. Moreover, I have strived to listen to the words – and silences – of the poets themselves.

Humour is not simple – nor is irony – and to treat either as such would be to miss the point of this book. Humour has been given short shrift in favour of irony precisely because, as Linda Hutcheon puts it, 'the language of irony has seemed a somewhat more appropriately "serious" object of academic study' (1994, 26). In order to situate the readings in the chapters that follow, this introduction explores theories of humour and irony by combining the work of recent Native and non-Native academics with the perspectives of the women poets who are the focus of this study. My aim is to provide workable definitions that create a space for reading a wide array of poems, and yet still respect the complexities of both discursive strategies, whether used individually or in conjunction with one another.

While King notes the growth of Native humour as 'a minor subject of discussion' (2005, 169) over the past five years, marked by the publication of the provocatively titled collection *Me Funny* (2005), edited by Drew Hayden Taylor, and Eva Gruber's thoughtful survey of Native humour of all genres on both sides of the border, *Humor in Contemporary Native North American Literature: Reimaging Nativeness* (2008), Native humour has traditionally been dismissed or ignored altogether. According to Native-American scholar and activist Vine Deloria, the cultivation and perpetuation of 'the image of the granite-faced grunting red-skin' dehumanizes tribal populations and ensures a lack of sympathy from outsiders (1969, 146). The recent studies of everyday tribal interactions (such as Keith Basso's *Portraits of 'The Whiteman': Cultural Play and Linguistic Symbols among the Western Apache*), and the written literature produced by Native populations on both sides of the border, prove that the 'grunting red-skin' is a mere stereotype and that Native humour is, as always, alive and well. Deloria, a Standing Rock Sioux, expresses the fundamental significance of a comic perspective to Native life:

> I sometimes wonder how anything is accomplished by Indians because of the apparent overemphasis on humour within the Indian world. Indians have found a humorous side of nearly every problem and the experiences of life have generally been so well defined through jokes and stories that they have become a thing in themselves. (1969, 146–7)

Gerald Vizenor, who is a member of the White Earth Anishinaabe, accords with and extends Deloria's perspective on the subject by critiquing social scientists for having ignored the prevalence of humour, which, he argues, is part of Native peoples' daily lives and integral to their sense of community:

> You can't act in a comic way in isolation. You have to be included. There has to be a collective of some kind. Sometimes things just *happen* and when they happen, even though they may be dangerous or even life-threatening, there is some humor ... And it's a positive, compassionate act of survival, it's getting along ... Tribal cultures are [fundamentally] *comic*. Yet they have been interpreted as tragic by social scientists; tribal cultures have been viewed as

tragic cultures. Not tragic because they are 'vanishing' or something like that, but tragic in their worldview – and they're *not* tragic in their worldview. (1987, 295)[5]

As both Deloria and Vizenor suggest, humour, and the laughter it evokes, takes on a life of its own in a Native North American context by bringing communities together, facilitating conflict resolution, and establishing shared bonds between otherwise divided groups.

This comic perspective is especially helpful to Native North Americans given the legacy of colonization and racial destruction that has shaped the history of various tribes over the past several centuries. However, Native humour, which as various Native scholars point out, predates colonization, has also been a crucial tool for ensuring internal reconciliation and self-regulation among communities. Deloria explains that 'for centuries before the white invasion, teasing was a method of control of social situations by Native people. Rather than embarrassing members of the tribe publicly, people used to tease individuals they considered out of step with ... tribal opinion' (1969, 147). In doing so, 'egos were preserved and disputes ... were held to a minimum' (147). Not surprisingly, then, self-deprecating humour became a significant part of Native cultures, as people began to strategically mock themselves in order to show 'humility ... and advocate a course of action they believed in' (147). Hence, post-colonization, the ability to joke about oneself, and especially about 'living as an exile in one's own land,' also provides Native populations with an opportunity to reconfigure their status as 'other' in relation to the white western settlers who came and claimed the New World for themselves (Gunn Allen 1986, 158). Kenneth Lincoln argues that the humour that infuses contemporary Native life can effectively bridge the gap between Natives and non-Natives without ignoring the past: 'Indi'n humor is a way of recalling and going beyond tragedy, of working through the hurt of personal history, of healing old wounds and hearing the truth of what's happening among Native Americans. It is the most vocal and effective voice among Indians today' (1993, 116).

Though Thomas King may hesitate to define Native humour, those who have recently written about it offer a laundry list of characteristics, centred on the notions of contradiction and incongruity: 'frequent teasing, outrageous punning, constant wordplay, surprising association, extreme subtlety, layered and serious reference, and considerable compassion' (Ryan 1999, xii). In particular, Barbara Babcock argues in her study of symbolic inversion among Pueblo clowns that such reversals cannot be dismissed as or reduced to merely an outlet for inappropriate behaviour; rather, the ambiguity that results from symbolic inversion is intended not only to spark creativity, but to 'prompt speculation about, reflection on, and reconsideration of the order of things' (1984, 122). Here, the perception of incongruity may lead to new ways of thinking about society. Whether to curb deviance and reinforce normalcy or to challenge the solidity of existing structures, 'humour plays with, negotiates, and exaggerates reality' for a variety of purposes (Fagan 2002, 11). And according to some contemporary Native studies scholars, Native humour shares similar traits to the '*Galegenhumor*' described by Sigmund Freud in *Jokes and Their Relation to the Unconscious* precisely because, as in the Jewish persecution, Native peoples have had to cope with an ongoing history of genocide and often do so with a comic touch (1905, 229). As Deloria explains in his groundbreaking essay 'Indian Humor,' published as part of his *Indian Manifesto* ironically titled *Custer Died for Your Sins*, 'The more desperate the problem, the more humor is directed to describe it ... Often people are awakened and brought to a militant edge through funny remarks' (1969, 147). Laughter, in other words, 'leads to community survival,' providing a means of coping in 'the face of danger or tragedy' (Fagan 2005, 25, 26). But Fagan, herself a member of the Labrador Métis Nation, is rightly cautious about treating humour exclusively as a survival technique, stressing that it is not focused solely on challenging non-Native dominance, but is intended to show the complexities of Native people and their communities.

Until relatively recently, the marginalization of scholarly work on Native humour was paralleled by the paucity of work on women's humour – and women's use of irony – more generally. With the exception of Gunn Allen, who specifically explores the relevance of both discursive strategies for Native-American women poets, the significance of gender in the context of Native humour and irony is virtually unexamined. Yet, as Nancy Walker explains in her groundbreaking books *A Very Serious Thing: Women's Humor and American Culture* (1988) and *Feminist Alternatives: Irony and Fantasy in the Contemporary Novel by Women* (1990), these devices have provided women generally with the opportunity both to express subversive and potentially revolutionary ideas within an apparently complicit and often lighthearted context and to reinforce the norms of their own communities. And while Walker notes the similarities between women's humour and irony in her respective texts, she is careful not to equate them, instead noting the ironic dimensions of humour and the potentially humorous aspects of irony in their paired reliance on incongruity. Her definitions of each discursive strategy are especially helpful; irony, she explains in *Feminist Alternatives*, 'is a way of negating the truth or validity of a received tradition and pointing to its incongruity or absurdity' (1990, 22). By emphasizing irony's ambivalence and its potential for use by both dominant and oppressed groups, Walker makes plain the risks involved for those who incorporate it into their texts: 'the fact that irony challenges our notions of reality means that it may be misunderstood' or missed altogether (28). Nonetheless, irony is appealing to those who, like the women poets in this study, want to explore the benefits and pitfalls of writing from the perspective of a Native female in the colonizer's language of English, even if it is their 'mother' tongue.

In *A Very Serious Thing*, Walker outlines the communal aspects of humour, stating that 'it is a means of both establishing and testing the boundaries between groups of people' (1988, 114). She makes clear distinctions between the use of humour by ethnic and racial minority groups and white women, focusing in particular on the comic strategies of black American women – and the legacy of American slavery. African-American women, as she explains, are doubly marginalized by virtue of race and gender. Although Walker does not touch on this, the writings of Native women on both sides of the forty-ninth parallel can be seen similarly. Drawing on anthropologist Mahadev Apte's cross-cultural work in *Humor and Laughter*, Walker discusses the conditions that 'appear to provide women with the freedom for humor: advanced age, which removes some of the pressure to behave as a "lady"... and situations in which women are segregated from men,' and thus can be 'more aggressive and ribald than ... in mixed company' (126–7). Both of these criteria are relevant to Native women writers. For instance, Marilyn Dumont explains that she learned how to use humour, irony, and sarcasm from her mother, who was from a generation of females that 'had to find other ways of being able to say something without alienating themselves,' but also belonged to a Native community in which humour between the sexes was commonplace:

> It must be a cultural thing too, because I notice that when I'm with a Native crowd the women are quite often making fun of the men. It's something that's kind of admired – a woman who can undercut something that's been said ... I think it's cultural, the joking, the kind of competition between men and women about who can be the wittiest and undercut the other ones. As I say my mom was very good at it. (Andrews 2004b, 155)

Likewise, Kimberly Blaeser describes how 'the whole process of everyday life was this lively oral exchange' within her tight-knit family and local community, which led to her acquisition of a raft of discursive strategies that she employs in her writing to this day (Andrews 2007, 3). What becomes clear is that humour and irony are pervasive in Native communities, among both men and women, in ways that inflect gender stereotypes differently. Native women's humour and irony is perhaps absent from analyses like those of Walker precisely because, although there are similarities with other ethnic and racial minorities (such as African Americans), there are also differences that predate the arrival of settlers to the New World.

Humour is indeed a useful strategy for the contemporary women poets examined in this book, because it acknowledges the complex status of individuals who may or may not identify themselves with a multiplicity of different Native and non-Native communities. Similarly, irony enables the recognition of incongruities that may otherwise go unidentified, yet are fundamental for these women writers in order to articulate the voices and visions of their speakers in a wide array of contexts. As Helen Hoy notes, however, there are always problems in 'organizing a book around the racial identity' and gender of those writers being studied. She cites M. Nourbese Philip's notion of 'cultural apartheid' and Claire Harris's description of such approaches as 'marginalization by literary category' to highlight the difficulties of such an analysis (2001, 20); both concerns are equally valid here. Hoy explains that one runs the risk 'of creating simple Native/non-Native binaries, of using race as explanatory, of reducing these texts to cultural documents ... [especially by] those at greater distance from Native life' (20). Yet to shy away from such a discussion would be a great disservice to the eight women poets studied here, whose work explores and reflects on the intricacies of Native identities in a manner that challenges standard representations of 'authenticity' in seeking their own grounds for self-definition (21).

Hoy describes the challenges posed by gender in the context of Native writing: '... feminist mobilization around the category "woman" has not always coincided with the priorities of Native women, for whom national/tribal sovereignty can be more pressing than gender politics' (21). While some Native female writers 'identify themselves in feminist terms, ... others do not' (21). Canadian political scientist Joyce Green, who is of English, Ktunaxa, and Cree-Scots Métis descent, elaborates on this seeming contradiction in the introduction to her edited collection, *Making Space for Indigenous Feminism*:

Over the years that I've been studying Indian women's political organizing, I noticed that Aboriginal women who organized on apparently feminist issues rarely identified as feminist. Yet, I knew Aboriginal women who had dedicated a large part of their lives to political activism who deployed an explicit or implicit feminist analysis. These women sought to claim rights for Aboriginal women. (2007, 14)

As Green explains, while Native women writers, scholars, and activists may not always overtly embrace the term 'feminism' in their work, they have often served as 'catalysts for some very powerful and interesting movements and for original and insightful academic work' which has a 'valid political stance' though it may not readily conform to standard (meaning white western) definitions of feminist thought and praxis (14). Such an approach is necessary when Native women face sex and race oppression within a colonial framework, as is the reality in both Canada and the United States. Of course, the differing legal status of Native women on both sides of the border makes such analyses even more vexed; in Canada, for instance, the dominance of the Indian Act from 1876 to 1985 removed Indian status from Native women who married non-status men, while giving status to the 'non-Indian wives of Indian men' (21).[6] Green's diverse collection of essays and interviews highlights the individual and complex nature of defining and understanding what feminism can mean for Native women, particularly in Canada, by probing the impact of the Indian Act on Native Canadian women's lives, the eventual success of Native women's groups in overturning the Act's discriminatory treatment of Native females who married non-status men, and the continued efforts of these same women to resist colonization and oppression at all levels of community. Further, as we shall see in the case of Wendy Rose, tribal regulations about matrilineal heritage (the Hopi, for instance, grant tribal status based solely on the mother's bloodline) suggest that government legal measures, often imposed on all tribes living in a particular nation-state, are not the only means of excluding women from their communities; tribes themselves may also institute potentially discriminatory policies.

'Woman' and 'gender' are categories that are fundamentally in dispute. Several of the writers discussed here turn to what Hoy calls 'historic matrifocal definitions of women's roles and responsibility' (22–3). Rose, for instance, identifies herself as a 'feminist' but notes that 'for me, that's a political construct' derived from the historical colonization of Native peoples (Hunter 1983, 80). As she explains, 'I am an Indian feminist and that gives me a different perspective from white feminists' (80). And, of course, the roles and responsibilities of women have varied from tribe to tribe throughout history. Moreover, the outright rejection of, or resistance to, feminism by Aboriginal women because it can minimize and even erase important 'social, economic, and political differences between vastly differently positioned women' is a logical political position (St Denis 2007, 33). As Métis education professor Verna St Denis explains, 'I could not and would not prioritize gender inequality over the political and economic marginalization of Aboriginal peoples' (33). Thus, readers need to keep an open mind and remember that affirmations of difference may be understood as being as radical as those who challenge 'gender roles ... [in] some white feminist contexts' (Hoy 2001, 23). The incongruous discursive strategies of humour and irony complement the fundamental destabilizations of definitions of race and gender, creating a space of mutual exploration, interrogation, and reflection on what alterna(rra)tives[7] may exist.

The term 'alterna(rra)tives' is designed to create a strong visual pun and to convey the interaction of the 'said' and the 'unsaid' that creates irony (Hutcheon 1994, 12). It is inspired by the title of Drew Hayden Taylor's play *alterNatives*, in which a mid-thirties Toronto-based female Jewish professor of Native literature, Colleen Birk, and her lover, a younger Native writer, aptly named Angel Wallace, host an intimate dinner party for a group of Colleen's white vegetarian friends and a Native couple from Angel's past with unexpected consequences (2000, 8). Taylor himself is a well-known playwright, essayist, newspaper columnist, stand-up comedian, television scriptwriter, and documentary filmmaker, as well as the editor of and a contributor to *Me Funny*. In this play, Taylor draws on his own experiences as a blue-eyed, fair-skinned Ojibway writer, who is often mistakenly identified as white, to probe and subvert pervasive stereotypes about Native peoples.

In *alterNatives*, Taylor takes aim at white presumptions of intellectual supremacy and the colonial temptation to instruct racial minorities about how to achieve 'a better life,' as well as critiquing the links between class and race prejudice and the struggle Native peoples face to define themselves and understand their own differences, even between members of the same reserve community. For instance, Colleen attempts to 'educate' Angel by insisting that he read either 'quaint legend[s] or ... yet another adventure in an oppressed, depressed and suppressed Native village,' a task that Angel resists, explaining, 'If I'm told that I'm oppressed one more time, I'll end up a drunk' (37), a comment that turns blame for a long history of Native alcoholism squarely back where it belongs: at the feet of white colonists who treated Native peoples and their cultures as lesser in order to gain lands, labour, and natural resources for themselves. Likewise, Colleen solicits her white male vegetarian friend, Dale, to help cook the moose she has procured for dinner. This task results in Dale breaking from the strict adherence to vegetarianism imposed by his well-meaning wife, Michelle, a discovery which forms the climax of the play and causes a fellow cook to burn his hand in the roasting pan. Having drunk far too much, Michelle soon reveals her own race and class prejudices, opening the door to a series of uncomfortably personal revelations about each of the character's past lives and future aspirations, which often defy the expectations of their partners and fellow guests. In particular, Angel confesses his desire to write science fiction, in direct opposition with Colleen's assertion that he 'could create the great Canadian aboriginal novel,' a wish that would bolster her legitimacy as a Native scholar and ensure that he was 'taken seriously by the literary establishment' (102). In a moment of intertextual play, Colleen cites the work of Thomas King as exemplary of what Angel could become, forgetting that King has actually written several short stories that parody the science fiction genre from a distinctly Native perspective (including 'How Corporal Colin Sterling Saved Blossom, Alberta, and Most of the Rest of the World as Well' and 'Where the Borg Are').

The evening ends with the dinner party dissolving into harsh words and the revelation that Colleen's early academic efforts as part of an anthropology team to gather authentic Native 'legends' were thwarted by Angel and another Native dinner guest who as children made up 'fantastic stories' to tell the anthropologists in an effort to protect their traditions (2000, 129). The result is a book that Angel uncomfortably notes is in its seventh printing and being taught at universities, despite its grave inaccuracies; as Angel explains to his old reserve 'Buddy': 'I don't want to be an alterNative Warrior anymore ... Too many people get hurt' (131). In the case of Taylor's play, the alter-Natives or other Natives must find their own alter-narratives, stories that they tell on their own terms, and in the case of Angel, in conjunction with or perhaps even despite his links to the world of academia. In adapting and reconfiguring Taylor's title, the term 'alterna(rra)tives' is employed here to convey the complexity of humour and irony in the work of the women who form the centre of this book and to probe the multiplicity of their stories.

Native North American Humour and Irony:
Acknowledging the Edge

Describing the interrelatedness of humour and irony is a difficult task, particularly because 'not all ironies are amusing' and some humorous texts lack an ironic edge (Hutcheon 1994, 26). But these two discursive strategies share many characteristics and often produce similar responses from audiences and readers. In *Irony's Edge: The Theory and Politics of Irony*, Linda Hutcheon points out that 'both [humour and irony] involve complex power relations and both depend upon social and situational context for their very coming into being' (26). Many descriptions of humour, in fact, closely parallel discussions of the forms and functions of irony. Perceiving incongruities, expressing feelings of superiority over another person, and experiencing a sense of relief and triumph as a result of this perception are all characteristics that have been used to define humour *and* irony. The similarities between the 'affective' and 'formal' dimensions of humour and irony have resulted in an occasional conflation of the two terms (26). The mocking aspects of irony, when used within a humorous text or situation, can temper or even undercut what is usually perceived as funny. Conversely, irony may remind readers of the ridiculousness of a situation or stereotype that might otherwise be entirely devoid of humour.

Both humour and irony rely on and reinforce already existing 'discursive communities' (91); without a community there is no context for the interpretation and reception of humour and irony. Rather than being static entities, these communities are flexible and constantly changing formations that reflect the multiple and shifting relationships individuals and groups have with each other. Moreover, humour and irony involve a process of interpretation. But because of the 'dynamic and plural relations among the text or utterance,' its author, its audience, and the larger context of reception, neither discursive process can guarantee a single definitive response (11). My own readings of how humour and irony operate in the chapters that follow are influenced by my position – a white female middle-class academic who has studied Native literature on both sides of the forty-ninth parallel – and offered here as one approach to the works of these eight poets, intended to garner attention for and provoke further discussion about these talented women and their works.

Traditionally, humour and irony have 'reinforce[d] rather than question[ed] established attitudes' and ensured that communities function in a cohesive and orderly manner (Hutcheon 1994, 10). The power to establish and reinforce the primacy of a particular perspective through humour and irony typically rests with white, middle- to upper-class heterosexual males whose race, class, sexual orientation, and gender are constructed as normative. However, both discursive strategies may be used to challenge dominant paradigms (and reinforce new paradigms) by juxtaposing conflicting elements or perspectives within a text. Humour and irony – either separately or together – can enable otherwise marginalized groups to destabilize traditionally uncontested voices. Racial and ethnic minorities (such as Native North Americans), lesbians, gays, and women from a wide range of class affiliations continue to create their own oppositional versions of these two discursive strategies. But those who employ humour and irony to articulate their typically neglected viewpoints risk being ignored, dismissed, or misunderstood; audience members and readers may miss the ironic and humorous dimensions of a text altogether.

The fragmentation and plurality of responses that these strategies invite can also pose challenges to segments of the population that are still struggling – as Native North Americans are – to claim a 'firm and stable subject position in the political arena' (Hutcheon 1994, 31). Negotiating an individual or group identity through humour and irony in a society that has ignored and degraded certain segments of the population on the basis of race, sexual orientation, gender, or class is a tricky business fraught with its own set of challenges. To presume that humour and irony are exclusively oppositional tactics when taken up by marginalized populations, such as Native peoples, would be naive indeed. Fagan reminds us of this when she states that 'humour offers a way to deal with change, chaos, and complexity, while maintaining a sense of continuity and identity' (2002, 16). And Gunn Allen goes even further, insisting that 'the interesting thing about the use of humor in American Indian poetry is its integrating effect: It makes tolerable what is otherwise unthinkable ... [and] allows a ... breathing space in which an entire race can take stock of itself and its future' (1986, 159). By providing a place for reconciliation, bonding, and celebration, the 'ironic humor' of the Native women poets Gunn Allen studies becomes the basis for reinforcing community structures and values, especially when faced with the 'stark facts of racial destruction' (158, 159).

One way to discuss humour and irony without collapsing the two terms is to conceive of irony as a miniature semantic version of the textual incongruities that shape a humorous poem. While irony and humour share structural characteristics, in the case of irony these overt and implied meanings can and do typically emerge at the level of language, particularly through puns and the relationship between the denotative and connotative meanings of words, where the latter usually develops from and depends on the context of community use. Humour mirrors this on a

larger scale. As Kenneth Lincoln explains, by way of Arthur Koestler's
theory of 'bisociation,' humour happens when mutually incompatible
codes or perspectives are put together and 'the incongruous parts edge
each other' (Koestler 1964, 35–6). Coined by Koestler, the term 'bisociation' calls attention to 'the creative act, which ... always operates on more
than one plane' (35–6). For Koestler, humour is a prime example of this
movement beyond 'the routine skills of thinking on a single plane' (35).
He claims bisociation involves *'the perceiving of a situation or idea, L, in two
self-consistent but habitually incompatible frames of reference, M_1 and M_2'* (35).
To make sense of these 'incompatible matrices' which have been placed
side by side, readers usually create palimpsests to help them grasp and respond to otherwise baffling juxtapositions (59). Similarly, Hutcheon contends that irony involves a rubbing together of the said and the unsaid,
a process that leads to the creation of a third meaning and gives irony its
edge. Both are 'relational,' operating between people and meanings, and
involving the recognition of a relation of difference; through this process,
irony and humour build and reinforce an array of community structures
and social systems through the creation of a shared set of contexts even
as they make space for alterna(rra)tives. When paired together, humour
and irony layer texts with linguistic and situational incongruities that encourage readers to negotiate multiple, often conflicting perspectives and
lead to both recognition and reconsideration.

Writers and scholars in the field of Native North American humour
have repeatedly emphasized that Indian humour has an ironic 'bite' or
edge (Lincoln 1993, 26; Hutcheon 1994, 26). In *The Trickster Shift: Humour and Irony in Contemporary Native Art*, Allan Ryan notes that the works
he examines are characterized by 'serious play,' which is intended to
shift a viewer's perspective by 'imagining and imaging alternate viewpoints' that are not always comfortable or easy to accept (1999, 5). Moreover, Kristina Fagan, in her study of humour and community-building,
contends that 'there is always an edge to community, an edge that lies
between inclusion and exclusion, identification and alienation, power
and victimhood, harmony and conflict' (2005, 43); humour, 'with its basis in incongruity,' thus becomes a tool to 'face, examine, and play with
this edge' (44, 43): an edge, I would argue, that is ironically charged.
The playful joking and self-deprecating teasing that are an integral part
of most Native North American communities come out of a legacy of destruction and poverty that cannot be ignored. In Laura Coltelli's *Winged
Words*, Gunn Allen outlines the significance of humour's bite when
she talks about the transformational nature of much Native-American

humour: 'So there's this tradition of ... funniness, and then there's this history of death. And when the two combine, you get a power in the work ... It creates a metamorphosis in the reader, if the reader can understand what is being said and what's not being said' (1990, 22). Gunn Allen's description suggests that Native humour, at least as she defines it, couples the use of playful incongruities and the power of irony to reinforce or subvert norms to explore the tribal histories and conditions that Native North Americans continue to face, depict, and revise. According to Gunn Allen, part of the process of interpretation and participation in the reading of such texts is an active consideration of the relationship between the said and the unsaid that encourages those engaged with the work to recognize and negotiate often startling or uncomfortable juxtapositions of cultural paradigms or belief systems.

Theory to Text and Back Again: The Poets in Question

In selecting the women poets for this study, I have tried to provide an eclectic cross-section of writers at various stages in their careers and included individuals who, despite their prolific output, remain virtually unacknowledged in the field of Native North American poetry. Notably, there are no single-author studies published on any of the poets included in this book, a reflection of the relative marginalization of these women despite their talent, innovation, and the sheer volume of their work. These women are joined together by their shared interest in religious and generic transformation; language and identity; history and memory; land, space, and home-place; and intertextuality. All employ humour and irony – to varying degrees – in their poetry to explore this collocation of themes; these two discursive strategies are conduits for examining issues central to their lives and identities. While each poet may use these discursive strategies somewhat differently, their texts often dialogue with one another, creating an inter- and intratextual web of relations that reflects their mutual concerns and commitment to poetry as a vehicle for reflection and change. Moreover, these writers cultivate vital connections between their life histories and the writing of poetry from their diverse perspectives as Native women.

Janice Gould illuminates the significance of these links in *Speak to Me Words*:

Writing ... must have an end, a meaning. I would say that for many Indian poets that end is to reclaim and rebuild the identities that the Euro-Ameri-

cans wanted to annihilate ... Poetry often serves to tell us about the places
we've been as a people or about the places we wish to be. What we admire
about it, ... [and] about the poets who make it, are the ways poetry may
succinctly distill and render human experience into language. (Rader and
Gould 2003, 11)

For Gould, the ability of these writers to convey the particularities of their
lives through poetry becomes a source of inspiration and motivation for
Native and non-Native readers alike to reflect on the challenges of what
it means to be a Native woman. Paula Gunn Allen extends this assertion
by arguing in 'Answering the Deer' that American Indian women who
write poetry draw on the ancient bardic tradition by primarily employing the themes of love and death, 'themes' that 'encompass the whole
of human experience' (1986, 143); she contends that 'like the bards we
are tribal singers' who draw on humour and irony to make 'tolerable
what is otherwise unthinkable' (143, 147), creating life stories that resist
extinction by emphasizing resilience and fortitude against all odds. And
the gendered nature of this perspective is one that is readily embraced
by the poets examined in this study, as exemplified by the poem that concludes the groundbreaking anthology of Native North American wom-
en's poetry, *Reinventing the Enemy's Language*, titled 'Perhaps the World
Ends Here,' by Joy Harjo.

   The poem, which is the final piece in Harjo's *The Woman Who Fell from
the Sky* (1994), playfully locates the beginning of the world at 'a kitchen
table' on the basis of necessity, with the narrator pragmatically explaining, 'No matter what, we must eat to live' (68). It is this domestic scene,
shaped by the presence of Native women, that frames the lives that unfold – from birth to death, over and over again:

   The gifts of earth are bought and prepared, set on the table. So it has been
   since creation, and it will go on.

   We chase chickens or dogs away from it. Babies teethe at the corners. They
   scrape their knees under it.

   It is here that children are given instructions on what it means to be human.
   We make men at it, we make women.

   ... Wars have begun and ended at this table. It is a place to hide in the
   shadow of terror. A place to celebrate the terrible victory.

We have given birth on this table, and prepared our parents for burial here.

At this table we sing with joy, with sorrow. We pray of suffering and remorse. We give thanks.

Perhaps the world will end at the kitchen table, while we are laughing and crying, eating of the last sweet bite. (68)

Throughout Harjo's poem, the daily life of raising families, working, warring, celebrating, praying, singing, laughing, crying, and writing are given centre stage, offering a strategic reconfiguration of the world and its presumed centres of power by acknowledging the individual experiences of Native women who shape the world fundamentally by virtue of their otherwise invisible gestures, roles, and routines.

Harjo couples humour and irony from the outset of the poem with her speculative title, 'Perhaps the World Ends Here,' which hints at the grandiose nature of the world's collapse while framing it in highly provisional terms with the word 'Perhaps'; it is this 'Perhaps' that also alludes to the pragmatism of the poem itself, which locates the world at the kitchen table and bases its significance on the need to eat to survive. Whatever romantic illusions readers might have of the world's demise are undercut by the domestic scenes that follow, which depict the lives of the narrator and her community of family and friends, through nursing and teething, cooking and teaching, gossiping and dreaming, as the table becomes a site of shelter, conversation, and education. The profane and the sacred are combined to offer a valuable and compelling alterna(rra)tive for Native women and readers of the poem whose lives are shaped by these domestic moments, both individually and communally. Appropriately, even the end of the poem blends humour with irony, as the final lines return once again to the title but with a marked difference. 'Perhaps the World Ends Here' has become 'perhaps the world will end at the kitchen table,' bringing the poem itself full circle from its first line in which 'the world begins at the kitchen table' (68). The final moments of the world are thus no longer filled with grandiose promises or elaborate visions of destruction but instead the quiet reality of a life well lived and filled with the sustenance of human experience – the 'laughing and crying' that is part of that 'last sweet bite' (68). Harjo's poem is thus emblematic of this broader link between life history, poetry, and gender central to all of the women explored in this study.

Harjo (b. 1951) is perhaps the best known of the group I have selected, having published nine volumes of poetry between 1975 and 2002, produced several CDs, co-edited the landmark anthology *Reinventing the Enemy's Language,* and written a children's book. Her last three collections of poetry have been published by W.W. Norton, a large and prestigious house, and she is the recipient of numerous awards for her work, including several lifetime achievement awards and grants from the National Endowment for the Humanities. An English professor at UCLA who now lives in Hawai'i, Harjo remains an outspoken political activist, reader, and musician, who toured the country with her last band, Poetic Justice, and is now cultivating an independent singing career, a step that she sees as a natural extension of her poetry. Harjo has garnered the attention of literary scholars for over a decade, and her work has formed the subject of numerous critical articles; as well, a collection of interviews with Harjo, edited by Laura Coltelli, has been published as *The Spiral of Memory.*

Most of the other poets selected are contemporaries of Harjo, born post-World War II, who also have witnessed massive changes in the treatment and representation of Native peoples in North America. Their poetry becomes a vivid record of this period of transition and redefinition. For instance, Wendy Rose (b. 1948) is the daughter of a mother of Miwok/European descent and a Hopi father, but she had virtually no contact with either tribe until she was eleven. She began writing poetry and painting in the late 1960s while living in San Francisco. Rose later completed a PhD in anthropology at the University of California at Berkeley, and has explored the contradictions of her education and tribal affiliations extensively in her work. She has published fifteen volumes of poetry and several key scholarly essays on Native-American writing, including her now famous critiques of 'white shamanism.' Rose has continued to paint and draw, often illustrating her collections. And as the head of the American Indian Studies program at Fresno City College, Rose has used her position and her creative writing to rethink curricular distinctions between anthropology and literature. Rose's lack of recognition within the Hopi tribe (due to the absence of matrilineal blood ties), her mixed-blood status, and her anthropological training have led her to be critical of western versions of memory and history in her poetry; in particular, Rose argues that the 'halfbreed condition,' as she calls it, is not merely an issue of genetics but rather 'a condition of history, of society,' that transcends individual marginality (Hunter 1983, 86).

Rose's interest in history and memory is echoed and reconfigured in the work of Kimberly Blaeser (b. 1955), an enrolled member of the Minnesota Anishinaabe tribe who was born and raised on the White Earth Reservation in the northwestern part of the state. Though also of mixed blood – of Anishinaabe and German descent – Blaeser grew up in a much more rural and primarily Native community, one to which she is still strongly connected and writes about extensively. Blaeser emphasizes in her poetry the importance of storytelling and memory in her upbringing, noting that as children she and her siblings 'were given the sense of being responsible for ourselves ... They [my parents] did it by telling us stories. We may never have met the people in some of the stories, but they're part of our family history' (Vannote 1999, 5). The need to hold onto and rewrite those narratives – and to cultivate a creative relationship to her past, present, and future – is central to Blaeser's poetry as well as her scholarly writings. But Blaeser, like Rose and Harjo, does not see her work limited merely to written texts; she also incorporates family photographs in her first volume of poetry and has experimented with singing some of her poetry in performance. A full professor at the University of Wisconsin at Milwaukee who has published an academic study of fellow White Earth writer Gerald Vizenor, three volumes of poetry, numerous scholarly articles, and (as editor) an Anishinaabe short story collection, Blaeser talks quite openly about her struggle to negotiate multiple – and often conflicting – world views: '... my whole life is a balancing act. I've always been in the border. I'm a mixed-blood, I'm educated, and I live on the res. There are countless ways in which I'm always crossing and recrossing those borders' (Vannote 1999, 6). For both Rose and Blaeser, wrestling with history and memory is critical to their efforts towards self-definition. And as Blaeser argues, humour with an ironic edge is especially helpful in this regard: 'Because historical stories, imaginative stories, cultural stories work to form our identity, the disarming of history through satiric humor liberates and empowers us in the imagination of our destinies' (1992, 363).

For Louise Halfe (b. 1953), like Wendy Rose and Kim Blaeser, the history of her family is central to her poetry. A Cree woman, born on the Saddle Lake reserve in Alberta and raised there by her paternal grandmother until she was sent to residential school at the age of seven, Halfe has published three books of poetry, *Bear Bones & Feathers* (1994), *Blue Marrow* (1998), and *The Crooked Good* (2007), whose titles reflect her interest in the narratives of those who have been silenced – or buried – by history. Halfe explains that while '[g]rinding bones makes medicine...[,] stories are also medicine. Stories are the marrow of our culture' (Armstrong and Grauer 2001, 240). Her experiences of residential school, where her parents were also educated, and her subsequent training in social work at the University of Regina, from which she received a BSW in 1991, have also affected the subject matter of her poems, which are intended to be sites of self-exploration, healing, and potential reconfiguration through memory. Halfe sees herself as a vehicle for these alterna(rra)tives, stating that 'memory is spirit. I allow this spirit to be my guide in writing' (239). Her second collection, *Blue Marrow*, pairs the concepts of memory and history in a more sustained form; it is a book-length narrative poem (complete with family photographs) told from the perspective of a contemporary Cree woman who incorporates the stories of her Native ancestors and their encounters with European traders and settlers to create a multi-dimensional account of pre- and post-colonial life for her Cree predecessors. Perhaps most powerful in these narratives is Halfe's exploration of the various registers of language use among the people she portrays. Halfe incorporates Cree words, including terms of endearment, traditional songs, and names, as well as her father's hybridized Cree, English, and French to depict the particularities of language and its impact on how stories get told. *Bear Bones* also looks at language through a variety of voices, including that of Halfe's mother, whose Cree-accented English dialect renders linguistically the religious, political, and cultural divides that mother and daughter struggle to overcome. Halfe provides a glossary of Cree terms in her early collection but leaves out such a guide in the first edition of *Blue Marrow*, published by mainstream publisher McClelland and Stewart, granting 'insider' status in the latter volume to those who can move between and among the Cree and English languages fluidly. In doing so, she inverts the assumption of the dominance of native English speakers. Yet her strategy of distancing readers through language is balanced by her sustained interest in conveying the humour, as well as the anguish, of the topics she explores. Her latest collection, *The Crooked Good*, is inspired by the gruesome but also wittily subversive Cree narrative titled 'The Rolling Head,' in which a husband takes revenge on his wife, who has been seduced by a snake, and eventually beheads both his wife and her lover; her head continues to roll around the world, calling her children to come home. Through the legacy of 'The Rolling Head,' Halfe portrays the lives of a group of Cree women who, despite years of sexual and racial exploitation, continue to pursue their 'Dreams': 'No one expected us, the brown-skins, to get anywhere. / Especially us women' (2007, 7). In Halfe's texts, her poetic speakers often use humour and irony to ensure that their voices are heard.

The challenges and rewards of linguistic border-crossings, such as those represented in Halfe's collections, are fundamental to all of the women discussed in this book. Jeannette Armstrong (b. 1948) was born and raised on the Penticton Indian reserve in British Columbia, where she learned to speak Okanagan fluently as a child. Armstrong has become a well-known novelist, poet, visual artist, and activist with a special interest in finding venues for the development of First Nations writers. To this end, she helped found the En'owkin School of International Writing in 1989 in Penticton, the first Aboriginal-run institution to grant credit for creative writing courses. Armstrong, the author of one poetry collection entitled *Breath Tracks* (1991), asserts that the oral basis and generic fluidity of her first language, Okanagan, has imprinted much of her work:

> I compose Okanagan song and poetry and I use mostly songs in the community in a social setting. I create images with words and with the enunciation of words, because ours is an oral-based language. You can do a lot more with an oral-based language, since you already have that legacy of how sounds work. They work much differently than in English, which ... [is] a written language. (Beeler 1996, 148)

Here, Armstrong suggests that the 'brevity and clarity' of English has likely been compromised by the predominance of the written language, in a way that is not true of Okanagan (148). Armstrong's intimate understanding of Okanagan as an expressive, communicative tool that functions primarily at the level of the spoken word and depends on exchange among community members makes her acutely aware of how contextual specificities shape language use and audience response. Some of her work attempts to bridge the gap between oral and written texts by turning poems into songs or other forms of musical collaboration, creating living 'soundscapes' (149). And not surprisingly, much of her work is characterized by humour and irony – a highly sophisticated double-talk which is fundamentally shaped by context, both in its oral and written forms. By moving between languages, Armstrong challenges white western presumptions that English conveys the life experiences of Native peoples most effectively. Armstrong often employs what she calls 'Rez English,' which, as she explains, is 'syntactically and semantically closer' to Okanagan and thus more accurately portrays a specific tribal perspective (1998, 193).

For each of the poets in this study, trying to locate oneself is an ongoing challenge, especially when raised in an urban setting rather than a reservation. In contrast to Armstrong, Marie Annharte Baker (b. 1942) is the product of mixed-blood parents and learned two languages (Anishinaabe and English) as a child. Baker was born in Winnipeg, Manitoba, to an Anishinaabe mother and a father of Irish/Scottish/English descent and was raised in the city; situating herself according to reservation ties (as some mixed-blood poets do by virtue of being raised there) is not an option. Well aware of her tricky status, Baker, the author of three collections of poetry, is wary of those scholars who try to define Native people in absolute terms of tribal affiliation. She contends that 'maintaining an Indian identity is a [daily] struggle' but also a source of great fascination (1994a, 115). According to Baker, 'I do enjoy the mention of cultural purity but I quickly get bored because it does not seem to have anything to do with the hodge-podge reality that makes up my world' (115). To adequately convey the 'celtic confusion' that defines her heritage, she argues that writers like herself need to approach English differently (115). Rather than simply seeing it as the 'enemy's language,' Baker insists that writers acknowledge that 'the enemy' is *within* the individual person – within one's own language use and how one is programmed to look at things' (1993, 61). Questioning language use then becomes an ongoing process that requires self-awareness and a willingness to scrutinize not just white western voices but also those of Indigenous writers who have been colonized by English.

While Baker admits that 'English is the language I have used in order to become a published writer,' a pragmatic decision given the industry, it does not mean that she passively employs English (1993, 66). And moving between Anishinaabe and English has made her acutely aware of the limiting syntax and vagueness of the latter language. As a result, Baker's poetry is a deliberately subversive mix of ironically overloaded lines, constant wordplay, and visceral images that come from approaching English with an inherent distrust, a position that is reflected in her latest book, evocatively titled *Exercises in Lip Pointing* (2003). Underlying her cautionary approach to language is Baker's belief that ultimately it is the recognition of individual differences that provides a basis for such skepticism and a place from which to explore her distinct heritage.

Baker's desire to both maintain and challenge the multiple boundaries that designate identity is not surprising given her mixed-blood heritage. While Baker is suspicious of the vagaries of English, she has the ability to move fluidly between two languages and uses these to create a liminal space for herself, at least on the page. However, several poets, by virtue of their life situations, do not have that same opportunity and have worked hard in adulthood to acquire some familiarity with their Native tongue even as they too question the limitations of the 'enemy's language.'

Marilyn Dumont (b. 1955), of Cree/Métis descent, wrestles with the reality of having grown up in a bilingual family, where English and Cree were spoken, but in which she never acquired a working knowledge of Cree. Dumont explains that Cree was 'the language that my parents always defaulted to ... It was the language where you spoke about really important things' (Andrews 2004b, 146). As an adult, Dumont has learned to use Cree at least sporadically in her work, particularly when discussing Native stereotypes and dialoguing with other people who may have been raised in Cree-speaking households but never became proficient in the language. She explains, 'I employ language to subvert, expose, empower ... I see language as a tool, and I do not underestimate the politics of the English language to silence us' (Armstrong and Graucr 2001, 255). By often including untranslated Cree phrases in her poetry, she foregrounds her own struggles to exist and thrive in the gap between languages, without having full access to her tribal tongue. Like Halfe, Dumont challenges the confidence of non-Cree speakers who may come to the text presuming to have full access to her world; the inclusion of words without translation forces these readers, myself included, to acknowledge their outsider status by actively reversing which language (and audience) is constructed as marginal. Language thus becomes a way to explore identity and the difficulties of self-definition. Given her interest in subverting the dominant tongue (English), it seems fitting that Dumont often employs humour and irony to enact those struggles on the page in a dialogic fashion; it is a powerful 'rhetorical strategy ... It's the way to point at prickly kinds of issues and to get at them' (Andrews 2004b, 155). Even the photograph of a young Marilyn and her mother that appears at the beginning of her first collection pointedly frames the double-ness that she has faced as someone who looks Native but lacks access to her 'Native' tongue. Having completed a BA and MFA at the University of British Columbia in 1991 and 1998 respectively, she has since published three books of poetry and been the recipient of several awards, including the Gerald Lampert Memorial Award from the League of Canadian Poets for a best first collection (1997). Dumont now combines teaching, student services work, and writer-in-residence postings in order to support her writing career.

The most senior of the ten poets, Diane Glancy (b. 1941), is also perhaps the most prolific, having published over thirty books and won numerous awards, grants, and fellowships. Born in Kansas City, Missouri,
to a Cherokee father and an English/German mother who rejected her
husband's Native identity, Glancy began to explore her Native heritage
through writing in the 1980s after the breakdown of a nineteen-year
marriage that produced two children. Glancy's opportunity to pursue an
MFA at the University of Iowa in 1988 was a personal and professional
catalyst, leading to a professorship at Macalester College in St Paul and
the chance to write and teach full-time. As she explains, the MFA 'gave
me a job; it gave me a way out of the backroads ... It gave me a life that
I wouldn't have had without it,' and granted Glancy 'the academic authority, the permission to do what I'm doing' (Andrews 2002b, 652). She
has published over a dozen volumes of poetry since 1984, collections
that deal with a wide array of issues, including space, history, memory,
language, and identity. In particular, Glancy is a practising Baptist, who
explores the merging of Christian and Native religious beliefs on paper.
Pivotal to her work is the idea of listening to those voices that are located
at the borders and frontiers. As a mixed-blood woman writer situated at
the crossroads of multiple borders, she must constantly negotiate and
reconfigure them to suit her own needs:

> All the Native writers I know are saying, in our own way, what it is like to
> be Native American, and all the writers are mixed blood. Are there any
> pure blood authors? I don't think so. All of us are mixed with many other
> cultures. And then we have found our own ways to live. Many have gone
> back and tried to recreate a traditional way: Sherman Alexie and Joy Harjo
> just to name two. Others have accessed Christianity, the academic world.
> Many of us are housed in academia. And we've all had to begin to listen to
> other voices. America had to throw out the melting pot and realize we are
> a multiplicity of voices. Each voice has its own words, and you have to listen
> to the whole group to understand. There are many different borderlands.
> I don't have access to what the pure Cherokee was like. I work in a border-
> land; the students who listen to the culture walk in a borderland. America is
> a borderland of these many differences. The melting pot, the oneness, the
> one nation under God, never was and never will be. (Andrews 2002b, 649)

Here, Glancy pointedly deconstructs the symbolic dominance of the
American nation for Native Americans by stressing the range of tribal
heritages within the United States and the importance of attending to

marginal populations as distinct entities. Rather than presuming to impose a unified reading of America's past, present, and future, she sees
writing as a way to create alternative (hi)stories that recognize the shifts
that have taken place in Native Americans' lives.

Glancy notes that humour and irony are qualities that she defines as
inherently Native – 'along with the importance of nature, the importance of the Great Spirit, the importance of family … anger, and loss,
and sadness' – but also specifically associates with her Cherokee heritage
(Andrews 2002b, 653). In an essay called 'A Fieldbook of Textual Migrations,' Glancy includes a section titled 'Over Who Will Rein Chief of
Words,' which explores 'the Cherokee influence of knowing how many
things can mean' (1998, 83). Glancy claims that 'when one is confused,
there is always an understanding of something imbedded within it. Even
if it is not always the understanding of what you wanted to understand'
(83). This apparent riddle reinforces the need to look again at words
and phrases by paying attention to their 'other' meanings. Likewise,
she sees humour and irony as ways of overturning dominant discourses
and reflecting the bitterness of tribal legacies without merely surrendering to that history; both discursive strategies express the intricacies of
her vision and allow for interpretive flexibility, demanding that readers
engage with and participate in this ongoing process of articulating and
repositioning one's poetic voice. For instance, when discussing one of
her poetry manuscripts, later published as *A Primer of the Obsolete* (2004),
which merges Cherokee and Christian perspectives, Glancy describes
her ironic response to the discovery that it had been awarded the prestigious Juniper Award for poetry from the University of Massachusetts
after years of rejection: 'After I got over the pain of the erasure, and always being pushed down, and not mattering and not ever hearing a voice
like my own, and now that I've got on top of the pile, things are kind of
funny, kind of ironic. You struggle your way up and you get a different
perspective on it' (Andrews 2002b, 653). As Glancy points out, the passage of time and her growing confidence in her poetic talent have given
her a different outlook on her writing and identity as a mixed-blood
woman.

While Glancy has produced texts in a range of different genres, she repeatedly returns to poetry, claiming that 'it's a very elastic genre. There
are the narrative poems, and then there's the very experimental, subconscious dream world that you can bring forth too' (Andrews 2002b,
645). She suggests that the less plot-driven form of poetry makes it ideal
for exploring subjects such as religious beliefs or language that may not

be easily transferred between cultural contexts. As well, poetry becomes, according to Glancy, a way to create, clarify, heal, and document one's experiences in the world. Poetry, as a genre, has a much smaller audience, is more difficult to publish, and yet is also more suitable to lifestyles in which writing is sandwiched between work. And because it evokes the subconscious world, those thoughts, ideas, and beliefs that are not typically articulated, it becomes an ideal form for exploring the perspectives of those who, as Glancy notes, were 'always outside the generally recognized voice' (645). More obviously, the fact that in many Native communities song and poetry are not differentiated makes it a textual form that honours tribal customs despite externally imposed generic definitions. If listening, as Glancy argues, is what counts, then the continued blurring of a distinction between song and text makes writing and reading poetry, rather than other generic forms, an especially appropriate choice for these women.

For those poets who have been born and raised within a tribal community, such connections are even more overt. Take, for example, Jeannette Armstrong, who sees poetry and song as intimately linked: 'Poetry is music to me. It's rhythm, and it's sound and it's imagery and it's metaphor ... poetry is another word for what I understand when I sing and when I create and compose music' (Beeler 1996, 147). Poetry thus becomes a way of acknowledging and sustaining Native oral-based traditions, even when working in a written form. Humour and irony are particularly useful tools for conveying these complexities because they can challenge dominant scholarly paradigms and reinforce new ones in a manner that is playful and engaging yet also forceful and provocative, creating a space that recognizes and celebrates a more diverse understanding of what poetry means to these women writers and their reading communities.

Aboriginal Poetry: The Telling of Choice

Despite its popularity, as attested to by the writers just profiled, Native poetry has not garnered the same sustained critical and popular attention as novels; even Eva Gruber's wonderfully wide-ranging investigation of Native North American humour relegates poetry to a secondary position, claiming that 'the short story is arguably the most fertile ground for humor in Native writing' (15) and concentrating primarily on prose texts. Dean Rader, the co-editor of *Speak to Me Words: Essays on Contemporary American Indian Poetry*,[8] expresses his bafflement at the lack of scholarly responses to Native poetry, pointing out that 'until the year 2000 no full-length study of contemporary American Indian poetry existed' (2003, 125).[9] The publication of Robin Riley Fast's *The Heart as a Drum: Continuance and Resistance in American Indian Poetry* (1999) and Norma Wilson's *The Nature of Native American Poetry* (2001) have begun to address that lack. Much to my delight, *The Salt Companion to Diane Glancy* (2010), edited by James MacKay, a rich collection of essays on Glancy's writings, including her poetry, appeared shortly after this manuscript was completed and hopefully marks a shift that will result in a plethora of new critical materials about Native American women's poetry, in particular. There is a similar paucity of work done on Native Canadian poetry; Susan Gingell's 'When X Equals Zero: The Politics of Voice in First Peoples Poetry by Women,' Méira Cook's 'Bone Memory: Transcribing Voice in Louise Bernice Halfe's *Blue Marrow*,' and Cara DeHaan's '"Exorcising a Lot of Shame": Transformation and Affective Experience in Marilyn Dumont's *green girl dreams Mountains*' are notable exceptions.[10] In addition, there are an increasing number of doctoral dissertations that examine Native North American poetry exclusively, including a recently completed thesis by Molly McGlennen on Native aesthetics and spirituality in the work of four contemporary Native-American female poets (two of whom are Blaeser and Glancy) and Amanda Cagle's dissertation, titled '"Pushing from Their Hearts a New Song": The (Re)construction of the Feminine in American Indian Women's Poetry' (Harjo and Rose are among the six writers whose poetry she analyzes). However, much of the published scholarship on Native North American women's poetry has taken the form of anthologies, a necessary first step to garner attention and put texts into wider circulation.[11] And though there are large numbers of articles on a few Native-American women who write poetry and prose (such as Leslie Marmon Silko and Louise Erdrich), typically the bulk of these studies examine the author's novels. Yet as Beth Brant (Mohawk) notes, the genre of poetry remains extremely popular with Native Canadian female writers:

> Poetry seems to be the choice of telling for many Native women. In our capable hands, poetry is torn from the elitist enclave of intellectuals and white, male posturing, and returned to the lyrical singing of the drum, the turtle rattle, the continuation of the Good Red Road and the balance of Earth. We write poems of pain and power, of ancient beliefs, of sexual love, of broken treaties, of despoiled beauty. We write with our human souls and voices. We write songs that honour those who came before us and those in our present lives, and those who will carry on the work of our Nations. We

write songs that honour the every-day, we write songs to food; we even incorporate recipes into our work ... No wonder the critics have so much trouble
with us! How could food possibly be art?! How can art remain elite if these
Native women are going to be writing poems in recipes. (1994, 12–13)

Brant passionately describes the power of poetry as a genre that is highly
flexible and able to accommodate a myriad of issues and ideas – and
acknowledges the song tradition that, as Armstrong, Harjo, and others
claim, is part of many Native tribes' heritages. Not only does poetry, in
her words, bridge the past, present, and future, but the forms it takes
challenge the very foundations of the genre.

Brant's suggestion that Native women's poetry is subversive and disturbing for many critics is not surprising. As Eric Gary Anderson points out,
much Native poetry is challenging for literary scholars because it does not
accord with traditional ideas about genre: 'Genres are forms of identity
imported from outside Native cultures and at times imposed on them'
(2003, 35). Rather than replicating what he calls the '"Eurocentric trap"
– a means of measuring and evaluating all things Indian by Euro-American standards' when analyzing Native poetry – Anderson offers a way to
sidestep this western genre-centred approach (35). He notes most Native
poets move among multiple forms of written expression (prose, poetry,
non-fiction essays, playwriting) as well as other arts, including photography, singing, music, painting, and drawing. Certainly the women whose
poetry is being explored here do just that – and are hesitant to see their
work categorically labelled and divided rather than acknowledged for
its dialogic possibilities. Anderson suggests that 'the *places* of American
Indian poetry ... differ in significant ways from the *placings* of Euro-
American poetry,' and to fully explore those places means taking into account the multiple communities from which these authors write and paying attention to how Native poetry and poets situate themselves (41). At
the same time, as Kimberly Blaeser explains in 'Native Literature: Seeking a Critical Center,' Native North American 'literary works themselves
are always at least bicultural,' having come from an oral-based culture but
rendered in written form, typically English (1993, 56). Blaeser is careful
to note that though these texts often 'proceed at least partially from an
Indian culture, they are most often presented in the established literary
aesthetic forms of the dominant culture (or in those forms acceptable to
the publishing industry)' (56). And because so many of the writers she focuses on are mixed-blood, Blaeser sees them as especially well equipped
to understand and rethink generic classifications to their benefit. From a

pragmatic perspective, Susan Gingell argues that the selection of 'either poetic style or form' by Native female writers enables them to appropriate 'to their own purpose the Western hierarchy of genres that places poetry above prose,' while still countering yet 'another Western hierarchy – that of written over oral' (1998, 458). For practical purposes, the idea of poetry as a distinct genre remains useful – but the work of the women under consideration in this text also invites questions about whom such generic classifications serve and how they might be creatively reconfigured to recognize other perspectives.

Examining contemporary Native poetry poses particular challenges for non-Native academics. Dean Rader has argued that 'Anglo critics shy away from writing about Native poetry because they can't characterize it. It doesn't fit any category or movement' (2003, 125). Such resistance to labelling does indeed pose problems. For scholars like myself who are trained to work within specific literary frameworks and whose teaching is often structured by generic distinctions among prose, novels, poetry, and drama, encountering works that are not easily contained can be unnerving. Not surprisingly, then, Rader speculates that 'there are so many interviews with Native poets and so few essays that engage their work ... [because] it is easier to have the other discuss her poetry than to try to inhabit the discourse of the other' (125). Without presuming to 'inhabit the discourse of the other,' which is an impossible task, this book approaches the subject of Native poetry through humour and irony, discursive techniques that I have chosen because of their centrality to the Aboriginal communities and writers under examination. Helen Hoy's *How Should I Read These? Native Women Writers in Canada* elegantly explores the challenges faced by non-Natives who work on Native texts.[12] Like Hoy, who borrows Trinh T. Minh-ha's term, I see myself as merely 'speaking nearby' (Minh-ha 1989, 101), providing one perspective on a wide range of poems in an effort to build a conversation with an expanding community of readers and writers that includes Native and non-Native people. And the conversation I hope will continue far beyond the pages of this book, precipitating exchanges and arguments across a variety of populations.

Using the framework of humour and irony, in the chapters that follow I examine five critical themes that have emerged from reading the works of, writing about, and speaking with these eight poets: (1) religious transformations; (2) generic transformations; (3) history, memory, and the nation; (4) photography and representational (in)visibility; and (5) land and the significance of 'home.' This structure borrows, in part, from that of Robin Riley Fast's book, which employs thematic strands to discuss a wide array of texts rather than relying on a poet-by-poet examination that would ignore the interactive and associative dimensions of the works. It also reflects the topical concerns of poems by contemporary Native Americans as outlined by Kimberly Blaeser in her essay on poetry for *The Columbia Guide to American Indian Literatures of the United States since 1945*:

> The poems have been seen to demonstrate a historical awareness, invest themselves in a political struggle, have a significant spiritual and/or physical landscape, [and to] search for or attempt to articulate connections with the tribal or pan-tribal reality or legacy. (2006, 192)

For example, chapter 1 explores the significance of religious transformation by attending specifically to how religious beliefs and practices are probed and reconfigured in the poetry of Glancy and Halfe. The second chapter, titled 'Generic Transformations,' offers a reading of works by Harjo and Armstrong that challenge the foundations of literary categorization by looking to forms of self-expression that bridge the gaps among music, poetry, and other media, or fundamentally rethink the question of generic categorization within – and beyond – the field of literary studies. Chapter 3 provides a discussion of how history and memory have played fundamental roles in the poetry of Rose, Halfe, Glancy, Dumont, Baker, and Armstrong, enabling these women to rethink dominant ideas of nation. Titled 'Haunting Photographs, Revisioning Families,' chapter 4 explores how several poets, among them Blaeser, Halfe, Glancy, and Dumont, draw on collections of family photographs in their works to raise questions about what constitutes family, identity, and a sense of belonging; in turn, the incorporation of visual texts enables these poets to probe notions of sight, blindness, and haunting in relationship to their mixed-blood identities. The fifth chapter, titled 'Space, Place, Land, and the Meaning(s) of Home,' considers the links between home and community, land and identity, and space and place within the poetry of Armstrong, Dumont, Blaeser, and Harjo, paying particular attention to how these women reconfigure the recent scholarship of select feminist geographers and cultural critics, including Doreen Massey and bell hooks. The conclusion returns to the image of Harjo's 'in the belly of a laughing god' by tracing, in a very preliminary fashion, the intricate web of intertextual conversations between and among several of the poets examined in this study; this last chapter briefly examines the last lines of the final poem in Kimberly Blaeser's *Absentee Indians & Other Poems*, titled 'Y2K Indian,' a text which invokes and reconfigures a collection of well-known phrases and lines from the work of contemporary Native North American poets for her own purposes. These women are influenced by their families, communities, and other writers; they look beyond tribal and national differences to create an ever-expanding set of dialogues that continue to shape and sustain Native women's poetry in Canada and the United States.

In the Epilogue to *Absentee Indians & Other Poems*, Kimberly Blaeser claims that 'the energy of poems constructs a community' (2002, 127). While Blaeser is referring primarily to the myriad sources that inspire poets to write, her comment is equally applicable to the critical analyses of poetry within this book and the conversations that have shaped it. The poetry of these eight women is compelling, evocative, thoughtful, and often disturbing even as it evokes laughter; it refuses passivity, provokes responses, and demands action by making the page a place of dynamic interaction. There are many other female poets who could have been included in this study. I have chosen to focus on these eight Native North American women whose work and lives straddle academia and creative writing, who incorporate humour and irony in a sustained fashion into their volumes, and who are relatively neglected by scholars. With the inclusion of other poets, such as Connie Fife, Nora Naranjo-Morse, Rita Joe, Chrystos, Beth Brant, Lee Maracle, Catron Grieves, Lenore Kees-hig-Tobias, Roberta Hill, Joan Crate, Kateri Akiwenzie-Damm, Marilou Awiakta, Carol Lee Sanchez, Denise Sweet, Luci Tapahanso, Beth Cuthand, Linda Hogan, Emma LaRocque, Paula Gunn Allen, Gail Trem-blay, and Ofelia Zepeda, this book would certainly be different. But as Blaeser quite rightly asserts at the end of that same epilogue, poems are constructed 'of the many connections my writing and living has to the stories, experiences, and writings of others' (2002, 128). If the humour and irony of the poetry in the pages that follow is, as I will argue, nec-essarily dependent upon interaction and dialogue, one can only hope that such an exchange will provide a useful foundation upon which to build an extended and ongoing conversation between female poets and scholars, both Native and non-Native. If this conversation can encourage speaking and, more importantly, listening, we will hear the laughing god and what those inside its belly have to say.

chapter one

Spiritual Transformations

Transformation: a marked change in form, nature, or appearance.[1]

Transformation, or more directly, metamorphosis, is the oldest tribal ceremonial theme ... And it comes into use once again within the American
Indian poetry of extinction and regeneration that is ultimately the only
poetry a contemporary American Indian woman can write.

Paula Gunn Allen, 'Answering the Deer'

'Transformation' is a central term for the women writers examined in
this book.[2] The poets have used it to describe their teaching strategies, to
talk about the purposes of their poetry, and, in several cases, to explain
how they reconcile or challenge the Christian faith with Native spiritual
beliefs. For instance, Kimberly Blaeser, Marilyn Dumont, Louise Halfe,
Marie Annharte Baker, and Diane Glancy all, to varying degrees, are concerned with the relevance of Christianity to their writing. Cree/Métis
writer and educator Kim Anderson explains that 'the church has been
heavily implicated in all aspects of colonization and it played a critical
role in undermining the role of women in Indigenous societies' (2000,
146). As the Native women interviewed in Anderson's *A Recognition of
Being* suggest, humour and irony are two of the most effective discursive
strategies used to reflect on Christian colonization and its lasting impact. Sto:lo Elder Dorris Peters recalls the disparity between her family's
extreme poverty and her father's insistence that he always contribute to
the collection plate; likewise, Gertie Beaucage describes being too poor
at eight years of age to afford to light a candle at a Catholic mass, an in-

cident which led her to conclude 'that I couldn't afford God. [laughs] It was the ... down side of being Catholic' (147).

In their latest collections, *That Tongued Belonging* (2007) and *Exercises in Lip Pointing* (2003), Marilyn Dumont and Marie Annharte Baker illustrate how humour and irony are used by contemporary Native women poets to explore religious identities. Dumont's 'She Carries the Pope in Her Purse' traces the story of an older woman who has managed to combine Catholic doctrine in the figure of the Pope with Métis religious practices, such as visits to Lac Ste. Anne, an Aboriginal shrine to the mother of the Virgin Mary.[3] In Dumont's lighthearted and playful poem, the Pope 'doesn't take up much room' and readily mingles in the depth of the purse with 'Pilgrimage medals,' 'rosaries,' and 'vials of Holy Water' from Lac Ste. Anne, which are thought to heal and bring good fortune (Dumont 2007, 14). Moreover, these symbols of religious practice are readily juxtaposed against the accoutrements of daily life for the older woman, whose life is contained in her purse, which holds tubes of unused lipstick and pieces of identification alongside a bank card, 'mad money,' and 'obituary clippings,' a mélange that ultimately resonates with the reality of her daily life and economic status, as the poem's speaker – in an ironic twist – reveals that 'her purse smells of Jergens, Juicy Fruit and second-hand stores' (14). Here, the Pope becomes compact and portable (presumably taking the form of a photograph or news-clipping tucked into a prayer book), and his centrality is displaced by other necessities of life, including a reclamation of Native spiritual practices.

Baker's 'It Was Like,' in contrast, depicts the speaker's struggle to survive on what she wryly calls the '666 Beast of Welfare,' the governmental program that the poetic 'I' associates with the Number of the Beast or Antichrist in the Christian New Testament, the central figure in an apocalyptic narrative. In this case, getting a welfare cheque 'takes an apocalypse' (2003, 80), meaning that it is about as likely as the end of the world, a reality that provides no real solace for the speaker facing eviction because she cannot pay her rent. Baker's poetic 'I' sarcastically laments that 'this cheque day was the last day / on earth if angels wanted to sing' (80), an imagined 'resurrection' that is soon reduced to a series of clumsy gestures as 'soul music feathers aflight / wings aflap do wop' (81), in a failed parody of the celebrated Christian transfiguration of Jesus Christ; the incident leaves the speaker chasing down the stereotypical Native welfare meal of a 'baloney sandwich' and reflecting upon the 'commercial drive' which underlies her own struggle to survive the beast that is 'capitalism' (81), a world where nothing is what it seems despite the title's promised proviso to describe what 'It Was Like' (80). This slippage between what is ideal and what occurs in reality is just one powerfully irreverent and compelling example of the colonial legacy of Christianity that has taken a particular toll on Native women. Although each poem approaches its speaker's struggles differently, the texts of Dumont and Baker embody several of the key strategies used by the female poets in this study to develop a flexible, inclusive, and often critical perspective of the relationship between institutionalized Christian religions and long-standing tribal spiritual beliefs and practices. More generally, Marilyn Dumont, Marie Annharte Baker, Diane Glancy, and Louise Halfe use religious transformation for their own purposes: to make sense of their own complex relationships to Christianity and Native spirituality, and to forge links between the disparate worlds they straddle. For others, such as Joy Harjo and Jeannette Armstrong, transformation is critical to their spiritual and artistic self-expression, enabling them to challenge generic boundaries, as I examine in chapter 2.

Aesthetics and Transformation

Transformation is an important dimension of Native cultural and spiritual beliefs and practices. For the women poets in this chapter, the idea of transformation offers a way to articulate their mixed-blood identities and, concurrently, explore traditional Native aesthetics and contemporary cross-cultural reconfigurations of those practices. In *Indigenous Aesthetics: Native Art, Media, and Identity,* Steven Leuthold argues that Eurocentric scholars need to acknowledge the imposition of foundational western values on Native cultures, which have been typically judged as not living up to those 'standards,' and devote increasing attention to the shifting strategies Native writers and artists employ to represent themselves and their subjectivities (1998, 52). Wendy Rose concurs, asserting that 'taken as a group, Euroamericans consider themselves to be uniquely qualified to explain the rest of humanity, not only to Euroamerica, but to everyone else as well' (1992, 406). Moreover, as Craig Womack wryly notes, 'Indian cultures are the only cultures where it is assumed that if they change they are no longer a culture' (1999, 16). Paradoxically, Leslie Marmon Silko reminds us that 'Europeans were shocked at the speed and ease with which Native Americans synthesized, then incorporated, what was alien and new' (1996, 73); while Indigenous art developed, much of it was either overlooked or dismissed outright because it did not accord with specific constructs of the 'primitive.' One of the key steps that Leuthold identifies as integral to altering such marginalizing perspectives of Aboriginal art is to look carefully at the 'reconstruction and transformation of cultural identity' as it occurs within and between different Native artists and their works, without relying necessarily on western evolutionary models of development (1998, 23). For Leuthold, in the case of Aboriginal artists, '"[n]ormal" portrayals of the cultural other are … challenged through the presentation' of alternative forms of self-representation; this 'juxtaposition of styles,' both familiar and unfamiliar, provokes audiences to negotiate their relationship to the various components of the text through a series of comparisons and contrasts (23). In other words, readers and viewers must work to make sense of the various stylistic components of Aboriginal art, without necessarily possessing knowledge of all of the formal and thematic aspects that may be in play. It is the tension between what is known and not known, and the need for audiences to make sense of a work, that provokes a shift in one's frame of reference; those interacting with the text supply 'new symbolic association[s] for…unfamiliar … elements,' and thereby discover new perspectives (Francesconi 1986, 38).

The impact of humour and irony on readers is both central to this study and a critical tool for the Native North American women poets who form the focus of this book; the writers in question employ both in complex and diverse ways to explore a variety of issues – from history and memory to land and space. Leuthold's concept of transformation creates space for humour and irony; both function on a microcosmic level to challenge expected perceptions by using juxtaposition and implication. Thus, changes in perspective and/or form, which operate at a macro level, are anticipated, mirrored, and reinforced by the humour and irony of a work of art, especially when it is identified as such by readers or viewers, as we shall see shortly. Because Leuthold is so intent on finding a way to talk about the differences that mark Aboriginal texts, he may be read as reducing Native aesthetics to a series of essentialist claims. Yet his interest in 'cognitive dissonances' as explored through the juxtaposition of 'incompatible constructs' and the need for western readers and viewers (like myself) to reconsider the Eurocentric definition of art are crucial steps towards an understanding of Native art (1998, 55).

Leuthold deepens his analysis of transformation, explaining that 'frequently, indigenous arts involve performance or participation designed to produce a transformative experience for the artists [and/]or the viewer' (1998, 58). That metamorphosis can involve a shift from human to animal forms (or vice versa), a movement between conscious and unconscious states, or simply an altered perception of an event. While western-trained scientists or historians 'may be able to provide a material or rational explanation for some aspects' of these transformations, the meanings of such metamorphoses for the artist and audience are not always readily categorized or easily deconstructed (58). Yet Leuthold points out that the relationship between art and the sacred has been increasingly maligned in western aesthetics, despite the fact that 'art in the West was primarily religious until the mid-to-late nineteenth century' (57); paradoxically, however, 'it is the developed, industrialized West that is an exception by not viewing art as an expression of the sacred' (57). And for all of the women poets studied here, spirituality (whether in the context of Christian religions, Native belief systems, a combination of the two, or resistance to both) is vital to their texts. Leuthold goes on to question how Native art disrupts attempts to frame and contain its concerns through metamorphosis, especially when religion is its primary subject:

> Is it possible that art's transformative power in these contexts ties it to spiritual realities not accounted for by scientific explanation? How do these different beliefs systems 'work' – through means such as transformative art – in ways that have profound meaning for members of indigenous cultures, but which we cannot grasp through Western theories of art? (58)

In doing so, Leuthold draws attention to the need for a different approach to Native works, citing transformation as a concept that, though often 'downplay[ed] in Western cultures,' provides both the terminology and flexibility to examine Native art on its own terms (58).

Defining transformation and explaining how it works in theory and in practice is a potentially self-defeating task. Kimberly Blaeser describes the importance of metamorphosis to her teaching and writing lives but, not surprisingly, resists imposing a fixed meaning on the term:

> The whole idea of transformation is of course a spiritual notion. And it's somewhat illogical, so people want to pin it down – is it literal? is it figurative? how do we mean it? – but I think it has to mean everything or we couldn't believe the possibilities it offers. With my students, just to have them be open to the possibility of transformation operating on many levels, I'll start by describing something very physical like the transformation of a caterpillar to a moth … And then I try to open up the possibility of there

being things we don't understand. How do we know what happens ceremo-
nially in any religion? I'll often use a Christian example like transubstantia-
tion and ask whether that's something they can believe or understand and
whether it's metaphorical or literal, and what it does to us when we accept
it in one way or in all ways. And then what happens when we are recipients
or participants in the life of imagination, story, poetry, or song? (Andrews
2007b, 13–14)

Blaeser's need to convey the idea of transformation to her students, and
its importance to her pedagogical aims as a teacher of Native texts, suggests its power. For Blaeser, metamorphosis offers a way of reading the
natural world, religious practices, and literary texts as part of a larger
community-centred framework in which the possibilities of imaginative
change – through story – are integral to daily life. At the same time,
stories and histories about transformation themselves become teaching
tools, providing instruction by example.

Blaeser's poetry offers one model for understanding transformation
in texts like 'Where I Was That Day' from *Trailing You* (1994), in which
the first-person speaker describes an encounter with the natural world
that becomes a lesson in looking and seeing the world differently:

> It was partly that day when I stopped at the little creek
> and noticed the funny little bumps on that floating log
> and how they seemed to be looking at me
> and how they were really little heads with beady bulging eyes
> and how when I came back a half hour later
> the bumps had been rearranged on that log
>
> ... And it was me who fit and saw one minute so clearly
> and then stumbled blind the next
> that made me think we are always finding our place
> in the great sphere of creation
> that made me know I could learn a way
> to pull the world around me too
> to colour myself with earth and air and water
> and so become indistinguishable
> ... to be both still and wildly alive in the same moment (1994, 19–20)

The spiritual dimensions of this realization are not lost on the speaker,
who concludes the poem with the reassurance that 'we are all / in this

puzzle together /... just learning / to hold the spell / a little longer /
each time' (21). In this case, the poetic 'I' explores how transformation
becomes a mode of shared survival, ensuring not only that the tree toads
live by virtue of their effective disguises, but that the speaker recognizes
her own need to do so. In addition, the poem values the power that
comes with being able to participate in this magical process of metamorphosis, one that Blaeser's speaker connects back to the Apache leader
and warrior Geronimo, who was known for his ability to travel through
and blend seamlessly into the mountains of the southwestern United
States and Mexico, which made capture by the American 'cavalries' virtually impossible (20).

  This same transformative power becomes critical for Blaeser, who as
a practising Catholic of mixed-blood parentage has always 'been on the
border' (Vannote 1999, 6) and is acutely aware of how useful this flexibility of vision can be for those who straddle various worlds; it is a survival skill and a way to respect the multiple traditions that she struggles
to negotiate and embrace: 'I hold many Indian teachings very sacred
– and many Christian teachings as well' (6).[4] Such challenges are overtly
portrayed in a deeply ironic poem titled 'Housing Conditions of One
Hundred Fifty Chippewa Families' from Blaeser's *Apprenticed to Justice*
(2007). In this text, Blaeser revises a housing report originally written
by the Catholic sister M. Inez Hilger in 1938, which fails to account for
the reality of life for these families living on the White Earth Reservation. As Melissa Meyer notes in *The White Earth Tragedy*, historically the
White Earth population was referred to by white western 'outsiders' as
the 'Chippewa' rather than the tribally favoured term, Anishinaabe, as
part of the process of colonization and religious conversion (1999, xiv);
Hilger's choice of title for her report is no exception. Part of Hilger's
problem, according to Blaeser's speaker, is that she is unwilling to ad-
just her perspective to account for individual and communal conditions
on the reservation, as well as her own white western biases. Instead, the
poetic 'I' directs her anger at the inflexibility of this Catholic woman,
stating, 'You left Mary Inez, the Latin Mass / and rosary zipped safely
in one pocket – / the names of each Mid wiwin elder / drumming and
chanting in the other' (2007, 83). These concluding lines embrace the
need for a more pliable perspective by depicting, through this ironic
juxtaposition, how Hilger attempts to keep Catholic and spiritual practices separate despite the fact that in this instance they are uneasily but
also inescapably intertwined. Sister Mary may relegate the Chippewa residents (including Blaeser's mother, who was a child on the reservation at

the time) to the realm of the 'sub-human,' but Blaeser's speaker knows better as a descendant who has been raised and nurtured by this same community (83). Thus, what was originally a Bureau of Indian Affairs report, authored by a Christian outsider, has been reclaimed and transformed into a poem authored by a 'Chippewa' woman who imaginatively deconstructs the power of the written word, once treated by Sister Mary as gospel (79).

What most interests Blaeser about transformation is its relationship to orality and writing, particularly because white western cultures have traditionally judged the former to be a primitive means of expression. Blaeser asserts that 'Native people for centuries have believed in the possibility of language [generally] being transformative' and sees this perspective as valuable to the classroom experience because of the impact that oral and written poems, songs, and stories can and do have on their audiences (Andrews 2007b, 14). Thus, for students to fully engage with the Native texts they encounter, they need to recognize and become comfortable with the concept of metamorphosis in its literal and figurative forms. Blaeser explains that 'if language has that power to really move us, to ... change our thinking, and if who we are depends on what we think, and I think it does, then we are transformed' (14). Even more specifically, she asserts that there is a friction or edge that is part of that process of change, and that may radically alter an individual's or a community's perception of the world: 'When things bump against each other, they transform each other, and that happens in many places including texts' (14). Blaeser suggests that the understanding of transformation is necessary for reading Aboriginal texts. It is a concept that should be taught but paradoxically remains difficult to deconstruct because in doing so, the power of change may be lost entirely.

Several other Native North American scholars/poets – most notably Gerald Vizenor and Paula Gunn Allen – have also attempted to describe the transformative nature of Native art in an alternately playful and serious fashion that avoids imposing reductive definitions on the term or its relevance to Native communities. Vizenor not only incorporates the erotic metamorphosis of humans and animals in his first novel, *Darkness in Saint Louis Bearheart*, but he continues to use this notion of change (of states of being and/or perceptions) throughout his extensive scholarly and creative oeuvre in combination with what he terms 'imagination' and a 'trickster consciousness' to ensure the 'survivance' of tribal peoples (Blaeser 1996, 11). In an effort to resist the imposition of what he calls 'terminal creeds,' beliefs that impose static definitions on the

world, Vizenor insists that new self-imaginings are central to psychic survival, especially for mixed-bloods like himself (1990, 185). In his own
work, Vizenor turns to 'mythic stories of transformation,' rather than
relying on more traditional literary modes of realism and naturalism
(Vizenor and Lee 1999, 110). Blaeser also notes Vizenor's interest in
and commitment to 'the mythic tradition of tribal trickster narrative' but
with a contemporary twist, which involves putting trickster[5] ideas into
written form while resisting stasis: '... he centers his energy on inviting
involvement, creating momentum, eliciting responses – he centers his
energy on breaking out of print' (1996, 162–3). And in his writing and
artistic practices generally, Blaeser suggests, Vizenor 'symbolically vivi-
fies the Indian identity, picturing it in an endless process of transformation' (163). Metamorphosis thus becomes a form of resistance to static
constructions of Nativeness, enabling Vizenor and others to subvert
figuratively and literally such limiting definitions and to embrace their
mixed-blood identities.

Writing from a gynocentric perspective, Paula Gunn Allen speaks
to the usefulness of transformation for Native North American female
poets even more directly. In the epigraph above, she contends that the
challenges of extinction and promises of resurrection are often addressed through metamorphosis in the works of these writers, who having 'located a means of negotiating the perilous path between love and
death, between bonding and dissolution, between tribal consciousness
and modern alienation must light on the transformational metaphor to
articulate their experience' (1986, 150). Finding a middle ground where
difference is more than marginally acceptable becomes critical. She suggests that by observing, accepting, and embracing change, particularly as
represented in the natural world through animals or even the seasons,
these women writers affirm the vitality of life and give hope to people
who might otherwise give up. Gunn Allen has written her own poem
called 'Transformations,' in which her speaker urges readers to pay attention to the 'patterns of continuance' and find strength in them, an
act of faith that she links back to her ancestors (152).

In her most recent collection of essays, *Off the Reservation*, Gunn Allen
returns to metamorphosis as a dominant theme in Native life and story;
when describing the old narrative cycle of the Pueblo peoples, which
consists of creation, emergence, and migration, Gunn Allen asserts that
'transformation is, after all, the heart of the people, the heart of the
tradition, and the heart of the life process of Thought' (1998, 13). But
she also offers a cautionary tale about change, especially sacred change,

by linking the story of a scorned sister in Laguna cosmogony, Naotsete, with the use of the New Mexican desert as a test site for the atomic bomb, which was subsequently dropped on Hiroshima and Nagasaki. Having quarrelled with Spider Woman over who was the eldest, Naotsete is said to have left the area with the local metals (including the key ingredient, uranium) in her medicine bag and is thought to have returned with a vengeance, at least symbolically, in the form of nuclear testing. For Gunn Allen, 'the approach of the sacred is fraught with great danger,' and the 'liminal state, which one enters at the moment of transformation, is as likely to yield disaster as its obverse' (106). Gunn Allen's argument ultimately takes an ecological turn; she asserts that the destruction of the earth needs to be stopped, and to do so, change needs to come most obviously through responsible treatment of the physical world rather than its contamination. Hence, the romance of Gunn Allen's vision is countered by the tangible eradication of nature and its explicit impact on human behaviour, a circle that endlessly loops back on itself. Thus, transformation becomes a vexed concept, both promising in its ability to heal through shape-changing and dangerous in that it does not always deliver what is desired. Transformation is ultimately not controllable and thus can be productively discomforting to readers.

While most of the poets in this study engage with the concept of transformation to some degree, interest in how religion and belief in the sacred intersect with transformation is most explicitly explored in the work of Diane Glancy and Louise Halfe. Both see it as vital to their work. However, while Glancy offers a provisional definition of the term and its usefulness to her project, Halfe uses her poetry to articulate a concept of religious transformation that relies upon readers to negotiate and make sense of her evolving relationship with her Roman Catholic education and Cree roots. In the case of Glancy, transformation becomes a means of exploring her identity as a Native Christian whose sustained commitment to Christ and interest in many of the peripheral female figures in the Bible has led her to write several volumes of poetry that specifically examine the paradoxes of Native Christianity and give voice to these otherwise silenced women. In *A Primer of the Obsolete* (1997) and *(Ado)ration* (1999), Glancy weaves together Christian and Native notions of metamorphosis to explore a wide variety of personal and religious issues. Her most sustained treatment of literal and figurative transformation, however, comes in *The Closets of Heaven* (1999), which is narrated by one of Christ's disciples, Dorcas, who dies and is resurrected by Peter but is given no voice in the Bible.

As a Native woman writer, Glancy is especially interested in the links between gender, writing, and transformation. In an essay titled 'SHEdonism,' Glancy describes her personal struggle to leave her marriage and become a writer in the following terms:

> It has taken YEARS for me to find my way. But my Native American heritage is also a strength (especially the images I get from it for writing). So my structure has always been One of conflict and ambivalence ... Aren't we all fragments of opposition, especially women? A composite for which we have to find the connecting threads. (1992, 52)

For Glancy, exploring the paradoxes of her mixed-blood heritage and religious beliefs through her writing has enabled her to give voice to a variety of women (including herself) who might otherwise have remained silenced (53). As she explains, 'the imaginative impact of combined images, of seeing the familiar in a new way,' is critical to her understanding of writing, living, and even her definition of feminism or what she calls '"SHEdonism": the enjoyment of oneself as a woman' (53). And humour and irony – which employ incongruity to challenge readers' perspectives – are integral to this personal and textual transformation.

While Glancy pointedly renegotiates her relationship with orthodox Christianity by reconfiguring the terms of her engagement with the sacred and incorporating a distinctly female-centred vision of key Christian figures and concepts, Louise Halfe, who was educated in the Canadian residential school system from the age of seven, has a significantly different approach to Christianity and, in particular, Roman Catholicism.[6] Halfe has been much less vocal than Glancy in analyzing her works through interviews and essays, yet like Glancy, her three poetry collections focus on reclaiming female voices, specifically the Cree female voices of her ancestors, whose experiences have been lost or forgotten. By attending to the bones of her foremothers, Halfe ironically seizes upon the Roman Catholic Church's historical reverence for the relics of saints to create her own homage to these women who were marginalized because of their race and spiritual beliefs. The result, in *Bear Bones & Feathers* and *Blue Marrow*, is an ironically charged transformation of memories and bone marrow into stories of their lives and legacies. And Halfe couples this reclamation with a deeply witty and often sarcastic look at how one Cree woman writes a series of missives to the Roman Catholic Pope in a vernacular style, based on the wildly unlikely premise that the Pope has apologized for the Church's shameful treatment of the Cree in Canada. By positing this absurd situation in the form of a series of 'ledders' to 'Der Poop,' Halfe not only stresses the scatological dimensions of this exchange – the female 'I' composes one of the letters while sitting in an outhouse – but she also turns the irreverence of these fantastic encounters into moments of transformation that empower the speaker while disarming the audience with her use of outrageous humour (1994, 103, 102), a strategy that is explored in much more detail in chapter 3. Likewise, Halfe's use of photographs in *Blue Marrow* to create a multi-layered, playful, but also poignant narrative about her family is discussed at length in the fourth chapter of this book.

What I am interested in here is Halfe's latest collection of poems, *The Crooked Good*, which extend and complicate Glancy's notion of religious transformation by producing a series of texts that rework 'The Sacred Story of the Rolling Head,' part of an epic Cree account of Creation that Halfe first heard as a child (Halfe 2006, 66).[7] Halfe delivered a keynote address on the Rolling Head at the 2004 '"For the Love of Words": Aboriginal Writers of Canada' conference held in Winnipeg, Manitoba, which concluded with a poem titled 'The Rolling Head's Promise' (2006, 73). The lecture and the poem give voice to the female figure of the Rolling Head, a woman whose husband severs her head from her torso after he discovers that she is having an illicit romance with a snake, which has resulted in a group of slithering offspring. The beheading leaves her able to speak but vulnerable to the changing terrain as she rolls over the ground in search of her two human sons, who are also intent on harming her. The woman's body eventually ascends to the heavens, becoming '*the evening star, her gown a purple sun*,' which chases after her husband in the form of the '*morning star*' (67); her head, however, remains earthbound, eventually ending up in the depths of a lake, and 'perhaps ... [becoming] the manifestation of the creatures that inhabit the deeper waters,' namely 'monsters' (73). This woman's horrific transformation is especially loaded because, as a wife and mother, the Rolling Head is demonized for her search for nurturance elsewhere (much like the Christian figure of Eve is blamed for Adam's downfall and their expulsion from Eden because she succumbs to the temptations of the snake). Paradoxically, as Halfe notes, in this case the husband's emotional negligence is not criticized; he ascends to the heavens with his body intact and is still venerated as a 'great hunter and provider' for his family (72).

In the poem that concludes Halfe's keynote address, the Rolling Head speaks, giving her listeners an opportunity to experience 'good grace' through her words, which notably become musical: 'In this death / I sing you this' (2006, 73). Here, the Rolling Head blurs the traditional disciplinary boundaries between music and poetry, a strategic move that echoes Glancy's efforts in her writing to combine poetry and song, and accords with the work of Joy Harjo and Jeannette Armstrong discussed in chapter 2. Moreover, the Rolling Head asserts her own right to receive God's grace, and enact the work of God, in spite of the efforts of her husband and son to impede access to this relationship with the divine. Just as white western institutional and disciplinary distinctions are being eroded by Halfe's speaker in this poem, she also uses the voice of the Rolling Head to explore the imaginative possibilities that emerge in the states of sleeping and dreaming that are beyond conscious control, promising, 'I will harvest your bed' (73). Here, Halfe recalls both the Cree's traditional use of harvesting to feed their people, a relationship that is fundamentally spiritual for the tribe given their intricate connections to the natural world,[8] and the high value placed on dreaming and the subconscious by the Cree people.[9] With this closing line, Halfe strategically embraces the power of the Rolling Head, as a part of the Cree story of Creation, to provide a pliable and compelling alterna(rra)tive to imposed Christian versions of Creation.

In an interview about the story of the Rolling Head, Halfe asserts that 'we are the dreamers of this rolling head. We continue on' (Andrews 2004a, 4). Halfe overtly acknowledges the ironic and humorous dimensions of this self-positioning by describing her own engagement with the Rolling Head narrative and providing a model of reading for others who encounter her texts. She explains that 'my efforts to unravel the story's philosophy, its psychology and spirituality in my language did not lead me any closer to definitive truths. If anything, I am left with more questions ... I will be scratching "my head" for a long, long time' (2006, 73). This willingness to explore her own vulnerability as a creator and listener, and her realization that change and persistence are valuable but may not bring easy answers, embodies the need to tell the stories of women who have been silenced or relegated to the status of a fallen woman, like the Rolling Head, in new ways. In particular, in *The Crooked Good*, Halfe employs a narrator called 'Turn-Around Woman,' based on the Cree term 'kwêskî,' which is to 'turn around or change; change your ways.'[10] And it is through her voice that Halfe explores the legacy of the Rolling Head, offering an(O)ther account of a Cree woman's cross-cultural exploration of her religious, sexual, and cultural identity.

Glancy's Transformation Band

Diane Glancy, who is of Cherokee, German, and English descent, acknowledges that her mixed-blood heritage and Bible Belt upbringing have had an enormous impact on her writing. Glancy grew up in 'the white culture' but was always aware that she was different by virtue of her darker complexion: '… even in the white schools and churches I attended, I was always asked the inevitable question by teachers. What nationality was I? … They knew I was something other, but they weren't sure what' (1997, 11). She explains that even as a child she knew that her father's claim that 'we were Indians' was not specific enough, prompting her to ask 'what kind?' (11). Glancy notes in a recent interview that the challenges of defining 'Indianness' are much like those of Christianity 'with its many different denominations and beliefs' (Andrews 2002b, 648). Her self-positioning as a Native and a Christian writer may seem paradoxical, given the historical motivations of Christian conversion and the legacy of residential schooling. Glancy acknowledges the pain of listening to those who attended residential schools talk about the lasting impact of this 'education' on multiple generations of Native peoples, but also explains her desire to embrace Christ, to find something to occupy the 'vacuum that needs to be filled' (1997, 32) because of dispossession and racism. Although Glancy did not attend residential schools, Halfe did, and her inclusion later in the chapter offers a different perspective on religion, focusing particularly on the impact of an institutionally imposed relationship to Christianity that was fundamentally tied to a rejection and even damnation of the Cree language and culture. Glancy, in contrast, was brought up regularly attending church and without any knowledge of her Native language and heritage. Yet the Christ she portrays is not merely the biblical figure contained 'in the religion that the priests and nuns brought with cruelty in the name of *saving souls*' (32). He is also a 'life-force' who crosses the boundaries of religious differences, and can be incorporated into both Glancy's tribal and Christian beliefs, as she demonstrates by labelling 'Christ. The True Buffalo. The One Who Danced on the Cross. Who was the final Sun Dancer' (32). Here, Glancy suggests what Native Christianity can mean for those who are situated between often conflicting cultural and social belief systems – and how necessary metamorphosis is to her understanding of Christ in relation to her own identity.

In *The West Pole*, a work of creative non-fiction with autobiographical elements, Glancy treats the concept of transformation very broadly; she notes that there are parallel histories of Christian and Cherokee transformations, ranging from the biblical figure of Nebuchadnezzar, who was changed from man to beast by God, to 'Cherokee conjurers and magicians': men who became birds (Andrews 2002b, 652). Yet, for her, daily life also offers avenues for metamorphosis, especially in the act of writing: 'I see transformation of my own life, of books … things that I could never have said or been just a few years ago I can do now through work, through craft, through writing, the best way I can. That's a magical transformation' (652). Glancy, like Blaeser, regards words as critical to change, noting the performative functions that the spoken utterance once served for the Cherokee prior to the introduction of English by missionaries and the development of a Cherokee syllabary in the nineteenth century. As she explains, 'There was a time when what you said actually happened. If you needed to hunt, you spoke the herd into the woods or prairie … When there were no books or written laws or any way to write them. When this word/object relationship was intact' (1997, 65). And thus she attempts in her own writing to try to recapture the idea of word as 'spirit … When … [what] we spoke actually served as a causal function. Words as transformers' (66). Though her knowledge of Cherokee is minimal and most of her poetry is in English, the belief that language is a precious commodity, invested with sacred meaning and the ability to bring about metamorphosis, is necessary and even vital to her survival and self-articulation. Further, Glancy is acutely aware of how important it is to provide readers with a context for understanding her language use and to convey her interest in the power of words. The fact that what she calls an 'alive' word can be both 'good' and 'bad' at once is especially valuable to her:

> Language doesn't work with a harness. It has to move … So we are renewed. Language has a holy-clown element that goes backwards or contrariwise. To give possibilities. To lose the bonds. So the tribe isn't stuck with hunger. Or unalterable, negative situations. (69)

It is this doubling-back upon one's words in a transformational context that opens up strategic possibilities for both embracing and rethinking Christianity in Glancy's poems. Metamorphosis, for Glancy, relies on the contradictory nature of language, with its potential for multiple meanings through often edgy juxtapositions and reconfigurations. Irony and humour can be seen as microcosmic textual strategies that reveal the 'holy clown element[s]' of language and cumulatively work to provoke transformation in Glancy's works, challenging readers to examine their own assumptions about Native Christianity and what forms that spirituality might take (69).

Appropriately, Glancy has written a poem called 'The Transformation Band,' which portrays the speaker's relationship to Christ as a process of metamorphosis that is both highly spiritual and pointedly irreverent. The poem itself is contained within a collection that foregrounds the need for such alterations through its punning title, *(Ado)ration*, and vibrant cover layout. The front cover consists of a dark red background, bright yellow lettering, and the colour reproduction of a painting titled *Navajo Resurrection II*, by Father John B. Giuliani. Giuliani is an Italian who immigrated to the United States as a child, subsequently becoming a theologian, chaplain, and commune founder; his painting combines a Russian Orthodox iconographic style executed in acrylics with an interest in Native-American figures and their place in Christianity. Giuliani has stated that he is trying to 'expand the notion of Orthodox sacredness in order to express the idea of Native-American Indians as the original, indigenous presence of the holy in this continent' (John B. Giuliani Gallery, http://udayton.edu/mary/gallery/johngallery.html). Giuliani's works have been well received by many Native-American Christians and hang in churches, often located on reservations, throughout the United States. The image that appears on Glancy's text exemplifies her desire to depict Indigenous peoples as holy figures. Giuliani's painting is of a haloed Native-looking figure, with dark skin and a strong profile, wrapped in a Navajo striped blanket, and floating above a traditional southwestern pueblo – in a stance that is like that of Christ, but not quite. The painting is strategically framed on the cover, with Glancy's name placed below it and the parenthetically divided title right above it, creating an explicit set of juxtapositions between words and image. The title evokes the act of worship and, more specifically, the power of Christian love and admiration for Christ above all others; when split in two, however, adoration also recalls the rationing of scarce resources (including food), a practice that had direct historical ramifications for Glancy's Cherokee ancestors, many of whom starved to death due to severe food rationing during their forced relocation from the southeastern to the midwestern United States during 1838–9. Although some Christian missionaries ostensibly fought alongside the tribe for the retention of Cherokee sovereignty, they, in actuality, took advantage of a vulnerable population to gain converts. With this cover, Glancy visually redefines key Christian terms of worship in a mode that can be described as transformative. She alters their meaning by dividing the title itself and evoking a multiplicity of complex and even contradictory resonances through the juxtaposition of image and text; in doing so, she exposes the hypocrisy of terms like 'ado-ration' and makes a careful distinction between the actions of Christian missionaries and the power one can find directly through loving God. She also ensures that the Christ-like figure is rendered in the form of an Indigenous body – thus, the possibility of being Native and holy is made visually explicit.

In the poem 'The Transformation Band,' Glancy relies on words and accent for effect, with the speaker taking on the voice of a country bumpkin, whose colloquial language and rural farmland lifestyle make the act of salvation a surprisingly informal affair, with the poetic 'I' agreeing, '*Yez*, I could have washed out / like the Creek County bridge / but Christ redeemers me / the *phlung phlung* of his cross / my Savior' (1999b, 52). Instead of being swept away, in this instance, the speaker is saved or at least is offered the potential for redemption by the pounding of the crucifix, which ironically echoes the thumbing of guitar strings. Having borne the 'the lonesome bundle of these two worlds he gave me to walk,' the speaker laments the feeling that s/he has 'been behind so long,' that there is no hope of ever really catching up, or finding release from the burden of that load (52). While Christ has relentlessly tested the speaker's faith, there is an end in sight: a band of angels, a holy contingent of musicians, offers the promise of 'glory' (52). In the final lines of the poem, driving displaces music as the dominant metaphor for the journey towards salvation; the discovery of Christ's 'luv' is conveyed not only through music, but also by the companionship that is otherwise missing on the lonely roads that the speaker travels: 'how the car stumbles over the hill / that long road he took me / more times than I remember' (52). But that love has its own limits, as the speaker's colloquial affirmation of Christ's affection – '*yez* Jesus' – becomes a reflection on the intimate connections between such affection and the inevitability of death (52).

Glancy spent years on the roads of the midwestern United States, building her career as a writer through writer-in-residence positions as well as by commuting between Iowa City and Minneapolis/Saint Paul to complete an MFA in creative writing while starting her professorial career at Macalester College in the Twin Cities. These experiences of movement are evocatively portrayed in much of her poetry and prose. Integral to this process of self-discovery through travel is the ownership of a vehicle, a sustained faith in Christ, and the writing of poetry. As Glancy explains in *Claiming Breath*, 'Always on these harder [writing] residences when I feel that I'm the only one in the universe, Christ is the rope I hang on to. That faith has never failed me. Who could travel with less?' (1992, 28).

Further, she has repeatedly recorded the challenges of driving long distances to care for her ailing mother in poems like 'Migration to Summer Camp,' which puts another twist on the natural migratory patterns of many Native tribes, given that she is visiting the Anglo-German mother who rejected her children's 'Indianness':

> There is anger still between us. But now in storms I hear the prayer song as tribes migrated to summer campgrounds ... In Bucyrus, I see Christ's steeple above the trees. I feel sympathy for the first time & she, for once, is glad I am there. I wipe her as she did me when I was small. I hold the crossed trails of white settlers & Indians, endure two heritages, & in these trips, the healing of our tribes. (41–2)

The act of driving and of imagining the prayer songs of travelling Natives, when juxtaposed with the sighting of the crucifix, gives Glancy's speaker in 'Migration to Summer Camp' the strength to close the distance between herself and her mother. By drawing on some of the dominant clichés about Native Americans, Glancy uses travel as a means of undergoing a transformation, and more broadly reflecting on her life; although she is from the Cherokee, 'a sedentary Woodland tribe,' she strategically employs the historical migration of the Plains Indians to describe her death-bed reconciliation with her mother (1997, 2). Thus it is fitting, if one chooses to read 'The Transformation Band' autobiographically, that the music evoked by driving metamorphoses into a complex set of symbols for Glancy and her poetic voices, putting '*luv*' in all its colloquial resonance together with death, transforming the angels of Christ into a country band, and delivering redemption with its own shade of darkness (1999b, 52). This music of transformation enables the overarching dichotomies of life and death, salvation and damnation, belief and doubt to co-exist rather than clash in Glancy's poetry.

Such playfulness is also manifested in Glancy's dialogic treatment of key Native and Christian traditions, which she does by juxtaposing, for example, 'A Hogan in Bethlehem' and 'A Confession or Apology for Christian Faith' in *Claiming Breath*, poems that create a conversation about the credibility of Christian beliefs while trying to assert a middle ground. 'A Hogan in Bethlehem' traces the birth of a holy son with solemnity, foregrounding Cherokee as well as pan-Native symbols alongside Judeo-Christian references. The accretion of tribal descriptors is punctuated by biblical terminology, creating a distinctly cross-cultural portrait of Christ's arrival:

> & so it was in a country across the water, she gave birth to a son & wrapped
> him in a buffalo robe. The raccoon & elk & deer gathered in the hogan-
> manger. & there were shepherds, or animal-watchers, in the field, & lo,
> an angel, a spirit-being with wings, a bird-person, appeared the way a coy-
> ote or tumbleweed crosses the headlights on a reservation road at night …
> suddenly there were other angels & hosts of spirit-beings in war-paints &
> feathers shouting their war cries & praising Wakan Takan, the Great Spirit,
> who had sent a Chief to walk among us. (1992, 93)

In this case, transformation takes on literal and figurative dimensions.
Flying angels are joined by 'spirit-beings in war-paints' whose presence
in the night sky may be missed without careful scrutiny (93). The manger, which serves as a crib for the holy baby, is located within a hogan,
a sacred, traditionally multi-sided timber and earth structure used for
ceremonial purposes by the Navajo. Glancy strategically inverts Christian
claims of domination over Native peoples by placing the make-shift crib
inside the hogan, altering the relationship between the two populations
by highlighting the individual and collective significance of these layered cultural and religious symbols. Even the Three Wise Men who follow a shining star to locate Christ and deliver precious gifts to honour his
arrival are depicted in 'A Hogan in Bethlehem' as '3 scouts, 3 Medicine
Men' who 'made their vision quest under one star,' recalling the puberty
rites of many Native-American young boys (including the Cherokee)
who undergo physical hardships in order to gain insight through a spirit
helper (93).

Yet with the turn of a page, Glancy's poetic voice alters dramatically, a
shift that is anticipated only by the somewhat contradictory title of the
prose poem that follows, 'A Confession or Apology for Christian Faith,'
which begins with the rhetorical query: 'How could I believe this stuff?
A white child in a manger' (1992, 94). Despite the racial emphasis and
ironic tone of this line, especially when placed on the verso of a work
that portrays the significance of Christ's birth in decidedly Native terms,
the rest of the poem makes a provisional attempt to present a series of
parallels between Aboriginal belief systems and Judeo-Christianity without favouring one over the other. Glancy is well aware of her somewhat
tenuous position as a mixed-blood Cherokee Christian who connects the
survival of her people to the European importation of the Christian faith
and thus 'may make some Native Americans who read this mad' (112).
But she is careful to map out a critical vision of her own Native Christianity that is decidedly active. Glancy develops readings of biblical events

and their significance that weave a strong web of relations between tribal identity and Christian identity, at least for their author.

Even the choice of the poem title, which places 'Confession' and 'Apology' side-by-side, foregrounds the doubled nature of her task. Confession is traditionally associated with the disclosure of sin; apology, in contrast, is both a declaration of regret and, less commonly, an intellectual defence of the Christian faith. Glancy's poem is both. The poetic 'I' acknowledges the value of the arrival of Christianity, while retaining respect for Indigenous belief systems. Likewise, her poem refuses to wholeheartedly embrace all aspects of Christianity; she counters reductive presumptions about the effectiveness of Christian salvation for both Natives and whites by noting that 'the white man brought the gun & horse, two beloved possessions. Why not also a spirit message ...? Even though it seems that the white man no longer believes his own creed' (1992, 97). Nonetheless, the speaker insists on embracing the importation of Christianity and celebrating tribal religious practices, acknowledging that 'in that imperfect vehicle came news of the light. That is a hard lesson ... Maybe it's easier if ... Christianity is a fulfillment of the old ways. But who can be fulfilled without the star quilts on the church walls, the burning of cedar at the altar, & the drum hymns' (98). Glancy's poetic vision transforms the relationship between Native traditions and the Christian faith, rethinking a tendency to see them as antithetical. Without accepting all of the precepts of Christianity, particularly those that offend or anger the speaker's sense of equality and justice, Glancy's poem exemplifies Leuthold's assertion that transformation and the sacred in art go hand-in-hand. Her text becomes a series of shape-shifting moments, a collage of alterations that explore how and why faith matters through the written word.

To explore the complexities of faith through transformation, Glancy combines the strategic juxtaposition of different perspectives on religion with a dark sense of humour. In *Primer of the Obsolete*, Glancy includes a poem titled 'Caint Aint Abel: Pastel on Brown Paper Bag,' which alludes to the Book of Genesis, chapter 4, in which Cain kills his brother out of jealousy after God favours Abel's offering of a lamb over Cain's fruits. The title highlights the differences between the two brothers through wordplay – Cain becomes 'Caint' who 'Aint' his brother, or is un-'Abel' – and this is continued in the poem proper with a variety of misspellings that stress the speaker's informality and the liberties that he or she is taking with the story itself (2004, 30). The competition between the two brothers is rendered in crayons on a lowly brown paper bag. Although

the encounter with God is modernized considerably, the outcome remains the same: Abel brings the lamb's blood in a Tupperware container
and is rewarded for his tidy offering, unlike Caint, who literally cannot
satisfy God's wishes. But the poem's speaker clearly believes that s/he
can, noting in parentheses at the conclusion of the first verse, 'God says
I'm goint to get an A on my story the structure with no sudden turns you
know but plotted for' (30). However, the budding writer subsequently
takes on God as 'the instructor in this writing class' (30), criticizing him
for being uncompromising; the poetic 'I' asserts the need for individual self-expression, which clearly is not lacking in this instance, with the
twists and turns of the revised story of Caint and Abel. The speaker also
laments the modern-day results of this biblical tale, noting 'we find a
time / now of trouble everybody suing and saying so what it / wasn't
their fault just like no brother's keeper' (30).

   In this poem, the story of Cain and Abel is given a series of postmod-
ern twists: God is a writing instructor, the sheep's blood is transported in
Tupperware, and the moral of the story is rendered in pastels on a brown
paper bag. The mangled logic and conversational language of the poem
alter what was a traditional narrative of brotherly revenge into a pointed
critique of Christianity's relentless moralizing and general inflexibility.
And the value of a story that is 'plotted for' and even predictable also
becomes a source of frustration for the young speaker, who recognizes
the rewards of such conformity (the coveted A grade) but wants to resist
being like everyone else. As the speaker reminds us, 'Caint Aint Abel,'
but neither is this poem a conventional rendering of the biblical story –
the writer has decided to do 'what works well for me' (2004, 30), taking
responsibility through action in a manner that reflects both the seriousness of a brother's betrayal and the irreverence of a young speaker's hon-
est voice and uncompromising vision.

Listening to the Story of Dorcas: Code-Switching Transformations

In her 1999 book-length prose poem, *The Closets of Heaven*, Glancy develops a variation on Keith Basso's concept of 'code-switching'[11] to address
her complicated self-positioning as a Native Christian and, more specifically, a 'Christian-feminist' (Andrews 2002b, 654). Glancy acknowledges
the potential contradictions inherent in that latter pairing of terms, noting that, being from a Christian background, the women are seen as the
'minor beings' (654). It is this absence of voices of women that has led
Glancy to produce a volume of poetry that offers a first-person account

of the life of Dorcas, a seamstress and disciple living in Joppa, whose brief appearance in the Bible (Acts 9:36–43) focuses on her death (from illness) and subsequent resurrection by Peter.

Code-switching, as discussed in the introduction, has been extensively studied by Basso in relation to the linguistic humour of the Western Apache. He argues that the movement between the Apache and the English language is 'an indirect form of social commentary' that allows for the ironic redefinition of the dominant group (1979, 9). If humour is a tool for managing social relations, jokes are especially useful for the Western Apache. As Susan Purdie explains, jokes usually 'involve an intrinsic mechanism' designed to '"trap" the Audience into a situation where their proper activity of "making sense" inevitably entails' transgression (1993, 37). Jokes thus provide an opportunity for the Western Apache to temporarily 'transform themselves into Anglo-Americans through the performance of carefully crafted imitations' (Basso 1979, 6). The formulaic quality of joking marks the movement from one social and linguistic context to another, signalling the altered position of both the joke-teller and the audience. Integral to Basso's discussion is transformation – the changes that occur through these joking imitations and that are shaped, in part, by the linguistic codes the joker takes on to fulfill both his joking identity and that of the 'butt' or target of mockery (who may or may not be present). Basso includes among his various categories of Western Apache jokes the situation of the 'double transformation,' which happens when both the joker and the butt are placed in social categories to which they do not belong but are linked by virtue of their assigned roles in this 'tiny world of make-believe' (41). The catch, however, is that the scene is not entirely imaginary; rather, it is modelled on 'slices of unjoking activity' that are the 'raw materials from which the joking performances are fashioned' (41). Basso notes that joking is a way to reconfigure one's relationship to another, even just momentarily, because jokes, when recognized as such, offer an imaginative framework that allows for social transgression and even humiliation, if those participating will permit it. Yet irony also underpins code-switching jokes, because ultimately this 'transformation is only an illusion' (76).

In *The Closets of Heaven*, Glancy juxtaposes the formality of biblical quotations, indented and in italics, with the conversational voice of Dorcas, whose intimate account of her daily life destabilizes the silence of many women in the Bible and challenges the truthfulness of the Holy Word; her poems may produce ironically charged and occasionally humorous moments for Christians and non-Christians alike. But there is no guaran-

tee that all readers will get the joke; some may be offended or unwilling
to participate in an imaginative framework that grants Dorcas a voice
that does not conform to her brief and silent biblical depiction. The
code-switching that Basso so carefully observes in the Western Apache
context is thus reconfigured in Glancy's volume with biblical quotations
becoming the 'slices of unjoking activity' that provide the basis for the
text's humour (Basso 1979, 41). Dorcas is the joker who identifies and
mocks her own series of butts, typically male disciples, who are located
within her imaginative framework, which combines aspects of the world
she would like to live in with the reality of the patriarchal world which
she has been brought back to. It is these juxtapositions between what is
ideal and what is real that provide further fodder for her jokes and give
her accounts of daily life an ironic edge, particularly in relation to her
unwanted resurrection. In Glancy's rendering of Dorcas, English domi-
nates; it is the common language, though there are occasional words
in other languages that reflect Dorcas's heritage and are untranslated:
'I come from two worlds: Greek and Hebrew' (1999c, 20). Moreover,
Dorcas inflects her speech to reflect the different situations that she encounters privately and publicly; as part of a community in which men
talk and women listen or talk among themselves, she is very aware of the
power of the word and the constraints of gender. Thus explicit joking,
which she identifies as such, becomes a primarily private affair, shared
with the text's readers and aimed at the men who govern her life. For
instance, early in the collection, Dorcas recalls the presumptuousness
of Peter in relation to Jesus, stating, 'When Jesus wanted to wash Peter's
feet, Peter asked to be washed all over. I laugh under my breath when I
hear this' (21). But she also delineates the boundaries of what she deems
funny, pointing out in the very next line, 'Before he died, Jesus told
Peter to feed his sheep. That doesn't make me laugh. Am I a sheep? The
daughter of a craftsman. The wife of a merchant. The granddaughter of
a woman who talked to me of the ideas men thought' (21). This ironic
turn, when the first biblical situation is compared with the second, is especially bitter, highlighting the marginality of women and the arrogance
of men.

While Dorcas may be expected to remain silent in her dealings with
biblical male leaders, *The Closets of Heaven* allows for a world of make-
believe to emerge that repositions both this female disciple and her male
counterparts, making the men into the butt of the joke and giving her
the power of the Word even as she professes her inadequacies as a disciple of Christ. Dorcas describes her struggle to speak in tongues to God,

and wryly asks, 'Is tongues not a gift the Holy Spirit gives to his believ-
ers? If they are good little donkeys. If they carry the burden they should'
(1999c, 31). Here, Dorcas jokingly implies that she is trying to be the
bearer of burdens as expected. Yet she quickly inverts her self-positioning as the naïve donkey when she subsequently recalls her reaction to a
biblical passage delivered by a man at a Christian meeting in Joppa:

> *Forty years God sustained them in the wilderness. They lacked nothing. Their clothes
> did not get old* (*Nehemiah 9:21*).
> 'Their clothes did not get old?' I asked suddenly. 'Their clothes did not wear
> out? What kind of threads made them? Did some angel remake or mend the
> robes as people slept? Did God breathe upon the cloth at night? How could
> cloth not wear out? Just look at the ragged children in the marketplace.'
> The people look at me. Why don't they say something?
> 'Cloth wears out,' I say. (31)

This final line provides its own ironic reversal because it is Dorcas's
ability to sew, and the need to create new garments and mend worn ones,
that secures her unwanted resurrection after she reaches heaven. While
there is no record of Dorcas's words in the Bible, in Glancy's text Dorcas
asks questions, probing her religious leaders and suggesting that their
knowledge is surprisingly limited when it comes to practical matters. She
also goes on to position herself as a font of information who is burdened
both by the relentless requests of young women to become her appren-
tices and her rapidly deteriorating health.

 This is nowhere more evident than in the latter part of the collection
when a dead Dorcas is brought back to life by Peter and expresses her
anger at this miracle, done at the behest of her fellow disciples and without her consent:

> Why couldn't they leave me alone? I was pulled back into a room where a
> man said *arise*. He didn't even use my common name. Dorcas. Why didn't
> he bring someone else back, if he had to bring someone? ... Someone who
> has something to do? ... What do I do now? Tolerate these women? Wait for
> another death? (1999c, 78)

Treated as evidence that miracles can happen, Dorcas becomes an object
of fascination for the local population. Yet the joy expected from her by
virtue of her resurrection is explicitly countered by Dorcas's fond – but
quickly fading – memories of heaven and the realization that she has

been brought back because Peter admired her sewing talents, the same
Peter whom Dorcas overhears advising an abused woman to stay with her
husband because 'heaven is obedience to God' (66). Dorcas expresses
her anger at Peter's arrogance, countering his claim with a pair of rhetorical questions that undermine his authority by ironically juxtaposing
his lack of experience with her implied first-hand knowledge of heaven:
'Who has been to heaven already? Is it him?' (66). She subsequently
turns to the example of Christ, citing lines from John 8:6–7, in which
Jesus is tested by the Pharisees and the teachers of law at the temple
courts by being asked whether an adulterous young woman should be
stoned. Christ tells them, '*He that is without sin among you, let him cast the
first stone on her,*' to which Dorcas comments, 'Just imagine' (80). Again,
gendered presumptions of arrogance – the impossibility that any of the
men presented are indeed as pure as they pretend to be – are undermined by the 'unsaid,' as it is precisely what cannot be imagined that
reveals the truth. With that pithy and biting response, Dorcas illustrates
Peter's unnecessary arrogance and his own lack of perceptiveness, despite Christ's example. Notably, Glancy's representation of Peter through
Dorcas complicates renderings of this apostle as a trickster figure in the
Christian folklore of the Yaqui and other Native cultures in the American Southwest. As William Hynes and Thomas Steele suggest, there are
a variety of 'San Pedro' tales from the region in which Peter behaves as
a Native trickster figure, indulging in lewd behaviour, employing scatological humour, shape-shifting himself for the purposes of deception,
and generally breaking every taboo, in ways that may seem counterproductive but are ultimately beneficial to the community (1993, 166).
If, as Hynes and Steele suggest, the trickster serves as 'a social steam
valve that can vent ... pent-up emotion,' typically through 'laughter at
the profanations of the trickster,' and enable both a return to order and
its transformation, then Glancy's reconfiguration of Peter here can be
read as a highly ironic comment on popular versions of this male apostle
as trickster (170). Dorcas may damn Peter for his self-centred resurrection of her, but ultimately the world is transformed, at least in Glancy's
text, by her return.

   In *The Closets of Heaven*, Dorcas does not hesitate to express her frustration with other male biblical figures and the scriptures more generally,
in part because 'there's a lot of tearing off and renting of clothes,' the
very items that she has been brought back to continue to produce but
that seem to hold little value for the men who wear them (1999c, 83).
Dorcas offers up the scriptural example of Paul and Barnabas, who re-

move their clothes in Acts 14:14–15 to prove that they too are human, and she contemplates the travel of these men in their role as missionaries (albeit often under threat of death) with the routine of her own life, asking mockingly, 'How would they like to sit in their house all day and sew?' (84). Rather than providing space for these men to relay their experiences, Dorcas again implicitly displaces their prominence with irony through careful self-positioning as a woman relegated to the home and domestic duties. She also cultivates the strength of her Christian faith, raising questions as to whether travelling and fleeing do indeed constitute more important acts of faith than her own toiling, which has resulted in her resurrection.

Scriptural quotations in *The Closets of Heaven* thus become a catalyst for Dorcas's own counter-discourse, transforming the Bible from a source of all wisdom to a springboard for her intimate account of her life, death, and subsequent resurrection. As a woman without a voice in the Bible whose physical return to life is a means of convincing the people of Joppa to believe in God, Glancy employs her own version of code-switching between passages of scripture and the imagined voice and thoughts of Dorcas to challenge constructions of male authority and to offer potentially irreverent yet compelling perspectives on biblically rendered women's roles. At the conclusion of the collection, while attending an assembly, Dorcas hears yet another scriptural passage about Jeremiah's rescue from a dungeon by Ebedmelech, with the help of Jeremiah's '*old rags and worn-out garments*' which serve as bungee cords (1999c, 100). As a seamstress, Dorcas mocks the obviousness of this revelation: 'I could have told them that. It's clothes that pull us up' (100). But rather than stopping there, Dorcas goes further, asserting that, having herself seen holy garments in heaven – 'the closets of coats, the robes of the ephods, the ephods, the breast-plates, girdles, and mitres' – 'even women could be priests like Samuel and Aaron … Women the same as men' (101). In a final act of defiance against the queries of locals who want details about her brief time in heaven, Dorcas asserts that 'in the end, I will tell them, it's what we sew' (101). Here she deliberately puns on the doubled meaning of sew/sow and the biblical concept of reaping what one sows or sews – in the case of Dorcas's handiwork – in order to stress both the fertility and power of womanhood and to assert women's significance beyond serving as vessels of reproduction, labour, and resurrection. The joke is hers, and she claims the right not only to be a joke-teller but also to transform the male disciples into the 'make-believe' roles of her choosing, and to make them into her individual and collective butts as she sees fit.

Dorcas, of course, is not a Native woman, but Glancy is a Cherokee-German poet, and her decision to write *The Closets of Heaven* is explained in some detail at the conclusion of the collection, again through the juxtaposition of scriptural passages and Glancy's own sustained commentary on her position as a self-identified Native-Christian and feminist. In particular, Glancy stresses the sense of 'severe admonition' she felt in writing a book that countered the scriptural instructions of Revelation 22:18: '*If any man shall add unto these things, God shall add unto him the plagues that are written in this book*' (1999c, 104); in defiance of this instruction, Glancy insists that she, as a woman, had to 'fill-in the blank places in the scriptures, even if they were only the imaginary happenings of Dorcas's ordinary daily life' (104). But she also acknowledges the self-serving nature and limits of such a project and the impossibility of ever fully realizing Dorcas's voice: 'I had the feeling of being where I didn't belong, which all writing is, maybe, even when it isn't putting words in the mouth of someone who lived' (105). For Glancy, this collection, with its moments of irreverence and sustained ironic edge achieved in part through code-switching, becomes a way of articulating her own distinctive Native-Christian vision. While scriptural quotations become a road map for many Christian readers of the collection (because of their familiarity), Glancy employs Dorcas's voice to offer her own social commentary on behalf of one kind of marginalized individual – the female disciple – who becomes a stand-in or figurehead for all those relegated to 'otherness' in biblical writings, particularly Native-Christians. And by virtue of the book taking the form of a published text, Dorcas's transformation becomes more than merely an illusion; it gives her a powerful voice. If, as Glancy has suggested elsewhere, 'seeing the familiar in a new way' is what writing as a feminist does, then such an account of an otherwise forgotten female figure from perhaps the most widely read book in the world, the Bible, becomes not only a 'revelation of words' but a way of understanding one's mixed faith (and mixed-blood self) and communicating that notion to readers as a transformation with lasting consequences (1992, 53).

Reading *The Crooked Good*

For Louise Halfe, *The Crooked Good* represents the power of 'The Sacred Story of the Rolling Head,' which continues 'to live in our imagination and puzzle those attempting to unravel her mystery' (2006, 73). The resulting collection explores the bodily transformation of the Rolling

Head, as a result of her beheading, and her legacy for Cree women. But Halfe's book also engages explicitly with the impact of an imposed Catholic conversion, primarily enforced through the residential schools system, on multiple generations of Cree families. As Katherine Pettipas argues in *Severing the Ties That Bind: Government Repression of Indigenous Religious Ceremonies on the Prairies*, when first instituted in the 1880s, residential schools were designed to produce 'new, moral, self-support-ing Christian citizens' through 'a Victorian regime of discipline and school regulations' (1994, 80). Missionaries were deemed to be suitable teachers in these schools precisely because, from the Canadian govern-ment's perspective, they were seen as having already made a strong com-mitment to educating Native children. In particular, Pettipas's choice of language to describe this process of forced assimilation is worth not-ing; she explains that 'the transformation of Cree children began the moment of their arrival in the schools' (80), starting with a dramatic physical alteration – accomplished through scrubbing, haircuts, the don-ning of uniforms, and new Christianized names – and was followed by an imposed linguistic, cultural, and spiritual re-education process during which the children received instruction in 'Christian religious ideology' (80).[12] The result was that 'Indian religious rites were ... replaced by the rites of Christianity' (80). The transformation and recuperation of the Rolling Head comes through the mediating figure of *ê-kwêskît* – Turn-Around Woman in Halfe's collection – whose voice rises from the depths of the lake where the Rolling Head drowned. The story of her people becomes a pivotal counter-narrative to the silencing of Cree women, and the Cree population more generally due to the painful legacy of residen-tial schooling.

Like Glancy, Halfe sees the pliability of language, its ability to double-back, as fundamental to her project, which pointedly displaces Christian-ity – and especially the damnation of Eve because she has surrendered to the temptations of the snake – with her own Cree-centred account of Creation. While there are striking similarities between Eve's fate and that of the Rolling Head, there are also critical differences. For exam-ple, Halfe specifically employs code-switching, often between Cree and English, to destabilize the presumed dominance of Christianity and the English language, and to create moments of cross-cultural humour for those readers who can engage with both the English and Cree meanings of words. As with *The Closets of Heaven*, in which Dorcas acts as the joker, mocking the male disciples who surround her, Turn-Around Woman takes aim at the arrogance of men, especially white Christians such as

'Father Francis Du Person' (2007, 8), a real-life seventeenth-century Jesuit missionary whose voice Halfe appropriates in order to explore what happened when religious authority was imposed on the Cree without knowledge of Cree values and traditions. Notably, Halfe uses linguistic code-switching much more abundantly than Glancy by incorporating a wide range of Cree words and proper names into her text, which – although they are translated in a 'Glossary' at the back of the collection and sometimes in the poems themselves – come to represent an alternate world view that resists comprehension by any reader who is not willing to do the extra work of looking up the translation, and even then cultivates a slippage between the word and its meanings by only defining individual terms. In other words, to get the joke requires 'insider' access, which is reserved for those who are fluently versed in English and Cree. And ultimately, by employing the voice of Turn-Around Woman, who is Cree, rather than a Christian figure such as Eve or even Dorcas, Halfe explores the possibilities of transformation within the realm of her own Native community and heritage, drawing on Cree concepts and people to convey her familial, tribal, and spiritual history as she overtly mocks the limitations of Catholicism and the English language.

Halfe establishes a doubled framework for reading *The Crooked Good* from the outset, with the volume's cover illustration and layout explicitly invoking and displacing the story of Eve's fall with the 'puzzle' of the Rolling Head, a narrative that is much more resistant to quick resolution and easy judgments (2006, 73). In the acknowledgments at the end of the collection, Halfe thanks Paul LaPointe, a Saskatchewan-based painter, for 'your friendship,' noting that 'your art is our blessing' (2007, 134). It is LaPointe's 'Snake Woman' that adorns the glossy-black-on-matte-black cover of *The Crooked Good*. But the glossy black outline of the head of this snake comes with an unexpected twist. The snake's mouth and neck contain the head of a woman who is clearly visible to those looking at the cover; the woman has her eyes closed and her mouth wide open, as if she is calling out, just as the newly maimed Rolling Head does to her children. Moreover, the ends of the woman's two braids poke out of the snake's mouth, creating an optical illusion by appearing to form the reptile's forked tongue. This visual pun is mirrored by the book's title, which appears just below the image in bright red letters: *The Croo$_{ked}$ Good*. The title not only visually echoes the forked nature of the snake's tongue, but also enacts a pun of its own by making the word 'Crooked' literally crooked when presented on the page. By placing 'crooked' and 'good' side by side and forging a relationship between seemingly oppositional words, Halfe signals her desire for readers to wrestle with these ironic juxtapositions. According to the *OED*, 'crooked' is an adjective that not only describes something that is 'bent from the straight form, curved, ... awry; deformed' but also, in figurative terms, something that is a deviation from 'rectitude; ... dishonest; perverse.'[13] 'Good,' in contrast, is used adjectivally to praise what is 'commendable; right, [or] sound' in a person's behaviour, or to refer to a thing that is 'useful, reliable, ... or efficient in a function, pursuit.'[14] When coupled, these two words clash, undercutting one another to forge a slippery bond. Indeed, *The Crooked Good* is ostensibly about one story within the Cree creation narrative that does not conform to standard white western definitions of good and evil. But in tracing the literal and figurative curves that are central to the Rolling Head's legacy, Halfe's poems also mock the arrogance and righteousness of those good Catholic missionaries who claimed to be civilizing the Cree people, by making their presence in her text peripheral and revealing their logic to be simplistic and ultimately faulty.

While the snake's head (with the Rolling Head inside) rests on the top part of the cover, with the head looking down towards the title, the bottom half of the cover is adorned with the same snake's tail, creating a sense of circularity; the snake seems to be wrapped around the book of poems, squeezing it tight, and both tempting and threatening readers who break the binding to look inside. And imprinted across the snake's tail are the two sets of names Halfe uses to identify herself, again in bright red: the italicized *Sky Dancer* appears just above the block capitals of LOUISE BERNICE HALFE. This doubly inscribed identity makes her straddling of the Cree and white western world visible and gives primacy to her Cree culture. As Halfe explains in the poem called 'Listen: To The Story' from *The Crooked Good*, '*sky dancers*' are the stars in the sky which are produced by figures like the Rolling Head, ensuring their eternal survival (2007, 24). The verbal and visual cues offered on the cover of *The Crooked Good* gesture towards a doubled reading of the poems that are contained inside. The decapitated snake and human heads release blood, in this case manifested as red ink that imprints the cover with the power of fertility in the form of menstrual blood (the shedding skin), but also recalls the white western legacy of Eve's fall because of the snake's tempting offer of a red apple from the Tree of Knowledge of Good and Evil, a bargain that led to the end of human immortality. In her 'Keynote Address,' Halfe draws on the work of antiquities scholar Kenneth Lapatin to explain that snakes are themselves regarded as contradictory and duplicitous by many cultures, precisely because they

'combine in disturbing ways the comforting and the familiar with the ter-
rifying and the repellant' (Lapatin 2002, 79). This stereotypical reaction
motivated Halfe in childhood to 'take ownership over my fear of snakes'
by handling garter snakes and using them to chase away 'a man who
made my skin crawl' (2006, 70). In the Cree culture, women such as her
grandmother recognized that 'the gifts of the snake are powerful' (70);
the Cree used snakeskins, particularly for healing (70). This text then
arguably becomes an act of cultural recovery and healing that embraces
the crookedness of the snake, its ambivalent but powerful legacy for the
Cree, and replaces less nuanced white western associations of the reptile
with temptation and evil with a more complex, female-centred understanding of its potential, especially for figures like the Rolling Head.

    Halfe reiterates this ironic and sometimes playful portrait of snakes
and the women who love them in the poems that make up *The Crooked
Good*, starting the volume with a text that signals its duplicity and resistance to closure through its title: 'The End and the Beginning' (2007, 1).
Rather than replicating white western linearity, Halfe inverts the order of
her narrative, which is in keeping with the pliability and circularity of the
snake that adorns the cover.[15] This approach also accords with Halfe's
exploration of 'Traditional Cree Philosophy,' where she notes that 'traditional Cree spirituality ... strongly reinforces the principle of the circle
of life' (Halfe and Jaine 1989, 11), as opposed to a linear and strictly
chronological journey. Halfe's first poem in this collection traces her
speaker's journey across lakes and hills to a traditional 'Talking Circle,'
where healing and reconciliation with the speaker's 'ancient roots' take
place; the speaker even sits with 'Rib Woman,' who for white western
readers like myself recalls the Christian description of Eve's creation in
Genesis, but functions outside of the constraints imposed by God and
Adam (2007, 1). The result is a poem about the speaker's efforts to come
to terms with and honour her ancestors through a process of metamorphosis and rebirth: 'Some of us have learned to: / Incubate, / hatch
those million eyes, these million / ears, these million noses, these ancient roots / that stem through our bodies. / It is these sun-runners who
go deep' (1). The poetic 'I' refers here to a long history of running in
Native North American cultures as a means of communication and a
system of protection.[16] These runners, who faced all kinds of extreme
weather, acted as emissaries for their people by supplying and exchang-
ing information with other populations, but they also became critical to
a tribe's survival by warning their communities of approaching danger,
be it soldiers, missionaries, or both. And the act of running has often

been linked by Native peoples across North America to the creation of the world through origin stories. For Halfe, the actions of the sun-runners, through their repetition of ancient ceremonies, maintain constant links with the 'ancient roots' that are part of the speaker's heritage and her being in the present (2007, 1). The holy roles of the sun-runners and their value to tribes because they can access the sacred inspire the speaker, who concludes the poem with the claim that 'perhaps, I am one of them' (1). Here, her speaker enacts the 'crooked-ness' that characterizes the text as a whole by speculating on her place within Cree society, an act that resists closure and certainty. Halfe's narrator embraces the potential of transformation, whether through literal rebirth by incubation and hatching or a figurative renewal that comes from connecting more strongly and directly with her Native heritage. Moreover, in this poem, Halfe's poetic 'I' can be read as pointedly displacing the primacy of the Bible, and specifically, the Book of Genesis. If, in Genesis, the snake's success at tempting Eve marks literally the end of human access to Paradise, forcing Adam and Eve to vacate the Garden of Eden because of their violation of God's trust, Halfe's speaker refuses to see her people as being systematically damned because they will not abandon their Cree spiritual beliefs.

Instead, Halfe frames the presumptive authority of white male Christian voices (as expressed in a poem like 'Father Francis Du Person, *27th of April, 1639*,' in which Halfe draws on the published diary entries of this missionary, complete with his descriptions of the heathen 'savages' he ministers to) with the voice of Turn-Around Woman, a figure who experiences and then describes the historical and contemporary significance of the Rolling Head's legacy for Cree women (2007, 8). In contrast with Du Person's fear of what he perceives as the Native willingness to be dictated to by the '*devil*' (8), a shape-changer whom the missionary describes as turning in an instant from '*a crow*' to '*a flame / or a ghost*' and imposing wishes on the '*savages*' through the medium of dreams (8), in the self-titled poem '*ê-kwêskît* – Turn-Around Woman,' Halfe's speaker embraces the potency of dreams and visions, and describes the ways in which her teachers have helped her to become a storyteller and writer, to 'dream awake. Asleep. On paper,' and to give voice to an ever-changing universe, a project that inevitably remains 'half done' (4). Turn-Around Woman, unlike Du Person, has no illusions of grandeur or belief in her righteousness above all others. In the third stanza of this loosely structured poem, she stresses that her narratives should not be compared to the talents of those '*gifted mysterious people of long ago*,' the '*ancient story keepers*' (3), stating explicitly that 'I, Turn-Around Woman, am not one of them' (3). This unexpected and even jarring ironic turn underlines the speaker's modesty and self-doubt, but also reflects a style of poetic diction that – much like the snake who graces the cover – challenges readers to stay awake, pay attention, and reach their own judgments.

The humorous dimensions of such a rhetorical strategy emerge more clearly as the poem progresses, with the first-person speaker describing her efforts to aspire to the talents of her racially diverse teachers: 'Old people. / An Indian man, a White Man. / An Indian Woman, a White Woman' (2007, 3). Turn-Around Woman may seem to be little more than a 'wailing' student, unable to reach their lofty heights (3). However, readers soon discover that the narrator is savvy, mature, and manipulative in ways that defy her naïve and youthful pose:

> I am not a saint. I am a crooked good.
> My cousins said I was easy, therefore
> I've never been a maiden.
> I'm seventy, but still
> I carry my sins. Brothers-in-law
> I meet for the first time wipe their hands
> As if I am still among the maggots. I didn't
> Know their women wept when their men
> Slept in my bed. I am not a saint.
>
> I married Abel, a wide green-eyed man. Fifty years now.
> Inside Rib Woman I shook hands with promise.
> Promise never forgot, trailed me year after year
> His Big Heavens a morning lake drowns me in my lair.
> I learned how to build Rib Woman
> one willow at a time, one skin at a time.
> I am only half done. This is part of the story. (4)

Here, the poetic 'I' plays a joke on those readers who may presume to already know the speaker, and creates a counter-narrative that deliberately differentiates her from various biblical figures of female goodness, embodied by Catholic saints and even the Virgin Mary, whom Father Francis identifies as appropriate role models for wayward 'savages' (8). Halfe's speaker dismisses the possibility of being canonized a saint, and counters this goal with the reality of what she has become, describing herself as 'a crooked good' whose sexual promiscuity has been a way of life for decades. Indeed, the poetic 'I' is no spring chicken, revealing her age as 'seventy' and noting that she had no idea of the impact of her behaviour on the women whose husbands she bedded (4). Whether what Turn-Around Woman claims is true or not, she carefully frames and reinforces her actions with the line that opens and closes the stanza, 'I am not a saint' (4), which explicitly signals a movement away from white western Christian expectations of piety and towards a more complex and unpredictable version of femaleness, one that is neither dependent on death and canonization to establish her value to society nor forced to pay eternally for the sin of falling prey to temptation.

With this rejection of Christian sainthood firmly in place, Halfe's speaker relays the story of her marriage to the biblical Abel, the second of Adam and Eve's sons, who is murdered by his jealous brother, Cain. In this case, however, Abel is identified as jealous himself, a 'green-eyed man' who struggles with covetousness, presumably over his wife's behaviour (2007, 4). Halfe's depiction of Abel can be read as ironically echoing Glancy's 'Cain Aint Abel' in its revisionist aims; here, Abel takes on the fundamental characteristic of his brother, becoming un-Abel or Cain-like. By reshaping otherwise familiar Christian figures, giving them unexpected attributes, and echoing biblical narratives but with a twist, Turn-Around Woman undercuts the priority given to white western Christian stories in order to foreground her own. Halfe's speaker locates herself inside Rib Woman, a Native adaptation and reconfiguration of Eve (who, according to the Bible, was made by God from Adam's rib to provide him with a companion), where she shakes 'hands with promise' (4), an act with lasting consequences as the persona of Promise begins to trail Turn-Around Woman, threatening to drown her with the pledge of a wondrous Christian afterlife. But Halfe's speaker remains resolute that she will forge her own Cree-centred spiritual path, one that is inherently crooked and incomplete; the building of Rib Woman, which she describes as 'one willow at a time, one skin at a time,' remains purposefully 'half done' in order to allow her story to unfold and transform just as she does (4).

In a poem that appears on the facing page, called 'Everyday Is a Story,' Halfe's poetic 'I' reiterates this need to break from the Christian emphasis on the 'Promise' to obey and be faithful (2007, 4), describing instead the bonds created between a group of Cree women who straddle time and space in a manner that enters the realm of the mythic or fantastic. These women have travelled 'on brooms, / jalopies, luxury cars, airplanes, trains, ships,' all take 'snake-tongued lovers,' inherit 'laughter,

... [along with] working hands' and use 'dreams' as their 'medicine' (7).
While the first-person speaker recalls growing up on the eerily named
Cannibal Lake Reserve, where men ruled, dividing women and setting
them against one another in an effort to ensure that they behaved in a
saintly manner, her generation starts to resist such patriarchal dictator-
ship (which is attributed to the introduction of Christianity) by returning to traditional Cree practices. Although Turn-Around Woman may
not possess the 'roots' and 'herbs' of her ancestors, she has the ability
to dream (7); it is this skill that proves restorative and cultivates connections between these women, a point that Halfe herself reiterates in
an interview where she states that dreaming 'is very central to my work
... It gives me the story' (Andrews 2004a, 3). Moreover, this receptiveness to the spiritual world is complemented by the belief that access to
such experiences need not be mediated by an authority figure, such as
a Catholic priest.

Nor does the forced act of renaming Cree children after saints automatically ensure their redemption, as Halfe's speaker points out in a
later poem, 'My Tribe,' where this ritual is resolutely mocked through invocation of childhood nonsense rhymes that echo the derogatory treatment of these young boys and girls who are regarded as physically and
spiritually dirty, as well as unintelligent by their teachers and caregivers:
'Everyone in boarding school was named after a saint. / Mary Wash Your
Feet, Simple Simon, Peter Thumper' (2007, 114). Simple Simon's inability in the classic nursery rhyme to pay for a taste of a pie is followed
by a series of mishaps (at least in some versions of the poem), including
washing himself with a 'blacking ball' because he has no soap, and then
stating, rather ironically, 'I'm a beauty now, I hope.'[17] Similarly, 'Mary
Wash Your Feet' and 'Peter Thumper' wryly recall subservient religious
and cultural relationships. The Christian washing of feet is regarded as
an act of humility and faith undertaken in several places in the Bible
at Jesus's behest, and the term 'Peter Thumper' juxtaposes the name
of a saint, whose feet were actually washed by Jesus, with the image of
the cuddly Disney rabbit from *Bambi*; 'thumper' is also a disparaging
nickname given to women when perceived primarily as sexual objects,
relegating them to the status of pets. Access to sainthood at residential
schools is paradoxically pre-empted by the reality of racism as students
may be named after saints but are doomed to never attain their status.
This situation is best articulated by Homi Bhabha when he explains the
phenomenon of 'colonial mimicry,' which is 'the desire for a reformed,
recognizable Other, *as a subject that is almost the same but not quite*' (2004,

122). In his study, Bhabha attends primarily to the impact of this desire on the colonizer, but the slippage between the reformed object of colonization and the colonizer's ideal (embodied by him- or herself) becomes a productive way to understand Halfe's use of irony and humour in *The Crooked Good*. While the appropriateness of applying post-colonial theory to Native texts is the subject of ongoing scholarly debate,[18] in this instance, colonialism is at the heart of the speaker's experience of 'in-betweenness,' that speaker having been educated in a Catholic residential school and raised with Cree values and beliefs. Halfe enables this double perspective to emerge, flourish, and talk back to the dominance of white western Christian paradigms through sharp wit and keenly ironic juxtapositions, both in individual lines of poetry and with the positioning of texts within the collection. Hence, when Halfe's poetic 'I' celebrates the power of dreaming in the final lines of 'Everyday Is a Story,' asserting that 'No one expected us, the brown-skins, to get anywhere. / Especially us women' (2007, 7), she builds towards the collection's decisive undercutting of the white western presumption that, over time, these female voices, who were the antitheses of sainthood, were supposed to fade from prominence and eventually die out altogether.

Halfe furthers the ironic resonances of this claim to survival by placing 'Everyday Is a Story' immediately prior to the poem that partially excerpts the diary entries of Father Francis Du Person. This editorial choice is complemented by Halfe's decision to end the poem titled 'Father Francis Du Person' with a first-person interjection from Turn-Around Woman, who pointedly undercuts the missionary's assessment of the Cree '*savages*' as failing to '*make any distinction / between the good and the bad*' (2007, 9) by giving the 'crooked good' the last word. In this instance, 'I, *ê-kwêskît*' and her female companions triumph over the seeming dominance of Du Person's voice by asserting that they 'lived ... / Shared a story ... / Sang into the dark' (9). In this instance, the speaker describes the transformation that occurs in spiritual and generic terms by describing how the Cree women turn to the oral communal art of storytelling and song, as related forms of sacred expression, in an overt violation of the condemnatory sermon delivered directly above by Du Person.

The final alteration in this spiritual revisioning of Genesis, and more broadly the Catholic damnation of these 'crooked' women, comes in the last poem of the section, titled 'First Sound,' which is all about sound-play. Halfe's poetic 'I' employs what appear to be yoga chants as the basis for a series of lines that explore, and conversely make fun of, that pivotal moment in the world's creation. Instead of focusing on what God has made, the speaker depicts the sounds that emerge through the repetition of 'hoooooooooooo' and 'ommmmmmmmmm' (2007, 10). In yoga, 'ho' is part of the laughter chant, used to relieve stress and provide health benefits to practitioners, though when extended by the addition of multiple *o*'s the sound may be associated with a myriad of other contexts, including the delivery of a baby. 'Om,' a mystical syllable in Buddhism, forms the core of many yoga chants because of its significance as a most sacred mantra.[19] It, too, is drawn out in Halfe's poem, becoming not only the sound that the Rolling Head makes when she resurfaces from her watery grave to speak again, but also the basis for an intimate verbal exchange in the midst of a moment of sexual ecstasy:

> Beloved's sweet Ommmmmmmmmmmmmmmm
> The echo of my breath Ommmmmmmmmmmmmmm
> He asked...mmmmmmmmmmmmm
> Hooooooooooooooooo I'm having moooooooooooooooooooooooo
> my own.............Ommmmmmmmmmmmmmmmmm, as we came. (10)

In this instance, the identity of first-person speaker is not made explicit, though given the structure of the collection, it is mostly likely Turn-Around Woman, who – in this case – is reconfiguring the dominance of the visual in the biblical account of creation with an emphasis on sound, and what those sounds can convey, even when represented in print: sexual joy, the pain of betrayal, or a fundamental awareness of the body as a living being. Halfe's playful rendering of 'First Sound' becomes a reminder to readers to listen carefully to what is both presented on and absent from the page. Moreover, these 'first sound[s]' call on readers to hear the poem on the page and, in doing so, viscerally experience the processes and products of creation (10).

By the end of *The Crooked Good*, Turn-Around Woman's voice is intertwined with that of the Rolling Head in a parodic rewriting of the biblical story of Genesis that combines the Cree and English languages and cultures with relative ease. The vision that Halfe presents is fundamentally transformative and regenerative, yet also acknowledges the pain and suffering of colonization and, specifically, the legacy of residential schooling. The tragic story of the Rolling Head possesses some stark similarities to the experience of residential schooling and its legacy for parents, children, and subsequent generations, with a beheaded and disempowered mother figure struggling to reconcile with her two sons who have been turned against her by their father because of a perceived fall into temptation. The patriarchal structure of Roman Catholicism, the efforts made by the nuns and priests running the schools to eviscerate Cree culture and language, and the structure of the educational system that insisted upon the forced separation of young children from their families in order to better them, parallel the brutal physicality of the mother's beheading, search to reunite with her offspring, and her eventual drowning.

Yet Halfe resists treating the story of the Rolling Head as finite. The final poem of the collection, entitled 'Gave My Name,' starts with the lines 'In the beginning / when these words were born' (2007, 124), echoing Genesis but with a critical difference. Here Turn-Around Woman appears to become the Rolling Head, emerging as a 'sturgeon' from 'the depths of the lake since the day I drowned' (124); the speaking 'I' and the eyes of the Rolling Head seem to have transformed into two parts of the same figure, and this duality is rendered visible on the page through the presentation of the poem in two columns. The poem on the left, called 'Gave My Name,' is in the standard font of the collection, with the exception of one italicized Cree word, which is the Cree name for Turn-Around Woman. The text on the right, titled '*âtayôhkan*' (meaning 'spirit being; spirit entity; ancient legend spirit'), provides an abbreviated English-language account of the story of the Rolling Head in italics, including a vivid description of her '*hairy skull*' becoming '*a home for mice and snakes*' after centuries of tumbling (129, 124). The only Cree word used in the right-hand side of the poem is 'nitêh,' or 'my heart,' which is not italicized and becomes symbolic of the pain that the Rolling Head has undergone because of her husband's violent act: 'nitêh *my heart, / bleeding, / clutched in his fist*' (124). According to the Rolling Head, her spouse is a 'cursed man' who may have made it into the sky, swimming '*in stars,*' but she too has found a place for her voice and vision, in partnership with Turn-Around Woman (124).

This metamorphosis from Turn-Around Woman to the Rolling Head, as the poem reveals, is no ordinary change in shape, for 'When *ê-kwêskit* sinks, / head on the pillow' into dreaming, the 'I/eye' of the Rolling Head emerges, complete with her contemporary tools of technology: 'I surface / with camera, phone, television / and a big screen' (2007, 124). This media-savvy version of the Rolling Head/Turn-Around Woman may, at first glance, seem to border on the absurd. But the joke is on readers who dismiss the emergence of the Rolling Head as nothing more than Halfe's sleight of hand. The accretion of high-tech gadgets may be useful to survey the water and its surroundings, in an effort to keep Turn-Around Woman safe. It also reflects the contemporary reality of Cree women, like Halfe and Turn-Around Woman, who adeptly synthesize traditional spiritual beliefs with modern conveniences and sources of entertainment. Yet Halfe's ironic commentary on Rolling Head's relevance to the world today does not stop there. She further complicates this meeting of voices by adding a visual intertext and including a final stanza that returns the collection yet again to its beginning. A different LaPointe ink drawing of the Rolling Head woman within the snake appears on the page opposite to this last poem; in this drawing, the snake's body forms a fairly tight figure-eight shape but leaves a gap between the forked tongue and the tip of the tail, a metaphoric space of possibility. And Halfe ends the poem with an italicized stanza that is situated in the bottom middle of the page, forging a common ground or place to merge the two women's voices in this text:

> *I'm earth*
> *born each moon*
> *waxing and waning,*
> *bleeding eggs.*
> *I've painted red on rocks;*
> *I swim the caves in lakes*
> *where my head swims.*
> *And I drink to roll again.* (124)

In her 'Keynote Address,' Halfe emphasizes the ironic dimensions of the Rolling Head's story, explaining that it is virtually impossible to reconcile the relationship between the head and the heart: 'The Elders tell us that the longest and most arduous task that humans will ever undertake is the journey between the head and the heart. Perhaps this story reflects just how hard it is to seek and find one's heart's desire with simply the head' (2006, 72). Despite the loss of her heart, the Rolling Head still possesses her head, which is crucial because, as Halfe notes, 'it houses the brain' and allows us as human beings 'to create, imagine, and dream' (2006, 72). The Rolling Head thus becomes 'a muse,' inspiring 'the visionary, the poet, the dreamer, the singer, and the painter' through the subconscious, long after she is thought to have died (72). If in 'The Promise' the Rolling Head has committed to harvesting the beds of her readers differently, then the concluding stanza manifests this promise in the natural world through the cycle of female menstruation, the painting of blood on rocks, the production of eggs, and the eventual return to the watery caves where her head continues to inspire, and she drinks to 'roll again' (124), ensuring an eternally productive journey for those who listen to the words of this woman and her story of crooked goodness.

For Diane Glancy, spiritual transformation affords the opportunity to revise or, in some cases, write into being the stories of neglected and marginalized biblical women. Humour and irony offer the tools to displace some of the white western patriarchal aspects of Christianity, enabling her to represent 'the familiar in new ways' (1992, 53) without diminishing her own reverence for her Natively embodied Christ (as represented through the cover of and poems in *(Ado)ration)*. The result is that Glancy weaves her own web of relationships between her tribal identity and her Christian identity, and foregrounds the doubled nature of this task. In *The Closets of Heaven*, Glancy further complicates this challenge by exploring what it means to be a Native person, a Christian, and a feminist; code-switching and joking offer ways to juggle these multiple affiliations, without asserting the primacy of one over another. Louise Halfe negotiates between an intimate knowledge of Roman Catholicism and her commitment to Cree cosmology through the story of the Rolling Head. With *The Crooked Good*, Halfe employs the concept of spiritual transformation to literally rewrite the biblical story of Creation through a figure that has affinities with Eve but is willing and able to perceive her crooked goodness as a source of creative empowerment. The careful juxtaposition of texts and images, in combination with code-switching, enables Halfe to undercut the presumed dominance and righteousness of Catholicism, as imposed through residential schooling, with a series of alterna(rra)tives that return the reader to a female-centred vision of the world that is grounded in traditional Cree beliefs and practices. While Halfe's speakers in *The Crooked Good* may be no more irreverent than those in Glancy's collections, the need for a complete transformation is much more dramatic. Dorcas is silent within the Bible, and given voice by Glancy, but Halfe alludes to the character of Eve and her fall in order to move beyond the Bible and write her own account of creation. She asserts the sacred power of the Rolling Head and Turn-Around Woman, dreamers who are decidedly Cree and unwilling to be subsumed in any way, shape, or form by Christianity or the English language. What these poets do share is a commitment to depicting women's voices and an insistence upon the close relationship between poetry and song. In fact, the last line of *The Crooked Good*, 'and I drink to roll again,' can be read as musically inflected. The speaker's promise 'to roll again' may refer to the actual rolling of a head, but it can also be read ironically, as referring to a drum roll, a rapid succession of notes that form 'almost'[20] a continuous sound, in much the same way that Halfe refuses to close down or preclude potential alterna(rra)tives in her collection (124). The next chapter probes the work of several women poets who explore the notion of transformation through genre, employing humour and irony to dismantle established literary categories and to examine the links between poetry and music.

chapter two

Generic Transformations

I don't know what this has / to do with what I am trying to tell you except
that I know you / can turn a poem into something else.

Joy Harjo, 'Transformations'

the physical power in thought / carried inside silently / pushing forward in
each breathing / meaning wished onto tongues / transforming with each
utterance / the stuff of our lives ... / to become sound ... // reaching ever
forward into distances unknown / always linking to others / up to the last
drum / vibrating into vast silence.

Jeannette Armstrong, 'Words'

Because transformation explores the 'permeability of all boundaries,' it
also can be used to rethink western definitions of genre and medium, as
is exemplified by the work of Joy Harjo and Jeannette Armstrong (Donovan 1998, 143).[1] The efforts of these two Native North American poets to
bring music and poetry together in performance as well as on the page
have often been deemed inappropriate by literary scholars, or ignored
altogether despite the plethora of scholarly writing on them, especially
Harjo. In an effort to negotiate her urban mixed-blood status and alienation from her tribal language, Harjo has continued to cultivate the relationship between song, music, and poetry, and to blur the boundaries
that critics might try to impose on her work. Harjo's poetry readings
exemplify her ideas of transformation. She often combines the singing
of her work with the playing of her saxophone and has, on occasion,
brought other musicians to perform with her.[2] Likewise, Armstrong employs her spoken poetry, in conjunction with eclectic musical and vocal

arrangements, to assert her Okanagan identity, and works collaboratively
to articulate a cross-tribal call for resistance and action against Canadian
settler governments and to counter the dominance of capitalism and
the sustained destruction of the environment within North America. As
is evident from the second epigraph above, taken from a poem titled
'Words,' Armstrong's poetic speaker is acutely aware of the transformational power of the word, especially as manifested musically. Notably, this
generic definition of transformation is also applicable in varying degrees
to the work of Blaeser, Halfe, Dumont, Baker, and Glancy, all of whom
have experimented with genre[3] and are beginning to work in multiple
media, though not necessarily to the extent that Harjo or Armstrong do,
at least yet.[4]

While Harjo, like the poets in the previous chapter, employs transformation in some work to explore issues of spirituality and religion, her
interest in transformation extends to questions of genre in relation to
her creative efforts as a poet, musician, and singer. Despite having a paternal great-grandfather who was a 'full-blooded Creek Baptist minister'
and other religious relatives, Harjo has rejected evangelical Christianity
and instead embraces her own form of Aboriginal/Christian spirituality (Ruwe 1996, 125): 'I am reconnecting with the true image of the
sacred, I believe ... I'd rather have a god who is related than a stranger,
than a judgmental god who would destroy people from jealousy' (126).
In keeping with this, Harjo employs transformation to explore relationships between people and things without the imposition of a hierarchical structure, which she – like Glancy, Blaeser, Baker, and Halfe – sees as
prevalent in much of Christian theology. Similarly, Harjo also resists textual labels and generic classifications of her work, regarding the imposition of these as modes of colonization. As a musician, she uses published
and unpublished poems as song lyrics, performing at readings with her
saxophone or an accompanist on guitar, as well as producing albums
and touring with her band. Harjo co-founded her first band, Joy Harjo &
Poetic Justice, in 1992, and was the lead singer and saxophonist on their
only album, *Letter from the End of the Twentieth Century*, released in 1997.
The album consisted of ten songs, whose lyrics were adopted from four
books of Harjo's poetry and prose: *She Had Some Horses* (1983), *Secrets from
the Center of the World* (1989), *In Mad Love and War* (1990), and *The Woman
Who Fell from the Sky* (1994). With Joy's move to Los Angeles and, more
recently, Hawai'i, Poetic Justice has disbanded; Harjo is now pursuing
a solo career as a singer, songwriter, and saxophonist, while continuing
to publish books of poetry. Her album *Native Joy for Real* was released in

2004 on her own label, Mekko Records; lyrics for eight of the ten songs first appeared in her poetry collections. She has subsequently released another solo collection, *She Had Some Horses* (2006), which she has been distributing independently under her own label; this album, however, has only three musical tracks, all drawn from her previous discs.[5] The other twenty tracks are of Harjo reading her previously published poetry, without any music; with this new album, she is transforming the notion of song back to poetry.

This movement between music and poetry is equally familiar territory for Jeannette Armstrong, who is an accomplished sculptor, painter, writer, orator, and musician, as well as an Okanagan elder responsible for ensuring the transmission and sustained knowledge of traditional Okanagan songs and dances. As with Harjo, Armstrong certainly links what she calls 'the Native Creative Process' – documented in a book of the same title collaboratively created with Métis architect Douglas Cardinal – with the development and sustenance of an individual and communal spirituality. In particular, Armstrong explains that the 'Okanagan divides the order of human existence into four main activities' (Armstrong and Cardinal 1991, 70): physical sustenance, learning from the external natural world, the perpetuation of human life, and, finally, 'spiritual acts which ... [push us] out into the unknown' (70). This last activity is a fundamentally creative process that can be characterized as religious but also is reflective of an ongoing commitment to 'continuous deliberate change' (58).

While Native spirituality is integral to the creative process and its products for Armstrong, she is also fascinated by the challenges that genres pose for Native writers. As the co-founder of the En'owkin School of International Writing, Armstrong is acutely aware of the challenges that young Native writers face when trying to establish 'new frameworks for their work' (Anderson 1997, 52). In an interview with Kim Anderson, Armstrong notes that the writers who come to the En'owkin School of International Writing typically struggle with what she calls 'some "hard line concepts" in Canadian literature that Native[s] ... find limiting,' including the notion of 'categorization' (52). For Armstrong, a crucial part of the training that these budding writers receive is the opportunity to deconstruct the categories of 'fiction, poetry, and drama' (53), which do not always adequately reflect the texts being produced by Native authors. Instead, Armstrong encourages her students to 'find the linkages in the expression of poetry; as ... an art form within various First-Nations traditions' (54). As a member of the Okanagan tribe who was born and raised in a traditional tribal community and learned the Okanagan language first, Armstrong is familiar with the original semi-migratory lifestyle of her people. She is especially aware of the distinctions between, for example, West Coast tribes that stress visual arts because of the permanence of their home place, and interior tribes like the Okanagan who, by virtue of their seasonal movement, have learned to carry art forms with them, primarily through the distinct and complex use of 'sound ... [with] language,' and the combination of 'image-making with sound in language' (54). Through her discussion of curricular practices, Armstrong illuminates the challenges she faces as an artist whose writing is influenced by and converses with her tribal heritage, one that is primarily grounded in the portability and pliability of sound. However, it is worth noting here that there are several poems in *Breath Tracks* that can be read either horizontally or vertically on the page, including 'Glacier,' 'Wind,' 'Green,' 'Wings,' 'First People,' and 'Indian Woman.' Orality obviously plays a different role in these works, with readers making choices as to how to read them, which, in turn, affects the nature of the poems themselves.

To develop her interest in sound further, Armstrong proposes the concept of 'oratory' as a way to articulate the intersection of 'the genre of poetry' with 'oral traditions of expression' (Anderson 1997, 54). In the *OED*, 'oratory' refers to both the 'art ... of [public] speaking,' in all of its eloquence, and 'a small chapel, especially for private worship,' which draws together the spiritual and generic dimensions of what Armstrong portrays as a transformative act of creation.[6] When probed by Anderson about what she means by oratory, Armstrong explains that though oratory borrows elements of poetry – including 'metaphor, ... symbolism and allegory' – it also draws on the 'backdrop of the sound of music' and the combining of 'sound and body gesture' to create an art form that is both eloquent and highly political in its intent (55). What Armstrong describes strongly resembles her own creative endeavours in the world of music, where she has transformed poetic texts published in her one collection *Breath Tracks* (1991) into audio recordings, including a version of 'Mary Old Owl' on the audiotape titled *Poetry Is Not a Luxury: A Collection of Black and Native Poetry Set to Classical Guitar, Reggae, Dub, and African Drums* (1987); seven songs on a CD titled *Till the Bars Break* (1991), which was nominated for a Canadian Juno Award in the 'World Beat' category in 1992; and 'Grandmothers' on a CD called *Word Up* (1995), on which Armstrong sings, speaks, and plays drums. It is worth noting the irony here that Native music, at least according to the Canadian popular music industry, is classified as 'World Beat,' a term that continues to marginalize and colonize Native artistic achievements within Canada by relegating them to a non-western category.

From Text to Song: Transformation in Harjo and Armstrong

'Transformation' is a term not infrequently used to describe the poetry of Joy Harjo,[7] and has also been applied to the work of Jeannette Armstrong.[8] Kathleen Donovan, for instance, in a book chapter devoted to comparing Harjo with French feminist Hélène Cixous, reads selected Harjo poems through feminist legal philosopher Drucilla Cornell's definition of transformation. Donovan is primarily interested in how Harjo employs poetic language to examine the destructive aspects of 'Western cultural myths of gender and ethnicity' and to transform those 'abuses of power' from her own multiply marginalized subject position (1998, 157, 154). Donovan's analysis, while very fine, is less helpful here than Cornell's own definition of transformation: 'Change, radical enough to so restructure a system – political, legal, or social – that the "identity" of the system itself is altered' (1993, 1). Cornell's approach proves useful when exploring questions of genre in Harjo's and Armstrong's work precisely because she suggests that only radical transformation will bring about change within the system, a strategy that both poets have adopted, albeit to different ends and for varied reasons. Harjo is an internationally recognized poet with a well-established career who has received numerous grants and awards for her writing, yet her prominent literary status has not stopped Harjo from exploring new creative outlets. Armstrong is also a world-renowned Native activist, orator, essayist, educator, children's author, painter, sculptor, poet, short story writer, and novelist. *Slash* (1985), her fictional narrative about the Native North American protest movement as seen through the perspective of a young Okanagan man, Tommy 'Slash' Kelasket, is recognized as the first published novel by a Native woman in Canada and has become an important part of Native efforts to reform Canadian educational curricula. In particular, by coupling music and poetry in their work, both Armstrong and Harjo expose the limitations of traditional generic categories and the disciplines in which they are housed. Though Armstrong's commitment to sound recordings of her poetry is certainly not as systematic or as sustained as Harjo's, her work on generic transformations – and her use of humour and, more overtly, irony – offers another perspective on how to understand the intersections of poetry and song.

Having written a poem titled 'Transformations,' published in *In Mad Love and War* (1990), a volume that garnered her significant national acclaim, Harjo herself suggests the significance of metamorphosis in analyzing her works, as we will see shortly. Yet to confine examinations of change to her published poetry is to overlook an important dimension of her artistic productivity. In 1992, Harjo collaborated with her soon-to-be Poetic Justice band mate Susan L. Williams to write initial drafts of a song-poem called 'For Anna Mae Pictou Aquash' (based on Harjo's earlier published poem of the same name) to be recorded for *New Letter on the Air*, a nationally syndicated poetry program. Shortly after, in 1994, she released a cassette of her readings to accompany the release of her sixth volume of poetry; the bundled collection and tape-recording were published by W.W. Norton. Since then, she has become an accomplished lyricist, singer, and musician who over the course of her career has led the development of two touring bands (Poetic Justice and her solo band) and the release of three compact discs, in 1997, 2004, and 2006. Further, over the last two decades, Harjo has learned to play the tenor and soprano saxophone as well as the flute.

In contrast with Harjo, Armstrong is not focused on developing her career as a commercially viable musician, but instead draws on the centrality of music and song as understood by her Okanagan tribe to enrich her artistic endeavours generally. For the Okanagan community, in which Armstrong has been raised from birth, language and sound are intimately connected, a fact that is exemplified by her poetry; consider the aptly titled 'Words,' which describes the transformative power of 'utterance' in which 'meaning [is] wished onto tongues' (1991, 17). Armstrong illustrates how community values and beliefs are transmitted through the voices that are part of the 'landscape of grandmother,' offering 'continuance' and becoming a form of nurturing and sustenance for future generations (17); here, Armstrong contends that the land of her ancestors speaks to those who continue to share that home place, an idea that is explored more explicitly in chapter 5 of this book. In 'Words,' the transformative potential of language is manifested in playful and evocative terms with the so-called 'stuff of our lives' travelling in Armstrong's poem 'on wind / on air' before bumping 'wetly / against countless tiny drums / to become sound' and turn 'grey silence / into explosions of colour' that express the tender intimacy of physical interaction – 'the excruciating sweetness of mouth on mouth' – before settling into individual and collective memories (18). Paradoxically, however, even as the sound fades away Armstrong's speaker insists that it remains a tool of connectivity by 'always linking to others / up to the last drum / vibrating into vast silence' (18). Thus, the poetic 'I' ensures that sound continues through the vibrations that defy the claim to silence, articulating what Armstrong has called elsewhere 'a [double-voiced] process of resistance' that speaks to her Okanagan community traditions and tribal audience, as well as 'breaking stereotypes and informing' non-Native readers who might otherwise remain ignorant of specific tribal contexts and practices (Anderson 1997, 51). This ironically charged perspective has been extended into the realm of music by Armstrong through her various sound recordings of published poems, a strategic alliance between media that has been motivated by Armstrong's strong commitment to political activism. The recordings Armstrong has made of her poems are typically done in a collective fashion with other ethnic and racially marginalized poets through small government-funded and independent labels – such as the Composers, Authors, and Publishers Association of Canada and Irresistible/Maya/Revolutionary – that aim to expand and define the scope of what constitutes poetry and poetic expression through music and sound, while articulating a consistent message of resistance and education to non-Native listeners and readers and continuing to strengthen the bonds of Native audiences.

Armstrong's exploration of music and sound differs substantively from that of Harjo, precisely because Armstrong's first language is Okanagan and within her tribe both sound and language have very particular meanings and functions. For instance, songs are used by the Okanagan to heal through a psychological transformation: 'Certain sounds in our songs that we create are intended to relax and calm and create the kind of thought wave pattern to rebalance the person's emotions ... They have an impact on our subconscious mind, creating harmony because of the way rhythms are produced' (Beeler 1996, 147). This process of rebalancing is directly linked to the structure and sound of the Okanagan language, a phenomenon that Armstrong explains further in an interview with Karin Beeler called 'Image, Music, Text,' which, notably, focuses on the diverse forms of expression Armstrong's work takes, including her musical performance of the poem 'Grandmothers':

> Originally that poem was an Okanagan poem. I find that in the Okanagan, I don't have to use as many words, so in the English version of 'Grandmothers,' the creation of the words for the sounds that I wanted and the imagery that I wanted was a great literary exercise ... I compose Okanagan song and poetry, and I use mostly song in the community in a social setting. I create

images with words and with the enunciation of words, because ours is an oral-based language. You can do a lot more with an oral-based language, since you already have that legacy of how sounds work. They work much differently than English, which has been a written language. I think that at some point earlier, before the language was written, the sounds may have been quite different in the language, but I think the sounds changed once they were written. This may have affected the brevity and clarity of the language and changed it considerably. (148)

Armstrong clearly outlines the benefits of a sound-based language for easy movement between genres and modes of creative expression, suggesting that her primary knowledge of the Okanagan language and culture, and its grounding in sound, has motivated her to wrestle with the English language despite its limitations. Her perspective not only reverses conventional colonial presumptions that written languages are more sophisticated than oral-based languages, but also poses fundamental challenges to white western notions of what constitutes a text. In other words, Armstrong's analysis becomes itself a model for transformation.

Moreover, for Armstrong, transformation is partly linked to a process of translation. As an Okanagan-language speaker first and English-language speaker second, Armstrong is constantly negotiating between these differing cultures: 'I'm still trying to find ways to articulate what this difference does to me internally, what the two languages do to me inside' (1990, 26). One of the key challenges of this translation and ultimately transformation is the fact that the Okanagan language is fundamentally based in metaphor, which she describes in a 1990 essay called 'Words':

When we speak to each other, when we communicate with one another, we are communicating something that's coming from thought, something that is coming from no [physical] thing. You're taking something that is nothing and you are attempting to make it visual, familiar to another person's sense of touch, feeling, taste, sight or whatever. You're attempting to find something that's not physical and turn it into a physical experience for another person ... given this particular human being's already existing feelings.

We find ways to do that ... When I say a word that may have no meaning for another culture, it has huge meaning for me. When I say 'coyote' it has a huge 20,000 year meaning behind it that has been passed on and on and on. Our character, our world view, the relationship we have to each other

> as people, our humanness towards the world and how we relate to the spiri-
> tual is wrapped up in the metaphors we use. All things hold meaning only
> in terms I understand, so that when I say 'coyote' to you and in your mind
> you see some four-legged creature running around, usually pretty rag-tag
> looking, you know that coyote has a whole different meaning for you than
> it does for me. Your experience is different. (26-7)

Armstrong's detailed and evocative discussion of how languages employ metaphor differently, posing special challenges for Native-language speakers who, because of colonization, write and publish primarily in English, has special resonances in relation to transformation, as well as humour and irony. When Armstrong describes the difficulty of convey- ing the significance of 'coyote' to non-Natives, she not only alerts her audiences to the ways in which readers come to any text with significant but typically unacknowledged biases and expectations, attitudes that may need to be adjusted by the reader rather than the writer, but she also foregrounds the ways in which linguistic translation – or, more ac- curately, transformation – is a tricky business, one that requires paying attention (as with humour and irony) to both the said and the unsaid aspects of a text. In the same essay, Armstrong urges those who speak from a dual linguistic perspective to assume responsibility 'for speaking those words' and remembering that 'you are responsible for the effect of those words on the person you are addressing *and* the thousands of years of tribal memory packed into your understanding of those words' (27). By highlighting the power of speech, its weight and its connection to spirituality, at least for Armstrong, she also reminds readers of the ever- present possibility that 'words can be misconstrued' (28), whether ut- tered in Okanagan or English, a rhetorical strategy that essentially turns the tables on non-Native readers who may see themselves as merely ob- servers in this discussion of language and transformation. Armstrong's sound recordings extend these efforts to take the responsibilities of speech and sound creation seriously and to explore the challenges of being 'misunderstood' or, conversely, opening up lines of communica- tion through a variety of media, even when using 'the English language' which is not her 'own' (28).

The shared interest of Harjo and Armstrong in transformation places a difficult theoretical burden on literary scholars who have embraced their published works (including their poetry) but remain generally si- lent with respect to their musical careers, which integrate published lyr- ics into songs, creating what could be called 'oral poetry' (Foley 2002,

29-30).[9] Given long established Eurocentric (and ethnographic) biases which assume that 'oral literature ... [is] simple, formless, lacking in artistic quality and complexity, the collective expressions of unsophisticated peasants and primitives' (Bauman 1990, 7), this silence is not surprising. To view oral texts as possessing the same level of sophistication as written texts means refusing to sustain ethnocentric hierarchies. John Miles Foley puts it bluntly:

> But consider the scale of our parochialism. For anyone trained in North American or European academic institutions, poetry is and has long been almost exclusively the kind of poetry composed and consumed via texts. It does not include ... performance or aural reception except as something additional, something nonfundamental. (2002, 29-30)

Hence, the addition of adjectives, like 'oral,' that identify a poem's form of creation or delivery as not married to the printed page; likewise terms such as 'spoken-word poetry,' despite their redundancy, are put into service specifically to identify 'voiced verbal art, verse that is lifted off the page and into the world of presence and experience' (30). Harjo's and Armstrong's integration of music, of course, adds yet another dimension that does not accord with conventional Eurocentric definitions of the poetry reading – 'a performance (from a published text ...) before a well-behaved, academic audience' – or the poetry text, as a published collection of works to be purchased and read individually (30). As Harjo explains, 'Poetry and music belonged together. This was not new ... They are soul mates, not meant to be parted. It is only in the modern age they were separated: when the printing press was invented' (2002, xxv). Harjo notes that even those who do acknowledge her bridging of song and music often view this development negatively: 'The literary critics have said, "This is a travesty, you don't mix poetry with music because it's too emotional, the poems should stand by themselves on the page." But you know, I work out of a different tradition' (David 1998, 4).

As Craig Womack points out, such a blurring of boundaries is integral to Harjo's Muskogee culture: 'What might be "experimental," however, in light of the Western canon, is a natural extension of the oral tradition, where the lines between the arts are more fluid. In a traditional culture, a story may be acted out in a ceremony where it is danced, painted or sung' (1999, 172). Harjo reiterates this in her introduction to *How We Became Human*, where she states: '... poetry ... is the making of songs for ceremonial or secular use' (2002, xxv). And of course, this applies to other tribal contexts as well; Armstrong describes this same blurring of boundaries:

> I have trouble separating the disciplines, because the creative process that I use doesn't differentiate. So to answer your question really simply, poetry is music to me. It's rhythm, and it's sound and it's imagery and it's metaphor, except that poetry can be written. And poetry is another word for what I understand when I create and compose music which talks about water, trees, birds and people and talks about response, feelings and interactions, all of those things that make us human. (Beeler 1996, 147)

While Armstrong strongly locates herself within Okanagan traditions, her emphasis on cross-generic approaches to artistic self-expression is useful when examining both poets precisely because the two women regard the links between poetry, music, and visual arts as fundamental to their work. In 1989 Armstrong received a diploma in fine arts from Okanagan College, followed by a BFA from the University of Victoria, with a focus on creative writing; she is also an accomplished painter, book illustrator, and sculptor, who has moved fluidly between media since her teenage years when she published her first poem in a local newspaper and sold a painting to an art collector (who has since donated it back to the En'owkin Centre).[10]

Born into a family of Muskogee painters – her grandmother and great-aunt both received BFA degrees – Joy Harjo was primarily a painter until she switched her major from painting to poetry at age twenty-two. But the decision to 'work with words and the power of words' has not altered Harjo's instinct to 'approach the art as a visual artist,' which means paying attention to the sound *and* look of poetry, and over time, music (Kallet 1996, 111); this could also be said of Armstrong. Moreover, Harjo has always been influenced by a diverse array of music and oral and written texts, ranging from the lilting musicality of Galway Kinnell's poetry and Navajo Night Way chants to Muskogee stomp dance songs, the songs of Patsy Cline, and even John Coltrane's saxophone playing. It was Coltrane's music that first inspired Harjo as a child to revise her understanding of the relationship between words and music: 'My concept of language, of what was possible with music, was charged by this revelatory music' (Harjo 1999, 152). Harjo has repeatedly emphasized her own ties to jazz music, arguing that its creation 'parallels my own genesis into the world. Jazz was born via West Africa, mixed with the parlour music of Europe and then the last stop was by way of Muskogee country. My

Muskogee people interacted with African people. There was intermar-
riage, interchange' (Aull et al. 1996, 104). Apparently, Harjo's grand-
father, Henry Marsey Harjo, was at least half African, but this heritage
was never mentioned because her relations prized light skin; Harjo only
discovered this family secret as an adult. Likewise, her familiarity with
Muskogee stomp dances, used to celebrate special occasions, and the
female-only Muskogee ribbon dances, both of which involve chanting
and singing, and derive meaning through the rhythms created by 'turtle
shell rattles' affixed to the moving dancers' legs, has shaped the sound
of her work (Harjo 2002, 212). While at the University of New Mexico,
Harjo learned a great deal about Navajo philosophy and culture; she
studied the Navajo language for eighteen months and gained familiarity
with 'Navajo horse songs' and Beauty Way chants (Harjo 2002, 204-5).
Harjo insists that 'writing the poem is about a linkup with that larger
field of meaning, of rhythm, of music and meaning' (Gould 2000, 137).
Thus, it is not surprising that she treats poetry and music as 'one entity'
(137), which is evident in her poetry readings.

    While Armstrong's influences appear, at least at first glance, to be less
eclectic by virtue of her traditional Okanagan upbringing and focus on
Okanagan curricular development, her extensive travel, teaching, lectur-
ing, and essay-writing, her work as a consultant with various social and
environmental organizations, and her appointment to serve as an Indigenous judge in the Ontario court system and for the United Nations
create a series of contextual frameworks that are further complicated
by her constant transition between the Okanagan language and culture
and the English language and white western practices that she negotiates daily. Moreover, Armstrong sees her development as a visual artist
to be a 'work in progress,' explaining to Beeler, 'Actually I'm not an accomplished painter or sculptor although I've won awards at some major
shows. All of my works, I have felt, have been studio works' (1996, 148).
What Armstrong stresses is her interest and efforts to hone her skills
in particular media, a task that is pleasurable and rewarding, not only
because of the potential 'to make a statement' that is unique to 'visual
art' but also because of its cross-pollination into other forms of expression (149), including poetry. Armstrong has even explored the relationship between computer technology and what she calls 'music poetry,'
holding a residency at the Banff Arts Centre in Alberta during the summer of 1996 to bring together music and a 'soundscape' to create 'the
visual background' for her poetry (151). While Armstrong, as already
mentioned, equates poetry with music by lifting the visual and the aural

dimensions of the text off the page and into the realm of performance, she also acknowledges that there 'are some things that you can say in sculpture that you can't do in poetry or in prose or music' (149), an assertion that allows both for the possibility of transformation and the sanctity of individual artistic forms, particularly when moving between the Okanagan and English languages, which she regards as more and less pliable respectively.

As already noted, Leuthold insists that transformation is essential to many Indigenous arts, particularly those which involve 'performance or participation' (1998, 58). Harjo's and Armstrong's approaches to fusing poetry and music are no exception. But before turning to the particularities of each artist's oeuvre, exactly what transformation means and how it operates are questions that both Armstrong and Harjo explore in their poetry and music, offering reading strategies for their texts – on the page and in performance – that emphasize their individual and collective efforts to playfully and subversively undermine the limitations of genre and create a more inclusive and flexible context for engaging with their works. Harjo's prose poem 'Transformations' marks one useful point of departure for such an examination. As Harjo explains in a footnote to a later edition of the poem, 'Transformations' portrays the situation experienced by a friend of Harjo's who struggled with self-hatred after being 'caught between two lovers' (2002, 222). The poem describes and attempts to actualize the process of metamorphosis by exploring the love/ hate relationship between a first-person speaker and (an)Other. Notably the poem begins with the speaker describing the text's form in two different generic terms: 'This *poem* is a *letter* to tell you that I have smelled the hatred you have tried to find me with; you would like to destroy me' (Harjo 1990, 59). Harjo's speaker claims to be writing both 'a poem' and 'a letter,' a distinction that is blurred by the prose form of the text, with its long line lengths, sentence punctuation, and lack of versification. And although the poem lacks a salutation and signature, the formal markers of a letter, the body of the poem is an intimate exploration of the hatred between two people, addressed to 'you.' The poetic 'I' then goes on to explore the transformative nature of hatred by paralleling it to poetry and tracing some of the ways in which texts can change form: 'This poem could be a bear treading the far northern tundra, smelling the air for sweet alive meat. Or a piece of seaweed stumbling in the sea. Or a blackbird, laughing' (59). Using a series of metaphors, Harjo affirms and enacts the power of words through the speaker's imagination, which enables a poem to become a bear, or seaweed, or even a blackbird.

In this case, poetry takes on a life of its own, becoming an active part of the natural world.

Relying on instinct, the speaker in 'Transformations' asserts the significance of these alterations without really understanding their power: 'I don't know what that has to do with what I am trying to tell you except that I know you can turn a poem into something else ... What I mean is that hatred can be turned into something else, if you have the right words, the right meanings, buried in that tender place in your heart' (59). The poetic 'I' calls upon the listener's emotions, an ability to find the vocabulary and employ it effectively, rather than simply pursuing vengeance – the 'eye for an eye' that Harjo's speaker suggests is far more damaging to the vision of the one who inflicts it: 'Bone splintered in the eye of the one you choose to name your enemy won't make it any better for you to see' (59). The ability to look at and see (an)Other with empathy are primary lessons that the speaker tries to instill in the listener. In addition, the narrator emphasizes that change is both necessary and cyclical, constituting a natural part of life and art:

> Down the street an ambulance has come to rescue an old man who is slowly losing his life. Not many can see that he is already becoming the backyard tree he has tended for years, before he moves on. He is not sad, but compassionate for the fears moving around him. (59)

If Gunn Allen claims that transformation is a key strategy for Native-American women poets who are exploring issues of 'extinction and regeneration' (1986, 162), this scene is no exception. Moreover, Harjo's poem becomes educative without imposing singular conclusions; the 'old man' may be ill and moving towards death, taking on the form of the tree he tends with such care, but he is not gone yet. Harjo has stated elsewhere that 'transformation is really about understanding the shape and condition of another with compassion, not about overtaking' (Ruwe 1996, 127), and the example of the old man epitomizes this need for open-mindedness and understanding.

In the concluding section of the poem, the speaker finally asserts, 'That's what I mean to tell you,' and urges the audience to look and listen differently to the hatred which separates people from themselves and each other (Harjo 1990, 59). Harjo cleverly transforms the divisiveness of hatred by portraying it as 'a dark woman' who stands 'on the other side of the place you live ... She has been trying to talk to you for years' (59). She plays with the metaphoric associations of darkness

on several levels here by combining the negative resonances of dark
skin with the temptations of female sexuality, and countering it with alternative[11] models of female selfhood, which acknowledge, negotiate,
and find ways to rethink the racial differences between women through
their shared experiences as women. Harjo has argued that 'the word
"feminism" doesn't carry over to the tribal world' (Coltelli 1996b, 65),
but she does see her work as articulating a vision of female 'empowerment,' shaped by her Indigenous heritage (65). And as someone who
is herself light-skinned, Harjo is frustrated by the fact that being able
to pass as white also means that at times she is perceived as less than a
full member of the Muskogee tribe. It seems fitting that Harjo challenges and often inverts conventional assumptions about female darkness
throughout this poem. Harjo's dark woman, who has haunted the listener's nightmares, is not at all what one would expect: 'She is beautiful.
/ This is your hatred back. She loves you' (Harjo 1990, 59). With these
lines, Harjo collapses the distance between the speaker and the listener,
bringing together the otherwise dichotomous emotions of hatred and
love in order to suggest the imaginative possibilities that one may find
through a combination of knowledge and empathy. The dark woman
thus functions both as a threat to survival and the source of redemption,
a seemingly contradictory pairing that echoes the spiritual transformations explored in Glancy's, Blaeser's, and Halfe's work. In other words,
Harjo's poem reminds readers to respect and engage in 'understanding
the shape and condition of' (an)Other, without demanding uniformity
(Ruwe 1996, 127). The dark woman can also be read as representing
Harjo's own practice of mixing genres – combining two seemingly distinct and even opposing categories into a single figure or form, while
still appreciating what is unique about each.

   The poem, moreover, relies on both a wry sense of humour and various
ironic juxtapositions to complete its transformations, with the speaker
foregrounding the need for readers to look differently at the comparisons being invoked, particularly when metamorphosis is involved; for
instance, the speaker compares poems with bears in search of their next
meal, a levelling technique that acknowledges the sustenance that poetry
provides while exposing the base, animalistic aspects of hatred as well as
the drive for survival that no work of art, however elaborate, can conceal.
And the conclusion of 'Transformations' heightens this ironic unravel-
ling of logical pairings through the introduction of the dark woman who
haunts the speaker's nightmares but also possesses the beauty and wisdom potentially to repair fundamental rifts. The joke is on the listener

who may not have realized that hatred and love come in all shapes and
sizes – and can co-exist, even within a single figure or form – while what
is unique about each is still appreciated. The naturalness of this need to
change form, to alter oneself or one's text to reflect multiple influences
and traditions, is at the root of Harjo's work as a poet and musician.

Though Harjo admits that such a vision of hatred and love as one
may be too idealistic, her commitment to the concept is based on her
rejection of a (Christian) hierarchy between spirit and flesh and instead
her acceptance and accommodation of difference. As mentioned, Harjo
insists that transformation is not about overtaking (an)Other. Changing
form does not mean the erasure of individual elements, but the bringing together of various aspects of a culture in a single text, allowing
Harjo to acknowledge her complex heritage. Testing generic boundaries becomes a means of undermining the biases that confine women
and visible minorities to certain formulaic modes of expression. Her
work asserts the potential inherent in metaphoric and literal depictions
of border-crossing, which is what mixed-blood urban-born and -raised
people like herself do every day, moving between cultures in a delicate
negotiation between communities and belief systems. There is no one
right form for a text to take; the same work can be a printed poem, song
lyrics, or part of a performance piece, all at once.

Armstrong's *Breath Tracks* signals a similar yet distinctive approach to
transformation by virtue of its title, which, as Stephen Morton argues,
'attempts to convey a trace or "track" of First Nations oral performance
("Breath") through a print medium which always also threatens to co-
opt the voice of Aboriginal women' (1999, 27). The 'breath tracks' or
poems that Armstrong creates are designed to both foreground and
preclude this obscuring of Native female voices, and the texts themselves incorporate a variety of literary strategies to enable this message
to come through. As Armstrong has discussed previously, she writes for
both Native and non-Native communities, a necessity because she has
'been given an ability to speak two languages, to cross between two languages in my mind' (1990, 28); the result is that her texts are inherently
'double-edged' in that she writes for multiple audiences and cultural
contexts. Such an approach lends itself by design to both humour and
irony, though Armstrong's poetry is typically more ironic than overtly
funny in both its condemnation of colonial practices and its efforts to
heal the Okanagan community (particularly through a reconceptualiz-
ing of history and memory from a particular tribal perspective, which is
addressed in more detail in chapter 3 of this book). Here, I want to turn

to one poem, titled 'With Compassion,' which epitomizes Armstrong's ironically charged exploration of transformation and distinctly echoes – with a twist – Harjo's 'Transformations.' Included in a section of *Breath Tracks* subtitled 'Fire Madness,' which itself explores the death-defying possibilities of the speaker's physical transformation from human to animal, 'With Compassion' traces the challenges of surrendering that which the speaker most desires and reviles, a paradoxical relationship that calls upon every ounce of strength the poetic 'I' possesses to reach a satisfactory conclusion.

Armstrong's poem opens with the first-person speaker's imperative command – 'I set you free' – a promise to action that is complicated by the lines that follow, precisely because what or who is being released is not entirely clear: 'my love / my desire / my illusion' (1991, 77). In an intertextual allusion to one of Harjo's poems, which is examined in more detail shortly, the poetic 'I' of Armstrong's text begins the second stanza with the promise 'I give you back' (77), a line that first appears in Harjo's *She Had Some Horses* (1983), and is later turned into a song-poem with several recorded musical versions. By drawing on this influential poem, Armstrong creates a dialogue that is inherently ironic and playful; while the fear that a person can generate within him- or herself to the point of self-destruction is central to Harjo's poem, 'With Compassion' focuses solely on the challenges, and rewards, of letting go of that which would otherwise destroy the speaker and the object of her compassion. Moreover, Armstrong's choice of title anticipates Harjo's later comment that transformation is 'about understanding the shape and condition of another with compassion, not about overtaking' (Ruwe 1996, 127). Indeed, compassion is a complex set of emotions precisely because it involves not only, as Harjo explains, a deep awareness of and empathy for the situation experienced by a person or creature other than oneself, but also a willingness to try to alleviate that suffering.

Like Harjo's text, this Armstrong poem creates a sense of cumulative action by starting every stanza (with the exception of one) with a different command; these commands gradually give force to the possibility of liberation from some bondage, which is never fully described, but a literal and figurative struggle is hinted at between lovers, friends, or a mother and child. With a laundry list of commands, 'With Compassion' becomes a handbook of active surrender – and the paradoxes that entails – ranging from 'I return you / to the mother / who didn't want you / but loved you / nevertheless' and 'I unbind you / from this cradle / diligently fashioned over the years' to 'I pass you to him / to face him

/ to fight back / to say enough' (77). Further, by employing what Morton identifies as 'the self-conscious use of enjambment and the interplay between writing and blank spaces on the page' (1999, 27-8), Armstrong sustains the mystery of the speaker's relationship to the intended audience and opens up the possibility that every reader ultimately is a potential vehicle of change, by virtue of their decision to engage with the text. For instance, in the third stanza, Armstrong's speaker juxtaposes the speaker's desire to 'return you / to the mother' with the more abstract 'I hand you over / to the faceless / open senseless rage / the smashing fist / the mouth snarling incoherently / criticism spilling from bulging eyes / the eternal ceaseless anger' (1991, 77); the reader is here directly challenged to remember that underlying this process of release is the act of compassion, which involves not only an awareness of the suffering of another being but additionally a commitment to do something about it. Yet, while the poetic 'I' may seem, at first, to be innocent and even vulnerable to this thing of 'love / ... desire / ... illusion' and oppression, at the end of stanza four Armstrong's speaker reverses this trend by slipping in an ironic twist: 'to rock you to sleep / to nurse you to health / to hold you closely / to rob you gently' (77). Whatever commitment to nurture may ostensibly govern the speaker's behaviour, there is also the double-edged reality that even in a loving embrace, there are always ulterior motives at work.

'With Compassion' can be read metaphorically as a call for compassion – towards the self and others – but with the knowledge that no act of release is entirely selfless. Armstrong's speaker reiterates this very point in the last three stanzas of the poem, which explore the transformative nature of the poetic 'I' letting 'you go / to grow / to walk / to breathe / to sing clear and long / I give you back / everything // the burning rage / the living chaos / the excruciating beauty' (1991, 78). Not surprisingly, the speaker connects the ability to develop and thrive with the acts of walking and singing, which are critical elements of the Okanagan's traditionally semi-nomadic and musically rich tribal culture; however, survival is never easy, as the poem reminds readers in the stanza that follows with the promise that being set free means confronting the full force of 'the burning rage / the living chaos / the excruciating beauty' that constitutes the world in all of its complexities (78). Armstrong employs vivid and even violent adjectives to modify the experience of life, creating a series of highly poetic, tightly compressed lines that anticipate the final stanza of 'With Compassion,' in which the speaker describes the need for separation as a kind of (re)birth and, by implication, a transformation of the speaker and reader to enact compassion individually and collectively while fundamentally respecting each other, saving the sanity and integrity of the poetic 'I,' and moving beyond the seductions of the past. If, as Armstrong has argued, one of the challenges she faces as an Okanagan woman writer is the difficulty of conveying metaphor and its socio-cultural frameworks in English, of reaching readers when tribal beliefs and practices are not always familiar to non-Native readers, here she provides an example of transformation in action through the universal act of birth: 'I push you / from me / for you / for love / and finally / for me' (78). Her strategic use of enjambment conveys the ironic complexities of not only physical childbirth, with its attendant pain and joy, but also the intricacies of letting go and embracing change rather than resisting or fearing it.

Reading and Listening: Variations on 'Fear Poem' and 'Threads of Old Memory'

Several of the poems that appear as songs on the Joy Harjo & Poetic Justice compact disc, her more recent collaborative efforts with Michael Sena, and her debut solo disc, *Native Joy for Real*, epitomize Harjo's vision of text and song as modes of shape-shifting truth-telling that are intended to bring about change through vision and a commitment to a combination of traditional and non-traditional musical and poetic practices. Likewise, Armstrong uses her sound recordings of poetry on *Till the Bars Break*, which includes two different musical versions of the poem 'Threads of Old Memory,' published in *Breath Tracks*, to challenge the historical record and bring to the fore the ongoing marginalization and racism directed towards Native peoples in Canada, particularly by the Canadian government in the wake of the Oka Crisis, a three-month armed standoff which occurred when the town of Oka, Quebec, proposed to use sacred Mohawk lands for a local golf-course expansion.[12] In doing so, both Harjo and Armstrong employ what Yvor Winters has called 'the correlation between sound and feeling' (quoted in Gross and McDowell 1996, 10) to evoke an emotional response from readers, from those who have seen live performances of Harjo's texts (with a band or alone) or have heard Armstrong read her work, and from those who listen to the recordings made by either poet. As Richard Bauman explains, performance adds another framework:

Performance represents a transformation of the basic referential ... uses of language. In other words, in an artistic performance of this kind, there is something going on in the communicative interchange which says to the auditor, 'interpret what I say in some special sense; do not take it to mean what the words alone, taken literally, would convey.' This may lead to the further suggestion that the performance sets up or represents, an interpretive frame within which the messages being communicated are to be understood, and that this frame contrasts with at least one other frame, the literal. (1977, 9)

While Bauman sets up a binary opposition between literal and interpretive frameworks that seems reductive, given the complex metaphorical and figurative dimensions of the two women's published poetry, he emphasizes the need to attend to the differences between specific textual and contextual frameworks. And Harjo, in particular, complicates this further by publishing her poems, adapting them to song-performance, producing sound recordings and lyrics sheet for them, and even recording them a second time for her solo album. These multiple manifestations in the case of Harjo – and, to a lesser degree, Armstrong – mark a series of transformations that, like the 'dark woman' of Harjo's poem, retain categorical distinctions and yet simultaneously blur them to create new forms of text that elude containment within conventional notions of genre.

Further, by presenting their poetry in these different contexts, Armstrong and Harjo challenge anthropological assumptions about 'folklore' as the study of 'residual culture that looks backwards to the past for its frame of reference, disqualifying itself from the study of the creations of contemporary culture until they too may become residual' (Bauman 1977, 48). Harjo refuses to view the more traditional elements of her Muskogee heritage as confined to the past and instead employs them in her multiple renderings of texts, integrating her knowledge of Muskogee, Navajo, and other tribal cultural practices and beliefs into her poems, song lyrics, and music; likewise, Armstrong embodies the contemporary reality of being an Okanagan speaker and elder, as well as a writer who straddles two cultural worlds and languages, and articulates this heritage forcefully in her work, whether as published poetry or song lyrics. This incorporation counters the concept of a residual culture with what Raymond Williams has called 'an emergent culture' in which 'new meanings and values, new practices, new significances and experiences are continually being created' (1980, 41). These women undermine the long-standing treatment of Native North Americans as a dying culture without contemporary relevance, and demonstrate the inadequacy of generic categories to accommodate these multiple modes of expression.

The remainder of this chapter explores two particular examples of the metamorphosis from text to musical performance in the poets' respective oeuvres. The first is Armstrong's 'Threads of Old Memory,' which is recorded in two different styles on the album *Till the Bars Break*, creating a rich layering of significances that are tinged primarily with irony, though elements of humour emerge in the dub version. In musical terms, a dub version involves mixing together two or more sound or video recordings to create a composite, or what Armstrong might describe as a transformative recording. In the case of Harjo, who has much more vigorously developed her musical career, the originally titled poem 'I Give You Back' provides the basis for a series of shape-shifting texts that ends, at least for now, with the concluding song on her solo CD, which literally inverts the creative lineage constructed by the movement of poem on the page to performed song. If, as Kathleen Donovan argues in her examination of Havasupai women's songs, 'a coming to voice may occur in forms other than writing' (1998, 10), as in the case of song-poetry, then Armstrong's and Harjo's multiple versions of their poems as songs need to be included in analyses of their work. Here, Armstrong's and Harjo's varied uses of irony and what Freud called '*Galgenhumor,*' or gallows humour, demonstrate the changing emphases of their work. Freud's primary example of this kind of humour involves a man heading for his Monday-morning execution who comments: 'Well, this week's beginning nicely' (1905, 229). While both poets' speakers may not be threatened with literal death, the danger of being overtaken by fear, or being silenced by the loss of a Native language, looms throughout the song-poems, becoming enemies worthy of both serious attention and sustained mockery. Freud notes in his description of gallows humour that it is fundamentally 'rebellious' rather than 'resigned,' possessing a 'dignity' that is unusual because it refuses to be frightened off by the dangers of the world and instead embraces the vitality and possibility of the situation no matter how grim (1927, 163). Such an assessment accords with the subject matter of both Harjo's and Armstrong's poem and songs, in which the speaker refuses to be dissuaded from taking on what may be feared – and encounters it differently every time.

In its published textual form, Armstrong's 'Threads of Old Memory,' which is discussed again in chapters 3 and 4, explores the relationship between the first-person speaker and the creation of a poetic text that can convey adequately the power of an increasingly marginalized Native language and the histories and memories it holds. The poem begins by portraying the challenges of depicting the Okanagan language and culture in English: 'Speaking to newcomers in their language is dangerous / for when I speak / history is a dreamer / empowering thought / from which I awaken the imaginings of the past' (1991, 58). Stephen Morton analyzes the double-edged message of Armstrong's opening lines in ironic terms, noting that while the 'language of the newcomers' is seductive, it ultimately hinders the speaker rather than helping because there is no easy way to accurately or adequately translate between languages and cultures without acknowledging what is lost in the process (1999, 29). Moreover, if the Native language 'spoke only harmony,' English becomes a serious threat to the survival of the Native community that this speaker represents; indeed, English is 'a language / meant to overpower / to overtake / in skillfully crafted words / moving towards surrender' (1991, 58). But it cannot erase fully the tracks of a culture that continues to survive, primarily through its 'songs / hidden / cherished / protected' (58). Fortunately for Armstrong's speaker, 'the univocality and stability of the English language fails to silence the different threads of meaning which form the poem's subtext' (Morton 1999, 29). The unsaid and said come together in a manner that ironically displaces colonial domination by favouring a voice that, though it speaks in English, embraces the need to straddle the two languages and cultures and in the process recognizes how words – even those of a Native speaker writing in English – can bring about transformation. Moreover, at this juncture in the text, the poetic 'I' becomes more overtly visually oriented – in keeping with Armstrong's blurring of artistic boundaries – by insisting that it is through the 'secret singing' of these songs that 'I glimpse ... / an old lost world / of astounding beauty' (58). Armstrong uses irony in a less rebellious and flamboyant manner than Harjo, as we will see shortly, because of her primary commitment to preserving the Okanagan culture and conveying its dynamic beauty. And as she does in many of her poems, metaphor becomes a means of depicting this central union of sound and meaning for the speaker as the poetic 'I' weaves together the 'gossamer threads of old memory' to form a visible and tangible tapestry of history (in the form of the poem on the page) that can be carried into the present and the future (59).

In 'Threads of Old Memory,' Armstrong develops a subtly ironic twist in the lengthy second stanza of the poem, where the speaker becomes uniquely empowered by virtue of her access to the past, which is portrayed as 'a place of magic ... // a pure place / silent / wordless / from where thoughts I choose / silently transform into words' (1991, 59). This ability to draw on Okanagan traditions, practices, and language gives the poetic 'I' a unique opportunity that, in turn, paradoxically embraces a sense of collectivity; in other words, the individual is transformed into part of a community, and silent words, though initially seeming to lack any efficacy in the present, take on immense value and do bring about change, at least within the realm of the poem: 'I speak and / powerfully become actions / becomes memory in someone ... // I am the dreamer / the choice maker / the word speaker / I speak in a language of words / formed in the actions of the past / words that become the sharing / the collective knowing / the links that become a people' (59). This account of words becoming action also embraces a multiplicity of generic forms, with the speaker playfully drawing together diverse means of creative expression in a single voice that confidently proclaims, 'I am the artist / the storyteller / the singer' (60). By claiming the authority to break boundaries and juxtapose different modes of expression, Armstrong's narrator refuses to be confined to a singular identity, imposed by white western values; instead, she insists upon the validity and significance of artistic flexibility, and the willingness to explore transformation without merely becoming victim to its whims. The poem reflects the speaker's desire to value and respect her Native identity, by refusing to adhere to western notions of genre and artistic categorization or to accept the imposition of the western language and its values without acknowledging its colonial heritage. Hence, the poetic 'I' explains, 'When I speak / I sing a song called up through the ages ... // I search for the words / spoken serenely in the gaps between memory / the lost pieces of history / pieces mislaid / forgotten or stolen / muffled by violence / splintered by evil / when languages collide in mid air' (60). Armstrong's poem visually renders the cultural conflict between Natives and English-speaking non-Natives as a collision course that results in a chaotic explosion, again using the force of metaphor combined with the ironic slippage between terms like 'speak' and 'sing' to foreground the need for Armstrong and others to continue their project of threading together old memories in English, but with the proper attention paid to Native traditions and ideas rendered in Native languages.

The final stanza of the published version of 'Threads of Old Memory' portrays the commitment of the poetic 'I' to 'asking the whys' in English, a strategy that results in the 'releasing [of] unspeakable grief' and concurrently leads to the 'dispelling [of] lies in the retelling,' a corrective but also regenerative act through the enemy's language that secures the beginning of 'a new song' and the potential to build on 'a world / that cannot be stolen or lost / only shared / shaped by new words' (1991, 60-1). Silence is displaced by speech and ultimately a song that is physically manifested in the sky through a cluster of shining stars, defying 'an endless silence' and pointedly melding the visual and the aural together in what can be read as a deliberate rejection of the categorical confines of literary scholars (61).

   Not surprisingly, then, Armstrong includes this poem in those she has recorded on *Till the Bars Break*, producing two distinct versions – 'Threads of Old Memory' and 'Threads of Old Memory Dub' – with one on each side of the album. The record itself is a compilation of contributions from a variety of Native and black North American as well as black British writers, visual artists, and musicians, all of whom reflect on the marginalization and racism that these populations continue to experience in Canada and the United States. Performers include the Native alternative rock band Seventh Fire, acclaimed multidisciplinary Ojibway artist Rebecca Belmore, Rastafarian and performance poet Benjamin Zephaniah, the music producer known as the 'Mad Professor' (Neil Fraser), indie rock band The Fire Next Time, who created a dance track for the album called 'Oka Ain't Over,' Cree poet, editor, and photographer Greg Ing-Young, and Armstrong. *Till the Bars Break* is a multinational effort, distributed by Cargo Records, a British independent label, and produced by 'Irresistible/Maya/Revolutionary,' a co-operative label described on the back of the eight-page CD insert as a collaboration between Pat Andrade, 'a Rasta and anarchist' who is 'bringing out connections between people of color within North America' through his series of ten Maya records, and Don Paul, who founded the 'Revolutionary' label to counter the legacies of American presidents Ronald Regan and George Bush, Sr (8). As the insert explains, 'the Irresistible label reflects the powers of both music and sexuality' and the potential of both 'to produce freedoms – available to all races and genders – that threaten the insane, death-eating, workaday structures of the modern, technological-industrial-capitalist State' (8). The insert also includes a two-page essay by Greg Ing-Young titled 'Oka Ain't Over: A History Lesson,' in which he argues for the long-standing existence of self-determining nations in North America, prior to the arrival of Columbus, and the sustained exploitation of Native peoples by the Canadian government from the Royal Proclamation of 1763 onward. Paradoxically, this proclamation has become the basis for contemporary nation-to-nation negotiations between the Canadian government and individual tribes precisely because it claimed that 'all lands … not … ceded to or purchased by Britain and that formed part of British North America were considered to be "reserved lands" for the indigenes' (Dickason 1997, 161). The question of 'whether the Proclamation recognized a pre-existing title or created it' remains contested (Dickason 1997, 162). Yet, the Proclamation marks an important historical moment for Native peoples in pre- and post-Confederation Canada, one that Ing-Young recognizes when he asserts that tribal populations 'have never surrendered Aboriginal title to their lands and resources or the right to govern themselves' yet are treated as second-class citizens (5). In particular, he catalogues the systematic abuses Native children have faced for generations, having been 'forced to attend residential schools, where they were punished for speaking their own language' (5), indoctrinated with western ideologies, and became the victims of ongoing physical and psychological exploitation, the very elements of loss of community and heritage that Armstrong responds to in 'Threads of Old Memory' and 'Threads of Old Memory Dub.'

The recordings themselves transform the published poems into another format, one that closely resembles what Armstrong has previously described as the alterna(rra)tive concept of oratory, which melds together argumentation and narrative with the practice of spirituality:

> The oratory extends beyond poetry in its need to interact with, and persuade an audience. It is not simply political rhetoric, because of its link to traditional story. It is not drama because, at its roots, it is prayer. It is a distinct combination that defies Western genres. (Anderson 1997, 56)

The aural recordings of the poems, as Richard Bauman argues, adds to these texts yet another interactive framework that is inherently ironic because it draws attention to the slippage between the literal and figurative dimension of the language being used and the varied contexts in which it is delivered to the audience – through the printed word, which is then made into a vocal and musical track, and thus is accessed in a multitude of forms, particularly if the listener also then reads the CD insert that selectively stresses the political aspects of each artist's recordings.

Notably, not much is said in the insert about the side A version of 'Threads of Old Memory,' other than Armstrong's voice is coupled with the San Francisco–based band Suspect Many – an name that itself stresses the need to look again by 'suspect[ing] many' – whose members combine the acoustic bass and acoustic guitar with a steel pan, which originated in Trindad, and then add piano, violin, and extra percussion

(1992, 2). And the eclectic nature of this sound certainly gets less coverage than the side B version of the same poem/song, which is remixed by the Guyanese-born Neil Fraser, internationally known as the Mad Professor, who specializes in dubbing or remixing music digitally, often bringing reggae and electronics together. As the CD insert explains, '[a] Dub version of *Threads of Old Memory*' emerged from a studio engagement with the Mad Professor at his sound studio in September 1990, and 'the studio's very tight Robotics band enlivens [the] melody, as Maya Music's tradition of mixing reggae with Native lyrics continues' (7). What becomes clear, at least textually, is that the more overt and systematic the layering of unexpected or even dissonant sounds, the more radical and worthy of attention the song's political message becomes for those who have written the insert. But I would argue that both tracks engage in a Native oratorical tradition that is itself transformative by virtue of its ironic layering of text and sound and humorous reworking of the expected, without presuming that the more disconcerting the juxtaposition, the more impact it will have. Indeed, Armstrong's transformations are often subtle, yet highly effective in bridging the distance between multiple forms of expression, even as she draws attention to those gaps for the purposes of cultivating various communities of readers who may (or may not) 'get' the differing layers of irony and humour.

Both versions of 'Threads of Old Memory' are part of a much larger political project, one that is reflected in the notes of thanks which come after the credits in the insert to the CD, where the Maya Music label founder and producer of *Till the Bars Break*, Pat Andrade, acknowledges the contributions of various artists, starting with Jeannette Armstrong, 'for their inspiration, support and analysis in helping him to survive and truly begin to understand the connection between Black and Native people' (4). But even as Armstrong seems to be straddling the divide between black and Native populations, she is also carefully retaining a link to her own distinctive Okanagan traditions by creating oratory through the song-poem format. This is evidenced in her choice of recorded lyrics; rather than recording the entire poem, the side A version encompasses only the fourth stanza of lines, which is the section in which the speaker specifically explains that 'when I speak / I sing a song called up through the ages,' overtly stressing the juxtaposition of genres through her choice of language, and then describing in detail the need to look across the landscape of her memory and that of her people to recover those 'sacred words / spoken serenely in the gaps between memory' that have been 'mislaid / forgotten or stolen / muffled by violence / splintered by evil' (1991, 60). The stanza ends with the violent collision of languages, along with the chaotic explosion of the 'past and the present,' which results in the 'the imaginings of the past' tearing 'into the dreams of the future' (60). Armstrong resists including the more peaceful resolution which comes at the end of the published poem, one that listeners of the CD would not have access to directly without also purchasing the poetry collections because the lyrics are not reprinted in the insert; thus each version of the text ironically speaks to the other beyond the framework of the respective publication venue, yet also ensures that for savvy readers to really get it, one must have ready access to both. Further, non-Native and non-Okanagan readers and listeners ultimately lack complete access because they are not familiar with or privy to the precious and fundamental musical traditions of Armstrong's tribe, of which she is a keeper and teacher. Even the musical instruments used in the recording hint at this distance between description and experience, and the need to recognize and articulate the violence of the movement between Okanagan and English, even though non-Natives cannot fully access that experience.

The initially melodic piano scales which accompany Armstrong's reading of the first lines of the stanza become gradually more dissonant and tension-filled with the integration of a violin that rapidly jumps between notes and is occasionally punctuated with the acoustic bass and guitar. By the time Armstrong is describing the collision of languages 'in mid air,' the violin and acoustic bass are given centre stage, aurally speaking, as they leap between low and high notes, and the steel pan – an instrument built from used oil barrels which originated in Trinidad and was initially used as a form of communication by African slaves before being outlawed by British colonialists in 1883[13] – starts to be heard. At the conclusion of the recording, the steel drums reverberate beyond the violin notes and the last words uttered by Armstrong, offering a musical response to that final oral crescendo that couples the tradition of Okanagan singing and drumming with the legacy of black Caribbean drumming; like the history of the steel pan, the knowledge of Okanagan songs and music was jeopardized by the introduction of colonial practices, particularly the creation of residential schools and the institution of laws forbidding the continuation of long-standing tribal practices. Thus, what the first version of 'Threads of Old Memory' presents is a site of cross-cultural intersection through the juxtaposition of words and music that references multiple histories of colonial violence and enforced silence by enabling the steel drums to literally and figuratively continue to sound beyond the words. This not only demonstrates the sustained power of music to bring about change, but also suggestively and indeed humorously hints at what such cross-cultural and cross-national relationships may bring about when 'the imaginings of the past' are allowed to 'rip into the dreams of the future' (1991, 60). The choice of 'rip into' here is notable because one of its meanings is 'to make a vehement verbal attack on,' and hence raises the possibility that the so-called 'dreams of the future' are not only exclusionary but need to be torn up and revised, whether on paper or through music.[14] As well, the musical term 'ripieno' refers to that which replenishes or supplements, namely, the full body of the orchestra instead of a smaller group of soloists.[15] Armstrong's choice of the term 'rip into' suggests a movement away from exclusionary musical and poetic forms that ignore the full and rich resources available; her recording enacts that belief. To listen carefully and to attend to the unsaid are critical strategies when approaching 'Threads of Old Memory.' On this track, Armstrong offers a compelling version of what she calls oratory, and insists that transformation of words when coupled with sounds can lead to other fundamental changes in perspective.

'Threads of Old Memory Dub' extends and complicates Armstrong's undermining of generic classifications, with a collaborative creation that is much more overtly ironic and occasionally funny precisely because it is a dub track and thus foregrounds its own slippage between various versions of the song-poem. In this particular version, Armstrong reads stanza four of her poem once again, but her voice, taken from the previous recording, is overlaid with a persistent, quite loud reggae beat that is sustained throughout the track. Yet in a moment that pointedly riffs on 'Threads of Old Memory,' Armstrong's voice is cut off just after the lines 'I search for the sacred words / spoken serenely in the gaps between memory' (1991, 60), ensuring that the line that follows, 'the lost places of history,' is literally lost within the context of this song-poem. All that audiences can hear is the reverberation of the word 'the' as it is electronically fragmented, echoing in the musical interlude that follows. In addition, this actualization of the loss of the oral – which has been a primary mode for recording and passing on Okanagan history – is compounded by the removal of the six lines of poem lines/lyrics that follow that describe the 'violence' and 'evil' that characterize such ongoing colonial suppression of tribal voices and practices (60). By leaving out this section of text and having Armstrong's voice return with a fragmented version of the word 'explode' in which the 'ex' is dropped in favour of the sound 'plode,' followed by an abbreviated use of the last few lines of the poem/lyrics in which 'the future' fades away, the dub version of-

fers an alterna(rra)tive to previous versions of the song-poem: slippage
between the said and unsaid is routinely enacted, and closure is resisted
altogether. The 'future' may fade away, but Armstrong's voice returns,
in a parodic repetition of the previous version, to sing yet again the first
ten lines of the poem's lyrics; this time, the first-person speaker/singer
finishes in the middle of the published text, finding purpose and voice
in the 'heart' and 'mind' (1991, 90). This perspective emphasizes the importance of the individual's and community's commitment to nurturing
the population through sound and thought; in other words, audiences
need to listen repeatedly and carefully, with an ear to both similarities
and differences, as the Okanagan tribe (as manifested through Armstrong's words and voice) continues to sustain itself in complex and often
ironic and playful ways, through startling and evocative juxtapositions
with other contemporary cultures, such as Caribbean reggae music and
the world of electronic dubbing in which the manipulation of sound is
central. The future, as the creators of 'Threads of Memory Dub' (namely
Armstrong and the Mad Professor) remind listeners like myself, necessarily combines speech and song, blended together in an 'ex-plosion' as
different languages, along with the past and future, meet and jostle for
space in an energetic, provocative fashion that celebrates cross-generic
innovation and resists the tendency to dismiss Native artists and their
works as mere 'folklore,' representative of a 'residual' rather than a dynamic culture (Bauman 1997, 48).

Listening to Harjo

The genre-crossing texts of Joy Harjo extend and complicate the work
of Jeannette Armstrong, whose use of irony and humour are subtle but
strategic, given the Okanagan woman poet's efforts to situate her tribal
language and traditions within a twentieth-century context. Harjo seizes
more readily upon the defiant tone of Freud's 'Galgenhumor' in her musical recordings of 'I Give You Back' precisely because she is focused on
overcoming that which might otherwise push the speaker of the poem-
songs into the realm of silence, passivity, and further exploitation, both
personally and culturally. While Armstrong is fundamentally committed
to sustaining the tribal practices of the Okanagan people, incorporating points of cross-cultural intersection such as the steel pans, in order
to secure her community's survival and growth, Harjo's efforts are both
Muskogee-centric and more overtly pan-tribal, also drawing on Caribbean and African influences, which results in readers and listeners hav-

ing to be familiar with a wider variety of intertexts and references to get the irony and humour. In addition, Harjo has created, by virtue of her sustained musical career as a singer and musician, a much more intricate set of textual and musical conversations.

Knowledge of the frameworks of different versions of the song-poems are especially helpful in the case of Harjo for understanding how 'I Give You Back' has changed, yet remains the same. 'I Give You Back' was first published in *She Had Some Horses* (1983), a book that garnered Harjo considerable acclaim; it then became a song on *Letter from the End of the Twentieth Century*, Poetic Justice's compact disc, which not only incorporates the Native heritages of various band members but also draws on blues, jazz, and reggae for its sound. The poem has subsequently been adapted yet again for inclusion on Harjo's solo release, *Native Joy for Real*, an album that moves in a different direction, combining 'Native rhythms and singing with jazz, rock, blues and a touch of hip hop' (2004, 6). It is the only poem to have been recorded on both compact discs, and also appeared in her 2002 collection by W.W. Norton of new and selected poems. And on each of the albums, Harjo has renamed the song-poem, again raising questions about genre; on *Letter from the End of the Twentieth Century*, it is called 'Fear Poem,' and on the solo album, it is transformed once again, aptly titled 'Fear Song,' in a pointedly ironic reversal of its previous (musical) incarnation.

The structure of Harjo's published poem 'I Give You Back' (in *She Had Some Horses* and *How We Became Human*) is influenced by Navajo night chants, with their repetitive invocation of place, subject, and/or action, all in the service of restoring balance and harmony within the individual and the community. In the printed version of the poem, utterance becomes action, as Harjo's first-person speaker describes the process of embracing and releasing fear to reclaim a spiritual balance. The text strongly resembles 'Transformations' in its desire to find love through hatred or, in this case, fear. And like 'Transformations,' the dialogue between the first-person speaker and the second-person audience is intensely emotional and highly creative as hatred and fear are reconfigured or repositioned; the ability to overcome such powerful emotions rests, as Harjo suggests, with introspection and metamorphosis from within. 'I Give You Back' begins with the phrase 'I release you,' which becomes one of the crucial lines of the poem by virtue of its imperative form – it signals the beginning of the rejection of fear as a part of 'myself' by the poetic 'I' and anticipates the steps that need to be taken towards wholeness, a metamorphosis of self that requires acknowledging the power of fear and the willingness to face it head-on (1983, 73). In the poem, Harjo employs line breaks to create unexpected juxtapositions and turns in narrative events; for instance, the opening lines read: 'I release you, my beautiful and terrible / fear. I release you. You were my beloved / and hated twin, but now, I don't know you / as myself' (73). While the poem title, 'I Give You Back,' suggests return and healing, the movement from the first to the second line invokes a very different sort of reaction; the generosity of 'returning the gift' is countered with the desire to exorcise fear, in all its beauty and ugliness.

Fear, however, is not as easily returned as it may first appear, despite the speaker's efforts to hand it over to those who have provoked it: 'the soldiers / who burned down my home, beheaded my children, / raped and sodomized my brothers and sisters' and 'those who stole the / food from our plates when we were starving' (1983, 73). As a Muskogee woman, Harjo may be referencing specific historical incidents – such as the Trail of Tears – but the potential universality of the exploitation the speaker describes stresses the need to act, and to refuse to be a victim anymore. Hence, the middle stanza of the printed text consists of four identical lines that build their power through repetition and the lack of punctuation, an accretion of sounds that become ceremonial in their efforts to cast fear away forever: 'I release you / I release you / I release you / I release you' (73). The speaker then adds an ironic twist by countering the previous set of invocations with a lengthy list of pairs of opposites that s/he embraces, claiming 'I am not afraid to be …' (73). The fundamental nature of these pairings and their numerous metaphoric resonances – anger/joy, black/white, hunger/fullness, hatred/love – enable the poetic 'I' to reverse the dominance of fear through the presence of love. In the line that follows, Harjo employs repetition to literally overtake fear, pushing it to the edge: 'to be loved, to be loved, fear' (73). While the speaker readily admits to having assisted fear's destruction of herself, such acquiescence to this 'shadow' is about to end (74). Even the form of the lines that acknowledge the speaker's weakness provide an opportunity to rebalance power relations through rhythmic repetition and realignment:

> Oh, *you have* choked *me, but I gave* you the leash.
> *You have* gutted *me but I gave you* the knife.
> *You have* devoured *me, but I* laid myself across the fire. (74, emphasis added)

The juxtapositions between fear's ability to manipulate and the narrator's willingness to surrender are made ironic by the repeated inclusion of 'but,' which reveals the speaker's compliance with the process. This participation in one's own destruction, however, is cut short in the next stanza, which begins, 'I take myself back, fear' (74), returning the focus to the speaker's empowerment. Much like a pesky infestation, fear needs to be expelled from every part of the speaker's body and no longer given the freedom to manipulate emotions: 'You can't live in my eyes, my ears, my voice / my belly, or in my heart my heart / my heart my heart' (74).

Yet the last three lines reverse expectations once again by adding another ironic turn to the final showdown between the narrator and fear. The speaker takes on the sultry voice of seduction and bids fear to return with the promise of another sacrificial encounter: 'But come here, fear / I am alive and you are so afraid / of dying' (1983, 74). However, this time, it is the narrator who claims life and promises the destruction of (an)Other, presumably echoing the very rhetoric which initially made Harjo's speaker such a desirable target. Fear thus becomes vulnerable to the same fate as the speaker once faced. And Harjo's spacing of the lines on the page gives the anticipated death further weight; 'of dying' sits slightly to the right of the end of the previous line, creating a step downward that also ensures a sustained breath pause between them. Deliverance becomes death, an appropriate fate, given fear's ability to torment the poetic 'I.' The generosity that marks the poem's inception, with the promise of release followed by the speaker's increasingly bold self-reclamation and admittance of complicity, turns to revenge and destruction as fear is finally made fearful by the threat of death in a surprising inversion of events. While the poem may not seem to be conventionally funny, Harjo invests the final lines of 'I Give You Back' with a tone reminiscent of '*Galgenhumor*' by making fear into a figure of vulnerability, complete with a bleak future and impending death; the joke is played on fear and, more precisely, those who presumed that fear would take care of the speaker (including those who assumed that Native peoples would merely die out or assimilate once colonized). While killing fear may be merely a powerful fantasy, Harjo's poem suggests that it is a necessary stance given the history of destruction that the speaker and her people have faced individually and collectively. Thus, the magnanimity of the poem's title, 'I Give You Back,' belies the challenges of survival and the seriousness of what is at stake in such an encounter. The self-transformations that occur over the course of the poem, and the unexpected juxtapositions that are presented for readers to make sense of, become tools of what Gerald

Vizenor calls 'survivance' based on a comic and ironic rather than tragic vision of the world (1994, 4).

Released in 1997, *Letter from the End of the Twentieth Century* is a handsome looking disc, complete with a fifteen-page sleeve booklet containing substantial information about Joy Harjo & Poetic Justice as well as copies of all of the lyrics to the ten recorded songs. Produced by Silver Wave Records, an independent Colorado-based company specializing in contemporary Native-American music, World music, and New Age music, the disc not only reaches an audience who might never otherwise encounter Harjo's texts, but transforms the poems into song-poems by providing a venue for repeatedly listening to her work, separate from reading it out loud or seeing her at a reading.[16] In the case of 'I Give You Back,' the published poem is renamed 'Fear Poem' on the disc, and the printed information that follows suggests that other kinds of alterations have been made. The song is attributed in the Poetic Justice booklet to Harjo and two members of her band, John L. Williams and Susan M. Williams, but a list of credits located further down on the same page suggests that the collaboration is much more intricate:

Joy Harjo: Poetry
Susan M. Williams: Bass Drums & High Hat
John L. Williams: Bongos
Frank Poocha: Rattle
William Bluehouse Johnson: Powwow Drum & Bells

She Had Some Horses
(New York: Thunder's Mouth Press, 1983). (1997, 7)

Here, Harjo is attributed with authorship of the poetry and its performance, but not necessarily the chanting or singing of this particular song, though she does both on the track. The credits mediate between Eurocentric expectations that individual contributions will be readily defined and categorized, and Harjo's own desire to acknowledge and celebrate the collectivity of the album's creation. The act of recording draws on – and complicates – the notion that poetry is both authorship and performance; 'I Give You Back' undergoes a (live) transformation into 'Fear Poem,' a title that cleverly recalls its generic origins. And, of course, the band's name itself further complicates questions of 'authorship' and 'ownership,' with Harjo as the only explicitly identified member; Joy Harjo & Poetic Justice follows a long line of bands who rely on a single star member – usually the lead singer – to give the group a broader recognition.

In 'Fear Poem,' the song lyrics are identical to the published version in *She Had Some Horses*, with one crucial exception. While lines 8-9 of 'I Give You Back' read 'I give you back to the soldiers / who burned down my home, beheaded my children' (1983, 73), race becomes an explicit factor in 'Fear Poem': 'I give you back to the *white* soldiers / who burned down my home, beheaded my children' (1997, 7; emphasis added). This racial identifier alters the tone and focus of the poem slightly, tying it more solidly to the historical exploitation of the Muskogee people. It also anticipates the binary opposition between black and white that the speaker is trying to break down shortly afterward, by claiming that s/he is not afraid to be either black or white. Moreover, the inclusion of this adjective fits with the mandate of the record company, which is to be a leader in the field of contemporary Native-American music. The disc itself is packaged to emphasize the Aboriginal heritages of the band members, but with a few twists on that theme because of the band's interest in reggae music. The cover art is by Jaune Quick-to-See-Smith, a well-known Shoshoni painter and print-maker, and includes a black stick figure. To ensure that the figure is visible on a black backdrop, the symbolic colours of the Rastafarian religious movement – red, green, and yellow – frame the stick figure in a box, giving it definition; the so-called Rasta colours recall the Rastafarian reverence for Ethiopia, with its striped flag as a promised homeland for Africans, and serve as a reminder of the movement's efforts towards pan-African unity. The message of the Rastafarians has been most effectively and widely communicated through reggae music, which calls for universal suffrage, and conveys its unique sounds through its use of back beats (which involve striking the drum on the odd beats of two and four) and the incorporation of a bass drum on every third beat; this unexpected use of beats dramatically alters the reggae sound of songs and, in doing so, conveys a powerful message of liberation for blacks. In the case of this disc, the mixing of symbols and colours on the cover that have significance resonances for Native and African Americans is a strategic choice that draws in a broader cross-section of potential listeners but also signals the complex sounds and messages of the songs. Even the presentation of the band's name on the front cover of the disc – an ampersand that joins 'Joy Harjo' and 'Poetic Justice' encased in an arrowhead, which points upward – is multi-layered, serving as both a directional marker and a playful reminder of a clichéd yet also important symbol of Aboriginal survival in the form of a hunting tool.

The recorded version of 'Fear Poem' begins with traditional powwow drums and bells along with a rattle, reminiscent of Muskogee stomp dances. These instruments establish a strong and quick rhythmic beat, over which Harjo begins to recite the song lyrics. The line breaks, which appear in both the printed poem and the song lyrics, are elided in this recording, creating a somewhat different portrait of fear and its power over the speaker. At the beginning of the printed poem and lyrics, 'fear' is literally divided from the rest of its sentence:

> I release you, my beautiful and terrible
> fear. I release you. You were my beloved. (1997, 7)

In the printed poem, 'fear' remains presented throughout the text, visually countering the cumulative weight of the speaker's insistence that she is not fearful:

> I am not afraid to be angry.
> I am not afraid to rejoice.
> I am not afraid to be black.
> I am not afraid to be white.
> I am not afraid to be hungry.
> I am not afraid to be full.
> I am not afraid to be hated.
> I am not afraid to be loved.
>
> to be loved, to be loved, fear. (1983, 73)

The word 'fear' clings onto to the end of the sentence, potentially undermining the repetitive force of the narrator's desire to 'be loved.' The ironic potential of this textual ambiguity, however, disappears when the song is performed; 'I am not afraid to be loved, // to be loved, to be loved, fear' becomes 'I am not afraid to be loved, // to be loved, to be loved ...,' leaving the threat of fear and its incorporation aside. Moreover, the final phrase of 'I Give You Back' is altered both in the printed lyric and as song, with the juxtaposition of 'of dying' just beyond the end of the second-last line as a perilous last step for fear to take, revised and, in turn, made less visually and verbally ironic. Instead, these final words are blended into the sentence as a whole in performance, with Harjo taking only a very slight pause before delivering the phrase 'of dying.' And in the CD booklet, the same two words are moved into alignment with the beginning of the previous line. As a whole, the transformation in 'Fear Poem' is altered in its musical form on the Poetic Justice CD. The lyrics become less edgy and more incantatory, as words are elided or simply omitted. Nonetheless, the decision to include the word 'poem' in the song title suggests that there is an element of mockery in this poem's metamorphosis. The false magnanimity of the previous title, 'I Give You Back,' is replaced with 'Fear Poem,' a title that explicitly acknowledges the focus of the speaker's transformation.

In his fascinating study *How to Read an Oral Poem*, John Miles Foley attempts to divide the oral poem into relevant categories, including what he calls 'Voiced Texts,' which are 'aim[ed] solely at oral performance and are by definition incomplete without that performance' (2002, 43). He carefully contrasts voiced texts with written poetry, emphasizing that the 'spoken word is the necessary and defining outcome of the composition-performance-reception process' in the case of the former (43). In particular, Foley notes the ways in which live performances often lead to alterations in recorded songs; over the course of a band tour, 'the instrumentation may change, a harmony may be deleted or added, various members of the band may experiment with rhythms or insert instrumental solos ..., [and] the lead singer can modify phrasing or even lyrics' (44). He identifies the mass-market CD with its printed lyrics and fixed recording as the starting point for a variety of metamorphoses in an individual song, noting that '"live" albums ... often make their mark by taking advantage of the distance between "canned" versions and fresh reinterpretations of what is recognizably the same song, but with a difference' (44). It is this difference that is especially relevant in the case of Joy Harjo, because what we encounter with 'Fear Poem' is a song-poem already revised in its textual form (from printed poem to song lyric) that is then adapted yet again for musical performance. The recording does not mark the beginning of this work, and thus the variations that follow (both published and recorded) create a palimpsest of reinterpretations of the poem, which oscillate between text-on-the-page and musical performance. And this is further complicated by Harjo's decision to re-record the song-poem for her solo debut album.

Native Joy for Real looks and sounds different – the album is described on the second-last page of the accompanying booklet as her 'debut as a singer/songwriter, an album so strong, so brimming with soul and beauty that even long-time fans will be astonished by the power of its poetic vision' (2004, 6). Released independently through Harjo's own record company, Mekko Productions, the compact disc is less packaged than her album with Poetic Justice; the hard plastic case has been replaced by a cardboard sleeve; there is a shorter booklet of lyrics and acknowledgments; and all songs are credited to and copyrighted by Harjo. To add a whimsical touch, the disc itself has a picture of Harjo singing, saxophone around her neck, and a single phrase printed on the outer lip of the disc – 'May the pretty beast and all the world know peace' – which echoes the rhymes of children's nonsense poems, but with a touch of foreboding given that it is also a line from the first song on the album, which deals with the struggle to survive 'in the last world of fire and trash' (2).

Within the enclosed booklet, those lyrics that were previously published as poems are identified as such with full publication information, and the only name that appears on the disc cover is Harjo's, though there is a group of musicians who play selected instruments on the recordings. This time, Harjo takes on a much more prominent role with respect to the music. She sings, and plays saxophone, bells, Native drums, flute, rattle, percussion, and even an 'improvised guiro,' made from her daughter's van's broken gas cover (2004, 1).[17] As with *Letter from the End of the Twentieth Century*, the disc consists of ten tracks. In this case, however, not all of them are previously published poems. Harjo includes three new compositions, two of which bookend the album; the third, called 'Reality Show,' is a version of a Navajo beauty chant. Moreover, Harjo employs Native languages in sections of two of the recorded songs; the first, 'Reality Show,' includes a Navajo version of the chorus, and the second track, titled 'Eagle Song,' is framed by a chorus in the Muskogee language, and functions as a prayer to beauty. And in each case, Harjo provides either a very limited translation or none at all, creating an insider and an outsider group of listeners based on linguistic knowledge. Paradoxically, however, the album is intended to increase Harjo's audience base and garner new fans; as the description at the end of the disc insert states, 'With "Native Joy For Real," she makes a giant step towards mainstream credibility' (6). Harjo's album reveals her own contradictory agenda, one that relies on both her established reputation as a poet and the desire to position herself as a singer, songwriter, and musician. Even the title of the album itself underlines these paradoxes of language and meaning. Are we hearing and seeing *Native* Joy, the Muskogee woman, for real, exposed for the first time? Or is it *Native Joy* for real – the pleasure and delight of being Native, of exploring one's heritage? Are we to read the assurance of reality in 'for real' as a sign that the last album was not authentic or representative of Joy Harjo or her Native joy? The multiple ironies evoked by such a title anticipate yet another series of transformations in her voice and work.

This time, 'I Give You Back' is renamed 'Fear Song' rather than 'Fear Poem,' a title that asserts the completeness of its musical metamorphosis. Located early in the album, this latter version is also substantially longer, going from two and a half minutes in length on the first disc to over five minutes on the second. The single addition to the printed lyrics on *Letter from the End of the Twentieth Century* – the '*white* soldiers' – has disappeared once again, broadening the potential applicability of the speaker's narrative. Further, the final line of the song, 'of dying,' is given new life, as Harjo alters 'I am alive and you are so afraid / of dying' (1983, 74) to 'I am alive. And you are so afraid. / Of dying' (2004, 3). In doing so, Harjo stresses the assertiveness of the first-person speaker's claim in contrast with fear's vulnerability; fear does not know what is to come, until the very last moment. Even the musical instrumentation has changed, from two types of drums, a rattle, bells, and bongos to a guitar and a keyboard, along with Harjo's guiro and her vocals; the result is less rhythmic and incantatory and more reminiscent of soft rock music. Harjo too, having taken voice lessons, has revised the delivery of the lyrics. In this version, she relies more heavily on melody, moving away, over the course of the song, from spoken chant to include note changes, while retaining the breath pauses and intensity of delivery that make the song compelling to listen to. She occasionally deviates from the printed text, using the repetition of key words to cumulatively negate fear's perceived power, and ends the song with a combination of generosity and self-assertion, combining 'I release you' with 'I am not afraid' to finally undermine fear's reign.

Paradoxically, the very elements that bring new life to Harjo's latest version of 'I Give You Back' can be seen as further tempering the humorous and ironic aspects of the published poem analyzed above. Her interest in melody, the incorporation of different instruments, and even the tone of her delivery signal both a change of context and content that is dependent on listeners and their responses. Yet Bauman insists that 'performance represents a transformation of the basic referential ... uses of language,' demanding that audiences move beyond the literal to pay attention to how other frameworks are juxtaposed on and contrast with it (1990, 9); and here, the performative aspects of Harjo's poem-song give the work an ironic edge by virtue of its context. Admittedly, such a reading may not be shared by many. With an album, the visual placement of words on a page that is so critical to readings of the published poem,

'I Give You Back,' is, not surprisingly, superseded by the dominance of sound. Really, how many listeners will read the enclosed album booklet as they listen to *Native Joy*? How many will know that the song has been previously recorded by Joy Harjo & Poetic Justice? And of those, how many will look back to Harjo's published poetry to examine the lyrical basis of the song? Will anyone else but myself so avidly and carefully listen to the two versions of Harjo's song, with the various printed lyrics and original poem in print at arm's length so as to ensure that the multiple layers that frame 'I Give You Back' are acknowledged and accounted for in some way? Given my prior knowledge, I cannot help but do so, and hence my reading of Harjo is intended to challenge that separation of poem and song and to examine my own response to the complex juxtapositions she creates between different kinds of texts, readings that are cued by my familiarity with her work, her interest in humour and sustained use of irony, as well as her resistance to generic distinctions.

On an album whose title explicitly questions the veracity and, indeed, the authenticity of one's identity – *Native Joy for Real* – 'Fear Song' becomes a cautionary tale, suggesting that fear is not that overwhelming, paralyzing sensation that grips you in its claws, but rather something that needs to be framed and contained, respected and paid homage to, without being consumed. The immediacy and brutality of the speaker's seduction by fear – coupled with powerfully vivid images of war, poverty, hunger, and hatred – is presumably aimed at a privileged and likely primarily non-Native audience who can most easily afford Harjo's published books and CDs; it takes on a particular urgency when delivered aurally, demanding that larger groups of listeners pay attention. Perhaps it is only with an album titled *Native Joy for Real*, which so overtly signals a change of voice and vision, that the resonances of 'Fear Song' emerge as an ironically charged transformation in Harjo's career; clearly, she is fearful no longer of those critics who wish to categorize her works, or of the challenges of being a solo artist – singer, lyricist, and musician – who has primary creative control of her album. In that context, 'Fear Song' can be read as an embracing of Harjo's multiple, contradictory selves, the various speakers that populate her poems and songs.

But Harjo's darkly humorous vision of the world, which is not in evidence in 'Fear Song' or on much of the disc as a whole, re-emerges in the concluding cut on *Native Joy for Real*, titled 'The Down-to-There and Up-to-Here Round Dance,' which is a duet with well-known Oneida comedian Charlie Hill. This final track explores Native-white love relations through both lyrics and an intricate layering of riffs on various musical eras and styles, including disco tracks of the 1970s and traditional round dance songs; there is also a great deal of improvisation on the printed lyrics that appear in the album booklet, with whole lines added to the song in performance. Round dances are social dances traditional to the Plains tribes and beyond, in which men and women are both involved; the dancers hold hands and slide-step to the left, following the rounded shape of a circle. While Harjo's version of 'The Down-to-There and Up-to-Here Round Dance' begins with ceremonial singing, drumming, and bells, this framework is abruptly interrupted by a first-person female speaker who is in the midst of telling off her ex-boyfriend at a local bar, saying to him in a dismissive tone, 'I don't like your girlfriend and her / high-heeled shoes / And her skirt up to here and her blond hair down to there / When you dance right past it gives / me the blues' (2004, 5). To add drama to the song and the story behind it, Harjo juxtaposes her singing voice with Hill's, creating a call-and-response pattern between the unhappy ex-lovers as they banter back and forth, each informing the other of how much they dislike their respective new partners while secretly confessing their continued love.

What make this track humorous are Harjo's musical and vocal transformations, along with her choice of lyrics. Initially the traditional ceremonial chants and choral singing provide a backdrop for Harjo's rhythmically spoken complaints and Hill's off-key pleading as he laments her: 'How can I tell you when you don't talk to me' (2004, 6). Just as Harjo's speaker takes aim at the presumably white, blonde, provocatively dressed new girlfriend, Hill's character critiques his old girlfriend's choice of a new mate based on race: 'I don't like your boyfriend and his / white man ways' (6). But the intrusive nature of Hill's out-of-tune voice, in particular, is reconfigured when the traditional Aboriginal singing, drumming, and bells are suddenly sped up to replicate a disco beat. The mood changes dramatically as Hill takes on the voice of a smooth-talking dandy, who speaks over the chorus, hoping to win her back, only to discover that she is resentful of more than just losing him; she also does not like his other (Native) girlfriends, complaining that his choices have hurt her reputation as well:

> I don't like your girlfriend. I never liked any of your girlfriends. None of them. Not your Sioux, not your Comanche sweetheart, not your shining Shoshone, not your get-down Diné. Not your too-fat girlfriend with her up-to-here and her that down-to-there and her here-down-to-everywhere. You know, it looks bad on me. (6)

The accusatory tone of Harjo's female speaker and Hill's stumbling attempts to redeem himself suggest that competing egos may prevent this relationship from being rekindled.

The song itself ends with a return to more traditional Aboriginal music, though still in double-time in keeping with the disco rhythms, as the same final confession is delivered by both parties: '... If you come close to me honey hey yah / I will have to tell you / how much I love you hey yah ha' (2004, 6). Yet the end of the song, with its concluding chorus, gives a false sense of closure because as soon as the music stops we hear Hill's speaking voice asking, 'Are you done? Geeze' (2004). What follows is a short banter about the perils of too much drinking and partying, especially when you end up in the arms of another woman. Harjo's spoken voice provides a rhythmic counterpart to Hill's off-the-cuff comments, juxtaposing the quotidian with the poetic as she traces the 'uptime too much ... downtime too much ... downtown, runaround' circle of dancing, loving, and even life. Hill's speaker recalls waking up from his drunken stupor to find a woman beside him; he leans over to check her breathing, but the seeming innocence of this particular act is undercut by the compromising scenario he finds himself in. While his ex-girlfriend may still love him, she is familiar with his hard partying ways. Thus, the down-to-there and up-to-here in Harjo's title signal the see-saw action of love and the frustration that grows as lovers realize their partners' bad habits; the all too familiar phrase – 'I've had it up-to-here' – echoes throughout the song. Nonetheless, the conclusion of the track resists writing off the estranged couple completely as Harjo's voice finishes with an 'and,' which suggests that this saga of broken hearts and longing, no matter how contrived and fuelled by jealousy, will continue.

The juxtaposition of radically different musical styles – the slower ceremonial rhythms of Native choral song and drumming with disco's speedy 2/4 or 4/4 time, strong bass beat, and electric guitar – combined with the changing lyrics, create various aural dissonances that give the song an ironic edge. While the Aboriginal music provides a steady percussive beat and sustained melodic singing, the intrusion of disco, with its light and funky sound and emphasis on danceability via a relentless beat, turns what might have been a traditional round dance into something playfully subversive. Harjo's choice of disco also has significant political resonances; as an art form that rose to global prominence in the 1970s, disco became an anthem of sexual liberation for gay men, among others, and provided opportunities for ethnic minorities and women to find commercial success in the popular music industry. To have Oneida comedian Charlie Hill metamorphose into a disco hustler makes the round dance, which is often understood to be a courtship or friendship dance, into a site of sexual liberation and game-playing. Hill's speaker becomes a larger-than-life aural presence whose voice reflects his inflated ego and presumed sexual prowess, before being deflated by too much partying, drinking, and sleaziness. By combining disco with round dance music, Harjo not only resists the stereotype of the static Native by juxtaposing incongruous elements together, in defiance of the rest of the album, which favours a more traditional and subdued mood, but offers a new model of transformation through aural improvisation. In previous examples, Harjo has focused on the alteration of printed lyrics and their delivery. Here, however, the song escapes the confines of a published text by relying on extensive improvisation that creates the rhythmic exchanges between man and woman in both the song itself and its aftermath; it becomes what Foley calls a poem in 'oral performance' (2002, 40).

If Harjo's goal is to blend music and poetry, and to enact the imaginative possibilities presented by both, then 'The Down-to-There and Up-to-Here Round Dance' epitomizes these efforts. She challenges listeners of the song to wrestle with the incongruousness of disco-inflected Native music and to pay attention to the double-talk which takes place between these two ex-lovers, each of whom is trying to make the other jealous. Notably, the song itself deviates substantially from the enclosed book of lyrics. Without listening to the music, audiences miss the rhythmic call-and-response banter of the two main singers, the fusion of disco and traditional Aboriginal ceremonial music, and the song's aftermath, which tells a different story altogether, with Hill's speaker revealing that he is a man past his disco-era prime. What makes this song funny is its aural incongruities, and thus Harjo's album demands that readers of her poetry retrain themselves to hear the music and lyrics, the nuances of sound, rather than relying on the printed word. As a later 'publication,' *Native Joy for Real* marks yet another transformation, with poems being re-recorded as songs and songs taking on the rhyme schemes of poetry only to be improvised and expanded upon in performance. Foley rightly reminds us that 'a fixed, written text lies at the basis of most ... songs' (2002, 44), but the enclosed lyrics for 'The Down-to-There and Up-to-Here Round Dance' comprise less than half of what is sung on the track. What Harjo moves readers like myself towards, then, is a more flexible use of sense perceptions and an increasing acceptance of the 'shape and condition' of (an)Other, regardless of the form it may take.

Through their uses of generic transformation, Harjo and Arrmstrong establish frameworks for reading their texts that are grounded in Native traditions and celebrate their interest in and comfort with border-crossings of various kinds. Both poets employ humour and irony, albeit to varying degrees, to portray the processes and products of their trans-formational texts; these discursive strategies provide the opportunity to explore what might seem commonplace in a new way, to create new combinations and find ways of expressing themselves that provoke their readers to perceive the world differently. While the two poets share a commitment to rethinking genre and draw on their respective Native heritages as a basis for doing so, each woman writer employs her own strategies and has unique reasons for pursuing this artistic course. Armstrong sees the melding of music and poetry as natural and uses her sound recordings to illustrate what she calls 'oratory' to a wider audience (Anderson 1997, 54); in doing so, she highlights the importance of speech and sound to the Okanagan people and imbues this act of textual transformation with her own kind of spiritual significance. One of the key challenges Armstrong faces in her poetry and recordings is how to communicate effectively across languages and cultures, a difficulty that she links to the predominance of metaphor in the Okanagan language and the need to articulate ideas that are fundamentally dissimilar to or non-existent in a non-Okanagan culture. By employing the discursive strategies of irony and, to a lesser degree, humour, Armstrong can convey these cultural and linguistic differences textually and aurally in ways that are accessible to both non-Natives and Natives, yet demand that non-Native readers, in particular, engage with the text's difficulties without expecting – or getting – any easy answers. Harjo resists generic and spiritual labelling, relying on her ongoing musical development to create multiple published and recorded versions of various song-poems. While Harjo is strongly influenced by her Muskogee heritage, she is not a native speaker of the Muskogee language and thus is less concerned with linguistic translation and more interested in her cross-racial heritage that blends a variety of musical influences together. Moreover, Harjo has positioned herself as a professional musician, devoting increasing time and energy to her career as a saxophonist, bandleader, singer, songwriter, producer, and marketer of her own work. Having participated in the packaging of her poetry as song from the bundling of the poetry collection with a cassette of readings when W.W. Norton released *The Woman Who Fell from the Sky* in 1994 onward, Harjo has worked tirelessly to demonstrate that poetry and music are one and the same and that to engage critically with her texts necessitates recognizing, acknowledging, and celebrating that fact. Not surprisingly, then, Harjo cultivates a witty and ironic perspective in her work that accords more closely than Armstrong's texts with Freud's concept of '*Galgenhumor*' in its defiant playfulness and refusal to give up, despite all odds (1905, 229). Although their work may vary by degrees, these poets share a commitment to spiritual and artistic exploration that is sustained by a sense of humour and a desire to challenge dominant paradigms with creativity. In the chapter that follows, the women poets draw on the principles of religious and generic transformation to explore the subjects of history and memory, presenting their own complex and stimulating versions of the past, present, and future from their varied perspectives as mixed-blood women.

chapter three

Histories, Memories, and the Nation

Each time I tell a story I tell it in a new way.
That's what history is ...

Diane Glancy, *Rooms*

Writing is an act that can take place in physical isolation, but the memory of history, of culture ... is always present – like another being.

Beth Brant, *Writing as Witness*

Wonder if I'm what they call living history?

Kimberly Blaeser, *Trailing You*

History is just used Pampers on the / grave of Sitting Bull at Yankton ...

Marie Annharte Baker, *Exercises in Lip Pointing*

As Kimberly Blaeser argues in 'The New "Frontier" of Native American Literature: Dis-Arming History with Tribal Humor,' history has fundamentally shaped Native literature, serving as a basis for opposition and revision for contemporary Native authors who write 'against the events of Indian/White contact and ... more importantly, against the past accounting of those events' (1992, 351). Native writers are not the only ones who have expressed skepticism about the objectivity of history as a discipline; Hayden White famously asserted in 1978 that history texts are best described as 'fictions, the contents of which are as much invented as found' (1978, 82). Post-structuralists and postmodernists, in particular, have vigorously debated history's credibility over the past three decades. For Native peoples, however, the issue of historical representation is fundamentally complicated by the knowledge that they have been typically marginalized or ignored altogether in written historical narratives. In her recent collection of essays, *Indian Country*, Gail Guthrie Valaskakis explains that 'Native heritage is marked with memories of events that newcomers seldom remember and Indians never forget' (2005, 76); the result is a disjuncture between local knowledges and histories and the 'official' records of the past. Even for those historians who acknowledge the long-standing significance and impact of Native peoples within Canada and the United States, 'Native heritage [usually] marks the difference within dominant signifying systems rather than the historical substance of Indian experience' (76). Mark Dockstator explains that 'Western conceptualizations of the historical interaction' between Native and non-Native populations date back only as far as the arrival of Europeans and have focused primarily on assimilation (2005, 103).

Acknowledging the colonization of Native peoples and their existence prior to the arrival of European explorers is a critical first step towards changing the dominant historical record.[1] However, Calvin Martin, himself a non-Native scholar of Native history, points out the limitations of such a strategy when he self-reflexively states, 'Ironically, in writing histories of colonization we are proceeding by way of ideological colonization' (1987, 9). To treat European conquest as central to the recording of Native history is to impose a framework that is inherently colonial, with Native societies being depicted as too primitive to possess their own concept of history or their own narratives of past events. In particular, Martin contends that traditional historical renderings of Native populations remain 'more akin to posed, still photographs' than anything else (9). Martin's paralleling of white western accounts of Native pasts with the images of white American photographer Edward Curtis and others deserves more extensive consideration. Indeed, the next chapter moves from texts to photographs in an effort to explore how several of the women poets discussed here take control of photographic constructions of themselves and those about whom they write. But the women who form the focus of this chapter – Diane Glancy, Jeannette Armstrong, Marilyn Dumont, Wendy Rose, Marie Annharte Baker, and Louise Halfe – primarily identify themselves as writers, and thus it seems appropriate to begin by examining how they use the written word to challenge and refashion standard definitions of history. As we shall see, their poetic renderings of historical events in relation to memory and the creation of nation, as well as their efforts to recover personal narratives of their pasts through memory, take traditional white western patriarchal notions of what constitutes history in new directions.

Roger Simon provides an especially constructive model for readers/ critics like myself to approach the poetry of these Native women, and, in particular, their treatment of history and memory. He claims that 'in democratic communities, we should at least acknowledge *in principle* that previously established historical memories, informed and sustained by established practices of remembrance, should be open to critique and contestation' (2005, 17). Simon, as an education professor, is primarily interested in the pedagogical challenges of 'how non-natives living in Canada and the United States might embody within "living memory" the invasion, appropriation, exploitation, attempted genocide, and colonization of indigenous peoples' (17). What he calls for, from non-Natives like me, is productive listening, or 'listening differently,' which involves not only focusing on the actualities of violence of the past and present but also exploring discursive forms of resistance: 'who is listening, what is heard, and what is learned?' are all part of this process (17). More specifically, Simon argues that 'it is [in] the practice of attuning to what is not spoken' or unsaid 'that the possibility for listening to become a way of thinking exists' (90). While the tendency of dominant populations has been to focus on 'the consolidating identificatory effects of practices of historical memory,' this chapter attends 'to the eruptive force of remembering otherwise' (4), and does so by looking at how the specific tribal and pan-tribal textual strategies of humour and irony become tools for resisting various forms of colonization and formulating new versions of the past, present, and future.

While western historiography struggles 'against genealogical storytelling, the myths and legends of collective memory, and the meanderings of the oral tradition' (de Certeau 1986, 200), the six writers under discussion embrace these same elements in their poetry. Much of the work of Native North American writers involves reflecting on 'what it means and has meant to live in a present which is continually overwhelmed by the fantasies of others of the meanings of past events' (Deloria 1985, x). To simply dismiss or rebut these imposed histories seems inadequate for such a monumental task. As the epigraph from Diane Glancy above suggests, the alternative for both men and women lies with story-making. Blaeser provides a helpful explanation for why such strategies are particularly appropriate for Native poets, whether linked to a tribal community or not, when writing (about) history. She contends that many Native writers 'work to unmask and disarm history, to expose the hid-

den agendas of historiography and, thereby, remove it from the grasp
of the political panderers and return it to the realm of story' (1992,
353). Blaeser argues that those who do so through humour are most
successful and convincing because they provoke an 'imaginative reevalu-
ation of history,' one that is not predicated on 'the illusion of ... [a]
pristine historical territory' (353). In other words, Native writers expose
the ridiculousness of a fundamental presumption, namely, that the New
World was a barren land, whose sparse populations lacked the complex
political, cultural, economic, and social structures to move beyond a so-
called 'primitive' existence. The belief that 'there was "a point in time"
which was "prehistoric,"' and that 'traditional indigenous knowledge
ceased, in this view, when it came into contact with "modern" societies,
that is the West' (Tuhiwai Smith 1999, 55), is shown to be patently absurd. Through a process of deconstruction and re-examination, history
becomes a humorous business, one which requires serious thought and
a willingness to engage playfully in alternative modes of thinking about
the past, present, and future.

Marie Annharte Baker's 'An Account of Tourist Terrorism' provides
one such model for re-examining history, with her wryly evocative first
lines (see also the epigraph above): 'History is just used Pampers on
the / grave of Sitting Bill at Yankton' (2003, 29). Writing about the legacy of Sitting Bull's remains, which were originally buried at Fort Yates,
North Dakota, by order of the American government agent Major James
McLaughlin, and then supposedly secretly transported to Mobridge,
South Dakota, by the Sioux in 1953, Baker's speaker looks beyond the
paradoxical existence of these two sites that both claim to be Sitting
Bull's final resting ground to consider where one might locate history:
'What is history and what did happen / is a deeper question than tourists / dumping dollars in an empty memorial' (29). It is 'the words not
written on the plaque or / between the lines' that cry out for attention,
'ghostwritten graffiti' that are not readily visible or easily deciphered
(29). This combination of scatological irreverence – the used Pampers
that mark the grave as a literal and figurative dumping ground – and
provocative double-talk resists imposing singularity on the past. Clearly
history, in Baker's poem, is not just about the soiled diapers filled by the
next generation of these consuming, capitalist tourists. Equally disturbing is the fact that in coming to the grave and behaving as they do, the
tourists and their descendants still may presume to be more enlightened
in their engagement with Native history. Blaeser suggests that Native
writers, like Baker, who employ humour to rethink history approach the

subject with an acute awareness 'of the reality of the place where the diverse accounts of history come into contact with one another' (1992, 353); Baker correspondingly refuses to glorify the legacy of Sitting Bull when it is exploited for profit.

Further, as the following section will explore, gender and racial identity are central concerns for these women writers as they rewrite history to suit their own purposes. As Native and predominantly mixed-blood women, they have been multiply marginalized not only by white western patriarchal colonization tactics – which have undermined the foundations of many matriarchal Native tribal cultures – but also by racial and gender politics within their own Native communities. Marilyn Dumont powerfully illustrates this point in 'Leather and Naughahyde,' a poem in which the easy conversation between a female Métis speaker and 'this treaty guy from up north,' who shares in her mockery of white city folks, is ruined when the poetic 'I' reveals her mixed-blood heritage: 'he says, "mmh," like he forgives me, like he's got a big heart and mine's pumping diluted blood and his voice ... goes thin ... and when he returns he's got "this look," that says he's leather and I'm naughahyde' (1996, 58). The speaker is perceived as a cheap imitation, lacking the authenticity and richness of her male treaty companion's heritage. Likewise, Baker's 'Ever Notice the Women's Dance' exposes the gender imbalances that shape daily domestic life for many Native heterosexual couples:

> when it is time for the Earth-change
> medicine societies will come dancing
> men may prance around hard times
> practice fancy steps and talk movement
> never notice who is responsible for
> Grand Entry each day around the house. (1994b, 30)

The poem is juxtaposed with a black-and-white cartoonish rendering of a female coyote in the bottom right-hand corner of the page. Wearing a housedress to denote her gender and pushing around a vacuum, this coyote is not – but should be – recognized for her skilful handling of seemingly unceremonious tasks: 'her sensing ceremony / a dirty diaper / needs somebody changing his mind' (30). Despite being the biological producers and caregivers of future populations, the domestic contributions of these women remain unacknowledged. With all of the poets discussed here, many of whom constantly negotiate multiple positions in various communities as (ex-)wives, mothers, writers, academics, and Native women, using humour and irony to draw attention to border spaces is particularly appealing. These tactics help to undercut the fixity of traditional histories and provoke new kinds of revisioning by exploring the unsaid or implicit aspects of the national and tribal pasts in relation to the present.

Defy(n)ing History through Poetry

The word 'history' (which comes from the Greek *historia*, meaning 'to investigate') appears to ask 'the most natural, the most innocent of questions – "What happened?"' yet historical discourses traditionally have aimed to ensure the perpetuation of select master narratives (Ashcroft 2001, 82). In her groundbreaking book *Decolonizing Methodologies*, Maori scholar Linda Tuhiwai Smith explains that for Indigenous peoples, western history can be described as a modernist project 'which has developed alongside imperial beliefs about the Other' (1999, 30). Based on the understanding that only '*fully human*' literate subjects (i.e., white western men) could articulate the totality of world events in a single coherent narrative, history emerged as an 'innocent' discipline, dependent on the gathering of facts by those in power to create a clear picture of the past (31). White western history has been especially problematic for Indigenous women, given that it is inherently a 'patriarchal' enterprise which has systematically relegated women to the sidelines. In white western history, Tuhiwai Smith further explains, women have not been recognized as fully developed subjects, capable of self-actualization, nor given the opportunity to participate in most of the 'bureaucracies or hierarchies where changes in social and political life were being determined' (31).

In *Culture and Imperialism*, Edward Said claims that both colonialism and imperialism 'are supported and perhaps even impelled by impressive ideological formations that include notions that certain territories and people *require* and beseech domination, as well as forms of knowledge affiliated with domination' (1993, 9). The same paradigms that have supported the writing of official history have also fuelled the imperialist project from its inception, ensuring that the populations being colonized were perceived as too primitive or 'Other' to themselves build new nations or capitalize on their countries' rich natural resources. For instance, gynecocratic tribal systems that were fundamental to some Native populations were rapidly dismantled to make way for patriarchal governing structures that would eventually facilitate the creation of new westernized nations; Paula Gunn Allen notes the plethora of tribal 'women chiefs' (in the pre- and post-contact eras) whose existence has been ignored by most historians (1986, 34). By presuming that the New World was pristine and untouched, despite evidence to the contrary, traditional white western history ensured that Native peoples – particularly Native women – were positioned on the margins, and their access to state-authorized citizenship was either limited or refused altogether. And this was reinforced through social and political structures within the new nation-states, both in Canada and the United States. The sense of nationhood that western societies imported to the Americas was designed to ensure white superiority. As Mark Dockstator explains:

> From the duality of the Western perspective, Aboriginal peoples were [only] nations when necessary, for instance, in order to sign treaties required by Western nations; thus nationhood for Aboriginal peoples but not as conceived by Aboriginal peoples existed in some forms with the understanding that it would be temporary. After assimilation, the era of Indian nations would be over. (2005, 107)

The potential for extended nation-to-nation relations, and the ability to protect and sustain existing leadership structures within the tribal nations, were fundamentally undermined.

Native women, in particular, suffered the loss of tribal identity to varying degrees under these strictures. For instance, prior to the passage of Bill C-31 in the Canadian Parliament in 1985, Native women who married non-Native men (or even non-status Native or Métis men) lost their band status, could no longer live on the reserve, and were not able to pass on status to their children even if their marriage dissolved; Native men did not face the same penalties for marrying non-Native women. And as Joyce Green notes, although 'these sex discriminatory provisions were amended in 1985,' they 'were replaced with provisions that arguably continue sex discrimination and which permit sex and race discriminatory band membership codes to determine band membership' (2007, 145); in other words, giving more power over status membership to the bands did not necessarily alter the long-standing colonial legacy of separating women who married non-status or non-Native men from their Native communities. More broadly, the historical assimilationist tactics engaged in by national governments over the past several centuries have taken aim directly at Native women as the biological reproducers of future generations. In *Woman – Nation – State*, Nira Yuval-Davis and Floya Anthias explain:

Women are controlled not only by being encouraged or discouraged from
having children who will become members of the various ethnic [and
racial] groups within the state. They are also controlled in terms of the
'proper' way they should have them – i.e. in ways that will reproduce the
boundaries of the symbolic identity of their group or that of their husband.
(1989, 9)

This forcing of women off the reserve and alienating them from their
communities has ensured, gradually, that Native populations decrease in
size through a process of integration. More generally, in order to build
and strengthen the nation as a cohesive entity in both Canada and the
United States, the diverse histories of Native communities have been
rewritten to fit the goals of the colonizers or, more ideally, forgotten
altogether, separating the past from the present in a gesture of colonial
'goodwill' that was supposed to help eradicate the existence of Native
populations as distinctive and self-defining groups.

In *Manifest Manners*, Gerald Vizenor notes that 'entire cultures have
been terminated in the course of nationalism. These histories are now
the simulations of dominance' (1994, 4). The memorializing of a tribal
presence and writing of 'Indian history as obituary,' a term used by American literature scholar Larzer Ziff in *Writing in the New Nation* (1991),
did as much to destroy Native populations as those who were 'bent on
physical extermination' (quoted in Vizenor 1994, 8). But as Vizenor explains, 'the postindian ousts the inventions with humor, new stories and
the simulations of survivance' (1994, 5). Marilyn Dumont affirms this
perspective when she describes the role of history in her poetry: 'I think
it's certainly writing back to the history that I learned, but it is also a way
of creating a new history, too ... when we write stories we create worlds'
(Andrews 2004b, 147). Part of the challenge for Dumont and several of
the other women poets examined here is that many of the stories from
their communities have been circulated orally rather than in print and,
of course, continue to change over time. As a result, Dumont recalls her
feelings of being 'deficient in my Nativeness' because she did not have
a physical library from which to draw her knowledge of traditions (149).
To challenge her own misconceptions about where knowledge comes
from and elaborate on her own history, Dumont insists on the importance of humour and irony, noting that 'it is a real rhetorical strategy. It's
being kind of sly, kind of tricksterish. It's the way to point at prickly issues
and to get at them through humour' (155). And as mentioned in the
Introduction, for Dumont, humour is linked to gender, offering her a

model for her own revisioning of history, one that relays Native women's stories using their favourite 'rhetorical strategies':

> My mom was extremely sarcastic, I think brilliantly so, and I think I learned that from her. It's interesting because the women of her generation had to find other ways to be able to say something without alienating themselves and I think that this is one of the ways that my mom did it. (155)

In Dumont's case, humour and irony provide ways of expressing an inheritance that is grounded in familial and community interactions – and especially a woman's articulation of selfhood through joking, sarcasm, and attentiveness to what is unsaid or implied. Moreover, Dumont's continuation of this tradition enacts her survival through relational means that undermine white western versions of history as primary. The rhetorical tools and stories learned in childhood offer ways for Dumont to understand how history can be shaped and reshaped by its tellers.

Dumont's discussion of her mother epitomizes another crucial aspect of these women's poems about history and memory, namely, a need to acknowledge and respect the powerful impact that the past can have in shaping both the present and the future. Bill Ashcroft notes in *Postcolonial Transformation* that 'most non Western societies' are not merely concerned with 'what happened' because they see the events of the past as intimately linked to those of the present and the future (2001, 82). To make such black-and-white distinctions would be to ignore the flux of life and the potential for shifting and conflicting accounts of the same events. In his Massey lectures, *The Truth about Stories*, Thomas King further explains that to rely on a constructed past is to presume that there is 'no present' and 'no future' for Native peoples, despite the knowledge that we are 'very much alive, physically and culturally' (2003, 106). He argues that Native writers thus have begun 'to use the Native present to resurrect a Native past and to imagine a Native future' (106). The women poets discussed here see themselves and their individual experiences as an integral part of such a narrative. Diane Glancy, for instance, argues that 'history can ... be seen as the writing of one's own story into the fabric of the written text. Maybe even the *rewriting* of one's own story into the *rewritten* text' (1997, 115). She devotes a section of her generically hybrid poetry/essay collection *The West Pole* to the subject of history, ironically framing it with a series of entries before and after that are all placed chronologically in the here and '*Now*' (i–iii). This gesture firmly asserts the contemporary existence of contemporary Native voices, in spite of what Ward Churchill has described as the 'continuing genocide of North America's native peoples,' which he dates back to the arrival of the first explorers to the New World (1997, 251).

Linda Tuhiwai Smith also stresses the importance of re*writing* and re-*righting* the position of Native women in history; she notes that 'Indigenous people want to tell our own stories, write our own versions in our own ways, for our own purposes' (1999, 28). In *The West Pole,* Glancy draws parallels between a traditional Cherokee form of birchbark biting and her own efforts to record her history. She begins by describing an artistic practice called *Macenattowawin,* which means literally 'chewing the language' – in which women 'put their teeth into the work,' pulling the outer layers of a tree apart and folding them before biting various designs into the bark (1997, 115). As Glancy explains, 'I'm thinking now of history in terms of *chewing the language*' (115). She deliberately conflates the acts of biting and writing to emphasize how history, like bark, is shaped by language use and the artistry of its creator. In particular, Glancy emphasizes the spiritual connectedness of the female birchbark biter she describes:

> A woman ... taking the point of it in her mouth. Biting along the fold ... She chews a geometric design in the papery bark. A braille of sorts ... Maybe the pattern of woodland blizzards still in her head. The old woman has chewed so long her teeth are gone. The spirits come to her in bifocals. Together they enter the chaos before creation. They feel their way back through the dark. The birch-bark biter hears the ancestors in their graves. Sometimes they grind their teeth in sleep ... She holds to the spirit ahead of her. Her dentures chewing. Does it matter the earth has changed? ... Bringing her bitings back from the dark. (115)

Despite the physical impediments for the birchbark biter – her deteriorating eyesight and her false teeth – she possesses an understanding of history that enables her to travel backward and forward in time, and to use this knowledge to create patterns that reflect the complexity of that experience. Glancy pointedly positions her work alongside birchbark biting as woman-centred processes and techniques that Indigenous women can use to rewrite dominant versions of history (115). Writing poetry, like birchbark biting, becomes a tool for serious play. Glancy's inquiry into the history of her mixed-blood tribal roots and family mirrors this artistic form, strategically piecing together bits of information and precise linguistic choices to establish an account of her life that is

not linear or chronological but impressionistic and reflective of her ambivalence about her local and national identity.

Memory and the Nation

Like Glancy, Dumont, Halfe, Armstrong, Baker, and Rose all question
the presumed dominance of nation and national citizenship in the
context of their identities as Native women. As Daniel Francis explains
in his aptly titled *National Dreams: Myth, Memory, and Canadian History*,
'The stories we tell about the past produce the image that we use to describe ourselves as a community' (1997, 176). Borrowing from Edward
Said's famous phrase 'nations are narrations,' Francis contends that for
Canada – and the United States – the need to fashion 'images of communion' are especially pressing because both countries have such diverse populations (10). The writing of a collective and unifying history
has been a central part of this task, to the detriment of Native peoples
on both sides of the forty-ninth parallel. The images that are circulated
reflect the dominant culture's 'understanding of the Indian as noble
or evil, villainous or victimized' and support the notion that 'Indians
[are] historyless vagrants, without an authenticated written past' (Valaskakis 2005, 76). Valaskakis argues that 'the history that assigns these
images to Indians also constructs the nation-states they inhabit' or are
absented from, 'creating an imagined coherence and commonness
among newcomers that excludes' the land's original occupants (76).
Benedict Anderson's oft-repeated and romantically charged description
of 'imagined communities' emphasizes the power of these unifying narratives of identity: 'Members of even the smallest nation will never know
most of their fellow-members, meet them, or even hear of them, yet in
the minds of each lives the image of their communion' (1991, 6). Of
course, the danger of relying on such histories is that what gets forgotten or left out are the narratives of those who have been marginalized
and/or colonized. This is especially true of Anderson, whose concept of
nationalism relies on 'a deep horizontal comradeship' or '*fraternity*' that
figures women as the land to be conquered (16). By implication, both
Native and non-Native women are excluded from this homosocial bond
other than as objects of literal and figurative penetration. Yet, paradoxically, Anderson's work remains especially relevant to those Native wom-
en writers (especially Glancy, Rose, and Dumont) who may have had
little or no physical contact with their respective tribes, nor the matriarchal or patriarchal links to gain tribal membership, and thus need to

use their imaginative powers to create connections between themselves and their Native communities.

As a critical part of this deconstruction of the historical record and the creation of altern(arr)atives, the female poets in question evoke memory to prevent absolute forgetting. In *Decolonizing Methodologies*, Tuhiwai Smith explores the challenges of remembering within and beyond Native communities:

> The remembering of a people relates not so much to an idealized remembering of a golden past but more specifically to the remembering of a painful past and, importantly, people's responses to that pain. While collectively Indigenous communities can talk through the history of painful events, there are frequent silences and intervals in the stories about what happened after the event. Often there is no collective remembering as communities were ripped apart ... This form of remembering is painful because it involves remembering not just what colonization was about but what being dehumanized meant for our own cultural practices. (1999, 146)

This process of healing and recovery depends upon both the memories of those who were born and raised within Native communities that survived (such as Halfe, Armstrong, and, to a degree, Baker)[2] and those who are exploring their estrangement from and efforts at recovering their Native roots (Dumont, Rose, and Glancy). Blaeser describes the significance of memory, drawing on the work of Paula Gunn Allen: '... she hyphenates the word ... making it re-membering. By including that hyphen, she stresses the idea of putting something back together; I've always thought that's a really wonderful way of understanding that word ... serving as a kind of adhesive' (Andrews 2007b, 13). Blaeser sees memory as integral to making important 'intergenerational connections' that enable the refashioning of historical records to include familial and tribal associations, without presuming that there is a single way to rebuild the past (13).

The poets are also resolute in their desire to incorporate trickster humour into their works to facilitate healing and recovery through memory, rather than merely conserving 'the tragic' that Gerald Vizenor notes is so often identified 'as a common [Native] theme' by those from the dominant culture (1994, 83). The conclusion of Marie Annharte Baker's 'One Way to Keep Track of Who Is Talking' deliberately juxtaposes the tragic with the comic to undo such associations, and stresses the need to speak out, to remember differently. As the poem's speaker explains when recalling the massacre at Wounded Knee, 'Frozen Indians and frozen conversations predominate ... Our frozen circles of silence do no honour to them. We talk to keep our conversations from getting too dead' (1990, 78). Here, the vitality of talk metaphorically staves off death. By punning on the phrase 'getting too dead,' Baker's poem not only gives weight to the recording of alternate memories and the need to talk in order to pay tribute to those ancestors who sacrificed their lives for Native self-expression, but also lightens this burden by mocking those who talk without purpose, driving those who are listening to their graves (78). Likewise, the epigraph from Blaeser, taken from a poem titled 'Living History,' offers a wonderfully incisive yet lighthearted look at the generational and, more particularly, familial links evoked through re-membering. A young woman visiting her reserve encounters a 'big Indian man paying for some gas and a six pack' who is 'looking at' her 'hard' and dismisses him as a 'dreamer, I think. Too old for me' (1994b, 5). But when he approaches the poetic 'I,' it is to comment on how much she looks like her mother: 'Pinches my arm, but I guess it's yours / he touches / Hell, wasn't even looking at me' (5). Blaeser's speaker quickly has to shift perspective to make sense of the encounter, which she shares through the poem with her mother, Marlene, and comes to realize that she is a figure of 'living history,' the embodiment of a previous generation that defies traditional presumptions of Natives as a dying race and sustains their vitality as a community (5).

While memory may be seen as a seductive alternative to history because it provides access to tribal communities and cultures, the poets discussed here are careful not to simply treat the two as binary opposites. In *Present Pasts: Urban Palimpsests and the Politics of Memory*, Andreas Huyssen explores the traditional relationship of history to memory:

> For about two centuries, history in the West was quite successful in its project to anchor the ever more transitory present of modernity and the nation in a multifaceted but strong narrative of historical time. Memory, on the other hand, was a topic for the poets and their visions of a golden age or, conversely, for their haunting of a restless past. Literature was of course valued highly as part of the national heritage constructed to mediate religious, ethnic, and class conflicts within a nation. But the main concern of the nineteenth- [and twentieth-] century nation-states was to mobilize and monumentalize national and universal pasts so as to legitimize and give meaning to the present and to envision the future: culturally, politically, socially. This model no longer works. (2003, 1–2)

Huyssen suggests that the instructional value of history and its perceived stability have served the project of nation-building well, relegating memory – at least in western cultures – to a secondary status over the past two centuries. But he argues that with the interest in memory discourses 'in the wake of decolonization and the new social movements' of the 1970s, such an equation needs to be radically revised (12). Memory offers several alternatives; as Huyssen outlines, it can be used to look beyond the borders of national history in collaboration with 'cultural globalization,' expanding concepts of time and space, but it may also provide a means of imagining the future and serve as a tool 'to regain a strong temporal and spatial grounding of life,' despite globalization (6). For the women poets examined here, the flexibility of memory, along with the long-standing interest in and commitment to it in Native societies makes the act of re-membering an obvious tool of self-articulation. The opportunity for these poets to carve a space of in-between-ness for mixed-blood female voices and to find places to locate their family, both within and outside of the scope of nation, is particularly compelling.

Memory practices, as Huyssen notes, are a way to hold onto and sustain specifics: 'Lived memory is active, alive, embodied in the social – that is, in individuals, families, groups, nations, and regions' (2003, 28). Yet memory is tricky to use. It is notoriously unreliable and thus easily manipulated, even by those who fundamentally depend upon memory to cultivate tribal and familial links. Rose, for instance, highlights the ways in which her poetic narrators can and do alter their renderings of memory to suit their own visions of selfhood. In 'Margaret Opens the Bon Ton Salon' from *Itch like Crazy*, Rose traces the story of her great-great-grandmother's experience during the California gold rush. Margaret, who was born in Germany, came to California via Missouri, and ended up running her own restaurant/bar, expresses her frustration in Rose's poem with the writers who seek her out, wanting to hear a romantic narrative of immigration:

> Let hang the next story writer
> who comes to my table
> with notebook and camera
> to ask of my long memory
> …
> I will not say I did not hunger
> or that when the Indians came to the wagon
> I did not fear (though it was only berries
> they wanted to sell …). (2002, 33)

By foregrounding the provisionality of memory, Rose reminds readers of its flexibility and potentiality as well as its vulnerability to manipulation or even complete erasure. As Huyssen suggests through his close examination of German (and specifically Holocaust) memories, 'the *political* site of memory practices is still national' rather than global (2003, 16), and thus is shaped, in the case of Canada and the United States, by the framework of nationhood and citizenship that in many cases has figuratively and literally buried Native voices. Rose's insistence upon the significance of memories and her willingness to expose their constructedness is in keeping with a spirit of trickster liberation that refuses, however tempting it may be, to replicate white western paradigms of dominance without an element of self-reflexivity. The female poets studied here recognize and acknowledge the challenges of employing memory, incorporating its paradoxes in their efforts to secure an alternative past for themselves and their ancestors, especially when they have been separated from their tribal roots and thus may be excluded from the very heritage they wish to recover and connect with.

Memory, Blood, and the Body

In *Heterologies: Discourse on the Other*, Michel de Certeau figures the efforts of resistance against erasure in physical terms, as literally '*marked on the Indian's body*,' making these poets vessels of memory by virtue of the 'blood ties' that they have to their ancestors, links that defy the regulations of the nation-state as to who is and is not Native (1986, 227). The image de Certeau uses is ironically deployed by those contemporary Native North American women poets who may not meet government requirements to qualify for tribal status. Baker's 'In the Picture I Don't See,' from her latest collection, *Exercises in Lip Pointing*, aptly illustrates first-hand the problems with such demands from nation-states and even tribes for 'authenticity,' when her speaker wryly notes: 'I get told the identity problem / is 100,000 Indians do not know / tribes of origin but make up lies' (2003, 14–15). As a result, this poetic 'I' has gone to extremes:

> I have tattooed the verification
> of Indian status on my big toe
> band number without the photo
> ...
> I have provable identity in case
> clan membership expires annually

> or my traditional but urban story
> requires I reinvent my ancestors. (15)

Baker's speaker explores the ways in which the desire to define and fix Native identities by governing bodies ignores the complexities of mixed bloods. With her artfully placed tattoo card (easily concealed and lacking a photo precisely because the body it identifies is immediately present), the poetic 'I' has some insurance, however unorthodox, in case her status is challenged once again. The poem concludes with the speaker's assertion that 'a right to being Indian / is not a pretty picture / an identity made questionable / by invasion or evasion' (15), punning on the phrase 'a pretty picture' to make her point. Baker, and the other poets considered here, suggest that exploring the imaginative ties to one's ancestors through writing, and thus creating new narratives about the past, offers a viable alternative to primarily genetic measures of authenticity.

Kiowa writer, scholar, and painter N. Scott Momaday addresses the challenge of defining oneself as Native when faced with the lengthy history of U.S. government regulations regarding 'blood quantum' with his signature concept of '*memory in the blood* or *blood memory* ... which achieves tropic power by blurring distinctions between racial identity and narrative' (quoted in Allen 2002, 178). As Chadwick Allen explains in *Blood Narrative*, 'blood quantum' or the 'degree of Indian blood ... originally served as a device for documenting "Indian" status for the [American] federal government's purposes of dividing and subsequently alienating collectively held Indian lands' (176); the same is true of Canadian history, beginning with the introduction of a blood quantum proviso in 1869. However, Allen contends that Momaday's

> trope's provocative juxtaposition of *blood* and *memory* transforms that taxonomy of delegitimization through genetic mixing into an authenticating genealogy of stories and storytelling. Blood memory redefines Indian authenticity in terms of imaginative ... re-membering. (178)

The power of memory forms a basis for retelling history, or more accurately in the case of these women poets, 'her-stories.' While Momaday's insistence on the genetics of Native memory has been challenged by some scholars who are uncomfortable with its essentialist underpinnings (such as Arnold Krupat), Diane Glancy represents the perspective of most of the writers discussed here when she argues that 'racial memory, generational memory,' is central to the work of Native literature, and

Native poetry, in particular (Andrews 2002b, 649). Memory, she asserts, 'is the informer of the poetic text,' giving Native writers a critical foundation from which to explore their identities (651).

Wendy Rose exemplifies this need to find connections to the past through racial memory in her poem 'Naming Power,' from *Now Poof She Is Gone* (1994), which argues for the importance of being named into being and the struggle the narrator faces as someone who has not been named, because she lacks the Hopi mother who would legitimize her tribal status. Although Rose's poetry records the difficulties of such an exclusion, her poetic 'I' is also careful to emphasize the power that 'ancient words / [have] to bind you / to your people'; the narrator describes herself as 'a creature of blood / and it's the singing in the blood / that matters, songs to keep' (1994a, 35). The speaker may be starved 'not for rabbit stew / but for being / remembered' (35), but she does presume that through blood, in combination with the power of imagination, one can at least speculate on an ancestral line and make connections with a viable past. Rose's situation is a complex one. Because her father rather than her mother is Hopi, she cannot claim Hopi tribal status; and her mother's tribe, the Miwok, has no formal tribal organization and a tiny dispersed population, making a tangible affiliation to a homeland and community impossible. While Rose begins the poem with the lines 'a thirty-year-old woman / is waiting / for her name,' the collection as a whole, which Rose dedicated to herself with the statement 'this is my book,' suggests that she has indeed found a name in the spaces between traditional tribal designations and a memory in the blood that draws on her imaginative inheritance (35, 5).

The women poets in this chapter use their texts to dismantle the fixity of white western masculine histories and to examine the global appeal of memory discourses in an effort to interrogate nationalist ideologies and to return memories to the realm of the local and/or transnational, depending upon their specific relationship to a tribal community and its memory practices. By combining the strategic essentialism[3] of 'memory in the blood' with aspects of spirituality and a strong belief in the power of imagination, the writers in question are able to put themselves in positions of authority and claim access to memories that might otherwise be lost or buried, while also acknowledging that memories are, by their very nature, provisional and subject to change. In addition, the presumption that everyone can and does have a readily accessible history becomes a point of contention, as most of the women poets in question write about their struggles to learn about themselves and their families in the absence (or distortion) of such narratives. Thus, within their texts, cultural recall is treated as a malleable process that involves the performance of identity. And as part of this process, the poets in question employ the concept of what Roxanne Rimstead calls a 'double take' when examining the cultural memories of their families and communities; they engender new ways of thinking about Native histories by offering (an) Other look at constructions of the past (2003, 2). These writers provoke their readers to look again at seemingly innocuous events or situations and to probe the constructedness of traditional history through collective and individual memories, while simultaneously acknowledging the limitations of such strategies.

Male public figures from the dominant historical record are particularly appropriate targets for these Native women writers because they represent the power of white western masculinity and the deliberate erasure of Native voices from the scope of official records. As Roger Simon explains, '… historical memory is constituted through social practices of remembrance wherein specific images and narratives are put forward as the terms on which to articulate a collective historical imaginary' (2005, 15). Glancy, Rose, Halfe, Baker, Armstrong, and Dumont may be described at first glance as 'writing back' to the history of their predominantly male oppressors. But they go beyond the immediate task of deconstruction to examine both ingrained assumptions about individuals like Christopher Columbus, and the broader history of New World nations upon which the creation of Canada and the United States are built. Most obviously, these women challenge the presumption that when Europeans arrived, they found a huge and unoccupied land mass they could claim for themselves. As Daniel Francis notes, 'Memory implies its opposite – forgetting … For example, it is known but not often recalled, that the successful, and relatively peaceful, settlement of Canada by European newcomers was possible largely because a vast number of the original inhabitants, the First Nations, were wiped out' (1997, 11). Louis Owens furthers this argument by distinguishing between notions of territory – unoccupied space – and the frontier as a place of contact, asserting that Native writers start from a place of contact, possessing no illusions about the existence of a pristine territory (1992, 353). By insisting upon the existence of Native ancestors who suffered at the hands of soldiers, missionaries, and government officials, before and after the Declaration of Independence and Confederation, these women writers give voice to stories of marginalization through a process of imaginative retelling. They resurrect these so-called male 'heroes' and criticize them both as icons and individuals. The poets unpack the concepts and symbols of nationalism and national history, and their roles in enforcing Christian conversion. They also interrogate the very basis upon which dominant narratives of discovery and nation-building were constructed.

Who's(e) Columbus?

Christopher Columbus's historical prominence as a European explorer and discoverer of the New World has formed the focus of works by numerous Native writers who are eager to contest traditional representations of his arrival and subsequent exploration of the Americas, among them Thomas King's *A Coyote Columbus Story*, which was released in 1992 to coincide with the quincentenary of Columbus's arrival in the Americas. In *A Coyote Columbus Story*, a wily female Coyote's efforts to engage the newly arrived Columbus in a game of baseball fail, and the clownish Columbus, disappointed by his inability to find gold to take back to Spain, instead seizes a group of Coyote's 'friends' (1992, 23) to sell to 'rich people like baseball players and dentists' back in the Old World (26). Columbus's departure not only spurs the rest of the Native people living near Coyote to leave before the Genoese-born explorer returns but also leaves Coyote without friends with whom she can play ball – that is, until Jacques Cartier arrives on the final pages of the text and becomes the trickster's next potential playmate. King's book 'reveals the racial and cultural specificity of the traditionally accepted version of Columbus's voyage,' a message that was notably poorly received by U.S. publishers when King's Canadian publisher attempted to sell the foreign rights to the book at the Bologna Book Fair (Andrews et al. 2003, 78); one publisher deemed the children's story 'hateful,' and another dismissed it as too 'depressing' for 'American kids' (Ross 1992, C14). These reactions of horror and outrage on the part of U.S. publishers mask a more pressing issue, that of the 'cultural relativism of their own perspective' and the reality that 'alternative perspectives continue to be deemed intolerable,' particularly when those alterna(rra)tives question Columbus's centrality to birth of the New World (Andrews et al. 2003, 76).

As Winfried Siemerling notes, Columbus has become not only a 'foundational signifier of the "New World" but also of colonization and oppression' (2005, 3). In both Canada and the United States, the creation of independent democratic nations paradoxically depended upon the 'brutal practices of imperial dispossession [and Christian conversion] of Native peoples' (24). Not surprisingly, the Columbus Quincentenary in

1992 had a notable impact on Native male and female writers, on both sides of the border, including several of the poets who form the focus of this book: Diane Glancy, Wendy Rose, Jeannette Armstrong, Marie Annharte Baker, and Louise Halfe. Plans for the Columbus Quincentenary celebrations began in the United States a full decade before the anniversary of his arrival, with the creation of a Congress bill intended to secure funds to pay for a variety of events around the country and beyond.[4] Designed to pay tribute to Spanish Americans and their European heritage, the celebrations backfired with the overt and increasingly visible Native public protests over Columbus's arrival and subsequent impact on the Natives he encountered, as well as his contributions to the creation of a Middle Passage and the advent of slave importation.[5] Vizenor eloquently articulated the ambivalence encoded in Columbus as the discoverer of America in *Manifest Manners*, explaining that 'the quincentenary is a double entendre, the long gaze celebration of colonial civilization in his names, and the discoveries of his name in a constitutional democracy' (1994, 110). In this case, Columbus's visibility as a figure of nation became an impediment to the celebrations; his legacy was perceived as embodying the worst aspects of American conservativism, leading to funding withdrawals even from seemingly right-wing organizations such as the National Endowment for the Humanities.[6]

Glancy's *The Relief of America*, published in 2000, responds retrospectively to the resolutely positive depictions of Columbus in stories of the creation of the New World and the American nation, punning on geographic terms and exploring the art of cartography in order to re-vision the country from a distinctly Native and female perspective. Glancy had produced a prior prose poem about Columbus in her 1997 collection, *The West Pole*. Called 'Columbus Meets Thelma and Louise and the Ocean Is Still Bigger than Any of Us Thought,' the poem's narrator explores various constructions of the quincentenary Columbus, only to posit her own ironically charged claim that 'Columbus was the forerunner, the archetype of the new woman who sheds her boundaries' (1997, 120). Glancy's speaker compares Columbus's multiple voyages across the Atlantic Ocean to North America with the white working-class female protagonists of the 1991 American film *Thelma and Louise*, who at the end of the movie drive their car into the Grand Canyon in an attempt to escape the police, and more generally, a life of oppression based on sex and class. In 'Columbus Meets Thelma and Louise ...,' Glancy may be read as initially celebrating the construction of a female-authored New World geography and the resolution of white working-class women (who are fed up with patriarchal domination) to travel alone. But the poem foregrounds its own shifting trajectory:

> Setting out for new ground.
> Not interpreting the same only way, i.e. the text as a single authority ...
> The inward personal layered saying-of-one-thing-and-meaning-another.
> Apparent form, hidden meaning. Emerging and bleeding genres ...
> How to lie and keep secrets. Present the unsure as what is sure. (123–4)

Glancy's insistence upon the 'layered' meanings of her poem frames her ironic representation of Columbus, in the lines that follow, as 'the first feminist,' who possessed 'domestic sensitivity' but 'was too bogged with land. / ... he kept running into' (124). By re-visioning Columbus as Thelma and Louise's 'matriarch,' Glancy's speaker urges these white working-class movie characters and the readers of her poems to treat their interaction with the poem as Columbus would have, as an adventure to be seized: 'Take captainship into your own hands. Hear the text. Take it into consideration. Deconstruct it. Perceive it in your own way' (125). Glancy concludes her poem by refashioning the fateful conclusion of *Thelma and Louise* into a moment of Native self-assertion. Her speaker explains that 'once I envision the voyage nothing is ever the same' (126), a line which suggests that there are indeed other other altern(arr)atives available to Indigenous peoples and Native women, in particular.

She furthers this perspective in *The Relief of America* by innovatively envisioning the landscape over which her first-person Native speakers travel. The title of the collection refers to changes in terrain, the elevations and depressions which reveal the contours of the land; it also evokes the sense of a burden being lifted and compensation being offered for a legacy of erasure. *The Relief of America* explores alternative cartographies by attending to the lost and forgotten memories of those whose terrain was taken from them in the effort to build America. Anne McClintock reminds us that typically 'the knowledge constituted by the map both precedes and legitimizes the conquest of territory' (1995, 27). Geographer Christopher Board offers another viewpoint in his classic essay 'Maps as Models,' stating that 'maps [are] representational models of the real world ... They are also conceptual models containing some generalization[s] about reality. In that role, maps are useful analytical tools which help investigators to see the ... world in a new light, or even to allow them an entirely new view of reality' (1967, 672). By remapping

familiar land in new ways, Glancy juxtaposes colonial visions of the nation and their appeal to Euro-Americans with new versions of America,
and thus subverts the tendency to, as Vizenor puts it, reduce tribes 'to
the tragic in the ruins of representation' (1994, 83). Elsewhere, Glancy
acknowledges her own cartographies of migration by commenting on
the paradoxical nature of her family's movement to Kansas City and her
tendency to write as a migratory Native woman despite being descend-
ed on her father's side, as mentioned in the previous chapter, from 'a
sedentary Woodland tribe, the Cherokee' (1997, 2). As a result, she has
spent much of her life as a 'part-Cherokee living on land that belonged
to another tribe' (2). This acute awareness of land – its ownership, occupation, and withdrawal from Native control – adds another aspect to
The Relief of America.

The collection also may be read as ironically responding to the 1831
decision of Supreme Court Chief Justice John Marshall, who rejected the
Cherokees' claim to operate as a free and independent nation, instead
describing the tribe as a 'dependent domestic nation' that because of its
weakness had chosen to 'place itself under the protection of one more
powerful' (Deloria and Lytle 1984, 17). The Marshall decision did not
address the Cherokee's own concerns that with the passage of the Indian
Removal Act by Congress in 1830, the tribe would be unable to protect
itself from the land claims of white Georgians, which had begun to be
pursued by state legislators in Georgia in 1827. The result was the eventual removal of the Cherokee westward along the famous Trail of Tears,
which Glancy discusses in *The West Pole* as a radical shift in direction for
the Cherokee, both literally and figuratively:

> No longer
> would our ancestors be from the great salt-waters
> toward the rising sun.
> Now we faced the other direction. (1997, 156)

Hence, in *The Relief of America*, Glancy's depiction of Columbus becomes a catalyst for rewriting both the map of America and the specific
experience of the Cherokee people. As she notes in *The West Pole*, 'It was
different with Columbus ... After Columbus, the white man would keep
coming and forever change the life of the Native American' (1997, 155).
In *The Relief of America*, Glancy suggests that Columbus's arrival set into
motion, among other things, the Marshall decision, which established a
negative legal precedent for the future of Native-American sovereignty

and their efforts to reclaim land. Glancy's collection, in response, performs a process of reclamation that is grounded in the land itself rather than dicta from a distantly located federal government.

Glancy's attentiveness to America's geography is evident from the first page of *The Relief of America*, which contains a small, slightly faded, black-and-white contour image of North America, positioned far enough away as to play tricks on the viewer's eye. The lack of precise visibility of the image, and the narrator's claim that 'North America is an Indian's head. Growling' (2000, 5), provides initial context for (an)Other look at the history of the New World, especially with respect to Columbus. This other perspective is laid out in the first poem of the collection, 'Christopher,' a retelling of Columbus's arrival on the shores of America relayed by a colloquial Native narrative voice that slips between a broken English and Spanish phrases:

> Here come Christopher Columbus comming ober t'wabes.
> PUFF. PUFF.
> He think he come to the segund part of urth.
> His shups bump inter land at night
> y haze la senal dla cruz. (9)

Glancy employs capital letters and words written as they sound to visually and orally mock the naivety of the Spanish explorer, creating a text that is good-humoured yet sharp in its critique: the 'PUFF' of the boat, the sails being filled with wind, also can be read as a comment on Christopher's own arrogance, his hot air. Glancy has argued elsewhere that 'language has a holy-clown element that goes backward or contrariwise. To give possibilities. To lose the bonds. So the tribe isn't stuck with … unalterable, negative situations' (1997, 69). The contrariness of 'Christopher,' which is achieved in part by Glancy's *'chewing the language,'* is created through often bitterly ironic juxtapositions between the sound of a word, its appearance on the page, and its multiple meanings, as in the case of 'PUFF' (2000, 9). Likewise, when Columbus uses gold 'to buy our souls inter heaben,' Glancy replaces 'into' with 'inter' to remind readers of the long-term impact of this explorer's fateful arrival; 'inter' also means 'to obtain, take possession' and 'to bury or put a dead body into a grave,' both of which emphasize the destructive aspects of Columbus's first encounter with the Native peoples, whom he turns into objects for purchase and slave labour. Even Glancy's use of Columbus's first rather than last name in the title of the poem anticipates the destabilization of

accepted stereotypes. She forgoes the respectful distance of employing
his last name to create a sense of intimacy that reflects his own imperialist attitude towards the Natives he encounters; if he can name them with
such ease, why can't her speaker do the same?

In 'Christopher,' the narrator undoes Columbus's authority by stressing that his landing is not purposeful but accidental. Once there he
quickly tries to exploit the locals and their natural resources, asking,
'*Now whar find GOLD?*' and claiming the land for the Spanish monar-
chy in a broken Spanish tongue (2000, 9). Glancy's Christopher offers
the Natives 'glaz beads & bells' and his 'treasures' (9). Coupled with
his sudden arrival from the vast emptiness of the horizon, his seeming
generosity initially leads the local population to believe that he is a god
and to imitate his inflated rhetoric: 'We think he god from skie. Yup.
Yup. Wedu. / The blue oshen sprad like a table napkin by his shups' (9).
Glancy refuses to let Native peoples off the hook either. Their naïve wor-
shipping of Columbus and willingness to follow his orders proves both
positive (they load the ships and send him on his way) and negative (he
will return). But Christopher's single-minded search for gold, a request
couched in a garble of English and Spanish religious rhetoric ('*Gloria religion xpiana. / Gloria Yndias*'), and his presumption that he has reached
India, and hence can call the population '*Yndias*' (9), are revealed as
patently absurd.

In the closing lines of this poem, which needs to be read aloud to hear
the oral complexities of the dialogue that constitutes much of the text,
the narrator relishes Columbus's departure from the shore, a departure
which is facilitated by the Natives who pack up his ship. Glancy ironically
echoes the initial lines of the poem at its conclusion, creating a rhyme
that links the beginning and end of 'Christopher': 'Thar go Christopher.
Huf. Huf' (2000, 9). The huff and puff that are associated with Columbus invoke another set of memories in the form of a popular childhood
story from the western world about a wolf who tries to destroy the houses
of three little pigs – he succeeds with the first two but fails with the third,
a brick house, and is scalded to death in a pot of boiling water. In this
case, Columbus is fended off at least temporarily, but the poetic 'I' recognizes the darker aspects of the explorer's visit through the Christian
virtues that he espouses: 'Wid gold he own t'segund urth. / Wid gold
he buy our sould inter heaben' (9). The rhetoric of salvation through
exploitation that the narrator has heard and assimilated provides an oppressive final vision of Columbus's legacy – with the arrival of missionaries – but Glancy carefully balances this mood with the code-switching

that goes on throughout the poem, an exchange that reveals the cross-talk of this 'first' encounter as ludicrous. Columbus becomes the cartoon figure whose arrival and departure anticipate the beginnings of an America where capitalism, Christianity, and civilization trump the prior occupation of lands. And Glancy's readiness to refer to Columbus by his first name establishes an intimacy that belies the authoritarian behaviour he exhibits towards the Natives he encounters in what he thinks is India. While Columbus may order them to 'load his ships,' a task that the Natives take on to rid themselves of him, Glancy's narrator has the last word, exposing the economics of Christian patriarchal colonization for what they really are (9).

Much of the irony and humour in 'Christopher' depends on the evocation of altern(arr)ative constructions of memory that ironically refashion traditional white western perspectives on historical events by juxtaposing them with Native viewpoints. Wendy Rose also uses the figure of Columbus to explore not only national but also personal alienation and discontinuity in a work called 'One of Those Days When I See Columbus' from *Itch like Crazy*. As an academically trained anthropologist, the objectivity of this social science is undermined by her own 'half-breed' status and sense of alienation in the scholarly world, a discontinuity that she links back to Columbus. This poem suggests that Columbus's brokering of his voyages, his search for wealth in the New World, and his enslavement of some of the people he encountered, partly as specimens to take back to Europe, strongly parallel traditional protocols in anthropological research. The poem's title also serves as the first line of an intimate first-person exploration of how Native peoples continue to be sold out under the guise of anthropological study, a process that the narrator witnesses daily in her work as an anthropologist.

When asked about her own experiences as an anthropology student and later professor, Rose explains that she pursued graduate work in anthropology in part to gain the credentials and knowledge to be able to challenge the repeated 'exploitation' of Native sacred grounds for ethnographic study (Hunter 1983, 72). She has written about her academic studies using a strong dose of wry humour in several previous volumes, including the aptly named *Academic Squaw: Reports to the World from the Ivory Tower* (1977). As Rose notes, 'One of the things I learned growing up ..., as we all do when we become older, is that if I really wanted to get a political point across, to tell it outright ... won't be effective'; instead, Rose advocates introducing the topic to readers 'in such a way that it goes inside of them before they recognize it for what it is and when it

comes out it's coming from inside themselves. Very often, humor is a way
to do that, or taking something universal' and making it individual (Gray
1985, 14). Rose reminds readers that 'I am angry and I am bitter, and the
matter of having the poetry not come out angry and bitter [lies in] the
crafting of it' (14). While there are moments of bitterness and anger in
'One of Those Days When I See Columbus,' Rose relies on the accretion
of snippets that her speaker gathers from behind a closed office door to
create ironic and eventually more humorous moments in her text:

> Voices beyond
> my office door
> speaking of surveys
> and destruction,
> selling the natives to live among strangers
> to pay for the trouble of transporting them,
> or mastering this or that, perceiving entitlement
> good as gold for service
> or kinship to the Crown. (2002, 67)

The abbreviated middle lines in the first verse depict how the speaker's
area of academic expertise depends on the dissociation between personal
and professional lives; much like Columbus's conduct in the New World,
the discipline of anthropology traditionally has been characterized by
exploitation and pillage. To refute this, Rose's poetic 'I' refuses to presume that the New World is empty and uses her imagination to create a
whole series of powerfully evocative counter-memories grounded in the
body: 'Terror / crouches / in the canyon my hands make' (67). She lists
not only the names of places within the United States, Mexico, and the
Caribbean where large-scale massacres of innocent Native peoples occurred, but also the Vietnam massacre at My Lai of over three hundred
civilians by U.S. soldiers claiming to be on a 'search and destroy' mission,
reminding readers of the lasting impact of imperialism on America and
demonstrating the global price paid for such behaviour.[7] The irony of
her list is that it is complex and pointedly exclusionary, demanding that
readers know an enormous range of historical events involving Native
populations – many of which were hidden from public record for some
time. And to further complicate the significance of such a list, Rose's
speaker puts '[m]y mother' at the end of the list of massacre sites. The
death of her mixed-blood mother (Scottish, Irish, and Miwok) can be
read as marking the decline of a tribe (the Miwok) already in peril,[8] and

thus represents another kind of symbolic killing. By invoking a slippage between place and person, Rose's speaker reminds readers of the public and personal toll of such losses and refuses to fall silent in her grief.

Instead, the remainder of the poem offers a series of assertions that are anticipated by the word ' ... so,' which concludes the first half of 'One of Those Days When I See Columbus' (2002, 67). The physical layout of the text contributes to this ironic shift in perspective, as the speaker starts to hint at the power of survival: 'to rise where refugees have stepped / deep in the mud on the Turtle's Back ... so' (67). This 'so' sets off, on the flip side of the page, a list of anomalies from the natural world that survive despite all odds, ranging from a sunflower breaking through sidewalk concrete to 'bits of placenta' that breed new life as Native women continue to give birth (68). Rose's speaker also shifts from the singularity of her experience to a more collective voice, using 'we' to call upon Native readers, in particular, to 'choose our battles / and take our victories / where we find them' (68). Rose's speaker follows these exemplars of survival against all odds with a series of imperatives that encourage those whose beliefs and practices have been suppressed to rebel: 'So dance the mission revolts, / let ambush blossom in your lungs, / claim the enemy's finest night, sing, oh sing him into death' (68). Here, her poem recalls the long and frequent history of mission revolts by a variety of tribes in North, Central, and South America, who rose up against the forced incarceration of their populations and the concurrent imposition of Catholicism on Native peoples, including those in her home state of California. The cumulative force of this counter-vision is heightened by Rose's invocation of the trickster Coyote (a part of both Hopi and Miwok cultures), whose job it is to lure the missionary soldiers – who often brutally injured or killed those Native people who did not co-operate with the strictures of the mission system – away. The poem's final turn offers a thematic twist on the anthropological colonization that characterizes the beginning of 'One of Those Days When I See Columbus': 'Coyote will creep most quietly beneath / the ancient gallows that creak and creak' (68). It is Coyote who takes charge of this situation, creating a different kind of death site, one which counters the historical force of the Spanish mission system (and, by implication, Columbus's arrival in the New World) by hinting at alternative outcomes to this long-standing tool of conversion and domination; the possibilities of the unsaid open up the space for both counter-memories and altern(arr)ative visions of the present and future.

Columbus is a vexed symbol for contemporary Native-American women poets, but his significance also crosses national borders because he not only embodies the perils of First Contact but also represents the lasting aims of religious conversion and economic exploitation, as well as the subsequent impact of nationalism on Native sovereignty, on both sides of the forty-ninth parallel. Jeannette Armstrong's 'History Lesson' is perhaps the most pointed example of a Native woman's poetic challenge to the legacy of Christopher Columbus and the construction of Canada as a nation. In other poems from her collection *Breath Tracks*, Armstrong's first-person speaker describes her role as that of 'the choice maker' (1991, 59) who understands that

> Words are memory
> a window into the present
> a coming to terms with meaning
> history made into now
> a surge in reclaiming
> the enormity of the past. (17)

Armstrong elaborates on the significance of memory and the power of the word in an essay called 'Land Speaking,' where she describes how the Okanagan language, which she speaks fluently, 'carries meaning about a time that is no more' (1998, 181). Her obligation is to listen: 'The words are coming from many tongues and mouths of Okanagan people ... when my words form I am merely retelling the same stories in different patterns' (181). The weight of that responsibility and the need for survival through the speaking and writing of words are reflected in 'History Lesson,' which highlights the mythic dimensions of history-making by deconstructing some key events that shaped the British, French, and post-Confederation Canadian colonization of Native peoples. Armstrong employs contemporary marketing phrases, familiar clichés, and word puns, along with abbreviated line lengths and a richly imagistic vocabulary, to describe the arrival of explorers, missionaries, pioneers, and fur traders.

While several very fine readings of 'History Lesson' already exist,[9] what I am interested in is how Armstrong uses humour and irony to problematize not only positive renderings of Columbus's voyage but also official versions of Canadian national history. In her poem, Armstrong offers caricatured descriptions of those who colonized what were once Native lands. Her speaker portrays the Royal Canadian Mounted Police as 'red coated knights / [who] gallop across the prairie / to get their men' (1991, 28). As Renate Eigenbrod notes, Armstrong's poem offers 'a blunt parody of the grade school history lesson we have all had' (2005, 86), in particular, by mocking what Daniel Francis calls 'the narrative of the Mountie subduing the fiery spirit of the Indian and making the West safe for settlement' (1997, 30). The all-male RCMP officers in this poem not only reinforce Canada's ties to Britain through the monarch's granting of a royal title to the force, but also embody the stereotypical patriarchal Canadian values of 'safety and security, order and harmony' (Berton 1958, xviii). Armstrong's narrator, however, refuses to let these elegantly attired knights merely function as defenders of the realm; she also notes that their goal is 'to build a new world' despite the prior existence of an old one (1991, 28).

Even the pioneers and traders in 'History Lesson' bring 'gifts' that paradoxically kill or exploit the Native populations. Armstrong structures the poem to reflect that ironic disjuncture, countering the generosity of the newly arrived settlers with their negative impact. The poetic verse shifts from the promise of 'gifts' – with its shortened line length – to the alliterative appeal of 'Smallpox, Seagrams, / and rice krispies' (1991, 28). Armstrong's speaker also creates a cartoon vision of the natural world through vivid language and sensory overload. The poem specifically targets Canadian national pride by rewriting the efforts of pioneers who farmed the land, miners who searched for gold, and businessmen who established booming industries based on natural resources:

> Between the snap crackle pop
> of smoke stacks
> and multicolored rivers
> swelling with flower powered zee
> are farmers sowing skulls and bones
> and miners
> pulling from gaping holes
> green paper faces
> of a smiling English lady ...
>
> The colossi
> in which they trust (28–9)

As Renate Eigenbrod notes, 'if one reads the line "pulling from gaping holes" against Indigenous views about the earth as the sacred giver of all life,' it is not surprising that Armstrong's poem depicts 'the Europeans, in their non-spiritual search for dominating the people and the land, [as having desecrated] the earth in a "savage" way' (2005, 87). Certainly, the final verses of 'History Lesson' reiterate the perversity of colonial behaviour against 'whole [Native] civilizations,' with Armstrong depicting the settlers as poised and 'waiting to mutilate / ... ten generations at a blow' (1991, 29). But it is the juxtaposition of the poem's overtly cartoonish depictions of the polluted New World, quoted above, with the two lines that follow that turns the unsaid inside out, literally and metaphorically, and gives this poem a distinctly Canadian – or anti-Canadian – turn. The noisy smoke stacks and rainbow rivers, coupled with the farmers who sow bones rather than crops and the miners who discover buried money imprinted with the British monarch's portrait rather than the gold they are searching for, suggest that having faith in the largess of one's colonial reach can have devastating consequences for the land and those who live on it. In this case, respect for the memories of those who once toiled on the land is absent, displaced by 'the colossi' of industrialism and capitalism as epitomized in economic and political terms by the white female figurehead of the Queen (29).

Armstrong's speaker returns to the Christian basis of these colonial efforts to expose what is rotten in pre- and post-Confederation Canada (and North America more generally):

> Somewhere among the remains
> of skinless animals
> is the termination
> to a long journey
> and unholy search
> for the power
> glimpsed in a garden
> forever closed
> forever lost (1991, 29)

It is 'among' the almost extinct animal carcasses that Armstrong's speaker locates a point of closure for the settlers' 'long journey,' an end to the coveted re-entry to a garden that damned Eve – and all women – for eternity (29). This evocation of the Garden of Eden also recalls the legacy of Christopher Columbus, who strategically claimed to have discovered 'the precise location of the Terrestrial Paradise during the third voyage' in order to justify the costliness of his multiple trips in search of the Orient to the Catholic monarchs of Spain (Zamora 137). Paradoxically, Jeanne Perreault points out that in 'History Lesson,' 'the Europeans do not know what they have lost and cannot know what they ... are seeking,' namely, the memories of the Natives whose lands they covet, consciously possess, cultivate, and treasure (1999, 261). Conversely, the absence of memory 'creates brutal violations, [and] stupid destructions' of the kind exemplified by the Christian behaviour of figures like Columbus and, later, the missionaries, traders, and pioneers who settle in Canada (261).

If Rose favours the creation of counter-memories and Glancy overtly remaps the American nation, in 'History Lesson' Armstrong employs verbal ironies, puns, and darkly comic images of the colonized landscape and its occupants to document a history of European *and* Canadian loss and to hint at the power of Native women's memories, which contrast with Eve's damnation. In an interview with Kim Anderson, Armstrong describes how she often writes for multiple audiences within a single work, creating what she calls a 'double-edged' text:

> There are some Native writers who write for that [Canadian] audience. I decided in *Slash* to write from that perspective; to break down stereotypes, and make clear comments about some of the politics related to colonialism. Those comments are directed towards the Canadian audience as well as internally within my own community.
>
> But a large part of that book is written for my community. (1997, 51)

For a non-Native Canadian academic reader like myself, 'History Lesson' functions in precisely this way. While Armstrong refers here to her novel, *Slash*, writing to a dual audience is also an integral part of 'History Lesson.' Her poem exposes the fault lines of a Euro-Christian vision that remains blind to its own memories *and* provides a powerful counter-narrative to official histories of colonial settlement and the creation of the Canadian nation without providing definitive answers – in other words, reflecting the actual memories of the speaker's community. As the punning title of the poem suggests, 'History Lesson' relies on and plays with the multiple meanings of 'history' and 'lesson' to make its points – some of which may be more accessible or predominant for one group of readers like myself than another. The word 'lesson' can refer to a unit of teaching instruction in the classrooms where, historically, Native history has been unacknowledged; it also may be a punishment or source of moral education. Armstrong's poem depicts the twisted morality of the missionaries, mounted police, pioneers, and traders who believe that their paternalistic attitudes are serving a greater good, and the suppression of Native memories only heightens the damage that can be done.

The lessons of the poem remain complex and dynamic, as different discursive communities engage with what is both said and unsaid in the text on multiple levels. For me, the irony of the title emerges from my own internalized presumptions about what might constitute a traditional 'History Lesson.' The poem refuses to provide the comfort that historical distance gives to white western readers and proceeds to dismantle Eurocentric notions of chronology; the lesson is about those who have traditionally written history by turning subjects into objects of analysis and refusing to acknowledge the mess that they have made. Further, in a national context, Armstrong's narrator can be read as equating the creation of Canada to the coveted and yet impossible return to the Garden of Eden. The principles of colonization, industrialization, and capitalism under the watchful eye of the British Queen simply displace one structure of Euro-American patriarchal control with another – the Queen serves as a figurehead for God with her 'knights' controlling the Prairies (1991, 28). This creation of a male-dominated history, and specifically a national history by settlers to British North America, is revealed to be an imaginative exercise that fails to acknowledge the prior existence of Native peoples.

Insisting upon the importance of local tribal knowledges and collective memories, Armstrong is careful to limit non-Native readerly access in a poem that attends primarily to the dangers of European and Canadian amnesia through her depiction of a series of national and transnational symbols. In this way, Armstrong differs from Glancy and Rose, who are situated outside their Native communities and are searching for memories of their ancestors in an attempt to tell their individual stories and potentially connect with their tribal heritages. Armstrong wrestles with how to convey the memories of her Okanagan community, as evidenced by 'Threads of Old Memory,' in which her narrator describes her role:

> When I speak
> I attempt to bring together
> with my hands
> the gossamer thin threads of old memory
> thoughts from the underpinnings of understanding
> words steeped in age. (1991, 59)

The history that this speaker tells depends upon both the communal sharing of memories and an understanding of the past, present, and fu-

ture as an active continuum that the poetic 'I' is a part of and responsible
to, above all else:

> I speak and
> powerfully become actions
> becomes memory in someone
> I become different memories to different people
> different stories in the retelling of my place. (59)

In her essay titled 'Land Speaking,' Armstrong explains that through
her Okanagan heritage she has come to understand that words have the
power to 'shape-change the world' (1998, 183), an insight she describes
and enacts in 'Threads of Old Memory.' As an orator and writer, she
is obliged to wrestle memory 'into being through language,' whether
spoken or written (Perreault 1999, 261); to do so is a necessary and even
'sacred' task. By choosing to characterize her recovery of Okanagan
memories as 'sacred,' Armstrong can be read as fundamentally refuting
the white western presumption that Native populations needed to be
civilized and spiritually educated by those who have come to the New
World already fallen and corrupted by the 'unholy search' for 'power'
(Armstrong 1991, 28). As 'Indian Woman,' another poem from *Breath
Tracks*, suggests, Aboriginal women share a very different legacy from
the damned Eve; they are 'the keeper[s] of generations / ... [and] the
strength of nations' (1991, 106-7). Hence, Armstrong sees herself as a vehicle for the preservation of what is most sacred about her tribal culture:
the memories of her people, and especially of Okanagan women.

Juxtaposing the Sacred and the Profane

If the recovery of Indigenous memories and experiences is pivotal for
the poem by Armstrong, then Baker's decidedly irreverent treatment
of Columbus through the wily transnational and trans-Native figure of
Coyote in her 1994 *Coyote Columbus Cafe* brings the sexual and scatological dimensions of Native colonization to the fore. In a 2007 keynote address on the aesthetics of Native writing, Armstrong argues that Native
authors are especially skilled at symbolizing the 'juxtaposition between
what is sacred and what is humorous' and incorporating the profane
into their texts (2007, 26). She draws on the example of the Okanagan
jokers, clowns who attend short-house dances and who are responsible
for making 'laughter specifically *because* what is being presented is seri-

ous' (27). This ability to 'bring things that are sacred forward into the
human realm' is absolutely essential (27). As a result, Armstrong claims
to enjoy 'a world view that is unhampered by the long arm of sexual repression cast by Western notions of morality' (26). While Baker lacks the
access Armstrong possesses to her Native community and language, *Coyote Columbus Cafe* thrives on this meeting of the sacred and the profane
through the figure of a female trickster who is interested in conquests
of a different kind.

Coyote Columbus Cafe opens with two images, or what Baker specifically
describes as 'pictographs,' that establish a framework for re writing history with a profane twist by recalling the power of visual symbols (1994b,
5). The black-and-white cover of the collection, drawn by fellow poet
Cecile Brisebois Guillemot, juxtaposes a pole stuck in arid ground with
signs pointed in various directions (each of which displays one word of
the title) with a river upon which floats a turkey boat, complete with
a rendering of the flag of Genoa, Columbus's birthplace. Inspired by
the work of Ojibway conceptual artist Rebecca Belmore, the turkey ship
and the multidirectional signs graphically convey, to those 'in the know,'
that the poems inside are not sympathetic to conventional histories of
Columbus but instead play with and pun on those much circulated narratives; in addition, there is a set of animal tracks, presumably coyote,
on the cover, which go towards the pole and then pointedly head in
the opposite direction to the turkey boat, reorienting readers both geographically and ideologically by provoking them to look again. The
second full-page image appears just after the table of contents; it is a
wanted poster of 'Coyote Columbus,' a crudely drawn black-and-white
image of a coyote dressed in the customary garb of a well-to-do Medi-
terranean merchant or Renaissance nobleman with a doublet and soft
cap, brim turned up, and, in this case, with special holes to accommodate the trickster's ears. Again, Baker signals the confrontational nature
of her poetry in explicitly visual and highly ironic terms. This wanted
poster may appear to fit the conventional search for an illusive criminal,
but the evildoer in question is not Columbus himself but a tricky (and
furry) double. In Native North American cultures, Coyote, who functions as a chief mythological embodiment of the 'Trickster,' is known
for his/her creative transgressions. With enlarged genitalia, an interest
in excrement and flatulence, and a constant drive to fill primal desires,
Coyote is known for testing and even reconfiguring established moral
and social boundaries, often by looking again at the pretensions that
would otherwise be used to divide segments of the human population

according to categories such as race and nationality. And like the figure of the trickster, who is a cunning, playfully self-centred, impulsive, and shape-shifting creature, trickster discourse (a term coined by Vizenor to describe the uniquely comic spirit of many Native texts) favours multiplicity and open-endedness, and refuses completion.

In *Coyote Columbus Cafe*, Baker combines this trickster aesthetic in her collection with the literal representation of the female trickster as a figure of play – through both drawings and poetry – to exploit the possibilities of chance and reconsider the fixity of history. Hence, the search for Coyote in the guise of Columbus takes on its own series of (sexually) ironic twists in her text. For instance, the title poem of the collection is narrated by a female Coyote who frequents bars looking for her next 'cruise / & conquest' (1994b, 11).[10] In a role reversal of the traditional male explorer, she pointedly asks, 'why beat around the bush?' turning colonization into a sexual game:

> I have an attitude how to frequent
> with colonizers (dey got me surrounded)
> the right time is now
> to get discovered again
> & again very frequently
> on a repetitive basis. (12)

This Coyote, whose bosomy pencilled image appears in the bottom right-hand corner of page twelve, is no victim, with her 'Coyotisma' charisma and insistence that she is 'too damn direct / for the colonized coyote / poor oppressed critter' (12). As the title of the poem's first section suggests, 'once more it's Indian time,' but in this instance, the 'weasel [that] pops / in & out of old tunes' (11) is a 'Coyotrix' (rather than dominatrix) whose sexual skills and ability to question the world and assert her own needs counter the expectations of those around her (13). Inspired by 'the tough street women I knew as a child and ... found to be great storytellers,' Baker constructs a 'colonial frontier' in a contemporary bar setting with a female Coyote who refuses to be 'contained within the colonized images of Indigenous women' and instead uses 'the languages of social control' to her own ends and for her own pleasure (Baker and Grauer 2006, 122).

Baker further complicates the speaker's positioning by giving her an alternate voice, which appears on the right-hand side of the page in italics, creating a dialogue within the poem itself between the female

Coyote's inner thoughts and feelings and the voices and conversations she imagines taking place between herself and various men, or even in Christopher Columbus's own mind:

> it could happen in a Woody Allen movie
> Columbus gives a squirmy spiel

> > *I don't know anybody on this*
> > *boat. Strong chance we won't*
> > *make it to land.*
> > *The map I made shows the Indies*
> > *beyond the curve in the earth.*
> > *Most of the crew are already*
> > *around the bend.*

> Columbus did lack
> > cultural awareness
> > equity
> > affirmative action
> > political correctness

3. Discovery is a hard act to follow

> Colon would get comforted
> by a kindly Native who'd say

> > *Don't feel bad bro.*
> > *You're lost like the rest of us.*

> if Columbus was looking for turkey
> he came to the right place.
> he'd get the deserved treatment
> join our healing process

> > *Do you feel like a wounded*
> > *buffalo raging within?*

> mine's ready & raring to stampede
> right over a cliff. (1994b, 13–14)

The irreverence of Baker's speakers, complete with scatological references to Columbus as Colon and stereotypical images of Native people as wounded buffalo ready to stampede off a cliff, is juxtaposed with a piercing critique of the process and motivation for discovering the New World, as well as its legacy, which has necessitated the creation of public and private sector policies regarding 'equity / affirmative action' and even inspired 'political correctness' (14). Baker's poem depicts Columbus as little more than a salesman whose 'squirmy spiel,' his glib talk, reveals the ridiculousness of his goal to reach India, and the price he has paid for doing so (13). Once on land, in this version of events, the great explorer looks for a community to belong to, finding comfort in the presence of Native people who, because of Columbus, are *lost like the rest of us*' (14). The poet's use of conditional tenses and the subtitle that introduces this speculative vision – 'Discovery is a hard act to follow' – foregrounds the performative dimensions of conquest and its continued impact; Columbus/Colon's search for wealth, despite finding only 'turkey,' continues with what the speaker describes as the non-Native stalking of 'our organizations / get on the board of directors / become an Indian expert and / discover more Indians' (14). In this, Baker's poem stresses that the history of colonization has been appropriated in ways that service the dominant culture's need to feel less guilt about its long-standing oppression of Native peoples, particularly by learning how to be 'Indian,' at the expense of those Native populations who are themselves struggling to learn about their tribal traditions:

> if the class is full
> because too many Indians
> are just learning about
> their culture & identity
> then simply pick a popular
> bestseller HOW TO OUTINDIAN ANYONE. (15)

As Baker explains, 'our memories are getting bleached out by the implanting of colonized images of ourselves. We are now taught Native Studies which has been developed by white experts,' using Natives as informants rather than primary architects of the field (Baker and Grauer 2006, 123). Thus, the predatory stalking that Baker's sexy Coyote speaker undertakes at the beginning of the poem becomes payback for Columbus's journey, an ironic reversal of a screwing of the land and its people

– particularly Native women – that began over five hundred years ago when European explorers first arrived in the New World.

The concluding segment of 'Coyote Columbus Cafe' brings the past into the present through skilful wordplay and the voice of 'coyote girl,' who is not a flawless 'cover girl' but a welfare recipient who practises her tough stance in a mirror, covering up her 'big zit ... with a bandaid' before heading to pick up her cheque (1994b, 17). This contemporary speaker slyly laments her community's fate: 'I always forget to mention / we were too good way back when / to be real people before discovery' (17). Though she may not have mentioned it in the past, coyote girl speaks bluntly here, beginning with the section title, '4. culture vulture voyeur trips' (17). The title specifically exposes the voyeuristic attitudes of non-Natives who become 'culture vultures' when learning about Native tribes, and also recalls the external economic exploitation of natural resources that began with the voyageurs' selling of fur pelts hunted for by Native peoples (17). The result, as the italicized voice on the right-hand side of the page soon reminds us, is a Native economy of dependence under the Canadian government that necessitates the Native performance of stereotypical roles:

> *just thought I'd*
> *check out my cheque what happened to*
> *my cheque do you have my cheque*
> *just came to pick up my cheque I*
> *hope nobody cashed my cheque check ... give me my cheque* (17).

Money and monitoring become intertwined in a fast-paced language game that ends with a single blunt demand for payback. The punning on check/cheque extends to the final lines of the poem, where the speaker contemplates her position as someone who wants 'to educate the oppressor,' though she knows 'it's just about too late' and then asks, 'how does a coyote girl get / a tale out of her mouth?' (17). While potentially evoking both the vision of a tail that the coyote may chew on and the act of oral sex, which is in keeping with Christopher Columbus's masculinized conquest of the New World and his 'laying' of the land, the word 'tale' itself returns the poem to the questions of history and memory; whose narrative is being told, and is it merely a ruse or something more? Can this coyote be trusted, or is the point not that there is no one definitive tale/tail but rather multiple accounts of Native experiences of Columbus and his aftermath? Most striking is the speaker's choice of phrasing in posing this last question. Can a female trickster tell her story in a way that conveys the actuality of her gendered experience without discussing the sexual dimensions of this literal and figurative penetration of the land and its occupants, or is it, as the poem suggests, integral to the dynamics of colonization and thus an inevitable part of Columbus's bequest? The paradox of the poem is that the tale/tail does get recorded, moving from the mouth to the page in a manner that both mimics the conventional western valuation of the written over the oral and defies it by virtue of the poem's own dynamic sense of play.

Baker is acutely aware of the power of national memory and the need to marginalize or suppress those memories that counter the continuation of a culturally cohesive and dominant national identity. Not surprisingly, then, in section three of the poem titled 'Coyote Columbus Cafe,' Baker's speaker also pointedly comments on both the Indian Act and Columbus's legacy of fetishizing Native peoples as objects. But the speaker's frustration with this form of continued colonization is subverted by the multiple jokes made by her alternate voice:

> lo, the po'Indian

> Indian Act

> Tell Old Indian Joke
> like Indian Affairs

> Act Indian
> had an Indian affair lately? (1994b, 15)

Here, Baker's speaker puns on the word 'affair,' which can refer both to an illicit sexual relationship between two people for a limited period of time, and, more nebulously, to a 'matter' or 'concern.' Given that the federal government in Canada has a Department of Indian and Northern Affairs, founded in 1966 and designed to manage the country's recognized Native populations (meaning status Indians), Baker's choice of the word 'affair' enables her speaker to mock both the vagueness and bureaucracy of the nation-state, and the ways in which some non-Natives carry on a colonizing love affair with all things Native in order to legitimize their occupation of Native lands and the legislation of Native peoples' rights. At the end of the section, the speaker calls on the 'former Columbus clones,' while they 'still got a chance,' to 'discover a first

/ nation friend lover first nation first / for keeps person' (16), a tongue-twisting recipe for action that acknowledges the white western inherited tendency towards domination and reworks the task of claiming the nation for themselves by changing their notions of 'first.' In other words, rather than making the discovery of nation a first, perhaps the Columbus clones could instead alter their goals by putting the 'first nation[s] first' for a change. Thus, without being overly idealistic, Baker does offer a vision for change by drawing readers into her poems and demanding that they wrestle with both the said and unsaid meanings of her texts.

In speaking about her experiences as a mixed-blood female poet writing in English, Baker emphasizes the need to subvert the discourse of dominance, which is designed to give the subject primary importance and distance 'him or her from the humble listener' (1993, 59). However, in Baker's poems – like the other poets examined here – the undermining of such hierarchies through the manipulation of language is integral to the work. As she explains, 'I use the coyotrix persona (image) as a transformer of our internalized colonized mentality. The inner coyotrix "teases" or tweaks meaning out of the verbiage that surrounds us ... making it strange again' (Baker and Grauer 2006, 124). Not surprisingly, Baker has said: 'I "massacre" English when I write' (1993, 60). By wringing 'multiple meanings' out of words and employing 'wit' in her 'arsenal of word weapons,' Baker rejects the confines of what she calls 'the deadness of scholarly language,' turning instead to the vitality of 'the underclass English vocabulary' for inspiration in a relationship of linguistic reciprocity, which supports the continued existence of Native languages and refuses to let the necessity of writing in English undermine her efforts to convey the complexities of her own position (60). As Lally Grauer points out in her co-authored article with Baker, 'one of the ways Annharte sneaks up on the reader is by recontextualizing the languages of social control – of government, social work, therapy, self-help' – to reveal how perceptions and memories can be easily manipulated (2006, 122). And by provoking Native and non-Native readers to engage with the poetry and undertake a process of 're-discovery' through language play, Baker is able to both critique dominant colonial perceptions and encourage the reclamation of Indigenous humour and the cultivation of irony in the service of differently remembering individual and communal experiences, particularly those of women.

Writing Ledders to the Poop

In *Coyote Columbus Cafe*, Marie Annharte Baker uses an Aboriginal female trickster, with her linguistic irreverence and sexual prowess, to critique Columbus's colonial legacy. Like Baker, Louise Halfe also explores the gender politics of colonization through the juxtaposition of the sacred and the profane, but her focus is slightly different. In *Bear Bones & Feathers*, Halfe examines the historical impact of the Catholic Church on the memories of Native women who lived through the residential school era but now possess an (often painfully) ironic distance from the immediacy of that past. Rather than overtly referencing Columbus as Baker does, Halfe employs metonymy in a poem titled 'Ships on the Reserve' to connect this European explorer's voyages to the economic and spiritual colonization of Native peoples. 'Ships on the Reserve' examines how nation-building and the 'civilizing' effects of religion historically have gone hand in hand. The first-person female speaker explores the memories which have been buried in the reserve lands on which she lives. Although Halfe's speaker never mentions Columbus directly, the arrival of his ships in the New World alters the physical landscape permanently. She may not have seen 'a TV / never heard of ships / yet / ships were in the bowels of the earth' (1994, 70). 'Ships' thus becomes a chronicle of Columbus's legacy in the land-locked Prairies and the particular effects it had on the female narrator who realizes that her childhood innocence was itself contaminated by First Contact. The title of the poem itself also connects Columbus's voyages with the creation of reserve lands. Columbus's arrival marks the beginning of efforts to physically confine Indigenous peoples and create a clear slate for a new version of history based (at least implicitly) on national memories.

The most overt and destructive legacy of Columbus's voyage to the New World as depicted in Halfe's *Bear Bones & Feathers* is the importation of Catholicism, instituted primarily through missionary work and residential schooling. In *Bear Bones*, Halfe includes a series of six 'ledders,' correspondence between the head of the Roman Catholic Church – reduced to human waste as the 'poop' – and Aboriginal women in the section that follows 'Ships on the Reserve,' giving females from across the generations an opportunity to voice their anger at the Pope's belated regret for the Church's role in the lengthy history of forcibly converting Natives throughout North America (1994, 100). In contrast with 'Ships on the Reserve,' which relies primarily on ironic allusions to a traumatic past, the speakers in these poems explicitly critique the effects of colonization in material and spiritual terms, while exploring the challenges and insecurities these women experience as a result of being Native and female in a nation where they are second-class citizens. Like Baker's *Coyote Columbus*

Cafe, in these poems Halfe combines the sacred with the profane through 'metaphoric imagery' to evoke laughter (Armstrong 2007, 26). Halfe's 'ledders' underscore the inadequacy of the Church's long overdue apology to Native peoples through a series of graphic and playful puns. For example, the group of letters begins with a historical indictment of the Pope and his Indian agents and missionaries, whose material provisions – such as whisky, blankets, crucifixes, and 'a useless sack of scalped potatoes' – led to numerous deaths within the speaker's family (1994, 97). The speaker's vernacular voice hints at slippage between possible sounds and meanings when the word 'scalped' is used to describe a sack of potatoes sent by the Pope. This juxtaposition invokes the historical legacy of scalping, which has often been attributed only to Aboriginals when, in fact, Euro-Americans also collected and were rewarded for Native scalps as war bounty; it also has culinary resonances. Scalloped potatoes are a favoured dish at Thanksgiving, a holiday that began as a celebration of the Puritans' desire to gain religious freedom by coming to the New World, which is an event that, of course, discounts the prior presence of Native populations with their own religious practices.

Halfe depicts the 'poop''s hollow apologies for the suffering he has inflicted by proxy, outlining the rather ludicrous assumptions that justified colonization and genocide. The colonizers were dismissive of Native spiritual practices – 'the rock and twig / you smoked. / Blueberries, and sweetgrass / were your offerings' – and presumed that they 'could borrow land for a little / to plant our seeds, / raise sheep and build churches, schools,' without examining the impact of this on Aboriginal ways of life (1994, 98). The arrogance of such beliefs is compounded by the constant repetition of the phrase 'i'm sorry' from the 'poop' for everything from Columbus's arrival – 'too bad that man of sea, kelp, rancid pig / and starving teeth / came on your land' (99) – to the abuse of Aboriginal children at residential schools. To counter the Pope's voice, Halfe gives equal time to the frustrations of the female letter-writers themselves. In all six poems, Halfe, like Diane Glancy, employs highly colloquial dialect; in doing so, she actively undermines the presumption 'that letters to the authority of the Pope are written in formal English' (Eigenbrod 2005, 114). Halfe sets one poem, 'Der Poop,' in an outhouse, complete with newspaper for toilet paper, and proceeds to allow her female narrator to explore her unwillingness to abandon her traditional tribal practices and beliefs for Catholicism. Generally, scatological humour is intended to ridicule those codes of conduct that repress the free expression of bodily desires, and revels in the baseness of all human beings. For Halfe, the outhouse subverts established racial, class, and gender hierarchies and, in turn, may encourage the questioning of power relations by readers of her text. Although the use of outhouses can reflect class and/or geographical differences, her focus on a universal bodily function creates a framework that is both inclusive and highly irreverent:[11]

> der poop
> forgive me for writing on dis newspaper
> i found it in da outhouse, saw lines
> dat say you is sorry
> some of my indian friends say is good but
> some of dem say you sorry don't walk
> so i was sitting here dinking dat we
> maybe talk
> say, i always want to dell you stay
> out of my pissness (1994, 102)

The humour of the poem emerges from the structural juxtaposition of the speaker's legitimate concerns with forced religious colonization and the fact that she first reads about and responds to the Pope's apology for the abuse of Aboriginals in an outhouse, where the story has been relegated to a product of waste disposal, making clear the seriousness with which this gesture has been taken by the local community. Halfe's use of a vernacular English, with letter substitution and extensive sound play – coupled with the integration of several Cree terms including the words for Creator or God (*Manitou*) and the People (*Iyiniwak*) – forces non-Native readers to engage with the text aurally, to listen carefully for the double entendres that are invoked through this complex alteration of English that reflect on the vitality of a spoken dialect, without having 'insider' access to the poem in its entirety. The speaker's call for the 'poop,' himself rendered as excrement, to stay out of 'my pissness,' becomes layered with scatological implications: not only is the Pope charged with leaving her alone but he is, like Columbus, treated as a form of pollution, a cross-contamination in the outhouse, who has snuck in uninvited, much like the imposition of the English language on Native peoples by the church (102). Here, the sacred becomes the profane. Halfe's poetic 'I' thus seizes this moment of privacy in the privy itself, not to offer a confession, but to insist upon her rights as a Native person within Canada who is free to do as she wishes, with or without the Pope's apology.

Moreover, as Susan Gingell notes, in these poems Halfe employs 'code-switching,' which allows her to employ the Cree lexicon to depict specific aspects of Cree life in a manner that not only shelters the community from further access and exploitation but privileges those who are 'in the know' – namely, those who are familiar with both English and Cree (1998, 453). In *Portraits of 'The Whiteman': Linguistic Play and Cultural Symbols among the Western Apache*, Basso explains that the movement between and among languages in multilingual speech communities – where people are equally competent in both languages – is not random but rather used 'as an instrument of metacommunication' or 'an indirect form of social commentary' (1979, 8, 9). Basso focuses on the Western Apache's strategic deployment of English to imitate Anglo-Americans and to register, for those familiar with the significance of this shift, that 'a particular form of joking has begun' (9). Halfe also uses language as social commentary, but for different ends. In this instance, Gingell argues that Halfe likely draws on the Cree lexicon to refer to 'kinship or spiritual matters' because 'the most intimate and sacred aspects of that life cannot be adequately represented in a medium [English] in which that life has been so often perjorated and profaned' (1998, 453); joking thus takes place in English, or through the deformation of English, a deliberate revisioning of this oppressive language that ensures both an irreverent depiction of English as a source of authority and the securing of the sacredness of Cree life and practices from further degradation. As Gingell elaborates, the scatological images and references created by Halfe's persona who is writing to the 'Poop' on outhouse newsprint creates an 'orthography that represents the phonological differences of many Cree speakers of English from Euro-Canadians' pronunciation' (453). By reflecting the phonological and idiomatic aspects of Cree people who speak English, and giving the Cree language prominence, Halfe takes the incongruity of humour and irony even further. The joke is on those who are unable to hear and listen to those strategies of differentiation and individuation used by Halfe's narrator, who has mastered the two languages and shapes her use of both to suit her needs.

Halfe's speaker's rejection of Christian and specifically Catholic rituals that are not her own is given a final ironic twist in the last of the six poems, 'My Ledders,' which takes the Pope's influence on federal and provincial governments to task: 'well you must had some kind of bower / cuz da govment sure listen' (1994, 103). Here, the 'poop' is displaced by the 'pope,' and the scatology of the outhouse setting is replaced with a final poignantly angry plea from the narrator to end the exploitation of Cree culture. She juxtaposes the Pope's ban on 'da sweatlodge and sundance, drummin, singin and dancing,' which dates back to her grandparents' generation, with her recent encounter on the 'DV' with some 'whitemen / [who] sweat in da lodge' and mocks the absurdity of hearing a man 'on da radio / … dell us / dat some darafist was having a retreat / and to register,' explaining 'i never hear anybody before on da radio / dell da whole world dat' (103). The speaker then calls on the Catholic leader to stop the government from allowing 'whiteman from takin our '*isistāwina* [rituals]' by reasoning that he would not

> like it
> if i dook you gold cup and wine
> pass it 'round our circles
> cuz i don't have your drainin
> from doze schools
> I haven't married you jeesuz
> and I don't kneel to him,
> cuz he ain't my god. (103)

Halfe's speaker employs strategic essentialism here both to assert 'her special … knowledge' of Cree customs, ceremonies, and language, and to criticize the colonizer's appropriation of select elements of Cree culture for profit (Eigenbrod 2005, 116). As the poetic 'I' explains, 'dey don't know what fastin' mean / dey jist dake and gobble our *mātotsān* [sweat lodge] / as if dey own it' (1994, 104). Her inclusion of a Cree glossary at the conclusion of *Bear Bones & Feathers* highlights the need to be in the 'know' in order to get the text. She provides a dictionary so that, if only belatedly, non-Cree-speaking readers can access her work. Paradoxically, however, her efforts at motivating the Pope rely on the very tools that were used to convert and assimilate Aboriginals, including the Cree living within the Canadian nation-state. While the narrator assumes that the Roman Catholic leader would not want to see the Eucharist appropriated by non-believers, it is those very Catholic rites that were used to bring the Cree into the Christian fold, whether they understood and believed them or not. The unsaid presumption is that the Church, and by implication the nation-state, can pillage as it wishes, 'playing Indian,' in the words of Philip Deloria (1998, 7), to connect to a land and community that was never theirs for the taking; this is mostly explicitly targeted at the conclusion of 'My Ledders,' when Halfe's speaker states, 'dey don't know what it means to dake / from da earth and give some-din' back / i is so dired of all dis *kimoti* [stealing] pope' (1994, 104). For the speaker, the white western population's search for a primal connection to the land they stole and a culture they tried to destroy requires an equally harsh and highly ironic response, one that resists being reduced to a singular narrative of dominance:

> deach your children.
> eat your jeezuz body.
> drink his blood.
> dell dem to go back to dere own deachings. (104)

If, as Gerald Vizenor asserts, 'discoveries and dominance are silence' and 'tribal imagination, experience and remembrance' are the foundations of the literature of Native nations (1994, 10), then Halfe's metonymical rendering of Columbus in 'Ships on the Reserve' and her 'ledders' to the Pope become crucial alternative depictions of national memory and identity that use the juxtaposition of the sacred and the profane to insist upon the inclusion of Cree, and especially Cree women's, voices.

'We're Still Here and Metis': Re-membering Macdonald

In her 1996 collection, *A Really Good Brown Girl*, Marilyn Dumont further complicates what I have described as the border-crossing uses of irony and humour by these Native female poets. Rather than focusing on the transnational figure of Columbus, she explicitly writes back to a Canadian national history in 'Letter to Sir John A. Macdonald' as someone who is doubly excluded from visibility by virtue of her Métis heritage. Of course, defining the term 'Métis' is itself difficult, because it has been used to describe two different groups of people. It refers to a distinctive ethnic group that first emerged in the 1860s consisting of the French- and Cree-speaking descendants of the Red River Métis in Western Canada, which began with the relationships between French-Canadian fur traders and Indigenous women. However, since the 1970s, Metis (without the accent) also has been employed to describe a much broader segment of the population, namely, 'any person of mixed Indian-white ancestry who identified him- or herself and was identified by others as neither Indian nor white, even though he or she might have no provable link to the historic Red River métis' (Peterson and Brown 1984, 5). And the capitalization of the word 'Métis' also is politically charged. In a statement to the United Nations Working Group in Indigenous Populations, the Métis National Council (of Canada) explains that 'written with a small "m," metis is a racial term for anyone of mixed Indian and European ancestry. Written with a capital "M," Métis is a socio-cultural or political term for those originally of mixed ancestry who evolved into a distinct indigenous people during a certain historical period in a certain region of Canada' (1984, 6). Dumont, a descendant of Gabriel Dumont, Louis Riel's military commander during the North West Rebellion of 1885, identifies herself as part of the latter group. Until the Canadian Constitution Act of 1982, the Métis were not acknowledged as Aboriginal peoples, and it is only very recently that the Canadian government has formally recognized the Métis Nation as a distinct entity; the signing of the Métis Nation Framework Agreement in 2005 marks a first step towards federal government-to-government negotiations. Dumont's collection predates this Framework Agreement by nearly a decade, presenting a version of her – and her peoples' – history that is fundamentally resistant to the erasure of 'other' populations and insistent upon the specificity of her own heritage. 'Letter to Sir John A. Macdonald' appears in a section titled 'White Noise,' which provocatively puns on the concept of 'whiteness' as a pervasive colour: white noise is primarily known for its ability to conceal or cover up. Here, however, Dumont subverts white dominance and calls on readers to hear what has remained unheard and unacknowledged by deliberately foregrounding her 'invisibility' as a contemporary and historical subject.

It is this sense of 'otherness' even within tribal nations that shapes Dumont's poem to Macdonald, who served in a number of high-ranking federal government positions between 1867 and 1891, including superintendent of Indian affairs, minister of railways and canals, and prime minister. Responsible for the creation of the RCMP, the federal treatment of Louis Riel that eventually led to his execution, and the building of a transnational railroad that involved extensive land reclamation and led to mass dispossession among the Métis, Macdonald is a national political figure whose actions fundamentally altered the history of Dumont's forebears and had a dramatic effect on subsequent generations. In her poem, written in the form of a generic advice letter much like Halfe's 'Ledders' (though, as Susan Gingell argues, without the use of phonology to convey the particular pronunciation of Cree speakers of English), Dumont's speaker openly targets Macdonald and criticizes his self-righteous stance, identifying him as someone who had no hesitation in predicting the destiny of a group of people whom he did not know or understand. Further ironies emerge through the speaker's specific commentary on the fate of the Canadian railroad:

> Dear John: I'm still here and halfbreed,
> after all these years
> you're dead, funny thing,
> that railway you wanted so badly,
> there was talk a year ago
> of shutting it down,
> and part of it was shut down,
> the dayliner at least,
> 'from sea to shining sea,'
> and you know, John,
> after all that shuffling around to suit the settlers,
> we're still here and Metis. (1996, 52)

By rhyming the words 'sea' and 'Metis,' Dumont undercuts the rhetoric of Canadian intervention and reminds readers that the desire to join the two coasts of the country came at a heavy price. The Métis, in particular, were removed from their land to create a new nation that was not of their own making. In the poem, Dumont's speaker includes one of the prime minister's clichéd phrases, designed to sell the westward expansion of the railway ('from sea to shining sea'), places it in quotations, and dismantles its persuasiveness. She juxtaposes Macdonald's late-nineteenth-century rhetoric with her description of the contemporary situation: the closure of the railway and the continued existence of the Métis. The speaker's voice unmasks Macdonald's position, exposing the absurdity – in hindsight – of his presumption that the Métis would disappear.

In the second stanza of 'Letter,' Dumont's narrator brings together the said and the unsaid (which is now being spoken), creating an overtly incongruous relationship between official accounts of Canadian history and the speaker's counter-memories. In particular, the poetic 'I' quotes several lines from Canadian poet F.R. Scott's 'Laurentian Shield' (1954), which contemplates the impact of human beings on the national landscape. Scott, son of the Confederation poet Frederick George Scott, was known for his socialist politics, his work on constitutional law, and his commitment to civil liberty. In 'Laurentian Shield,' Scott examines the relationship between the land and those who visit or live on it, seeing it shaped primarily by 'exploitation' as people come to hunt, search for gold, create towns and cities, and eventually abandon it (1981, 58). The speaker of Scott's text also acknowledges the existence of racial and ethnic minority populations as part of this scene, living in 'the mines, / The scattered camps and mills, a language of life,' but does little to examine them (58). Here Scott is also, at least tangentially, responding to E.J. Pratt's nationalist epic, 'Towards the Last Spike,' which portrays the building of the Canadian Pacific Railway between 1870 and 1885, but leaves out any major reference to the thousands of Chinese immigrants who actually finished constructing the railroad, living in appalling conditions and continually threatened with the possibility of death due to malnutrition, disease, racial violence, exposure to the cold, or accidental explosion (as a result of the blasting done to clear surfaces for the tracks). Scott, of course, addresses Pratt's silence about the Chinese-Canadian and Chinese-American labourers more directly in his ironically titled poem 'All Spikes but the Last.'

In her poem, Dumont re-writes and re-rights Scott's and, by implication, Pratt's, white-authored version of the Canadian landscape and its nascent history as a nation-state by including the untold stories of the relocated Métis. The speaker's blunt language powerfully contrasts the rhetoric of railway expansion, Scott's eloquent depiction of the land that longs to speak, and the brash reality of Métis survival:

> We're still here ...
> One good for nothing Indian
> Holdin-up-the-train
> stalling the 'Cabin syllables / Nouns of settlement,
> /... steel syntax [and] / The long sentence of its exploitation'
> and John, that goddamned railway never made this a great nation,
> cause the railway shut down
> and this country is still quarreling over unity,
> and Riel is dead
> but he just keeps coming back. (1996, 52)

In this case, Dumont invokes the legacy of Macdonald and Scott, whose language either buries or aestheticizes the existence of the Métis, and acknowledges the ghost of Louis Riel as (an)Other important historical precursor whose desire to create a distinct Métis nation offers an altern(arr)ative to that of a unified Canada. Through the layering of this voice, Dumont urges readers to reflect on the exercise of nation-building and ironically inserts her own vision of the railway's impact on the Métis people, in the past, present, and future.

In the concluding lines of 'Letter,' Dumont's speaker provides a pun-filled reading of the railroad and its legacy: 'we were railroaded / by some steel tracks that didn't last / and some settlers who wouldn't set-tle' (1996, 52). The doubled meanings of 'railroad/ed' and 'settlers/settle,' when paired with the image of steel tracks that have failed the test of time, deflate the glory of Canadian nation-building. Such verbal play reflects the need to end a long legacy of linguistic double-talk that has been used to silence the Métis. Instead, Dumont employs her own discursive strategies to ensure that the irony and humour of the Métis population – 'it's funny we're still here' – and their survival despite all odds *are* communicated (52).

Dumont's efforts to interrogate the positioning of Métis people, par-ticularly Métis women, in the contemporary context of nation becomes even more overt in 'It Crosses My Mind,' a poem that comes shortly af-ter 'Letter to Sir John A. Macdonald.' In 'It Crosses My Mind,' Dumont presents a stream-of-consciousness first-person narrative about the iden-tity of Métis women in Canada that focuses on their access to and claim-ing of citizenship, a step that is paradoxically liberating and alienating: 'the job application asks if I am a Canadian citizen and am I expected to mindlessly check "yes," indifferent to skin colour and the deaths of 1885, or am I actually free to check "no," like *the true north strong and free*' (1996, 59). The speaker fears that by embracing Canadian multiculturalism in its legislated forms, she will lose touch with her 'own kin':

> … will they still welcome me, share their stew and tea, pass me the bannock
> like it's mine, will they continue to greet me in the old way, hand me their
> babies as my own and send me away with gifts when I leave and what name
> will I know them by in these multicultural intentions, how will I know other
> than by shape of nose and cheekbone, colour of eyes and hair, and will it
> matter that we call ourselves Metis, Metisse, Mixed blood or aboriginal, will
> sovereignty matter … (59)

As Dumont has explored elsewhere (particularly in her essay 'Popular Images of Nativeness'), the reality is that more and more Native people live in urban centres at a distance from their tribal community and the subsistence economy which once allowed tribal populations to support themselves. In her work, Dumont sees it as her responsibility to write 'out of my own urban experience' and examine ideas of Nativeness that counter the monolithic singularity of the image of the vanishing rural Indian, which continues to pervade not only white western culture but Native cultures as well (1993, 49). Part of that challenge involves figuring out ways to cultivate forms of self-definition that reflect contemporary life for people like Dumont without merely presuming that they are or want to be fully assimilated politically. In a special effort to rewrite history for future generations of Métis women, Dumont's speaker reflects on the difficulty of answering yes or no to the question 'Are you a Canadian citizen?' and the perils of having to do so without the chance to explain what it means for her:

> ... *yes but no*, really only means *yes* because there are no lines for the stories between *yes and no* and what of the future of my eight year old niece, whose mother is Metis but only half as Metis as her grandmother, what will she name herself ... (1996, 59)

According to this poetic voice, her eight-year-old niece needs to stop engaging in the process of labelling that has been imposed upon her by the nation-state and absorbed by Natives themselves. Dumont's punning title, 'It Crosses My Mind,' becomes resonant with contradictions and unsaid meanings when juxtaposed with the poem's final thoughts on her niece's fate: 'when will she stop naming herself and crossing her own mind?' (59).

Creating Alterna(rra)tives: Refashioning Nation

In *Red on Red: Native American Literary Separatism*, Craig Womack devotes considerable space to Joy Harjo as a poet, whose attentiveness to memory and history in both the context of her Creek roots and pan-tribal identity as an urban-born and -raised Indigenous woman demonstrates 'a belief that the Americas will once again return to some form of indigenous consciousness' (1999, 230). Womack explains that the movement of Native populations to urban locations led to the emergence of a 'new history ... that involved an indigenous awareness ... [across] tribal lines,' encouraging imaginative renderings of altern(arr)atives through prose and poetry that acknowledged the significance of those memories that have been suppressed under colonialism (230). Likewise Tuhiwai Smith suggests that part of the process of decolonization involves 'recovering our stories of the past ... It is also about reconciling and reprioritizing what is really important about the past with what is really important about the present' (1999, 39). She explicitly notes that decolonization is not 'a total rejection of all the theory or research or Western knowledge,' but that rather it is about centring Indigenous concerns and world views to avoid objectification (39). In this respect, the way in which the women poets examined here refashion history and, in particular, claims to historical knowledge, through their re-examinations of Columbus and Macdonald from Native perspectives, is pivotal to the effort of decolonization. These poets also construct their own – often humorous and ironically charged – narratives about history and memory which not only put nation into question, but also formulate new visions of what such communities might look like, even for those women who are estranged from their tribal roots.

Wendy Rose has written several volumes of poetry (such as *Long Division: A Tribal History*) that depict the challenges of trying to connect to tribal histories that are relatively inaccessible to her. *The Halfbreed Chronicles and Other Poems*, for example, consists of four sections, each of which explores a different aspect of her identity, moving over the course of the collection from her paternal links to the Hopi and Native peoples generally in works like 'Wounded Knee: 1890-1973' – in which she angrily reflects on the repetition of that massacre with the lines 'they shoot / at me / at all / my relations' (1985, 31) – to the specifics of being neither fully 'brown' nor 'white' in Part Three, ironically titled 'If I Am Too Brown or Too White for You.' Rose devotes Part Four of the collection to 'The Halfbreed Chronicles,' a series of poems in which she creates her own global web of relations, a procreative history for herself as someone who has had little chance to forge familial ties due to Hopi traditions and white racism. As she explains in her interview with Joseph Bruchac, 'I was in that situation where the white part of my [mother's] family had absolutely no use for any other races that came into the family' (Bruchac 1987, 255).

This section in Rose's text begins with two pencil sketches on the introductory page: one of a gorilla-human in profile, head in hands, and one of a forward-facing gorilla dressed as royalty. It is Rose's careful hand that conveys the contradictions of the faces she depicts. The profile sketch on the left conveys the pain and despair of an individual, its head supported by human hands in a gesture of defeat; the image on the right is of a gorilla wearing a crown and holding onto the corner of a veil that strategically conceals a presumably disfigured body, the hairy face looking out at the viewer. These visuals foreground the ironic dimensions of the poems to come, calling on readers to do a 'double take' as they try to make sense of the two images and their relationship to each other. As someone who is struggling to locate herself, Rose uses this set of images and the poems that follow to create her own extended family of 'half-breeds,' a term that she explains 'is a condition of history, a result of experience, of dislocation and reunions, and of choices made for better or worse' (1994b, xvi). Rose explains in the introduction to *Bone Dance: New and Selected Poems, 1965-1993*, 'I began to study the lives of individuals who, for reasons I didn't know, profoundly affected me. All were victims of their place in history in some way. All were colonized souls ... *The Halfbreed Chronicles* emerged from listening to those voices' (xvi). If Kimberly Blaeser favours Gunn Allen's concept of re-membering, 'the idea of putting something back together' (Andrews 2007b, 13), then Rose can be read as refashioning that notion by pulling together a set of ancestors, an intergenerational web of connections, that also encircle the globe. 'The Halfbreed Chronicles' enables Rose to listen to and look again at figures who have been marginalized, maligned, and even physically butchered because they challenged normative paradigms.

'The Halfbreed Chronicles' includes poems about several different individuals from around the world, among them Truganinny, the last member of the Tasmanian tribe in Australia, who was stuffed and displayed, contrary to her wishes, when she died, and Julia Pastrana, a Native woman from Mexico born with 'facial deformities and with long hair growing from all over her body, including her face,' who also underwent taxidermy after her death and was displayed along with her infant son by her husband/manager for profit (1985, 69). Rose's collective cataloguing of their stories weaves together a series of shared histories that not only reflect Rose's own experiences of being ostracized but explore how Indigenous women globally have been objectified, domesticated, and exploited for the sake of national harmony. For example, in 'Truganinny,' Rose explores the ramifications of this woman's commodification as an object of a presumably extinct tribe; by giving her a voice, Rose's poem refuses to accept that Truganinny can or should be silenced by her death and the absence of direct ancestors to carry on her tribe's history. Instead, the text offers up her imagined counter-memories and critiques the indignity of her treatment in the name of 'science,' which Rose, as a trained anthropologist, has repeatedly questioned.

Discovered by the Dutch in 1642, Tasmania was first settled by the English in 1803 and used primarily as a penal colony until 1877; as part of the process of colonization, the Native populations were the focus of a sustained genocide which eventually led to their removal from the mainland to Flinders Island, in an effort to keep the population from procreating with British settlers. Truganinny, who herself was part of the group sent to Flinders Island and eventually relocated to Oyster Cove, was dug up by the British-inspired Royal Society of Tasmania after she was interred in May of 1876. She was subsequently stuffed, and then put on display in the Tasmanian Museum, a national history and art museum, as an example of the now-extinct Native inhabitants of this British-controlled colony. She was taken off display in 1947, and finally in 1976, a century after her death, she was cremated in spite of the museum's objections, and in keeping with her wishes, her ashes were thrown into the ocean. Not surprisingly, then, the possession and stuffing of her body can be read as a powerful symbol of colonial dominance and the success of British efforts to ensure the genetic purity of those residing in all parts of the Empire, despite the fact that Tasmania was treated as a dumping ground for criminals. By displaying her in the National History Museum for residents and visitors to see and learn from, the Royal Society presumed they could use her in the service of a colonial and national agenda. As Jessica Evans notes, public museums were created in the mid-to-late nineteenth century to 'educate the national citizenry' by presenting a story of human progress in which principles of classification emphasized the hierarchical relationship between racial categories and favoured an evolutionary vision, whereby those who were 'other' had inevitably died off (1999, 238). Tony Bennett extends this line of argument, contending that, 'denied any history of their own, it was the fate of "primitive peoples" to be dropped out of the bottom of human history in order that they might serve, representationally, as its support ... [by] representing the point at which human history emerges from nature but has not yet properly begun its course' (1999, 351). In acknowledging Truganinny's importance as an object of scientific study and simultaneously showcasing her vulnerability as the last body of a population that was not meant to survive or be heard, the Royal Society appeared to have successfully silenced her. Paradoxically, the belief that she was indeed the last Tasmanian Aborigine has been exposed as false, with increasing numbers of Tasmanians today claiming Native status through their female ancestors, who often partnered with emigrant male colonizers.

The poem begins with the stuffed Native woman urging those who stand in front of her 'to come closer / for little is left of this tongue / and what I am saying / is important' (1985, 56); ironically, despite the multiple ways in which her express wishes have been ignored, Rose's Truganinny insists on the value of her words. The need to listen patiently becomes fundamental; those who take the time to hear her voice will learn about themselves from her experiences, creating a dialogue that empowers both the writer and those who engage with the poem to seize the opportunity to deliver Truganinny from her exploitation, if not lit-erally, at least figuratively through an imaginative leap of faith much like the one Rose has taken to bring the Tasmanian woman back to life. Moreover, Truganinny's rendering of history is distinctly female-focused in her assessment of her community's destruction:

> I whose nipples
> wept white mist
> and saw so many
> dead daughters
> their mouths empty and round
> their breathing stopped
> their eyes gone grey. (56)

The picture created is that of maternal loss, with Truganinny's nipples – the traditional source of milk-giving life – unable to save the women around her. After the 1833 resettlement of the Tasmanian Aboriginals to Flinders Island, the population of two hundred was decimated due to pneumonia, influenza, and starvation. Hence, even those who were typically expected to sustain the population could not do so. Midway through the poem, Truganinny – as rendered by Rose – further compli-cates this journey into historical memory by instructing the audience, 'Do not leave / for I would speak, / I would sing / another song. / Your song' (57). By making her narrative inclusive in its cutting across time and space, Rose highlights the fact that Truganinny's struggle, her silenc-ing and exploitation, are part of a larger pattern of repetition that rele-gates women of all kinds to positions of marginality within the nation. Yet the promise of a shared alterna(rra)tive and the faith that Truganinny shows towards readers, asking them to recover her body and take it to a sacred resting place, 'where / they will not / find me' (57), also suggests the possibility of hope that emerges from her words. By juxtaposing the epigraph from Coe, which details Truganinny's fate as a museum ex-hibit, with her first-person voice, Rose emphasizes the ironic dimensions of her life in death – even if Truganinny appears to have been 'found' as stuffed evidence of British colonial progress, what becomes clear from the poem is that such a possession is incomplete by virtue of her presence in this volume of poetry. Rose, at least, has indeed 'put her [some] where / they will not / find me' (57), in a context that interpellates the concept of the imperial nation and the place of Native women in the creation of colonies.

While it might be tempting to see Rose's project, at least from the perspective of a white female academic such as myself, as a version of 'global feminism,' the transnational dimensions of 'The Halfbreed Chronicles' not only pointedly deconstruct the fixity of nations and the centrality of a white western centre, but also bring together 'imagined communities of women' with their 'divergent histories and social locations, woven together by the *political* threads of opposition to forms of domination that are not only pervasive but systemic' (Mohanty 1991, 4). In their introduction to *Between Woman and Nation*, Caren Kaplan, Norma Alarcón, and Minoo Moallem note that 'the discourses of "international" or "global" feminism rely on political and economic as well as cultural concepts of discrete nations, ... always maintaining the West as the center' (1999, 12). Hence, Mohanty's call to critique the 'liberal underpinnings' of global feminism – and approach texts like Rose's differently – is a crucial step towards attending to the 'spaces between women and nation' rather than merely sustaining patriarchal and imperializing perspectives on nation (Kaplan et al. 1999, 12-13). In particular, Rose's attentiveness to the relationships between mothers and children, and the bonds they create between generations, draws attention back to those who are, despite being the producers of nation or at least national populations, the least empowered by the structures of nation.

In the last and perhaps most tragic poem of the 'Chronicles,' Rose gives voice to Julia Pastrana, whose deformed face and body are visually depicted at the beginning of the section in the 'gorilla' sketches. Having been 'stuffed, mounted and put on display' along with her deformed infant son by her greedy husband, Pastrana continued to travel the world after her death and draw crowds who wished to see the 'Lion Lady' (1985, 69), preserved and contained as a human aberration. Much like Truganinny's story, the story of Julia Pastrana is one of colonial dominance; her white manager, Theodore Lent, first took her to England in 1857 to exhibit her, claiming that she was the product of a Mexican Indian mother who cavorted with wild animals, which he used to explain Julia's dark skin colour, short stature, protruding jaw, and excessive hairiness over much of her body. Believing that he loved her, Julia married Lent in 1860 and had a child who survived less than a day. Rose's poem conveys Julia's frustration and anger at having been deceived by Lent and reduced to an object for profit:

> my eyes so dark
> you would lose yourself swimming
> man into fish
> as you mapped the pond
> you would own. (69)

Treated as little more than territory to be claimed and seeded for Lent's benefit, Pastrana becomes a portable colony whose profitability comes from her confinement to a box and her guaranteed silence:

> Oh, such a small room!
> No bigger than my elbows outstretched
> and just as tall as my head.
> A small room from which to sing
> open the doors
> with my cold, graceful mouth,
> my rigid lips, my silences
> dead as yesterday, ...
> and cold as the coins
> that glitter in your pink fist. (70)

But the humiliation of such exploitation is compounded by the knowledge that her most vulnerable dead baby, 'a tiny doll / that looked / like me' (71), is also an object of public scrutiny and profit gained by its father. Rose's Truganinny may beg to be buried in secret, away from public eyes; Pastrana, however, has no such luxury, no national or tribal affiliation to ensure her rescue. Instead, she must rely on both her maternal instinct and the ability to reconfigure herself in death, presenting a vision of herself that is not fixed in space and time nor readily framed by a box or mirror:

> I rose from my bed like a spirit
> and, not a spirit at all, floated slowly to my great glass oval
> to see myself reflected
> as the burnished bronze woman
> skin smooth and tender
> I know myself to be ...

and I was there in the mirror
and I was not. (70)

Here Julia Pastrana defies the conventional limits of self-representation without dismissing outright or ignoring the traumatic impact of her husband's manipulations. Her strategic and supernatural (re)appearance – intended, in part, to rebuild her own shattered sense of self – is coupled with the ambivalences of motherhood: 'It scares me so / to be with child' (71). On its own, this phrase can be read in multiple ways; it could refer to Pastrana's fear that she might produce a deformed child, or her struggle with the physical and emotional changes experienced during pregnancy, or even her knowledge of the infant's death, which is coupled with the reality of being exhibited beside the dead baby yet unable physically to protect it. Yet Rose ends the poem with two lines that simultaneously embrace and defy Lent's exploitation of her: 'It scares me so / to be with child, / lioness / with cub' (71). Julia Pastrana's motherly desire to embrace her son and keep him from such public humiliation is coupled with her own ambivalence about her appearance and her general fear of bringing a child into a world that exploits 'Otherness' of any kind. Rose's invocation of Pastrana as a lioness with her cub, when coupled with Theodore Lent's exploitation of his family, ironically conflates the objectification of animals and dark-skinned women. The basic units of lion society are 'prides,' groups of related females who share in the care and raising of their cubs and are viewed as prey by adult males; to ensure their protection, the lionesses work together, teaching the cubs to hunt for themselves and survive. Such a matrilineal vision of community and society counters Pastrana's admission that 'it scares me so / to be with child' by offering another perspective on her desire to protect her baby. While Lent may exploit his family, Julia suggests the need to look differently at the world and the judgments wielded against those who blur lines between animals and humans. In death, Julia embraces her monstrosity, her 'halfbreed' status, to assert her humanity (6).

    If western historiography's resistance to story-telling is a basis for Native women's adoption of story-making, then Rose's revisionist accounts of the lives of these otherwise often silenced individuals – a collection of physical or emotional 'halfbreed[s]' who challenge fundamental assumptions about national identity and allegiance, reconfigure conventional ideas about family and community, and create a global set of relations for the poet – provide a powerful model for rethinking what history is and how it has been traditionally defined (6). As Gail Valaskakis persuasively argues:

> Those ... who are excluded from or refuse to be absorbed into the cultural narratives of imagined communities – build their own [individual and] collective subjectivities and social boundaries in a politicized process that expresses not only their resistance but also their cultural continuity. (2005, 216–17)

The inherent contradiction of 'othering' the original inhabitants of Canada and the United States to build the foundations of a new nation is complicated by the fact that many 'Native North Americans [are] continually rebuild[ing] the basis of their nationhood, realigning borders in blood and culture,' and hence cutting across 'the imagined unities of the nation states' to construct their own tribal nations (218). For those who have been born and raised off-reservation and/or estranged from their tribal roots, the reclamation of such a nationhood is not necessarily possible; as a result, they turn to border spaces in order to tell their own stories about their past, present, and future in both individual and communal terms. And these communities, as Rose demonstrates, do not necessarily align with tribal efforts to build nations within nation-states. Instead, Rose's 'Halfbreed Chronicles' calls into question what constitutes 'Native history' and 'Native community.' The poetry examined throughout this chapter has – I am suggesting – relied on humour and irony to ensure that such lack of fixity is sustained throughout the works in question. The provisionality of memory also can be an effective tool for righting history, and for ensuring justice and equity, without merely reinforcing dominant paradigms of nationhood, particularly when marginalized Native women are used to interpellate on what grounds, literally and figuratively, nation-states were constructed. In the chapter that follows, I extend the consideration of history, memory, and nation by examining several female writers who combine poetry and photography to explore their relationship to ghosts.

chapter four

Haunting Photographs, Revisioning Families

For nearly two years I have been looking at these photographs and they have come to haunt me, not because of what I see, but by what I don't, and possibly can never, know.

Michael Katakis, *Excavating Voices*

Photography came along to memorialize, to reinstate symbolically, the imperiled continuity and vanishing extendedness of family life. Those ghostly traces, photographs, supply the token presence of the dispersed relatives. A family photograph album is generally about the extended family – and, often, is all that remains of it.

Susan Sontag, *On Photography*

The power of the visible / is the invisible.

Marianne Moore, *Collected Poems*

Ghosts are a powerful presence in recent Native North American women's poetry, as rendered through language and accompanying visual images, particularly photography. The invocation of ghosts can be a powerful tool for rewriting dominant (white western) histories of nation, whether by refashioning perceptions of key historical figures or by introducing otherwise marginalized individuals and communities into the realm of historical discourse. But the invocation of ghosts – ancestral or otherwise – is not just a tool for revising Eurocentric historical records. In many cases, as already exemplified by Blaeser's 'Living History' (see chapter 3), ghosts also celebrate the power of family ties, and the inspirational strength of those relations, beyond an individual's life cycle. Joy Harjo explains that in Native culture, life and death form a continuum: 'I know there is a world of spirits. I know there is a world going after ... The supernatural world is ingrained in our culture and it is another way of knowing' (Carabi 1996, 135). Harjo's emphasis on the links between the living and the dead suggests why ghosts are useful to the Native North American women poets under consideration, not just as figures of negativity but as sources of inspiration.

This chapter turns from an exploration of nation and national identity to an examination of photography and text in the work of Kimberly Blaeser, Marilyn Dumont, Louise Halfe, and Diane Glancy. All four follow in the footsteps of Leslie Marmon Silko's *Storyteller* (1981), a groundbreaking collection of poems, traditional Pueblo narratives, photographs, and her own contemporary short stories, published in a wide-page format that plays with white western formulations of genre by juxtaposing a multiplicity of textual forms with a diverse array of carefully placed black-and-white landscape and family photos. In particular, this chapter probes how the women poets specifically draw on collections of family photos – both formal portraits and more casual shots – to explore their individual struggles with and questions about what constitutes family, identity, and a sense of belonging when one is trying to find a place within and among multiple communities.[1] Notably, none of these women has extensively developed her skill as an amateur or professional photographer. With the exception of one photograph taken by Kimberly Blaeser, which she uses on the cover of her latest collection, *Apprenticed to Justice*, all of these poets integrate photographs taken by others (often family members) into their works. By selecting the photographs and placing them in relation to written texts, and in some instances determining the composition of the images of themselves in collaboration with a photographer, their collections become intricately visually layered products that probe notions of sight, blindness, and haunting.

According to Peggy Phelan in *Unmarked: The Politics of Performance*, there is a definite need to re-evaluate the prevailing assumption that representational visibility can be simply equated with political power;[2] think, for instance, of Edward Curtis's nostalgic images of late nineteenth- and early twentieth-century Native Americans, which provided great exposure (all puns intended) for Native peoples but confined the objects of the image to the realm of a dying breed. Curtis, as Thomas King explains, spent much of his life travelling throughout North America in search of the 'postcard Indian,' often going to extremes to get the shot he wanted by having his subjects shave their facial hair, don wigs, and even put on

the traditional clothes of other tribes (2003, 36). In contrast, each of
the four writers discussed here juxtaposes family photographs and the
occasionally formal portrait with prose poetry to demonstrate that they
are alive and well; they use their texts to explore their individual, mixed-
blood heritages and the intricacies of rendering memory on the page.
And if, as Blaeser and Glancy claim, the poetry of Native North American
women is rooted in paradox – the paradox of having to describe rituals
and memories that cannot be fully expressed through the written word –
then the coupling of photographs with poetry becomes especially worthy
of examination. It is in the liminal spaces between the poetic texts and
the photographs that a different kind of phantasmatic representation
occurs, one that I will argue resists the limitations of the written word
and creates the opportunity to revise dominant white western assumptions about Native family histories and identities. In this coupling, these
female poets call on their readers and viewers to consider how the paradox of (in)visibility is enacted through a dialogue with the photographs
that are an integral part of their texts.

Humour and irony are important conduits for this exploration of
(in)visibility; they encourage the subversion of traditionally neglected
viewpoints and demand the negotiation of incongruities by encouraging readers, as Arthur Koestler puts it, to move beyond 'the routine
skills of thinking on a single plane' (1964, 35). The inclusion of photographs and their complex relationship to the poetic texts of these female poets creates an opportunity for readers to understand the power
of images and the imagination from very different perspectives. The
naming and reading of one's ancestors through the photographs and
poems becomes proof of the survival of Native peoples, their families
and communities – a testament with its own ironic edge. Thus, the
works of Glancy, Dumont, Blaeser, and Halfe combine poetry with photography to create what Anishinaabe writer and literary scholar Kimberly Blaeser calls the 'ghost space – spiritual space' of familial memory
(Andrews 2007b, 19).

Blaeser specifically links ghosts with spirituality and a movement outside the confines of the temporal, suggesting that by focusing on ghosts
one can move beyond 'ego, ... [and] a lot of the things through which
we ground ourselves as humans' (Andrews 2007b, 19). While she argues
that to fully express the significance of familial ghosts may be 'beyond
the language that we have ... you can gesture toward it' (19). In Blaeser's
volumes, poetry and photography provide access to 'those ... ecstatic
moments' that, as she argues, 'we should build our lives around' (19).

Marilyn Dumont, like Blaeser, was raised as a Catholic and recalls learning about the importance of ghosts as a child:

> I grew up hearing about ghosts. My parents didn't actually say spirits, they
> said ghosts but when they said ghost I knew they meant spirit. I certainly was
> aware of that world – the intangible world. There's that aspect of it, but the
> other was just a sense of loss, a sense of grief, and a sense of estrangement.
> (Andrews 2004b, 148-9)

Dumont shares Blaeser's understanding of the value of the spirit world,
and like Blaeser, she views ghosts as a point of access to her Métis heritage precisely because in contrast with Catholicism, which 'was all formulated into doctrine' and consisted of published texts, she recalls that
'the Native religion or belief I grew up with wasn't formulated into doctrine but ...was equally present,' through figures like ghosts (149). Yet,
Dumont's Métis roots and her own nomadic lifestyle reflect a far more
ironic perspective about ghosts and what they may offer to present generations. Hence, ghosts are both precious evidence of the existence of
previous generations, and vivid reminders of this Métis legacy of dispossession and marginalization.

For Louise Halfe, the naming and reading of historical ancestors – the
foremothers she dreams about – are central to her poetry, particularly
her second collection, *Blue Marrow*, which begins with an invocation of
'the [Cree] Guardian of Dreams and Visions,' and explores the narrator's
relationship to her female 'grandmothers' through an intricate combination of poetry and photography (2004, 1, 7). Contrary to Dumont's
parents, in an article co-authored with Linda Jaine, Halfe uses the term
'Spirits' to describe the role of ghosts for Cree people, explaining that

> they are mediums through which we attempt to enlighten our understand-
> ing of the world in which we exist. And if we develop them properly, we find
> our answers.
>   Each of the Creator's gifts, particularly animals and humans, possess [sic]
> a Spirit. Because the Spirit is eternal we know that when we die, it is only a
> physical death and our journey continues on ... Separation from the body
> does not necessarily mean that all ties to people are disconnected. Spirits
> have the power to manifest themselves to the human eye and mind as well
> as to communicate with us. (Halfe and Jaine 1989, 11)

Halfe suggests that the Spirits impart wisdom; when looked for and listened to carefully, these ancestral ghosts convey memories of the past and provide strategies for coping with the present and the future, despite their physical absence. In a recent interview, Halfe explains that she communicates with the Spirits through 'dreaming' (Andrews 2004a, 3). By allowing the subconscious to freely wander in a dream-state, she gathers information about her personal and tribal history, a process that is enriched by the family photographs that provide a visual context for this interaction with her ancestors. But this juxtaposition of photography and poetry in *Blue Marrow* has its own ironic edge. The photographs are deliberately unlabelled, a gesture that conveys Halfe's anger at the presumptuousness of white western settlers who felt it was their right to take Cree lands and rename Cree people, especially Cree women, under the auspices of civilizing the population.

Like Halfe, Diane Glancy stresses the importance of listening to the ancestral voices that can be accessed through dreaming, viewing poetry as a conduit for these neglected narratives:

> We spend a third of our lives asleep, and in sleep there is a narrative, there is voice, there is something going on. We don't hold it fully ... We have our logical mind, and then we have this subconscious dream world without which we are not complete. It is a mystery; it is a bigger part of what we are than we can access, and it certainly shows up in dreams and vision in Native culture ... Poetry has the ability to get to that dream world. (Andrews 2002b, 646)

In *The West Pole*, Glancy further elaborates on how she connects with her Native ancestors, in spite of her mother's denial of Glancy's paternal tribal heritage, noting her receptiveness to both the voices of the land and the spirits who dwell on it. She explains that 'the ancestors come sometimes for supper,' and even travel alongside Glancy when she is on late-night driving trips: 'They were there beside the highway riding their spirit horses' (1997, 28). If dreaming and an openness to the spirit world of ghosts are ways to access a past that she has been denied, then bringing photographs into *The West Pole* deepens Glancy's efforts to understand her identity, and especially her mother's efforts to manipulate Glancy's childhood self-presentation to ensure that her mixed-blood daughter was not identified as Native. The myriad images and fragments of text that constitute Glancy's 'Photo Album' in *The West Pole* provide an ironic yet witty rejoinder to her mother's silence about Glancy's paternal ancestry, and enable Glancy to 're-image' and 're-imagine' herself by productively combining media forms to suit her specific path of inquiry (29).

Photographing Indians

In her now famous book *On Photography* (1989), Susan Sontag explores the links between nuclear families, the growth of urban centres, and the increasing popularity of the camera in North America during the twentieth century. She argues:

> Photography came along to memorialize, to reinstate symbolically, the imperiled continuity and vanishing extendedness of family life. Those ghostly traces, photographs, supply the token presence of the dispersed relatives. A family photograph album is generally about the extended family – and, often, is all that remains of it. (1989, 9)

Sontag's lament for the dispersal of extended families echoes the concerns expressed by Native North American women poets that print images, though potentially distorted, may be their only means of constructing a family tree and a sense of their ancestral past. Such a claim is complicated in a Native context because, historically, photography was used in North America to, as Katakis puts it, 'perpetuate the myths and stereotypes of Native Americans that still haunt us today – the noble savage, the monolithic group,' thus justifying their genocide (1998, 3). Conversely, white western stereotypes of the bourgeois family often influenced photographic portraits of Native peoples, inflicting what Julia Emberley calls 'representational violence' by deliberately refusing to represent familial configurations that strayed from the restrictive model of the nuclear family (2007, 13). It is these stereotypes and limitations that the poets contest through their inclusion of photographs and poems in their texts. Though each has her own particular approach to deconstructing stereotypical images of 'Indianness' and the concept of 'family,' all share in a desire to destabilize the fixity of the photograph and its frame by listening to what exists between or beyond a framed image and its accompanying printed text. They write about their own memories in poetic form and reflect on their own relationships to the photographs they have inherited, often with the help of humorous and ironic discursive strategies. These poets bring 'the power of the visible' to the invisible, suggesting that photography can move beyond surveillance and domination by being attentive to the voices of their particular familial histories (Moore 1951, 104).

At the conclusion of *American Indians: Stereotypes and Realities,* Devon Mihesuah deftly pairs two long-circulating and closely linked assumptions about Native peoples: that they 'are stoic and have no sense of humor' and that they 'like having their pictures taken' regardless of whether it violates a community's sense of privacy or not (1996, 110, 112). Mihesuah suggests that the notion of 'the humorless, silent, wooden Indian is [still] a popular image' because, typically, 'historic Indians' were not 'painted or photographed smiling, and with good reason'; many were photographed during treaty-signings, after being captured or jailed, or during portrait sittings in which the photographer paid subjects to look a particular way (110). Likewise, she contends that photography was historically treated by many Native peoples as 'intrusive' because so often non-Natives would disregard tribal rights to maintain closed ceremonies, and record sacred events for commercial or personal use (112). Such exploitation has, over time, been reversed in some instances, with reserve communities now charging visitors who want to bring cameras on site,[3] enforcing strict policies about what can and cannot be photographed, and even setting up staged photographic scenes to satisfy tourist curiosity, with the benefit of making a profit.

However, the predatory nature of photography as an act of acquisition has been especially damaging in the case of Native North Americans who have historically been viewed as documentary subjects of a dying race, one that was being displaced by the birth of a new nation. As Susan Sontag notes, 'a photograph is both a pseudo-presence and a token of absence,' which may be used to 'lay claim to another reality,' especially one that threatens the expansion of white western imperialism (1989, 16). By visually framing and fixing images of Native peoples through photography, a modicum of control could be established over what might seem otherwise to be unruly or threatening populations, while also furnishing 'evidence' for further regulation (5). Moreover, efforts to build national unity in the United States, according to Sontag, were often underpinned by photographs that recorded 'loss,' creating an apparently static past and, in doing so, 'steadily enlarg[ing] the familiar iconography of mystery, mortality, and transience' to give the country an instantaneous sense of history (67), strategies that were also part of the building of Canada. As Gail Guthrie Valaskasis explains, the importation of photography as a technology from Europe to North America occurred in 1839, followed by the introduction of postcards to the United States in 1873. The majority of these early photographs were portraits, used to record a vanishing race. The tendency has been to dislocate historical photographs of Native North Americans 'in time and space' and thus draw attention away from the context of their creation; by presenting the photos in a void (typically without the names of those in the photo or the location of the shot), viewers are oblivious to the 'plethora of missing information – personal, lived, local' (2005, 197).

In *The Imaginary Indian*, Daniel Francis argues that 'the Vanishing Indian' was a cross-border concept that fuelled national sentiment, but only when done in a manner that fulfilled the notion of 'a timeless Indian past where nothing much changed'; in other words, 'any evidence of contact with White culture contaminated this image' and thus was to be avoided at all cost (1992, 38, 41). As photography became increasingly democratized, tourists themselves began to gather photographic 'evidence' of the existence of Native peoples, before they disappeared altogether. Francis even points to memoir of Douglas Sladen, 'a British tourist who crossed Canada by rail in 1894,' and who later described in *On the Cars and Off*, how efforts to possess Native peoples were becoming rampant at precisely the same time that Canada as a new nation was revelling in the recently completed railroad that connected the country from 'sea to shining sea': 'Whenever you stop at a station all the steps getting down are packed with people taking pot shots with Kodaks ... Crossing the prairie, every operator imagines he's going to Kodak an Indian; but the wily Indian sits in the shade, where instantaneous photography availeth not' (1895, 226-7). The objectification of Native peoples and the selective vision of those who chose to photograph them, as well as the strategic efforts of Native populations to avoid the camera, suggest that the kind of exposure given to Native communities in North America was often more destructive than productive.

No doubt photography is a tool of power which has been, and continues to be, used to construct nations and, in some cases, figuratively eradicate individuals and communities that interrupt the presumed coherence of such projects. But photography historically has taken on a different role within families and communities, becoming an ever increasingly affordable way to commemorate 'the achievements of individuals' and their relationships to others, particularly when participating in significant social rituals such as births, weddings, and graduations (Sontag 1989, 8). Cameras in recent years have become a tool for creating personal histories by recording the quotidian events of family life, especially for those with children:

> Through photographs, each family constructs a portrait chronicle of itself
> – a portable kit of images that bears witness to its connectedness. It hardly
> matters what activities are photographed as long as photographs get taken
> and are cherished … photographs [also] give people an imaginary posses-
> sion of a past that is unreal. (9)

Notably, Leslie Marmon Silko inverts this focus on the child in her aptly titled 1996 essay 'On Photography,' which pointedly recalls Sontag's
groundbreaking text. In it, Silko describes the role that her father, Lee
H. Marmon, played in the local Native community. Marmon was a highly
accomplished photographer who 'photographed the land and the people of the Laguna-Acoma area' from the mid-twentieth century onward,
often taking pictures at the request of 'the families of old folks' (1996,
185). Marmon avoided using flashes, creating informal portraits taken
outside in daylight hours that reflected a reverence for the individual
subject. As Silko explains: 'He [Marmon] knew that these old folks, who
had loved him and watched out for him as a child, would pass onto Cliff
House soon … I think my father couldn't bear to wait that long to see
their beloved faces again' (186). Silko's description of her father's photographic endeavours conveys very powerfully how photography can
function as a labour of love, depending of course on who is behind the
lens; Marmon creates a visual legacy for the Laguna-Acoma community,
successfully cultivating and nurturing connections between and among
generations of Native families.

But even family photographs do not always have such positive resonances for Native people. Thomas King, who himself has undertaken a
parodic reworking of Edward Curtis's famous photographic expeditions
with his 'Medicine River Photographic Expedition,' outlines the specific
challenges facing Native people who use family photos in order to build
or affirm family and community links, while having already been trained
to see Native peoples in a particular way. He draws on the example of
mixed-blood writer Louis Owens, who when he examines old family photos, struggles to find evidence of his ancestors' Native heritage: 'To find
the Indian in the photographic cupboard, I must narratively construct
him out of his missing presence, for my great-grandfather was Indian but
not an Indian' (Owens 1992, 92). Not only is the past, in this instance,
treated as unreal in the sense of being imaginary or constructed, but because many Native people have been innundated with expectations that
their ancestors need to look appropriately 'Indian,' they must struggle to
make sense of photos that do not conform to these narrow assumptions.

Conversely, King explains that 'one of the conundrums of the late twentieth century ... is that many of our mothers and fathers, ... who were forcibly encouraged to give up their own identities, now have children who
are determined to be seen as Indians' (2003, 45). As Joy Harjo notes, in
an interesting variation on King's comment, it was only when she finally
was given photos of her great-grandfather, Henry Marsey Harjo, as an
adult that she understood why the images had not been circulated by
the family: 'When I saw the photograph I understood why the silence.
He is at least half African. My relatives prized light skin' (Aull et al. 1996,
105). For Harjo, however, seeing the photograph of Henry Harjo helped
her to understand her family's unexamined racial prejudices – being
Native was acceptable but being black was not – and to clarify her own
interest in African-American culture, especially music. In a broader context, then, although several of the women discussed in this chapter are
less concerned with visualizing their Nativeness in the present and more
engaged with representations of the past, the challenges of defining oneself through photography are, of course, part of the process of coming to
terms with one's identity.

Using Photos to Story

Diane Glancy reflects on the ancestral incongruity of her own family
album in an essay called 'Their Eyes Have Seen the Buffalo' from *The
West Pole*, in which she describes the difficulty of reconciling her paternal grandmother's portraits – included in a later section titled 'Photo
Album' – with her own stereotypes about Native peoples:

> I was raised at some distance from my Cherokee heritage. We made fre-
> quent trips to visit my mother's parents' farm in Kansas, but we rarely went
> to northwest Arkansas. It's where my father's mother lived in Viola, just un-
> der the Missouri border ... I remember a tall and bony woman with a long
> face and coarse grey hair. Not entirely white. Not entirely Indian. Especially
> not the image I had of the Plains Indians with a teepee and buffalo. My
> father's mother had a row of corn and some pigs. (1997, 28)

The subsequent 'Photo Album' includes a 1907 studio portrait of Glancy's paternal grandmother, Orvezene Lewis Hall, in which she is wearing
an Edwardian-style high-collared white shirt, necktie, floor-length skirt,
and long jacket, and is standing on a patterned oriental rug with a plain
dark backdrop. This is followed by two, more casual photos, both taken

decades later. In the first of the family shots, Orvezene stands between Glancy's aunt and father in 1936 in front of a car (often included to attest to the family's prosperity), wearing a shift dress that stops above the ankle and clearly visible dark dress shoes; rather than looking directly at the camera, as she does in the early portrait, Orvezene somberly stares out beyond the lens, evading interaction with the viewer, while her children seem to look right at the unnamed photographer (see fig. 1). Lucy Lippard argues that 'the only defense the turn-of-the-century sitter had against misrepresentation (aside from outright refusal) was the expression in his or her face'; she suggests that the stiffness and impassivity of early photographs 'can be attributed to the long exposures,' but also wonders 'if some of the "stoic" look, the "passive squaw," and stone-faced chief clichés were not voluntary defenses against yet another intrusion,' offering an ironic rereading of these Native stereotypes (1999, 138). While this photo of Orvezene likely was taken by a family member, neighbour, or friend, the gaze suggests a certain sustained distrust of the camera, even as it records the continued existence of her family.

The second family photograph of Glancy's paternal grandmother, which is titled 'My grandmother Orvezene and her pigs, 1940s' (see fig. 2) in *The West Pole*, shows a more bucolic scene, with her grandmother wearing a loosely fitted suit jacket and knee-length skirt, along with spectator heels and a fabric corsage on her right lapel, and holding a bucket and stick, presumably to feed the mother pig and her small band of piglets at the centre of the picture (1997, 134). Such elegant attire (including her spectator pumps) may appear to contemporary readers much too dressy for such a task. Moreover, the pastoral backdrop of rolling hills and trees can be read as ironic when juxtaposed with the props that she carries, which are necessary implements of regular farm life. But these photographs also capture critical moments in personal history; not only do they document changing styles in women's fashions and her shifting self-representation, but they also visually convey the varied circumstances of Orvezene's life. She was the young bride of a country doctor and was prematurely widowed; she initially depended on her son's wages for survival, but finally achieved a comfortable and relatively independent retirement. And the photographs are crucial to Glancy's efforts at 'storying' her familial history, especially given her own mother's distaste for her in-laws and thus the (in)visibility that is integral to such images: 'My grandmother had come from a removed race. Soldiers had even tried to exterminate the buffalo. The spirit animal of our country was supposed to be from my Indian past but wasn't. Making the certain-

*My father with his mother, Orvezene, and his sister, Effie,
1936*

1 A photograph from Glancy's personal archive.

My grandmother Orvezene and her pigs, 1940s

2 Another image of Glancy's paternal grandmother, who lived in Arkansas and
offered Glancy an important link to her Cherokee heritage.

ties more uncertain ... My grandmother's place in Arkansas was a big, unknown country my mother didn't like' (129). By foregrounding the tensions inherent in reading the photographs of her Native relations, Glancy highlights her own ambivalence as a Native woman writer who is acutely aware of the benefits and dangers of being visible, whether in word or image.

As Glancy's essays, prose poems, and photos suggest, the combination of more formal portrait photography and informal family photos offers a means of exploring her fragmented sense of community and family, and becomes a record of the changing economies of photography – the rarity and expense of earlier portraits is contrasted with the abundance and casualness of more recent images, typically taken with inexpensive portable cameras. Glancy, like the other poets examined here, seems very aware that the past as represented by photography is inherently partial or unreal and in need of narrative supplementation, if only to reflect further on what is absent from or escapes the limits of these images accumulated over time and passed on through generations. Sontag argues that the coupling of poetry and photography is particularly well suited to such investigations:

> Poetry's commitment to concreteness and to the autonomy of the poem's language parallels photography's commitment to pure seeing. Both imply discontinuity, disarticulated forms and compensatory unity: wrenching things from their context (to see them in a fresh way), bringing things together elliptically, according to the imperious but often arbitrary demands of subjectivity. (1989, 96)

Here, Sontag's discussion of the parallels between art forms – that alter contexts and create unexpected juxtapositions, as shaped by the subjective experiences of both author and reader/viewer, to provoke different ways of seeing – suggests why irony and, in some cases, humour can be found in the works of Dumont, Glancy, Blaeser, and Halfe when they combine photography and poetry.

Glancy, for instance, provides a pointedly ironic subtitle for her 'Photo Album' in *The West Pole*, just above the two photographs that begin the series of twenty-three pages of black-and-white familial images, briefly noted with dates and the names of those in the picture. The studio portraits of her paternal and maternal grandmothers, who stare starkly into the camera, are introduced with the following heading: 'Using Photos to Story as if They Were Teepee Drawings of Personal/Tribal History

(As if Having a Teepee)' (1997, 131). Having already provided a prose poem about her American-as-apple-pie existence and its limitations on the facing page that frames the 'Photo Album,' the heading reveals the weight of Glancy's own assumptions about her Native heritage and the inaccuracies inherent in those assumptions, especially in the case of her paternal grandmother, who has neither the requisite teepee nor buffalo. Thus, the subtitle becomes a commentary on the act of exploring her own (in)visibility through the photos of her family and her efforts to create a 'story,' to find 'a way to record the "migration" [of Native Americans like her ancestors] as they struggled across the moving landscape of their lives' without merely imposing or perpetuating dominant stereotypes (3). By borrowing from the very clichés that she herself has had to negotiate, Glancy formulates a series of interwoven jokes about her lack of a traditional tribal history; there are no 'Teepee Drawings' of her ancestral past, and even the notion of her Native relations having a teepee is ludicrous, having come from a sedentary Woodland tribe (131). Glancy's repetition of 'as if … As if,' and her bracketing of the possibility of 'Having a Teepee,' linguistically undercut the believability of such a fabricated narrative precisely because neither are the photos 'drawings' nor do they appear on teepee hides (131).

Instead, Glancy is left with photography, a medium that has been used historically to objectify Native peoples, and therefore cannot be trusted even though it is her primary way to connect with the past. And by putting the first two photos of her grandmothers along with the evocative subtitle beside a prose poem that appears directly beneath the 'Photo Album,' which documents the tension between darkness and light (literally and figuratively) in her own childhood, Glancy heightens the potential for both humorous and ironic readings of her texts:

> Our house on Woodland in Kansas City faced the west. Each day the sun pushed its way onto our front porch and into the house.
> I had a tricycle.
> When I was three my brother was born.
> We went to church.
> We went to the farm.[4]
> I was given piano lessons.
> I was a campfire girl.
> When I was eight I got a Schwinn.
> I had the idea from my parents that things should be done right.

We lived in America. My father voted Republican. My mother was a Democrat.

She made pot roast, mashed potatoes, and apple pie.

My father went to work each day.

They married in the Depression, but waited until it was over to have two children.

There was something in their lives that was not fun.

My father was dark and my mother light.

She was angry when I played in the sun.

Something was not explained. Something not told. What we wouldn't talk about was the way to make it go away.

But inside something said that I lived on the Great Plains of America. From the West Pole each day a light pushed itself into the house. I would look back someday. I would get through. (1997, 130)

As Glancy explains in an earlier essay in the same collection, the West Pole is 'what you are inside yourself without anyone else around' (105), a sense of belief that has enabled her to recognize and embrace her Cherokee heritage, despite her mother's efforts to bury that aspect of her identity. In the prose poem that appears beneath the title, 'Photo Album,' Glancy combines the play of light and dark with a cataloguing of key events in her childhood, a series of juxtapositions that enact her awareness of the unspoken racial tensions in her family. As a middle-class child who is able much of the time to pass as white, the narrator is provided with the material goods necessary to fulfill her role – a tricycle, a baby brother, regular church attendance, piano lessons, meals of 'pot roast, mashed potatoes, and apple pie,' and, on her eighth birthday, a Schwinn bicycle, an American symbol of tradition and quality (130). But despite all of this, her father's heritage continues to haunt the speaker, who is acutely aware that there is a distance between her parents that cannot be bridged; her mother's fear that her daughter's skin will darken in the sun epitomizes the anxiety the speaker faced as a child who was expected to hide her Native identity, while not even really knowing about it: 'Something was not explained. Something not told. What we / wouldn't talk about was the way to make it go away' (130).

Glancy explains in a recent interview that, in her words, 'my mother used to love to take photographs, only there was a cruelty about it. I was formed into her image' (Andrews 2002b, 656). Not surprisingly, then, the poem that begins Glancy's 'Photo Album' section is designed to deconstruct the fixity of her mother's imposed vision by ironically under-cutting her visual and verbal restrictions on Glancy. The formality of the photos that follow, with family members in elegant Sunday church dress, and staged childhood portraits, reveals Glancy's white, middle-class up-bringing – and her mother's efforts to confine her to a singular image. In most of these shots, Glancy is dressed in white and thus stands out against the dark background; her hair is neatly styled and often tied back with a bow or barrettes, and occasionally she wears some tasteful jewel-lery in the form of a strand of pearls or a decorative brooch. But Glancy also includes, as I have noted above, several pictures of her paternal grandmother, photos of herself with her father 'at the farm' after hunt-ing, and eventually more casual shots of herself and her own children (1997, 142). Moreover, she varies the detail and tone of the accompany-ing text of each photo, often giving merely names and dates of those in the picture, but sometimes adding her own ironic commentary. Both kinds of textual notations suggest that Glancy is reclaiming these photos as her own by creating, in Phelan's words, 'breaks in the reciprocity of visual exchange,' in particular, between herself and her mother (1993, 26). If 'in looking at the other ... the subject seeks to see itself,' then Glancy's efforts pointedly 'disrupt [what could be called] the neat substi-tution of the psychic economy of seeing' by fashioning her own album, one that is decidedly not in her mother's image (Phelan 1993, 16, 21). The brevity of some descriptions, such as 'Me, age 5' and 'Anna Myrtle Adams Wood, my maternal grandmother, circa 1904,' draws attention to the historical dimensions of the photos, providing a basic chronology while letting the photos 'speak for themselves' (1997, 140, 131). That succinctness, however, is elaborated by Glancy's own prose and the fact that the photos appear quite late in a book that she has authored; the photos have been selected and formatted by her, and blend together her paternal and maternal family trees, thus defying her mother's desire to keep her Cherokee husband's heritage invisible while highlighting the performative aspects of her own childhood 'whiteness.'

Certain photos in *The West Pole*, such as those of Glancy with her fa-ther, become the basis for her overt efforts to acknowledge visually and textually her mixed-blood identity. For instance, a photograph of a very young Glancy astride a pony with her father standing beside her holding her hand (see fig. 3), is given a revisionist twist with the line that appears below it: 'My father and me on my first war horse, August 1942' (1997, 138). Glancy's reference to her 'war horse' plays on the stereotype that all Native peoples were warriors who used horses for battle; in her own

My father and me on my first war horse, August 1942

3 A photograph of Glancy and her father, likely taken by her mother.

life, she playfully explains later in *The West Pole*, her cars have become
her 'war horse[s],' enabling her to travel across the country for work as
a writer-in-residence (163).

Glancy, touchingly, pays visual tribute to her war horses in *The West
Pole*. The final photograph of the album, called 'War Horse II,' comes
from a documentary titled *Without Reservations* and depicts a slaughtered
moose being hung from wooden scaffolding in the woods by several Native men with a Buick station wagon parked just behind it (1997, 153).
Glancy explains the significance of the photo in a section of the text
that follows the 'Photo Album' called 'Now,' which includes three 'War
Horse' poems. Specifically, 'War Horse I' mourns the loss of the Buick
station wagon, after thirteen years of use, when it failed an emissions
test: 'You know I think I left my husband more easily than I left that
car' (163). The speaker describes giving the Buick to an 'Indian friend'
who 'could use it for hunting' on the reservation, where there was no
automobile standards testing, and then recounts the shock and delight
of seeing her car in the documentary: 'And the car there as if it had had
a part in the hunt. As if maybe it held the bow and arrow' (163, 164).
The early photo of herself astride a pony with her father anticipates this
relationship with the Buick, and her own sense of herself as a modern-
day warrior and nomad who embraces the freedom that travel gives her.

Paradoxically, even in her apparent absence, Glancy's mother literally
and figuratively casts a shadow on her daughter; if one looks carefully
at the childhood photograph of Glancy astride a pony with her father,
there is a dark shadow in the bottom left corner that appears to be the
person taking the picture. If the photographer is indeed Glancy's mother, then her efforts to keep her daughter out of the sunlight in case her
skin darkened and her need to dress her in white become especially
ironic. Here, Glancy's mother becomes a ghostly shadow, a dark 'Other' whose determination to control the representation of her daughter
rather than acknowledging Glancy's individuality parodically echoes the
work of Edward Curtis.

Throughout 'Photo Album,' Glancy repeatedly explores 'the desire
to see the self through the image of the other,' a desire, which Phelan
notes, 'all Western representation exploits' (1993, 16). To this end, Glancy juxtaposes a picture of herself and her brother with her mother – all
clad in white and standing in front of the family home – with a more
casual shot of the two children and their father, beside a car, holding the
dead bodies of small animals that attest to the success of their hunt (see
fig. 4). This placement of photographs pointedly disrupts the narrative

Each day the sun from the west, 1948

"Something was there in knifing buckshot from the bird or animal." On the farm, 1949

4 Childhood photographs of Glancy and her younger brother with her mother and father respectively.

and visual continuity between Glancy's relationships with her mother and her father. The top photo of her mother, Glancy, and her brother is annotated with the line 'Each day the sun from the west, 1948,' which paraphrases the first few lines of the prose poem which opens 'Photo Album,' echoing linguistically Glancy's mother's fear of her children being darkened by the sun (1997, 142). The photograph itself is quite bright in tone, with all three figures clad in white outfits with neatly coiffed hair, posing for the camera and creating a vision of crisp cleanliness that is accentuated by the light backdrop of the house. Glancy's mother has her arm around Glancy, while her brother David stands to the side; the pose aligns mother and daughter, and with their similar hair styles and dresses, they become mirror images of one another.

The photograph below of Glancy and her brother David flanking their father, however, is a study in contrasts – all three people are wearing solid-coloured dark clothing, their hair is tousled or covered by a hat, and Glancy is not even looking at the camera. Each family member holds onto small dead animals, like trophies in celebration of their recent hunt. Beside this lower picture is the following caption: '"Something was there in knifing buckshot from the bird or animal." On the farm, 1949' (1997, 142). Though it is not clear as to which family farm the family is visiting, the act of hunting provides a candid moment of bonding between a father and his children – Glancy looks down at the animal she is holding, and her younger brother, David, proudly holds up a dead rabbit while his father protectively embraces him, in an ironic reversal of the photograph above.

The presentation of these two photographs on a single page in Glancy's *The West Pole* is an especially powerful and complex example of how humour and irony can work through unexpected visual juxtapositions. Glancy's placement of the two photographs with their stark visual differences alongside the similar positioning of the bodies within the pictures recalls Koestler's concept of bisociation. The incompatible edges of these photos invite readers to create palimpsests; as readers wrestle with the two frames of reference, each photograph represents a distinctive racial and social perspective on the world. Glancy's choice of photographic placement raises important questions about how and what viewers see, particularly given the historical allure of the 'postcard Indian' (King 2003, 36). King provocatively asks in *The Truth about Stories*, 'Yet how can something that has never existed – the Indian – have form and power while something that is alive and kicking – Indians – are invisible?' (53). Similarly, in one of the epigraphs that opens this chapter, Michael

Katakis laments the difficulties of learning about the lives of nineteenth-century Native North Americans through the formal portraits taken primarily by non-Native photographers: 'For nearly two years I have been looking at these photographs and they have come to haunt me, not because of what I see, but by what I don't, and possibly can never, know' (1998, 1). Glancy deconstructs the invisibility of 'Indians' in her 'Photo Album' even as she highlights the challenges of being raised in a family where being Native was not a point of pride. But by putting the two sides of her immediate family together on a single page, she creates a visual collage of her mixed-blood identity, a process that, as she acknowledges, is much needed because 'I had no clear image of myself as a Native person' (1997, 2).

As the 'Photo Album' shifts gradually from formal to more informal recent shots of Glancy and her family, this change in perspective is most radically marked by the pictures of Glancy travelling in her capacity as a Native author and tourist in Europe and the United States. In particular, Glancy includes an image of herself speaking at a 'Writer's conference in Freiburg, 1992,' with Acoma poet Simon Ortiz seated beside her. An earlier section of *The West Pole* is devoted to 'The Germany Trip,' which recounts in a candid-diary format the transatlantic journey, undertaken with a male companion, the conference in Freiburg, and a subsequent 'five-city reading tour' that Glancy went on in the summer of 1992 (1997, 43); in it Glancy explores the economic challenges of surviving as a writer, the tokenism of her presence at the conference – one of two Native Americans – and her efforts to negotiate her relationship with her companion in a setting loaded with historical anguish as a result of the Second World War. Further, because Glancy's mother was German, the trip takes on enormous familial resonances; by coincidence or fate, Glancy even ends up visiting the town where her mother's ancestors came from while on a bus tour of the Black Forest. Hence, the later inclusion of a photograph of Glancy delivering a talk in Germany, mouth open and eyes looking at her notes, becomes ironically charged, especially given the conference poster's caption visible beneath her, proclaiming, 'Home Abroad / Abroad Home,' for Glancy is both at home and abroad here (148). Paradoxically, she is no longer conforming to her mother's 'boundary of housework and children,' but instead sustaining an 'occupation' that acknowledges her Native heritage and gives her independence (1).

Glancy's declaration of her independence is enhanced in the final pages of the 'Album,' which bring together fairly recent shots of herself and each of her two children. Glancy's casual tourist pose at a canyon in Arizona is placed beside an image of her son at sea during the Persian Gulf War, with a caption that reads, 'Marine First Lieutenant David Glancy, my son, on board the USS Okinawa,' noting with pride his full title and status in the U.S. Marines (1997, 151). Although Glancy may not intend it, this later image can be read as an ironic comment on U.S. imperialism, given the history of the American government's efforts to colonize Native Americans and remove them from their lands, even as they expected those same populations to defend national interests abroad. And on the two pages that follow, the 'Album' includes a candid shot of Glancy's daughter playfully smiling at the camera at her university graduation ceremony, with a similarly detailed commentary, and a photograph of her beloved 'War Horse II.' The highly stylized portraits of previous generations, and particularly her mother's efforts to make her daughter in her image, are now displaced by the activity and obvious joy conveyed through the photos and captions that frame Glancy's own children, including the well-worn Buick, now happily housed on a Native reservation.

With these photos, Glancy gives 'form and power' to the 'Indians' whose invisibility King laments, celebrating her children in the midst of their own lives and situating herself as a Native writer and scholar who embraces the complexities of her mixed-blood identity (King 2003, 53). Glancy exploits the notion that 'looking ... both obscures and reveals the looker' (Phelan 1993, 16) by creating an album of images and texts in which she is both object and subject, and thus can expose the exploitation that can and does underlie, from her perspective, many of these family photographs that either do not accord with or indeed parody white western bourgeois notions of the traditional family portrait (with a patriarch at its centre). By locating herself in the interstices between and among the texts and their context, and employing humour and irony at various moments in *The West Pole*, Glancy demonstrates how looking again – differently – enables an exploration of her own in/visibility.

Reframing the Self

Glancy explores the challenges of re-framing the self in *The West Pole*, storying her family into being through photography in an effort to subvert her mother's desire to deny her father's Native heritage. But it is Glancy's choice of cover image that gives her meditation on photography – especially in relation to her mother – a final ironic (and playfully humorous) twist. The cover shot of *The West Pole* is a portrait taken by Native writer and photographer Thomas King in which Glancy, in a black T-shirt and dark jeans, stands looking directly at the camera, with a stark white cowboy hat and a black Lone Ranger mask at her side, directly addressing the politics of (in)visibility (see fig. 5). Both her body and the hat are cropped slightly, creating proportions that challenge typical constructions of photographic portraiture. Rather than having her body and face centred within the photo, Glancy's image blurs towards the edges of the book jacket; her long hair and the left side of her body disappear and are cut off by the sepia-toned background and side of the book itself. Taken as part of a series of portraits by King, who wanted to explore cultural assumptions about the racial identity of the Lone Ranger by photographing various Native artists in relationship to the famous mask,[5] Glancy selected this as her cover photo because, as she explains, 'I had a look on my face that said I dare you. It was a defiant look I liked, and I'd had to find that attitude when I wrote the book … The cover gives you permission to read the book in the way it should be read' (Andrews 2002b, 656). Of course, Glancy's removal of the Lone Ranger mask and white cowboy hat, two icons of the white Lone Ranger, poses a challenge to audiences who think that they know what Native people look like. The image of Glancy unmasked becomes a means of reframing the negative associations that she has with photography as a method of concealing or masking one's real identity. In contrast with her mother's manipulation of her daughter's image throughout Glancy's childhood, an act that haunts the family photo album, the cover is about self-re-presentation.

Reframing the Family

In an essay titled 'Independent Identities,' art critic and activist Lucy Lippard argues that 'self-representation is crucial to the construction of independent identity (at least in western minds),' a comment that is relevant to all of the Native women poets explored in this chapter (1999, 134). Lippard brings another dimension to the notion that traditionally stylized photographs of Native peoples are, as mentioned earlier, 'both a pseudo-presence and a token of absence' (Sontag 1989, 16); she describes the photographic archives of unidentified Natives as being 'like ghosts deprived of a rest' (Lippard 1992, 15). But Renée Bergland cautions that 'when we focus on Indian ghosts, we risk forgetting the fact that many survived' (2000, 3). Kimberly Blaeser and Louise Halfe employ photography in their texts to foreground their own resistance

5 Taken by Native writer and photographer Thomas King, this image of
Diane Glancy is part of a project called the 'Medicine River Photographic
Expedition.' King travelled across North America in the early 1990s taking
portraits of Native writers and artists, all with the signature props of a
black Lone Ranger mask and a white cowboy hat. Glancy liked this
photograph so much that she asked King if it could be used as the cover for
The West Pole.

to the stasis of the 'postcard Indian,' while opting to include historical family photographs in a context that subverts their easy relegation to a silent past. And both complicate Lippard's negative reaction to the unidentified Natives in photo archives by refusing to label the images they use in their texts, a gesture that has slightly different meanings for each poet. These poets embrace their ghostly ancestors, drawing on images taken by family members, neighbours, and friends, to situate their existence and affirm their survival through the voices and images of the poets themselves. In contrast with Glancy, whose past is shaped fundamentally by denial, Blaeser and Halfe view the past as a source of power; photographs offer another point of access to the past and remind readers that Native people are alive and well, while also making those same readers work to understand the specific relevance of the images to their respective poetry collections.

Blaeser, for instance, includes a photographic collage at the beginning of her first book of poems, *Trailing You,* a series of black-and-white candid shots that are glued onto a piece of cardboard and replicated on the page that faces the title page of the collection (see fig. 6). The photographs span several generations of family, a set of connections that Blaeser celebrates in her 'Preface' where she states, 'No voice arises out of one person. I know that I write out of a place, a center that is greater than what I alone am or could be' (1994b, xi). The overlapping images offer a visual catalogue of some of those links between and among family members, but Blaeser is deliberate in her efforts to avoid objectifying her relatives or limiting the potential connections or points of contrast readers might find when looking at the photo collage. In a recent interview, she explains why there are no captions, names, or dates to identify those who appear in the collage: 'That was part of my intention, because I didn't want the photographs to represent a single, identifiable person' (Andrews 2007b, 4). Blaeser ensures that the images are 'not fixed in time' and instead peak readers' interest and imagination, asking them to look again, particularly because in some of the photos relatives of different generations closely resemble each other, making it hard to determine who is who (4); the result is that 'the images ... open a dialogue with the reader and [do] not merely foreclose an imaginative interaction between reader and text' (5).

Blaeser's playful approach to the bisociative juxtapositions created through the photo collage is reinforced by her description of why she selected particular photographs for inclusion in *Trailing You.* She stresses that she 'wanted to avoid including any of those classic static romantic

6 Untitled family photo collage, created from Blaeser's personal collection
of snapshots, for publication as the frontispiece of *Trailing You*, her first book
of poetry.

Indian poses; instead some of the photos I selected are kind of funny'
(5), a strategy designed to convey the humanity of her family and her
fond memories of them. The photographs depict couples picnicking
and dressed in their finery, and children playing with toys and posing
with parents and grandparents. In one shot, a toddler is perched on a
sheep, as if riding it, while a mother securely holds the child in place.
In another, a photo that Blaeser explains she selected because it was
'funny,' three children who are cousins are lined up in a row facing the
camera; while two hold dolls in front of them, the third holds Blaeser's
little brother, creating a moment of rollicking fun through the juxtaposition of animate and inanimate objects, toys, and babies (5).

Not only do the quotidian aspects of these images convey the fact that
the individuals in the photos are people with full and rich lives, but also,
by bringing together several generations, Blaeser rejects the notion that
Natives can or should be confined to the past – instead, by seizing on
what she describes as 'a ghost space' or 'spiritual space' in memory, she
brings the dynamic power of her ancestors to bear on her own understanding of self (2007b, 19). She uses humour positively in this context
to express her love for and appreciation of her relations. Blaeser was
raised on the White Earth Reservation; thus her poems, many of which
are highly personal and dedicated to family members and friends, become another way to pay tribute to the vitality of her tribal heritage and
its impact on her development. It seems fitting, then, that the only other
photograph in the collection is the author's photo on the back cover, an
image that is not attributed to a specific photographer; the image shows
a happily smiling Blaeser in a pose that once again does not conform to
that of the stoic Native – she is alive and well, as the image attests, and
is proud of her family's ability to not only survive but thrive. The 'ghost
spaces' of memory, evoked by the photographs and the poems, become
productive rather than destructive, suggesting that (in)visibility, when
mediated by this Anishnaabe woman, encourages readers to engage
their imaginations and recognize the existence of Native peoples in the
past and the present, as well as into the future.

Louise Halfe, in contrast with Blaeser, offers a darkly ironic reworking
of her family tree in *Blue Marrow* through the incorporation of select
photographs into the text of this extended prose poem. *Blue Marrow* was
published first by McClelland and Stewart, a large and well-established
mainstream Canadian press, in 1998. In this edition, there are three
prominent images: the black-and-white formal oval-shaped portrait of
Halfe's great-great-grandparents, which appears on the cover of the collection (replicating the traditional model of the white western bourgeois

family); a casual unlabelled shot of family members, including Halfe herself as a small child, placed nine pages into the text; and, finally, a small author's photo on the back cover of the book, which, much like Blaeser's author photograph on the back of her latest collection, *Apprenticed to Justice*, shows Halfe gazing sideways. However, when the press decided not to produce another print run, Coteau Books, a small press located in Halfe's home province of Saskatchewan that had published her first collection, agreed to release a second, slightly altered edition of *Blue Marrow*. One of the notable changes to this edition is in the choice and form of the photographs that Halfe includes; as Halfe explains in the 'Acknowledgements' to the new edition, 'I was given an opportunity to revisit the text in a new way, and I am deeply appreciative of the vision that resulted from this' (2004, 101). The Couteau cover image splices a photograph of 'the author's grandmothers,' her father's mother and three sisters, with an image of the northern lights (iv) (see fig. 7). And the oval-shaped formal shot of Halfe's great-great-grandparents now appears inside the book, between the acknowledgments and the first page of the text, visually representing the focus of the collection: 'a Cree woman's' search for 'a past that is both personal and communal, remembered and imagined' through the 'stories her foremothers whisper, shout, and sing as their voices roll across the prairie' (Cook 2000, 85). Thus, her great-great-grandmother's stereotypical visage of stoic silence is framed by Halfe's dedication to her mother and grandmother on one side, and a prayer to the 'Voice Dancer,' the 'Guardian of Dreams and Visions,' on the other (2004, 1), the latter of which was absent from the earlier edition of *Blue Marrow*.

Halfe's direct invocation of the Cree Spirits on the first page of *Blue Marrow* is followed by a fragmented version of the well-known Christian hymn 'Glory Be to the Father,' which is also a new addition to the collection. In this case, however, the standard references to the Father, the Son, and the Holy Spirit are replaced by the Cree words for 'Mother Earth,' 'the Grandmother Keeper of the Sacred Legends,' and 'Dream Spirit,' as outlined in the book's Cree-English glossary (2004, 107, 108). Halfe reconfigures the Christian conversion tactics imposed on the Cree, in which the female power of Spirits (at least as depicted in *Blue Marrow*) was displaced by a singular male god. She brings renewed life to her great-great-grandparents' portrait by situating it between her textual efforts to embrace her Cree language and spiritual belief system and her visual invocation of her grandmothers on the front cover. Moreover, Halfe notes that the front cover also challenges white western notions of

7 The front cover of this second edition of *Blue Marrow*, created by Duncan Campbell for Coteau Books, combines a photograph of Halfe's 'grandmothers' (her father's mother and sisters) with a digital image of the northern lights.

family with a patriarch at the helm, explaining that 'it's [a picture of] my
father's mother and her three sisters so automatically they became my
grandmothers. They're not my great aunts as [the] mainstream would
perceive [them]. They're my grandmothers' (Andrews 2004a, 3). And
she continues this effort to reclaim her ghostly female ancestors' stories
and her role as a living descendant by including a different author photo
on the back page of the text, a shot of Halfe smiling and gazing directly
into the camera.

While the biographical note with the author photo is more detailed
in the second edition of Halfe's *Blue Marrow*, the other images within
the collection remain unlabelled, a deliberate and ironically charged
choice, which, as the poet explains in a recent interview, reflects the fact
that 'they [non-Native settlers and officials] wanted us nameless' (Andrews 2004a, 3). Her frustration with this historical tendency to not identify Native peoples by name leads Halfe to ask, 'Why should I provide
names when there is a litany of names that you guys figured out?' (3).
In *Trailing You*, Blaeser leaves her photographic subjects unidentified to
subvert time's linear progression and to engage her readers in a playful
guessing game. In contrast, Halfe expresses her anger at the imposition
of colonial names on her family tree in *Blue Marrow* by refusing to identify her ancestors in her own text, an ironic gesture that focuses attention
on the unsaid dimensions of her female Cree ancestors' lives, which she
reimagines throughout the collection. Yet Halfe's desire to avoid naming her foremothers in the photos is complicated in this new edition by
her insertion of a Cree glossary of terms with their English translations
at the back of the collection. Méira Cook notes that, unlike *Bear Bones
& Feathers*, which includes a neatly organized glossary of Cree terms,
there is no such aid for non-Cree speakers in the first edition of *Blue
Marrow*, 'an editorial choice that signals her acknowledgment that she is
not writing predominantly for a white English-speaking audience' (2000,
93). Although Halfe initially left out the glossary in *Blue Marrow* because
'as a voracious reader, when you are coming across French or Latin or
Greek nobody sits there and translates for you,' she was criticized for
this decision and decided, in order to expand her readership, that she
would include a glossary to aid those willing to do the work of looking
up words (Andrews 2004a, 1). Nonetheless, the absence of identifying
names and dates on the photographs in the latest edition of *Blue Marrow*
reminds readers that it is a collection that in many respects continues
to privilege those familiar with the Cree language, tribal traditions, and
history. For instance, Halfe's use of the image of her grandmothers that

is digitally juxtaposed with the beauty of the northern lights may be, for many readers, merely aesthetically pleasing, creating a sense of the power that these women possess even in death, as the women hover like ghosts in the sky above the nighttime horizon. But, as Linda Jaine and Louise Halfe explain in 'Traditional Cree Philosophy: Death, Bereavement, and Healing,' the Cree believe that 'the Northern Lights occur when the Spirits [of the dead] are dancing' (Halfe and Jaine 1989, 11); hence, Halfe's coupling of these two images takes on an added, culturally specific reference for those who are 'in the know' by reminding those readers of the significant roles that these women ghosts continue to play in the lives of their female Cree descendants.

Sontag makes the point that photos serve as 'richly informative deposits left in the wake of whatever emitted them, potent means for turning the tables on reality – for turning it into a shadow' (1989, 180). While Sontag here is talking about the ways in which photography challenges 'Plato's derogatory attitude toward images,' which he equates with 'shadows – transitory, minimally informative, immaterial, impotent co-presences of the real things' (179), her comments are especially relevant to Halfe, who employs her family photos ironically to make her foremothers less ghostly, and relegates those who do not acknowledge the potency of Native womens' voices and visions to the margins. In an untitled section that begins with the unlabelled photograph of Halfe as a child with her aunt, paternal grandparents, and father, her narrator explores the challenges of telling the story of her female ancestors by exploring the 'metaphoric dangers of weather and darkness' (Cook 2000, 89). By repeatedly employing the punning phrase 'My Cree-ing alone in the heavy arm of snow' (2004, 15), Halfe's speaker combines a direct invocation of the Cree language with the historical lamentation of her foremothers who have had to struggle to survive against the destructive racism of white missionaries, traders, and settlers, and anticipates bleakly, 'I won't have to live / in whiteouts much longer' (16). Cook explains that the 'image of the blizzard as "whiteout" cogently evokes the plight of the narrator at her window, alienated as she is by the prospect of living in a world of white values, coldness, and lack of vision' (2000, 89). Not surprisingly, then, the cover of the new edition of Blue Marrow combines a burst of colour with dramatic contrasts between the black typeface and white background to visually anticipate the narrator's longing for a different perspective on the world.

Halfe celebrates the 'vision' that she has gained in revising Blue Marrow in her 'Acknowledgements' to the second edition (2004, 101). The choice of photographs in this new edition gives the collection an ironic edge, especially through the visual impact of the cover image, which bathes the black-and-white photos of her grandmother and three aunts in a bright green light, and which suggests that their spirits are dancing in an effort to sustain their communication with the narrator and readers who may otherwise dismiss the potency of their shadows. In the opening page of the new edition, Halfe's poetic speaker reveals the sexism of the Roman Catholic Church practices that have been imposed upon her by rewriting a seminal hymn to show what is important to her: her links to her Cree foremothers. Halfe's collection traces the continued presence of her Cree grandmothers in the lives of their female descendants through the narrator's childhood 'crumbs of memory' and the imaginative force she derives from chewing at the bones of her grandmothers, literally and figuratively sucking at the marrow in an effort to hear and convey their stories (8). Halfe's use of the term 'marrow' in her title is an ironic invocation of the Cree's traditional practice of using buffalo bone marrow to create a highly nutritious and portable powder base for pemmican, which consisted of marrow, buffalo tallow, and berries; the narrator of *Blue Marrow* attempts to fill her need for a storied past by drawing on the riches of her foremothers' bones. And by fleshing out the narrative experiences behind the photographs, and the reality behind those shadows through her own combination of the Cree and English languages, Halfe ensures that their lives and their impact on subsequent generations are acknowledged and celebrated even through the recognition of their exploitation and suffering.

'Ghosted'

In contrast with Halfe's multiple images, Marilyn Dumont, who is of Cree/Métis ancestry and grew up off-reservation in rural Alberta, frames her first collection of poems, titled *A Really Good Brown Girl*, with a single carefully chosen family photograph. Dumont's poems recall the hardships of being dark-skinned and having to live a 'dual life' in which 'I had white friends and I had Indian friends and the two never mixed and that was normal' (1996, 15). The photograph, which appears on the left-hand side across from the title page, attests to the complexities of that liminal stance. Labelled 'Photo of author with her mother, Calgary, c. 1962,' the image is juxtaposed with the book's title, a loaded phrase that Dumont's poetic 'I' uses at the end of a poem called 'Memoirs of a

Really Good Brown Girl,' to mock an English professor's attempt to alter her speech patterns:

> I am in a university classroom, an English professor corrects my spoken English in front of the class. I say, 'really good.' He says, 'you mean, really well, don't you?'. I glare at him and say emphatically, 'No, I mean really good.' (15)

Dumont's choices of photograph and title page become ironically layered symbols of the historical challenges faced by the 'really good brown girl' on the streets of Calgary with her mother circa 1962, whose ghostly white face and hands and large body protectively shield the young child from harm (1996, 2). Notably it is Dumont who looks right at the camera while her mother turns her gaze away by looking into the distance, creating a palpable tension between bodily presence and emotional absence within the photo itself (see fig. 8). In a recent interview, Dumont explained that the picture was acquired from a city street photographer who peddled the shots he took of strangers: 'I think the picture really illustrated for me, more just in the physical relationship, how large my mother looked and how small I looked. It gave the sense that she was there protecting me and how innocent I look and how vulnerable to shame we are as children' (Andrews 2004b, 148). For Dumont, the photograph also reveals her childhood naivety about her brown skin, and specifically the fact that racism is not merely an individual problem, but rather 'the majority of it is just to do with the world we live in' (148), though as a child she tended to internalize and blame herself for that feeling of difference. Indeed, in the image Dumont's legs dissolve into the white background, suggesting that she too appears – and sees herself – as ghostly by virtue of her dark skin.

In *A Really Good Brown Girl*, the photograph that opens the collection becomes a tangible trace of past memories that is only fleshed out when put into poetic form; Dumont's mother died around the time when the book was published, and thus the picture and text become an active tribute to her presence – despite her physical absence. The title Dumont gives to the image becomes a way of talking to her mother's ghost, while also acknowledging the inadequacy of such a dialogue. Her text raises fundamental questions about how one defines or identifies a ghost, by suggesting that skin colour and gender are an integral part of the politics of ghosting. As well, by placing a photograph of her mother at the

Photo of author with her mother, Calgary, c. 1962.

8 This photograph appears at the beginning of Dumont's *A Really Good Brown Girl* and is from the author's personal archive.

beginning of *A Really Good Brown Girl,* Dumont challenges the 'spectral' violence that is integral to culturally hegemonic models of Native families (Emberley 2007, 12) and interrogates the naturalization of the white western bourgeois family unit, which usually locates a patriarch at its centre. Here, the relationship between mother and daughter is of primary concern, as both the subject of the photograph and Dumont's textual commentary.

However, 'ghosted,' from Dumont's second collection, *green girl dreams Mountains,* shifts the focus from her mother to her father by exploring her father's increasing (in)visibility as an 'Indian man' (2001, 34). Ghosts may make the dead visible, but they also can erase the living, an idea that Dumont explores through her poetic portrait of her father. Located near the conclusion of a section aptly called 'Homeground,' in which poems such as 'not Dick & Jane' emphasize the bleakness of the speaker's childhood in an ironic fashion by invoking the 1950s white brother and sister duo used in easy readers, 'ghosted' tells the story of 'a father who hid in a manly bottle, and / a mother who kept one eye on him / and the other on her suitcase' (28). The poem itself begins with the image of a 'liquor-grin' that turns the speaker's father into a caricature on 'the skid row streets' he frequents when away from his manual labour job and out for a night of fun (33). The narrator then describes the father's elaborate preparations for these weekend adventures and his wife's ambivalence about his binge drinking, which she understands is a reaction to his frustrations at 'the whiteman who is always boss / at his own cheap labour / at the money that never goes far enough':

> but this Saturday night he's clean-shaven
> having crouched over the washbasin and
> leaned his face into a small mirror
> as one would into a kiss
> to trim his mustache. (33)

Dumont's speaker is especially attentive here to the ways in which self-perception and visibility are altered once the father figure leaves the private domain of the household. Whatever self-love is suggested by the act of crouching 'over the washbasin' and leaning into 'a small mirror / as one would into a kiss' (33) to ensure the perfect shave and a handsome profile is undercut by the reality of the father's daily life, which is one of second-class citizenry. Moreover, the speaker makes it very clear that the visibility of the father within the household – even as an irritant to his wife – is trumped by the racism and resulting invisibility that he faces on the job, which he tries to forget with alcohol:

> so he drinks
> 'til he doesn't remember
> 'til his new shirt drips from his belt
> 'til his grin folds cast-iron bitter …
> 'til his spirit is sucked from his eyes. (34)

This paradox of (in)visibility has devastating results as the speaker's father is

> taken again
> ghosted away
> from the one who is my father
> into a stranger, into an Indian
> staggering down the street. (34)

By describing the shift from familiar family figure to Native stranger and ghost, the poetic 'I' makes plain how the father's increased visibility on the street erases her own private vision of him, sober, 'as the one who is my father' (34); thus perception and point of view become critical factors in determining who is visible and whether that visibility is indeed beneficial to the individual and his or her community. But the speaker's own invisibility, her lack of visual presence in the text, and her paradoxical control of the written words on the page, make her far more powerful than her father, exposing the dangers of presuming that to be seen is to be heard. Instead, her poem demonstrates that visibility needs to be used strategically, rather than destructively, as is the case with her father, who has become consumed by an image over which he has no control.

Glancy, Blaeser, Halfe, and Dumont recognize the problems with simply presuming that exposure will change one's social, political, economic, and racial status. By combining select photographs with poetry in their collections, these four poets create intricately layered conversations about the benefits and drawbacks of being (in)visible. In their works, they rely on the photographs of relatives and ancestors, the memories of their families, and the legacies that they leave in order to carve out new kinds of (in)visibility that are politically relevant and specific to the needs of individual writers, providing words and images that reflect the complexities of their lives and histories as they continue to be told and retold. Each writer's vision is fundamentally shaped by her own efforts at self-representation, and varies depending on the poet's relationship to her tribal community (or lack thereof) and the influence of her immediate family on her during her formative years. While Blaeser happily embraces her memories of growing up on the White Earth Reservation and uses the photographic collage in *Trailing You* to convey her feelings of joy towards her family and community, Halfe, Glancy, and Dumont urge readers to pay attention to the unsaid, ironic aspects of their childhoods, which provide clues to their own ambivalent struggles around the issues of identity and community. Halfe makes her foremothers visible by listening to the Cree Spirits; Glancy counters her mother's denial of her Aboriginal heritage; and Dumont explores the contradictory nature of ghosts – as figures that make the dead visible and, in the case of her father, consign the living to a ghostly existence. In doing so, they urge readers to think differently about how and what we see and read, and to attend to the 'ghost space[s]' of memory in ways that recognize and celebrate the textual power of spirits, and the rich but often paradoxical legacy they offer to these women poets.

chapter five

Space, Place, Land, and the
Meaning(s) of Home

this land is
my tongue my eyes my mouth

Marilyn Dumont, A Really Good Brown Girl

Indians are everywhere. On reservation and off, cross-border,
Boundary-unbound. Neither fences nor reservations can confine us.

Paula Gunn Allen, Off the Reservation

As the epigraphs from Dumont and Gunn Allen suggest, land is central
to Native identity whether one lives on reservation or is a second- or
third-generation city dweller. And the long history of Native dispossession continues to have devastating effects. Jace Weaver explains in *That
the People Might Live* that 'when Natives are removed from their traditional lands, they are robbed of more than territory; they are deprived
of numinous landscapes that are central to their faith and their identity'
(1997, 38). The land and body are intricately connected, particularly
through language. Likewise, the need for a place to call home is crucial
for the Native women poets in this book. Yet many of these women travel
extensively to sustain their writing careers, taking up fellowships, writer-
in-residence positions, and teaching posts all over North America and beyond. Most have either moved permanently off-reserve to improve their
access to employment or were raised in urban areas with limited links to
a rural tribal community. This chapter engages with these apparent contradictions between life and desire by suggesting that the complexities of
these women's varied relationships to land – and by implication their engagement with the interconnected concepts of space, place, and home

– are explored, in many cases, through the use of humour and irony.[1] As Gunn Allen defiantly states in *Off the Reservation*, 'Neither fences nor reservations can confine us' (1998, 7). Her irreverent treatment of the colonization of Native peoples in Canada and the United States, and her refusal to acquiesce to the white western desire to corral and marginalize Native populations, are representative of the sophisticated and witty strategies employed by the women poets examined here to reclaim their native lands on their own terms.

Since the European Enlightenment, white western civilization has regarded space, in the words of Michel Foucault, as 'the dead, the fixed, the un dialectical, the immobile' (1980, 149). Yet the dynamic dimensions of space are being revitalized by selected feminist geographers and cultural critics (including Doreen Massey and bell hooks), who regard space and place as sites of multiplicity and mobility that shape and are shaped by social relations. In her groundbreaking book *Space, Place, and Gender*, Massey, for instance, persuasively argues that because time has been so privileged by westerners, with its masculine coding and close alignment with history and civilization, the reconfiguration of space (and, in turn, place) and the increased mobility of women pose serious threats to a settled (meaning white, male, Christian) patriarchal order. Massey also explores what she identifies as the culturally masculine emphasis on place – 'a portion of space occupied by a person or thing'[2] – as bounded and thus defensively constructed to articulate a particular notion of identity. Yet traditional definitions of space may refer to both the delineation of an area and a 'continuous, unbounded or unlimited extension in every direction,'[3] especially when used in an astrological context. Thus, Massey urges readers to look at space and even place as 'multiple, shifting, [and] possibly unbounded' (1994, 7), an anti-essentialist stance that recognizes difference 'and yet can simultaneously emphasize the bases for potential solidarity' (8). But Massey is rightly cautious about the celebratory dimensions of such flexibility, noting that though colonized peoples can conceive of space and place in an anti-colonialist fashion, the reality of their circumstances may require using the colonizer's definition of these terms. For instance, for those Native peoples whose lands were taken from them, efforts to pursue land claims often mean employing, for the purposes of recovery, the white western understanding of space and place as objects to be owned, traded, and exploited for economic gain, whether or not they share such a vision.

As a radical black feminist trying to make recent critical theory relevant specifically 'to black folks,' bell hooks takes a different approach, stressing the importance of what she calls 'homeplace,' a private space of community and a site of resistance 'where we do not directly encounter white racist aggression' (1990, 23, 47). She couples the nurturing space of the family dwelling with the concept of location, suggesting the inherent value of acknowledging the contexts that shape the creation of individual people, specifically the black working-class women whom she writes about. The commitment hooks shows to changing the daily lives of those who are oppressed by their circumstances leads her to the 'margin,' a real and imagined space that she embraces for its oppositional possibilities: 'Spaces can tell stories and unfold histories. Spaces can be interrupted, appropriated, and transformed through artistic literary practices' (152). The oppositional creativity hooks invests in the margin may be appealing to those Natives who were born off-reserve or lack tribal status; the margin becomes a site of resistance from which, hooks contends, 'we recover ourselves, where we move in solidarity to erase the category colonized/colonizer' (152). And hooks makes a clear distinction between the margin she creates and that which is imposed upon her: 'We are transformed, individually, collectively, as we make radical creative space which affirms and sustains our subjectivity, which gives us a new location from which to articulate our sense of the world' (153). Yet Gerald McMaster notes that for many Native people, reserves are homeplaces that embody the heart of the tribal community, and thus travelling to them does 'not mean a return to the margins, but rather a return to the center' (1995, 80-1). This configuration of the reserve as centre reconfigures hooks's argument and negates the normative white urban assumption that the reserve is marginal.

Certainly, the efforts of feminist geographers and cultural critics like Massey and hooks to subvert the white western privileging of place over space is relevant to the poetry of contemporary Native women, some of whom critique such Eurocentric definitions. The female writers explored in this chapter – Jeannette Armstrong, Kimberly Blaeser, Marilyn Dumont, and Joy Harjo – bring their individual perspectives to the fore by combining innovative depictions of urban and rural Native women with Native-centred ideas about space, place, home, and identity that emerge from experiences of dispossession, relocation, and the establishment of reservations in the United States and reserves in Canada. Regardless of viewpoint, these poets unanimously regard homeland as precious, and as critical in determining one's understanding of reality. Further, as Gail Guthrie Valaskasis notes, 'Until Indians were relegated to reservations, "home" was often a territory, not a fixed site, and houses were portable'

(2005, 111). Such mobility varied from tribe to tribe, but regardless of its patterns of settlement, the physical location(s) of the population shaped its sense of identity. Sacred tribal stories emerged from a community's long-standing relation to place, typically explaining the creation of the local physical landscape and the appearance and development of its inhabitants. Land became both a general and specific cultural construct, as 'an expanse of territory in which the collective identity and practice of a respective nation or community is rooted' and a place that 'locates the ideology, identity, and practice of personal spirituality and collective memory' (103).

However, with the ongoing legacy of colonization, how contemporary Native women writers portray their relationship to land 'becomes [especially] complex' (2005, 103). In the case of some poets, including Armstrong and Blaeser, 'Indian Reserves' are spaces and places that signify their ancestral and childhood home, centres to which they can return from after their travels or during holidays to be reunited with their community; for others, like Dumont and Baker, who were born and raised in cities with little or no contact with their tribe, ties to land are based less on the specifics of a single geographic location and more on the flexibility of the concept of 'Indian Country,' which Valaskasis explains is 'recognized by Indians as a place that gathers Native North Americans together, wherever,' with 'a shared sense of cultural and historical experience' and a consciousness of 'living in a good way,' in 'physical, social, and spiritual health and harmony' (103). And writers such as Harjo create their own even larger poetic maps of the world, as they embrace legacies of enforced and chosen mobility. Harjo, for instance, constructs a personal, tribal, 'pan-tribal,' and ultimately 'spiritual' geography of her life (and those of her ancestors) that covers various regions within and beyond the United States, including Oklahoma, where she was born, Alabama, the original locale of the Creek people before the Indian Removal Act, and the Southwest, where she spent decades studying, teaching, and writing (Womack 1999, 231, 53). Valaskasis notes that, 'even in the ambiguous borderlands of urban and reservation experience, Native people express a primary attachment to the land and not to the nation-state' (2005, 122). This is not surprising given how the American and Canadian governments have treated Native efforts to retain and regain even small portions of their homelands, turning to measures that have often divided Native populations – such as blood quantum and status – in order to determine the so-called legitimacy of these claims. Hence, the seeming contradiction between the movement through space and the stability of a homeplace is subverted in the poetry of these women who focus on *their* relationships to land, recognizing that one journeys '*with* the land and not [merely] on it' regardless of what boundaries have been erected (111, emphasis added).

Our Home and Native Land

The opening line of the Canadian national anthem – 'O Canada! Our home and native land!' – seems especially appropriate to demarcate a section devoted to the complex and often contradictory meanings of home and land for three contemporary Native women poets whose tribes have struggled for recognition within and, in some cases, across the borders of the forty-ninth parallel: Jeannette Armstrong (Okanagan), Kimberly Blaeser (Anishinaabe), and Marilyn Dumont (Métis). 'Our home and native land!' presents a façade of inclusion that belies the historical slippage between the claiming of Native-occupied lands, the erasure of Native people's prior existence, and the creation of homesteads for the colonizers who came to the New World in search of prosperity; in other words, whose 'home' and whose 'native lands' are being celebrated, given the ongoing dispossession of much of the Native population of Canada and the United States?

Armstrong has authored an essay called 'Land Speaking,' in which she explains the powerful connection for her people between land, language, and home: '… language was given to us by the land we live within … the land constantly speaks … Not to learn its language is to die' (1998, 175–6). In an effort to illustrate this claim, she cites the Okanagan term '*Tmixw*' (loosely translated into English as 'grandmother'), which means 'something like loving-ancestor-land-spirit,' bringing together the various strands of her argument in a single word that enacts the very relationship she describes (176). But Armstrong does not make this assertion for herself alone. She notes that 'all Indigenous peoples' languages are generated by a precise geography and arise from it' (176). The fact that the Armstrong has been raised on reserve lands and taught her Okanagan language from childhood distinguishes her from the other women poets surveyed in this chapter. Her emphasis on listening to the land rather than objectifying it accords with geographer Yi-Fu Tuan's argument that sound is intricately connected to distance and movement through space. He contends that 'sound itself can evoke spatial impressions,' dramatizing 'spatial experience' in a manner that goes beyond the visual (1977, 15–16). This is especially fitting in the case of the Okanagan people, who, as Armstrong has argued in an interview with Kim Anderson, do not share the West Coast tribes' emphasis 'on visual arts' because of their migratory patterns: 'With the interior tribes, because of the semi-migratory lifestyles, it is difficult to take the art form with you, unless you carry it around in your mind. You [therefore] carry it around in the way you use sound, language, and the way you create image-making with sound in language' (1997, 54). Sound and language thus become primary tools for describing one's place in the world. The ability to listen to the land and the stories it tells and to conceive of a 'home and Native land,' despite dispossession and removal, involves working against what Jonathan Smith calls the 'aestheticized landscape of nostalgia' (1993, 78) that relegates Natives and their homeland to the realm of the past and silences their voices.

Armstrong's 1991 collection, *Breath Tracks*, engages with space and place as an Okanagan woman whose identity is intricately tied to where she lives and works. Seeing, hearing, and relaying the stories of the land is central to her life as a poet. While much of Armstrong's collection consists of landscape poems that may be read as descriptive and evocative rather than provocative, a reading that attends to the ways in which she employs irony sees these poems more politically as destabilizing white western renderings of landscape and presenting her dynamic voice and vision of her tribal home. Armstrong's own analysis of her work suggests the appropriateness of such an approach, because her writing addresses both Native and non-Native readers. She tries to deconstruct dominant stereotypes and provide her non-Native audiences with information while engaging with her own Okanagan community, 'writing with a purpose' that she describes as 'double-edged' (Anderson 1997, 51), and meta-textually mirroring the structure of irony. In *Breath Tracks*, Armstrong actively listens to the land and cultivates the spaces where, as Linda Hutcheon puts it, 'irony "happens"' (1994, 12), by exploring the relationship between the said and the unsaid, or the implied aspects of the places she explores.

The discussion of space in Armstrong's poetry is not entirely new – Stephen Morton describes the notion of 'rhetorical space' in *Breath Tracks*, arguing that her work 'negotiates the tension between the constraints of western print culture and poetics and the need to articulate the as-yet-unrealized experiences, agencies and cultural practices of First Nations communities' (1999, 27). Looking specifically at the limitations of post-colonial theories in relation to second-language use, Morton notes that Armstrong's often inclusive treatment of her readers in her poetry is complicated by the reality that employing English in her texts may endanger the 'semantic space' of Native people, and their opportunity to write in a language that fully and appropriately articulates 'their everyday lives and cultural practices' (30). Certainly such readings are invaluable and provide a basis for the approach I take here; my intention is to add to and extend Morton's work by thinking about two aspects of Armstrong's poetry with respect to space, place, land, and home. The first aspect is her representation of what landscapes and homelands mean to her speakers, as conveyed particularly through ironic juxtapositions; and the second is how such reconfigurations of space challenge western paradigms, especially the tendency to value place over space. Textual space in her collection becomes a metaphor for actual space, with the land that Armstrong depicts possessing the history, memory, and future of her people. The semantic and rhetorical spaces that she claims in *Breath Tracks* are an important part of Armstrong's efforts, through poetry, to tangibly regain the lands that have been taken from her people by providing alternate understandings of space, land, and home.

In 'The Lie That Blinds: Destabilizing the Text of Landscape,' cultural geographer Jonathan Smith examines how traditional Eurocentric landscape paintings typically provide the (male) spectator with 'the pleasures of distance and detachment and the personal inconsequence of all that they survey' (1993, 78). According to Smith, these paintings cultivate a voyeuristic relationship between the male viewer and the object of his gaze that has been critiqued by white feminist theorists such as Laura Mulvey and Griselda Pollock as invariably depicting the women and land as passive and ripe for exploitation (78). The nineteenth-century settlers' treatment of Okanagan lands in many ways parallels the dynamics between viewer and object outlined by Smith. Peter Carstens, author of *The Queen's People: A Study of Hegemony, Coercion, and Accommodation among the Okanagan of Canada*, notes, 'The Indian Act defines a reserve as a tract or tracts of land that have been set apart by Her Majesty for the use and benefit of a band' (1991, 67). The assignment of Okanagan reserves from 1858 onward typically involved marking off small parcels of land that tribe members used for only part of the year; authority for such designations was ultimately traced back to the colonial (later the federal) government and British crown, neither of whom were present for possible negotiation. And the settlers in British Columbia were quite comfortable pre-empting and illegally occupying Okanagan lands for economic gain, while the Okanagan people had no recourse for protection. Clearing the land, in this context, had two meanings for the colonial government and new settlers: 'It implie[d] ways of moving or resettling, and then dominating native peoples, as much as it suggest[ed] clearing bush and forest, and building towns, roads and railways' (55). As Smith explains, the land becomes an 'empty sign,' a space devoid of voice or vitality and evacuated of historical experience, becoming instead merely an object of aesthetic pleasure, meant for 'visual consumption' (1993, 86). But, as Leslie Marmon Silko argues in 'Interior and Exterior Landscapes' (included in *Yellow Woman*), the English-language term 'landscape' directs the settlers' performance: '"A portion of territory that the eye can comprehend in a single view" doesn't correctly describe the relationship between the human being and his or her surroundings' (1996, 27). Such a presumption of separation ignores the fact that 'viewers are as much a part of the landscape as the boulders they stand on' (27). Such a refusal to divide people from place not only highlights differences in perspective, but it also explains why for Natives, who see their land as shaping their identity and history, the politics of landscape are unavoidable and have pragmatic consequences. As Smith suggests, 'the unequal allocation of space which the landscape fixes both expresses and creates a more significant inequality,' namely, access to privacy, which, as he notes, is familiar ground to 'anyone who lives in a shoddy apartment building or tenement [and] knows when their neighbour uses the toilet, showers, copulates, argues or weeps through the night' (1993, 84). This is vividly depicted in the poetry of Marilyn Dumont (especially 'The White Judges'), which is explored later in this chapter. Dumont's texts explore the plight of those who have no place to call home as a result of colonization, a situation that Armstrong subverts (at least metaphorically) by reclaiming the vastness of her tribal homelands through the rich descriptions of space and the generous layout of her poems on the page.

Certainly the presumption that occupying and owning lots of 'cleared' land is desirable is rooted in western notions of capitalism. Nancy J. Turner argues in *The Earth's Blanket*, a study of Aboriginal ecological knowledge and practices, that 'real wealth ... is found among people who have a sound sense of their place in the world, who link their thoughts and actions with those of others and who are strong, vigorous and co-operative actors in their communities and eco-systems' (2005, 24); she deliberately contrasts a Native recognition of the vitality of an untamed land with European settlers, who 'were focused on their own vision of what this landscape should and could be,' based on their memories of their homeland (28). The need to destabilize easily framed and contained ideas of landscape is critical to Armstrong's project (and those of the other writers in this chapter) precisely because Armstrong is unwilling to regard the land of her community as devoid of its own history and voice. Hence, even the opening poems of Armstrong's *Breath Tracks* look to 'the landscape of Grandmother' – the title of the first section – to create concrete poetry that plays with the space on the page and establishes an oral mode of discourse in conversation with previous generations. Her invocation of the landscape of grandmother, I suggest, foregrounds the same principles that Doréen Massey uses to rethink space in feminist terms, by treating it as, in the words of Jennifer Kelly, 'a site of the construction of identity and as a process of reclamation,' which 'empowers a range of multiple transitional subjectivities and hails ... diverse voices ... enabling collective identification and marking individual difference' (1991, 113). And even the land, always invoked with its definite article in *Breath Tracks*, foregrounds both the uniqueness of the place Armstrong describes and the vitality of each inhabitant's interactions with the land as a subject in its own right. Most of the poems in 'the landscape of Grandmother' bring fundamental aspects of the natural world to life, including glaciers, wind, wings, light, butterflies, and the flow of blood (1991, 8). Several texts visually and aurally replicate the characteristics of the natural world being described; blood literally 'courses' across the page, weaving from side to side, and butterflies flutter by with the colours of their wings randomly scattered as if seen in flight (16, 14).

The primacy of the visual layout of *Breath Tracks*, however, is complicated by the need to listen to what these elements in nature can teach readers. Diane Glancy states in *In-Between Places*, 'I pick up stones or rocks in travel as texts that I can read,' emphasizing the link between land and story (2005a, i). Armstrong's similar focus on the world around her contains a crucial difference: she is able to write about the Okanagan homeland she still resides on, unlike Glancy, who has never resided on Cherokee lands. In 'Rocks,' for example, Armstrong gradually deconstructs the notion that her speaker should merely be a detached observer of the rocky landscape; the 'I' in the poem initially 'study[s] ..., scan[s] ..., and ponder[s]' the rocks and pebbles, veins of minerals, and semi-precious stones which appear, at least at first, to be easily manipulated, whether serving as ceremonial talismans, moved and blasted to make way for trains, melted down to create coins, or even mounted in jewellery settings (1991, 21). But the close links between the land and recent political events across Canada, including the standoff at Oka and the Lil'wat peoples' efforts to hold onto their burial grounds and pictograph sites despite the blasting efforts of timber companies,[4] turn rocks into diverse sources of historical and contemporary knowledge about Native people's struggles to retain their lands. Such efforts to resist multinational pillage are reflected by a shift in perspective as the 'rocks / strewn into the distance' are displaced 'in the foreground' by the 'rock pillared bridges [which] collapse under the groan of earths rock' (24). Notably, Armstrong's speaker leaves out the apostrophe that would signify the earth's possession of its rocks. This deliberate grammatical omission recognizes the impossibility of truly owning natural resources, despite the efforts of settlers to build a nation by turning 'ores liquefied / ... into ploughs / into swords / into moulds / polished into bullion / minted into coins' and to construct garrisons and train tracks which blatantly violate the landscape and displace its occupants (22).

By the end of the poem, Armstrong's speaker promises to 'study the rocks' differently (1991, 24), a commitment that has already been put into action. The speaker has arranged some of the rocks in the shape of 'a circle / opening to the east / on this mountaintop' (24). The gesture provides a model for how one ought to behave towards the landscape. The rocks form a circle, according with Armstrong's interest in this shape as representative of life processes. The positioning of the circle also highlights the importance of the East (as one of the four cardinal directions) to her speaker's understanding of the world. In turning towards the place where the sun rises, the circle anticipates a new beginning, one that is potentially inclusive and participatory if those who live on and study the landscape actually listen to the stories it tells and learn from them, as the poem's speaker demonstrates. This poem models possible altern(arr)atives to white western stories in which the land is merely an object to be possessed and controlled. It draws attention to the race and class privilege which leads to the unthinking domination of the natural world as well as the colonial inheritance that underpins this sentiment. The speaker in 'Rocks' performs her relationship to the land by moving the rocks, which, in turn, suggests the impossibility of fixing or claiming the land as settlers have tried to do. With the movement of the rocks comes the promise of stories about the past, present, and future, narratives that resist such objectification and yet also portray the challenges facing the Okanagan people in their efforts to maintain a homeplace despite the power of their connection to this land.

Armstrong reinforces the link between listening, speaking, and the survival of the land in ironic terms in several other poems in *Breath Tracks*, stressing repeatedly the need to reject a detached view of the natural world in favour of a more organic approach, one that is infused with

extensive wordplay and provocative imagery achieved primarily through
run-on lines. In 'Keepers Words,' 'the grandmother' is an integral part
of the landscape. Armstrong's speaker begins with the alliterative phrase
'makers are mockers,' which sets a darkly humorous tone with the overlap of sound and consequent slippage of meaning. She describes the
folly of European men who come to the New World presuming that they
can alter the landscape and leave their mark through the creation of
new words and 'sound songs' (1991, 91, 92). The speaker presents a vivid
picture of this white western arrogance:

> On this earth
> lives a cannibal monster
> who devours himself
> because he changes so much
> as he grows
> that he forgets what his tail looks like. (91)

The self-destructive narcissism of the monster is juxtaposed with the
grandmother's longevity and protective instincts:

> I'll be around she said
> soon after death lunges forward
> out of the rabble
> I will stand on a hilltop ...
> and my shadow will stretch
> long and narrow over the earth curve
> to seep into the little shadows
> even now
> skipping behind you. (91)

Despite being 'a [lone] black dot against blazing red,' the grandmother's shadow – and the 'sacred words' she whispers – are far more powerful than the monster's reach, as long as the grandmother's advice is
heard and understood (92). Looking, in this context, is deceptive. The
cannibal monster would appear to be the inevitable winner, based on
size and appearance, but using language properly ensures that 'what is
sacred' will remain and that 'forget[ting]' will not take 'its place' (91).
By resisting change and acknowledging her role as one of the 'keepers,'
the grandmother can guarantee the survival of her land and community
(91). As Armstrong's poetic voice reiterates at the conclusion: 'nothing

is new only changed / there are no men who are makers / just changers'
(92). The layout of these lines and extra spaces between words on the
page guide the breath of the readers and draws their attention to the fact
that 'new' is not as it as seems – it is 'only changed' (92). The appearance
of the poem on the page thus contributes to its ironic edginess and darkly tinged wit. The audacity of non-Native men who presume that they can
'make' the world is revealed as false; they do nothing more than make
changes to what already exists. Conversely, to be a female word-maker,
woven into the earth in life and death, is a point of pride and a means
of protection for future generations from such egotism. The slippage
between 'changers' and 'makers' and the space between 'new' and 'only'
serves as a reminder that landscapes are not spaces to be manipulated
and massaged into an ideal vision but rather partners in a life circle. This
is a concept that Armstrong elaborates on even more forcefully in some
of the later poems from the same section of *Breath Tracks*, which deal with
the subjects of creation and home.

Stoh:lo writer and activist Lee Maracle describes the fundamental
links between space and home in the preface to *My Home As I Remember*,
pointing out that 'stone is the foundation of the beginnings of the natural world. From stone springs all of our songs, our aspirations ... [and]
home is our first stone' (2000, i). For Maracle and Armstrong, space is
equated with home, in contrast with white western notions of home as
a place that is clearly bounded. Travelling through the land provides a
source of guidance and ongoing education for Native peoples – such
as Armstrong and Glancy – that is passed from generation to generation, and cannot be contained or quantified by the nation-state or the
church (regardless of what the Canadian national anthem claims). Maracle also stresses that home is a place 'of origin, the shell of nurturance,
... and [because it] is the domain of women ... it shapes our govern-
ance of the way we engage the world and shape our relationship to it'
(i). For Armstrong, space is dynamic and made meaningful through the
respectful interaction of land, people, and language. In the final poem
of *Breath Tracks*, called 'Untitled,' her speaker describes this natural dy-
namism (which contrasts the imposed attempts of white 'makers'): 'all
things right / yet all things change endlessly ... / there are tracks of
things / and the snow is disturbed / by the feet passing / and the land
changes again' (1991, 111). The 'breath tracks' of Armstrong's collection are themselves ironically charged, as they mark the historical yearly
movement of the Okanagan from place to place alongside the prints of
the animals they hunted; the title also alludes to the poems that create

tracks – in this case, words – across the pages of the text, and assert the
continued existence and survival of Armstrong's community. Whatever
fixity a white western viewer might seek in her landscape is subverted
from beginning to end, as we are shown that we are part of that space.
The fundamental values of Armstrong's people (acquired through her
knowledge as an Elder) are in turn offered up in the form of tracks that
traverse this space, continuing far beyond the covers of her poetry collection, teaching readers to think about land, space, and home differently.

(An)Other Absentee Indian

Jeannette Armstrong's treatment of home is unique among the writers
surveyed in this chapter. To be an ongoing resident on tribal lands is difficult if not impossible for many people, including Kimberly Blaeser, who
is distanced because of her chosen academic career. To be away from
home, here meaning one's birthplace, is particularly difficult for Blaeser, whose tight-knit upbringing and strong sense of tribal community
are constantly tested by the reality of being absent for much of the year.
The movement off-reservation to cities, which was precipitated at least in
the United States by 'relocation' programs of the 1950s, was part of an
integration policy that led to the majority of Natives living off-reserve.
Donald Fixico notes the paradox of this policy in the United States for
American Indians: '... they discovered that other people, immigrants
from Europe and various parts of the world, were like them in finding
new homes in American cities, but ironically this country was their native
home' (2000, 3). This phenomenon of displacement also resulted in a
shift from reserve communalism to foreign individualism and the rise of
a 'generic "Indian" identity' for those who did make the move and either
lost touch with their tribal roots, or simply had to find a community for
themselves within the urban setting (3).

   Blaeser self-reflexively examines the challenges of such a change
through the figure of the 'Absentee Indian' in her second and third
collections, offering yet another set of perspectives on space and place
that are based on her own boundary-crossing situation. For her, humour
and irony become crucial strategies for voicing unspoken feelings about
moving between and among urban and rural settings, the academic institution and reserve life, and the impact of these elements on her and her
family. Because she works in a university setting, it is not surprising that
Blaeser sees the language play that is integral to humour as also essential
to her poetry: 'It's ... another way of ... taking it [the poetry] out of the

solitary state' (Andrews 2007b, 7). At the same time, the 'more out-there humour,' which is evident in several of her poems about absence from the reserve, enables Blaeser to 'get a good laugh. But then I undercut that with a moment or a line that's very serious. Then the serious ... may startle a little bit more' (7, 7-8). Blaeser locates her speakers in a multitude of places and embraces this diversity, even when mocking her own absences and craving a sense of centredness. In 'Absentee Indians,' for instance, the poetic 'I' contemplates past assumptions about visitors to the reservation:

> Used to think they were white.
> Big cars,
> neat little
> quiet
> scrubbed-looking kids
> in matching tennis ...
>
> Back for a memory
> a fix if they could find it ...
> Old Man Blues ...
>
> Ain't no cure for it but home. (2002, 3)

The alien qualities of these misidentified 'foreigners,' who stand out in their desperate attempts to soak up the ambiance of home, is soon displaced by the narrator's own over-scheduled and inevitably brief visits from the city; likewise, the memories of mocking 'a city Indian' who brings his children from California to 'learn about their heritage' – 'We used to laugh / when he said heritage / like every book on Indians / instead of people or tribe or life' – are undercut by the stark reality that the speaker is now faced with the same dilemma: 'Ain't hardly laughing now' (4). The poignancy of what happens when life circumstances change is explored further on the facing page, with 'Twelve Steps to Ward Off Homesickness,' a poem title that has been already anticipated in 'Absentee Indians' when the speaker makes fun of the visitors' efforts to quantify and therefore better remember reserve traditions:

> Hoarding remainders
> things never meant to be counted
> like prayer breaths.

> some sequence of recall
> *twelve steps*
> to ward off homesickness. (4)

In a parodic homage to the twelve-step program of Alcoholics Anonymous, 'Twelve Steps to Ward Off Homesickness' describes a variety of so-called 'Native reservation' behaviours, including smoking, drinking beer first thing in the morning, driving a beat-up car, 'scattering machine parts around your lawn,' letting dogs loose to wander the property uncontrolled, and eating oatmeal and bacon for breakfast, eggs for lunch, and macaroni and canned tomatoes for dinner, for five days in a row (2002, 5). The absurdity of these actions, which both mimic and mock clichéd ideas about impoverished living on Native reserves, are tinged with a darker edge, as Blaeser's narrator interjects more disconcerting steps into the mix. The fourth stanza instructs readers to 'look in the mirror and say "Damn Indian" until you get it right' but insists that one should 'stop only when you remember the voice of every law officer that ever chanted those words,' a sentence that vividly invokes memories of all of the unreported instances of racist police officers who abuse their power and Natives who have resisted fighting back in order to get out alive (5). Likewise, Stanza XI, which follows the instructions provided by a 'call home to find out how all the relatives are getting along,' asks Native readers to 'recite the names of all the suicided Indians' (6). The friendly reminder is darkened by the knowledge that the relatives could have killed themselves. In other words, the desire to have a homeland, which is so elegantly and eloquently celebrated in Armstrong's work, is shown by Blaeser in 'Twelve Steps' to be an enormously vexed notion. The irony of Blaeser's poem lies in the depth of the pull to a place that in many ways is described as unhealthy; even in this, there is something life-giving, at least for those individuals who live off-reservation. As Eva Gruber notes, in this poem Blaeser portrays 'a caring community,' which – despite its shortcomings – may be 'the only home many Native people experience' (203). In a final ironic turn, the speaker of 'Twelve Steps' suggests exactly that: 'If all else fails, move back' (6). The suggestion, though initially amusing in its subversion of the whole point of the twelve-step system to recover from a disease, becomes disturbing when put side by side with the poem that follows, titled 'Recite the Names of All the Suicided Indians' (7), once again setting up a pattern of invocation and repetition between texts that highlights the need to attend to the ironic resonances of their individual and collective meanings, especially when the destruction of a community is at stake.

Home Is Downwind

The daughter of a German father and an Anishinaabe mother, Blaeser grew up in Mahonmen, Minnesota, located on the White Earth Reserve, while her dad worked in construction in Billings, Montana, for part of the year. This familial fragmentation, combined with living on the reserve, has led to a collective and flexible understanding of home:

> I suppose I had a strange childhood in a way, at least according to what was typical in the big world, the white world. We lived in many different places – not in the sense of being a transient, but really feeling at home. We spent summers in Montana, where my dad worked on construction part of the year. But we also spent a lot of time on the farm with my grandma and grandpa, where lots of other people might be staying at different times, or we spent time with relatives in Nay-tah-waush or Twin Lakes. It wasn't a big deal. We really did feel at home in all these places. For example, no one knocked on your doors; you just went on in because it was your home too in a way. (Vannote 1999, 4)

In contrast with Armstrong, who equates space with home, Blaeser identifies a multiplicity of places as home. However, Blaeser, like Armstrong, rejects white western notions of place as bounded or constrained. Blaeser's childhood experience of moving freely between and among homes conveys her community's desire to share their space and, hence, to define 'place' differently. The power of place, or in this case places, is affirmed by Blaeser when she discusses the inspiration for her poetry, stating, 'I know I write out of a place, a center, that is greater than what I alone am or could be. My work is filled with the voices of other people' (1994b, 1). Blaeser feels a fundamental responsibility towards her family, community, and ancestors because they have given her a strong sense of identity and the confidence to do whatever she wants. At the same time, she is acutely aware of the challenges involved for those who must leave the reservation for school or work, as she has done.

Blaeser has chosen to live a fair distance outside of downtown Milwaukee, where she teaches, and resides in the rural township of Lyon, Wisconsin, on a property that has both wetlands and woodlands much like the landscape of White Earth prior to its exploitation by lumber companies. Even though she spends most of the year away from White Earth, Blaeser contends that we all 'develop a landscape of sound that informs our verbalization, our vocabulary, and our poetic vision' (2001, 3). The experience of place creates an individual orality that is specific, and as with Armstrong's experience of space, the sound and power of words maintain the meaning of place despite her physical absence. To articulate the 'insane reality of being a mixed-blood' and her complex relationship to her homeland and place more broadly, Blaeser draws on her community's 'wonderfully ironic sense of humor,' a tool that enables her to address the joy and sadness of her family's experiences and to invite 'the reader to participate' in the process of playing with language (Andrews 2007b, 7). When describing the importance of humour to life at White Earth, she turns to spatial metaphors that reinforce the centrality of place to her writing: 'that many of the exchanges between relatives and in everyday settings are so filled with humor and playfulness ... I think that might be the *grounding* for it' (Andrews 2002a, 15; emphasis added). And her poetry itself, which draws on many different voices and sources of inspiration, enables her to cross 'boundaries of time and space, of ways of knowing, of what it means to be human ... my writing becomes an act that re-creates me' (Blaeser 1994b, xi). Blaeser's boundary-busting poetic perspective and interest in conveying the connections that land embodies reflect a constant negotiation between absent longing for the particularity of place and her efforts to remember its riches, which will ensure the recovery and the survival of both her tribal community and the land that she calls home.

In all three of her poetry collections, Blaeser devotes considerable textual space to the impact of dispossession on Native Americans: she explores the loss of traditional Anishinaabe lands, the subsequent creation of reservations, and the challenges of forced migration for a contemporary Native woman writer and academic. Although much of her work is inspired by her own life, Blaeser is careful about what she presents to readers because 'part of what I do as a writer is healing other people as well as myself' (Vannote 1999, 6). Moreover, she has repeatedly noted that as a child she learned to protect her Native identity from the world of 'the white community,' to keep them separate, and she has continued to do so even as she becomes more comfortable about moving between the reservation and her home in Lyons. As Blaeser explains, 'My perspective shifts almost the moment I return to this place [White Earth],' and while initially her husband would not recognize her voice when she was at the reservation, she has now found 'a voice that sort of goes with me wherever I am – but maybe not completely' (7). It is this movement between and among the places where she resides and the desire to find her multiple selves that form the basis for much of Blaeser's treatment of land, place, and home.

Like Jeannette Armstrong, Blaeser examines through irony the link between the domination of land and of the people who reside on it. For example, in her earliest collection, *Trailing You*, the first-person speaker of 'Downwinders' notes the slippage between American assertions of democracy for all and the reality for those who are located 'downwind' and thus on the receiving end of this deadly colonization under the guise of progress. 'Downwinders' historically has referred to those who are affected by nuclear testing due to their location, literally 'downwind' of the explosion site and thus vulnerable to serious health problems as a result of their exposure to nuclear fallout; these populations were not made aware of the dangers of their location, and were treated by those conducting the tests as readily expendable for the greater good of public security. But Blaeser expands this definition of downwinders, as the speaker draws parallels between the experimental dental treatments provided on reservations, the post-Second World War nuclear testing done on the Bikini Island Atoll by the U.S. government, the poisoning of female factory workers as a result of long-term exposure to radium, and the sustained exploitation of Native Americans that included forcibly removing them from their lands, confining them to reserves, and subsequently mining the natural resources of those reserves to the point of destruction. Blaeser's first-person speaker begins by recalling the words of another; however, the legitimacy of what is said soon becomes the object of scrutiny:

> I heard you say 'We all live downwind and downstream'
> and that sounded right and even profound,
> Only later when I learned that some of us had been selected for fallout,
> designated downwinders,
> it reminded me of the other profound saying
> about how in this land of equal rights and equal justice
> 'Some of us are more equal than others.' (1994b, 54)

In these initial lines, the narrator juxtaposes the seemingly logical presumption that everyone, in some way, is 'downwind and downstream' with the reality of a selective and much more malicious agenda. Emma LaRocque has argued that endeavours that put Indigenous peoples 'in their place' can be best understood as acts of 'intellectual genocide against contemporary Native people' (1984, 3). LaRocque's critique is directed primarily at those who insist on the static nature of Indigenous cultures in an effort to justify their destruction. Yet both LaRocque and Blaeser emphasize the differences between Native and white western definitions of place. For Native peoples, when artificial boundaries are imposed on land, with no regard for the people who live there, the desire to hold onto a homeplace can be a death sentence. Blaeser's poem literalizes this possibility when her narrator describes the mental and physical suffering of the Bikini natives who served as 'guinea pigs' in the name of colonial expansion (1994b, 54).

The vivid images presented in 'Downwinders' of the bodies and land that have been 'ruptured and contaminated' in combination with lists of atrocities couched in military terms – 'remnants chosen for test sites, weapons plants, nuclear burial' – make for a poem that is deliberately cumulative in its effect on readers (54). By placing an individual narrative about experiments in failed dental pain management on a Native-American reservation just before an account of the Bikini natives who were slowly poisoned by 'radioactive materials,' Blaeser demonstrates the pervasiveness of the assumption that Native people are merely 'guinea pigs' across space and time (54). Similar to Wendy Rose's 'Halfbreed Chronicles,' in which Rose forges imagined communities between women across the globe to challenge white western versions of history, Blaeser draws on a broad range of exploited populations to rethink how both people and land are viewed as mere commodities. By juxtaposing an array of examples of land abuse, in conjunction with the impact on its residents, the poem refuses to let the unsaid remain unacknowledged. Even the 'homeland' and 'family' of the speaker, 'whose lives are not fashioned in concrete and plastic' and who share the bounty of their designated reservation, are vulnerable to 'poisoning' through the contamination of their food sources in yet another instance of disrespect for the natural world (55). White Earth, too, has undergone sustained environmental degradation through 'lumber companies' destructive practices, state control of swamp lands, and state game laws' that led to the acquisition of large areas of land by non-Natives who promptly fenced them in and erected 'No Trespassing' signs, eventually destroying much of the tribe's ability to sustain itself through farming and hunting (Meyer 1994, 219). In recent years, testing conducted on tribal-area lakes has revealed mercury and heavy metal contamination of the fish populations as a result of 'coal-fire power plants and incinerators often located hundreds of miles away' (LaDuke 1999, 129) – yet another kind of downwind poisoning.

However, in a final ironic twist, Blaeser turns away from the speaker's homeland to the urban landscape of early twentieth-century America and the plight of working-class women in watch factories, such as the Elgin Watch Company (located in a Chicago suburb), where they were systematically poisoned by 'licking the tips of their brushes / as they painted the radium dials of clocks' (1994b, 55). These women, later known as the 'Radium Girls,' unknowingly 'poisoned the tongues they needed to speak' with the radium salts that were contained in the paints used for the timepieces (55); even after the dangers of radium had been recognized – based on the cancerous growths in the female workers' mouths that had been repeatedly misdiagnosed as syphilis – watch companies continued to deny the potential hazards of sustained exposure to and consumption of radium even in small quantities. Public pressure eventually led to the settlement of lawsuits on behalf of a number of the poisoned women.[5] Yet the compensation they received – much like the process of land allotments among Native North Americans – did not reflect the price they paid for their exposure, which was usually death.

While the plight of these women may seem to be an odd point of comparison, the narrator's imaginative rendering of the Radium Girls resonates with the issues of space and place raised earlier in 'Downwinders.' Certainly, the Radium Girls can be read as an example of the slippage between the colonization and exploitation of land and women's bodies as a site of literal devaluation through their imprinting by radium. In *Gender, Identity and Place: Understanding Feminist Geographies*, Linda McDowell argues that the 'body' needs to be treated as a 'place, the location or site, if you like, of the individual' and suggests that bodies may even be usefully understood as maps (1999, 34). This idea reflects the reciprocal relationship between the body and its environment, which 'produce each other' (Grosz 1992, 242). The female body as land is anticipated early in Blaeser's poem, when she describes how the land allotments given to 'the Indian people' were 'ripped open in searches for its gold heart, / its copper bosom, / its coal black eyes' (1994b, 55). Given Armstrong's emphasis on listening to the land and hearing its stories, Blaeser's choice of the Radium Girls (in conjunction with her rendering of Native reserve lands as physically assaulted women) seems especially appropriate because the poem portrays the literal and figurative silencing of those 'women' who are deemed as worthy of 'fallout' (54). The contamination of the Radium Girls had a particularly disturbing result: the loss of speech due to jaw and tongue cancers. In 'Downwinders,' the place of their bodies is poisoned in the colonial pursuit of space. Yet the absence of their voices is made present through the ironic juxtaposition of their stories with those of other exploited populations. Blaeser's poem suggests that the same destructive attitudes about place that led to the confinement of Native populations and enabled military and scientific experiments to be conducted are those that poison the bodies of young white working-class women. Such acts of colonization are a lasting reminder of the need for all potentially marginalized populations to resist white western efforts to define space and place and home as sites of domination. Instead, Blaeser's poetry works to reclaim place through its relationship to home. The physical boundaries of the White Earth Reservation are enforced by the American government, but the sacredness of the place where Blaeser grew up remains central to her identity and that of her community: it is a place that cannot be taken away.

This Land Is Not/Just

Blaeser and Armstrong both retain close links to their tribal homeland, but for Marilyn Dumont, as a Métis woman, such ties do not exist. Born in Alberta, near the Indian reserves at Hobbema and Morley, Dumont – a descendant of Gabriel Dumont – was identified as Native by locals as a child but had no official status. Nor was she raised to speak a Native language; though her parents spoke Cree during her childhood, Dumont only learned the language as an adult. Historically, the Métis in western Canada (descendants of European fur traders and Cree women) faced dispossession and were ostracized by non-Natives and even status Natives because of their mixed-blood heritage. Conflicts between status Natives, non-status Natives, and the Métis are ongoing. Métis demands for hunting and fishing rights, recovery of their homelands, and access to government funds are perceived as threatening the federal government's preferential treatment of status Natives. The historical desire for a Métis nation (led by Louis Riel) was seen as antagonistic to the project of British colonization in Canada and led to the long-standing marginalization of the Métis peoples and their rights up to the signing of the Canadian Constitution in 1982, which finally acknowledged them as part of the Aboriginal peoples of Canada. However, despite that official recognition, physical reparation for the removal of the Métis from their lands across Canada remains unresolved. As Olive Dickason explains, in the late nineteenth century, 'after all the confrontations over land, when it came to making a choice between cash in hand or an acreage, the overwhelming majority of Métis chose the money' (1997, 290). Because the land was often too marginal for farming and in places remote from land offices, selling their land scrip for cash seemed to be the best deal; however, that often meant that the Métis were given far less money for their land than they should have been. Dickason explains that 'fortunes were made at the expense of the Métis – "half-breed scrip millionaires," in the parlance of the time' (290). Dumont's childhood was spent in 'logging camps, where … [her] parents worked,' and later, 'a small southern Alberta farming community,' and she has spent her adulthood living in cities across Canada, working as a teacher and taking up writer-in-residence positions (1993, 46). It is this sense of profound dispossession and, paradoxically, a strong family unit headed by women who 'had to find other ways of being able to say something without alienating themselves,' often through humour and irony, that have shaped Dumont's changing poetic voice and ideas about identity and a homeplace or lack thereof (Andrews 2004b, 155).

Dumont is acutely aware of her ambivalent relationship to land and her struggles to find a homeplace. As she explains in a groundbreaking essay, 'Popular Images of Nativeness,' the 'experience of the urban native' is virtually absent from popular images of Indians despite the reality, as she puts it, that 'sixty percent of Alberta's native population now lives in urban centres' (1993, 48). Although now close to twenty years old, Dumont's essay remains timely precisely because she raises fundamental questions about domination, representation, and authenticity in the case of urban Natives like herself: 'This prevalent 19th Century notion of [Aboriginal] culture as static which is founded on the belief that there exists in the evolution of cultures, a pristine culture which if it responds to change is no longer pure, and therefore, eroding and vanishing affects our collective "self-images" as either: pure – *too Indian* or diluted – *not Indian enough*' (48). Instead of being held hostage by 'internal colonialism,' Dumont insists on writing from 'my experience as an urban native' (49). Yet despite the distinctiveness with which she asserts her difference from that of 'some natives in isolated communities [who] are still committed to the land in meaningful ways' (49), Dumont in her first collection, *A Really Good Brown Girl*, presents what she has subsequently described 'as a nostalgic sense about land and about nature' (Andrews 2004b, 157). More specifically, when drawing on her own childhood in her poetry, she both takes up and undermines the images of landscape as pristine, contained, and ready for consumption – as she explicitly depicts – by the white male gaze.

The opening poem in *A Really Good Brown Girl*, titled 'The White Judges,' foregrounds how a family of nine Aboriginal children and their parents, living in poverty in a converted schoolhouse, are regarded by the local (white) community. Narrated by the children, the poem recounts their relative lack of privacy and the sense of being constantly watched by white neighbours, who leave boxes of used clothes on the porch and seem to observe their every move. In contrast with Jeannette Armstrong's attention to tribal space in *Breath Tracks*, Dumont here stresses the limited space available to her poetic Métis family, an inequality that mirrors the history of the Métis people as non-status in Canada; this makes the children acutely aware that they are regarded by the local white population as objects rather than subjects, to be observed and judged for their heathen ways. As a result, the children seek privacy for themselves – away from the eyes of the white judges – when opening the unsolicited boxes of donated clothing:

> Or waited until cardboard boxes
> were anonymously dropped at our door, spilling with clothes
> waited till we ran swiftly away from the windows and the doors
> to the farthest room for fear of being seen. (1996, 11)

Likewise, they lament their own 'white' traits, 'for having heard or spoken / that which sits at the edge of our light side / that which comes but we wished it hadn't' (12). The arrival of 'settlement' relatives who visit for several months of the year but do not live full-time under the surveillance of the local community is another reminder of how this Métis family is forcibly confined to their home, with no chance of reprieve from their neighbours' watchful eyes (12). Dumont's poem can be read as suggesting that the nurturance and protection that Blaeser associates with her home community, although White Earth's physical perimeters are externally imposed by state and federal governments, are not readily available to those Native communities that lack status as legitimate Native tribes. As a result, Dumont's speaker is made to feel constantly inferior.

This internalized colonialism is given a more ironic spin in subsequent poems, including the title poem, 'Memoirs of a Really Good Brown Girl,' and 'The Halfbreed Parade,' which directly follow 'The White Judges.' In 'Memoirs,' the female Métis speaker recalls how she kept her white friends and 'Indian friends' geographically separated because of the institutionalized racism of the playground:

I lived a dual life; I had white friends and I had Indian friends and the two
never mixed and that was normal. I lived on a street with white kids, so they
were my friends after school. During school I played with the Indian kids.
(1996, 15)

And in 'The Halfbreed Parade,' the poetic 'I' describes her father taking
the nine children into town:

> a parade of snotty-nosed, home-haircut, patched halfbreeds ...
> The only thing missing was a mariachi band
> and a crowd of pilgrims stretching
> miles down the gravel road
> which offered passage to our grand mansion
> of clapboard. So magnificent. (16)

Using extensive line enjambment and an ironic tone, Dumont subverts
the shame associated with the family's home by ridiculing the absurdity
of the whole situation, including 'the mystery of white judges / who sat
encircling our two storey schoolhouse,' and are present without justification (16), and the participants in the so-called parade whose residence
and appearance are circus-like by virtue of their perceived marginality
or otherness.

In 'Circle the Wagons,' which appears near the end of *A Very Good
Brown Girl*, in a section titled 'White Noise,' Dumont uses irony and biting wit to explore some of the broader assumptions made about all Native peoples – Métis or not – including the significance of the circle as
shape and symbol in Native texts. The phrase 'circle the wagons,' which
frames the poem by operating as both the title of the text and its last
line, recalls the historical custom of bringing horse-pulled wagons into a
circle when stopping to rest overnight while travelling or when attacked
in order to minimize injuries. To 'circle the wagons' also describes the
tendency to pull into or stick with one's family and community, thereby
excluding others, just as the Métis have been excluded throughout Canadian history. Unlike Armstrong's use of the circle, which grounds her
speaker and represents the possibility of a more respectful relationship
with the natural world, in this poem, Dumont writes from the perspective of a sophisticated and cynical city-dweller who, as 'a fading urban
Indian caught in all the trappings of Doc Mar- / tens, cappuccinos and
foreign films,' feels trapped by the cliché of the circle and its seductive
appeal for non-Native readers, precisely because it is not part of the nar-

rator's world: 'There it is again, the circle, that goddamned circle, as if we thought / in circles, judged things on the merit of their circularity // ... Are my eyes circles yet?' (1996, 57). Dumont also uses an accretion of long-standing stereotypes about both what Native people consume – 'bologna ... bannock, [and ...] Tetley tea' and what constitutes their dominant cultural symbols – 'so many times "we / are" the circle, the medicine wheel, the moon, the womb, and / sacred hoops' (57) – to express in humorously pointed terms the difficulty urban Native writers face in trying to thwart such expectations, particularly when white western scholars have come to recognize and value such markers in Native texts. Here the speaker's frustration with the presumption that Native writing has such uniformity is no longer unsaid but instead explicitly stated, but with a twist, because as the poetic 'I' ambivalently notes, 'Yet I feel compelled to incorporate something / circular into the text, plot, or narrative structure because if it's lin- / ear then that proves that I'm a ghost and that native culture really / has vanished' (57). Hence, the final lines of 'Circle the Wagons' become an ironically charged gloss on poems like 'The Halfbreed Parade,' in which 'the white judges / ... sat encircling our two storey schoolhouse,' a home that has been dragged into town on a skid by a team of horses, followed by a 'parade of ... halfbreeds / trailing behind it' (16). The linearity of this procession is conveyed through the image of the moving schoolhouse, a 'floating prairie structure' that travels through the landscape with its Native occupants right behind, defying the expectations of white community members, who then circle the home in an effort to control and contain the building and its inhabitants (16).

By writing this poem, Dumont depicts her own efforts to resist the imposition of circularity onto her work, even as she paradoxically admits later in the same text that it is often tempting to include circular motifs in her poetry to ensure that her work is not lost in the literary landscape. In the concluding lines of the poem, her speaker transforms the material dimensions of this circularity as manifested on land by launching it into the sky, where it appears to be 'orbiting, / ... encompassing your thoughts and canonizing mine, / there it is again, circle the wagons' (1996, 57). While the circle remains in the solar system, serving as a visual reminder in the sky of the clichés that circulate (all puns intended) about Native literary symbols, Dumont's speaker appears to reject its primacy. However, the poem itself enacts the challenge of eradicating this stereotypical conception of Native literature, with the poet falling prey once again to its seductiveness. The title, 'Circle the Wagons,' comes full circle when it appears as the final phrase of the poem. Dumont's text illustrates the impossibility of escaping or even reconfiguring such clichés, especially as a Métis woman who is struggling to locate her urban experiences and her community's individual beliefs and practices given its history of dispossession.

Thus it is surprising that Dumont, on occasion in this collection, does romanticize (with only a touch of irony) the power and significance of land and especially homeplace for her. For instance, in 'Not Just a Platform for My Dance,' the speaker passionately celebrates 'the land' as much more than 'just a place to set my house my car my fence' (1996, 46), creating a run-on line that resists reducing the land to property to be occupied, while also echoing linguistically the need for just(ice) to be done regarding questions of land claims, for all Native peoples. In this case, the land, as the poem outlines, becomes the body: 'this land is / my tongue my eyes my mouth' (46). Such reciprocal interaction with the land in this poem closely resembles Armstrong's texts. Yet Dumont is also someone who sees herself as fundamentally an urban dweller without a tribal homeplace to return to. Hence, in both *A Very Good Brown Girl* and her subsequent collection, *green girl dreams Mountains*, she devotes considerable textual space to the idea and reality of city living.

Dumont describes her shifting ideas about home, space, place, and land in an interview where she explains, 'At some point I realized that I'm never going to go back to that [a nostalgic sense of land and nature], and I don't want to because I like the city. I've now lived in the city probably close to twenty-five years of my life, and that's what I know' (Andrews 2004b, 157). For Dumont, to know the city is to wrestle with the fundamental challenges of locating oneself in spaces and places that can provide anonymity, diversity, and sophistication. But the city also may prove to be as inhospitable as the experience of living in a semi-rural community where one's race and the location and condition of one's house determine one's social status and consequent treatment by the local population or government institutions – much like the plight of the child who undergoes dental surgery on a reservation and the residents of the Bikini Island Atoll who have been exposed to radiation in Blaeser's 'Downwinders.' Dumont is an especially interesting case because she has moved frequently, and she finds herself embracing the notion of 'globalization' because it reflects her own experience, despite the potential peril it poses for those communities who do want to recover their lands (Andrews 2004b, 158). Dumont notes, 'I could go to several cities now in Canada, and I feel relatively at home because I've been there before.

I've walked the streets and I know people. I have friends there' (158); but this movement from city to city means that 'home becomes a much more nebulous place' (158). Dumont parallels Armstrong's position by re-creating tribal space through her urban migratory patterns. The result is a doubled – and, I will argue, ironic – self-positioning that reflects Dumont's own efforts to make sense of her complex relationship with space, place, home, and identity.

Dumont lacks a place to call home and instead must find this space for herself in the myriad cityscapes where she dwells. For example, in 'It Crosses My Mind,' a prose poem about the identity politics of urban Native people in *A Really Good Brown Girl*, Dumont's first-person speaker begins by asking where 'we fit in this "vertical mosaic," / this colour colony; the urban pariah, the displaced and surrendered / to apartment blocks, shopping malls, superstores and giant screens' (1996, 59). While I have already examined this poem in another context in chapter 3, here I am interested in how Dumont represents cities. She uses images of the city, combined with the rhetoric of inclusion that characterizes Canadian multiculturalism on paper, and the desire of the nation-state to name and claim its citizens for itself, in order to expose the ongoing colonization of the Métis and many other populations who are absorbed within and often silenced by the city. While the city may provide employment and the lure of an urban lifestyle replete with big-ticket items,[6] the poetic 'I' is troubled by the dominance of the nation-state in her job search. As a descendant of the Red River Métis who sought recognition for their distinct nation status from Canada and wanted to govern their own lands in the late nineteenth century, Dumont's poetic allusion to this history is pointedly ironic: if the speaker acknowledges herself to be a Canadian citizen, she surrenders her Métis identity; and if she refuses, she knows that the rhetoric of nationalism articulated in the italicized line of the Canadian national anthem she includes in the poem – *the true north strong and free* – is not one available to the Métis people. This ironic rubbing together of the said and unsaid leads to the speaker's lament for her growing distance from her ancestors as Métis descendants continue to intermarry, and to her critique of the provincial and federal governments' smug assertiveness that the land that was taken from the Métis need not be returned:

... will it matter that we call ourselves Metis, Metisse, Mixed blood or aboriginal, will sovereignty matter or will we just slide off the level playing field turned on its side while the provincial flags slap confidently before

me, echoing their self-absorbed anthem in the wind, and what is this game
we've played long enough, *finders keepers / losers weepers*, so how loud and
long can the losers weep ... (59)

Dumont's poem highlights the failure of multiple levels of government
in Canada to recognize Métis land claims and their inherent right to
self-government; the slippage between and among words enacts the
frustration that the speaker feels as a marginalized entity, whose status
remains perilous precisely because of the government's unfair sports-
manship. What should be an issue of justice and rights has become
nothing more than a case of childish bullying, as exemplified by Dumont's choice of the rhyme – '*finders / keepers / losers weepers*' – which
recalls the lack of justification given by the Canadian government and
its provincial counterparts for the Métis loss of land and governmental
independence (1996, 59). But Dumont's speaker is not about to simply weep at this situation. Rather, she ponders how to respond to the
question of 'Are you a Canadian citizen?' and reveals the inadequacy
of the choices offered: '*yes, by coercion, yes, but no ... / there's more*, but no
space provided ... / there are no lines for the stories between *yes and
no*' (59). It is the absence of these alterna(rra)tives that is made present
here in the space between 'yes' and 'no.' The poem refuses to merely
accept the checked boxes as adequate and instead speculates on the future of Métis women, whose mixed-blood ancestry has made them particular targets of government efforts at assimilation. As Gail Valaskakis
explains, the Métis may have been recognized as Native people in the
1982 Canadian Constitution, but the 'double-grandmother clause' remains, ensuring that two generations of marriage between a status and
non-status person will lead to the loss of Native identity (2005, 228).
The speaker thus rightly queries the fate of her 'eight-year-old-niece,'
who by marking the 'x' in the box that ensures her recognition by government systems is also undermining her tribal sense of self (Dumont
1996, 59). While the lure of an urban lifestyle and the challenges of
playing government games to her advantage are important to the speaker, the poem also creates its own textual space, encouraging an exploration of 'the stories between *yes* and *no*' and anticipating the possibility
of carving out some tangible geographical space in a cityscape that is
otherwise relatively hostile (59). She explores the possibility of finding a
homeland in the city in her next collection, *green girl dreams Mountains*,
where Dumont turns her attention to her Métis female speaker's experiences in one Canadian cityscape.

Linda McDowell argues that places are 'defined by the socio-spatial relations that intersect there and give a place its distinctive character' (1999, 4), much like a person. And as mentioned earlier in this chapter, Elizabeth Grosz makes a closer link between person and place, asserting that 'the body and its environment ... produce each other' (1992, 242). Though philosophically such an idea is extremely appealing, it is also problematic for someone like Dumont, who is acutely aware of the inherent racism and sexism of many urban power structures. As a result, the question of what constitutes an acceptable body within a cityscape remains central to Dumont's text. In particular, in the section of *green girl dreams Mountains* titled 'City View,' Dumont can be read as reconfiguring the traditionally white male gaze of the landscape viewer as theorized by Jonathan Smith to examine her own ambivalent relationship to Vancouver. Having moved to the city after spending a decade in Edmonton, Dumont explains that the poems deal with 'where I am and my connection or disconnection to it' (Andrews 2004b, 157). She is careful to note her familiarity and comfort in cities generally, noting, 'I've now lived in ... [them for] close to twenty-five years of my life and that's what I know,' but in the case of Vancouver, 'I think those poems really demonstrate how alienated and how foreign I felt there. It's a beautiful city, but I just don't feel any connection to it' (157). The poems of 'City View' examine some of the main arteries of downtown Vancouver, chosen because, in Dumont's words, they are 'boundaries of class and race' (157). Deeply ironic and occasionally darkly humorous in their commentary on this west-coast Canadian city, Dumont's poems explore the politics of urban space in relation to her mixed-blood identity, paying special attention to those 'unacceptable' bodies that litter, literally and figuratively, the streets of Vancouver. Located right on the Pacific Ocean and blessed with a generally mild climate compared to much of the rest of Canada, Vancouver has earned in recent years a reputation for being a beautiful but very expensive coastal centre; it is also known for its large homeless community and drug problems, prevalent in Vancouver's Eastside, which had once been a vital part of the city's early growth. Dumont uses street names, many of which honour politicians, as well as early settlers and benefactors of the city – predominantly white men – as titles for the ten poems in this series. Moreover, she writes the poems from a first-person perspective as she moves along each street in question, placing her bodily experiences and feelings at the centre of the text.

'City View' begins with a poem called 'Main & Hastings,' which immediately places the speaker at one of the most controversial and troubled corners in the bustling city. Known in recent years as the home of Canada's first safe injection site, Main and Hastings is the main corner of Eastside Vancouver. Now populated primarily by homeless people, drug users, beggars, and prostitutes, prior to the Second World War it was the centre of Vancouver, housing the public library and city hall in its vicinity. The area's economic deterioration came about with the increased gentrification of several neighbouring areas, which led to the sandwiching of these impoverished populations within a small radius in the downtown core. Several clean-up projects at the municipal and provincial levels have been launched in an effort to make the corner more appealing for tourists visiting the city for events like Expo '86 and the 2010 Winter Olympics; these attempts, however, have done little to address the challenges of life on the street, instead simply clearing the unacceptable bodies out of the area for the duration of the event.

For Dumont's speaker, the city adopts different personas depending on location; here, for example, her narrator begins by noting, 'I feel the city sweat / closeness and / the drift of urban indians / hot pavement, dried condoms, deals' (2001, 39). The stifling atmosphere, with its heat and dirt, is combined with the presence of Natives who, like Dumont, are urban dwellers and part of this 'tunnel of trade,' what Dumont calls the 'foreign exchange of / skin for paper / paper for pills or powder / paper for cloth, cloth for sex and sex for power' (39). The speaker, who takes city transit along with many other racial 'Others' – 'latinos, blacks / and asians' – through this intersection, wryly observes that 'everything here can be bought or exchanged / Some things cannot be refunded' (39). Dumont's poem reflects on the unsaid reality of an urban economy: life cannot be bought back. When this poem is read in relation to the previous section of *green girl dreams Mountains*, called 'homeground,' in which a young female narrator laments the pain and loneliness experienced by various family members because of their mixed-blood status, the final lines of 'Main & Hastings' become ironically charged. The ability to buy and sell 'everything,' including people's bodies, and the fact that 'some things cannot be refunded,' explain not only the 'drift of urban indians' who may have no home thanks to the loss of their ancestral lands, to Main and Hastings, but also the lure of drugs, prostitution, and money in an economy where being 'Other' can and does limit opportunities (39). As these urban dwellers get desperate and become willing to sell anything, they lose perspective on the consequences of the losses incurred, for which there is no adequate compensation.

The narrator reinforces the precariousness of her status in the city a number of times in the nine poems that follow by reflecting on the economic disparity between those who have and have not. For instance, in 'Powell' she observes homeless people digging through street litter while riding 'the dull-circuit / to my day-job,' and then contemplates her proximity to the 'two young, pierced, tattooed, and shivering skins' who are begging outside of the 'Cafe' where she drinks a coffee on 'the drive,' located at Grandview and Woodland, where the Canadian Pacific Railway site was set up in the 1880s (2001, 40-1). A later poem, titled 'the drive,' refers to Commercial Drive, a trendy and increasingly gentrified Vancouver neighbourhood of small businesses, restaurants, and residential homes. Here, the speaker presumes a collegiality with her servers at what she playfully calls 'Cafe-du-Because we know / we could be panning on the street in minus 10 Celsius ... / sitting a cardboard's thickness away from icy cement with / their CV's' (41). Using enjambment, Dumont's narrator mocks the café's French name, undercutting its pseudo-elegance with the pragmatism of the speaker's observations – here, the movement from coffee patron to homeless beggar is literally a few steps away. And on the next page, Dumont's speaker expands on her analysis of this class divide in a poem called 'Robson,' a street in Vancouver named after the premier of British Columbia from 1889 to 1892, which developed from a collection of small boutiques, delicatessens, and patisseries owned by European immigrants into the premiere shopping street in the city:

> wouldn't it be tidy to think that this city cop and royal-blue redhead sipping coffee beside me were at fault for the two thin 'streets' who scavenge nearby and wouldn't I be blameless if all it took to alter this divide were to dissuade the cop and the royal-blue redhead from buying two hundred thousand-dollar condos for the sake of the two thin bums who beg and fry on the concrete (42)

In the final lines of this poem, the narrator offers up a seemingly easy strategy for altering the growing divide between the rich and the poor in Vancouver. Dumont's narrator includes a series of ironic juxtapositions that implicate herself and anyone else who participates in this economy of consumption as responsible for the existence of an underclass, in this case, 'the two thin bums who beg and fry on / the concrete' (42). The relationship between land ownership, price inflation, and homelessness puts, if only momentarily, the burden of change on those who have the money to be consumers. Yet, the rhetorical questions in the form of speculations ('wouldn't it'), the line breaks ('if / all it took'), and unexpected pairing of the 'the cop and the / royal-blue redhead' as potential purchasers of expensive condominiums also keep readers guessing, for much of the poem, who and what exactly are being critiqued (42). Here, what is implied about the relationship between the police officer, the blue-blood redhead, and the two beggars becomes as significant as what is stated. But Dumont's efforts to alter the growing distance between the rich and the poor are thwarted by what the narrator continues to encounter in the rest of the 'City View' series.

Ultimately, Vancouver thrives on its class and race distinctions, as Dumont suggests throughout this section through her use of street names such as Powell and Oak. Powell Street, named in honour of a white doctor who was involved in establishing the first public school system in the city and who donated the land for the first city hall, was known as the home of the local Japanese-Canadian population from 1890 until 1942, when, interned by the Canadian government, most lost their properties. Likewise, Oak Street, though originally the site of the winter villages for the Musqueam and Squamish as well as the Tslei'wauthuth tribes, became the thoroughfare for a number of exclusive neighbourhoods which were deliberately priced high to keep out the working class. Not surprisingly, then, when the poet describes 'Oak' street, her speaker is located outside of the homes being observed, only able to see 'the light from small windows,' a limited view that leads to the imagining of an idealized family supper scene, complete with all of the accoutrements of class privilege, including table cloths and water glasses (2001, 45).

The 'City View' presented in the ten poems thus becomes an implicitly subversive record of the land's previous functions, and an account of the poet's often ambivalent interaction with a city that she perceives as both alienating and intoxicating. When exiting the 'last-call express' bus, filled with late-night drunken partiers, the speaker contemplates the fact that 'so many things lost in this city' are 'never found,' but also embraces the city streets as potentially liberating: 'The bus opens, air like my breath rushes in and I am safely released to the street again' (2001, 47). The concluding poem of the section, 'Broadway,' pays homage to a central thoroughfare of Vancouver built specifically to meet the needs of an expanding population and renamed after the New York City theatre district in 1911 to give the city a more sophisticated aura. In this poem, the body and the city merge; the body becomes a map of experiences that travels through time and space, being shaped by and in turn shaping what it encounters through careful observation of those who are not usually included in depictions of Vancouver: drug addicts, beggars, and street people, many of whom are Aboriginal. And rather than being consumed by it, lost in it, never to be found, Dumont's narrator displaces 'the received fixity of social and geographical location' (Smith 1993, 77) by imprinting it on her body in an act that makes her 'more city' than anything she has observed (Dumont 2001, 48). Her interest in unacceptable or marginalized bodies, including her own, continually inverts and displaces the idealized, framed, and contained landscape expected by the white male gaze, and here she fully claims this sprawling and inclusive vision of those who live in and experience the streets:

> I am now Hastings and Main, tattooed, pierced, shaved, and dyed; the rain and rhododendrons and the Lion's Gate Bridge; I am now the panhandlers, the junkies, the hookers, the homeless, all of them, the Vancouver city transit, crowded and crabby, 'the Drive' ... (48)

The catalogue of things and places, seasonal events, and communities that are included in the poem do not obviate either the narrator's struggle to deal with the economic disparity she observes, or the fact that she regards her own life as closer to those who are struggling to survive than the populations that move through the city without any thought of what their economic and social privilege affords them.

As Liz Bondi outlines in an essay titled 'Locating Identity Politics,' a focus on space often shifts concerns about 'Who am I?' to 'Where am I?' (1993, 98). Although Dumont, like many other Native people who have experienced forms of colonization, would not be willing to surrender her sense of Métis selfhood, Doreen Massey's call for a redefinition of place as multiple and shifting, particularly for women, is enacted in these poems, which ostensibly promise an objective view of the city but present a highly subjective and visceral account of her narrator's interactions with this urban landscape: 'I am too, the disquieted waters / of the Fraser, the factories and mills that fidget next to it; I am / the ferry line-ups, the plum tree blossoms in March, the green smoke over Abbotsford, the blueberries, humidity, three weeks of rain' (Dumont 2001, 48). 'City View' offers a personalized portrayal of various urban locations, formed, as Massey explains

> ... out of the particular set of social relations which interact at a particular location ... the specificity of the interactions which occur at that location (nowhere else does this precise mixture occur) and in part out of the fact

that the meeting of these social relations and that location (their partly happenstance juxtaposition) will in turn produce social effects. (1994, 167)

Put in the context of the collection, place becomes dynamic and provisional for Dumont. Vancouver may not be an appealing homeland for this frequently moving urban dweller, and yet by stressing the ways in which place, position, and location are created and produced, Dumont's narrator is able to creatively imagine herself in relation to these urban spaces and reflect on the politics of being Métis. Moreover, Dumont ultimately ensures that her ironic distance from Vancouver is conveyed even in 'Broadway.' The speaker's body in this concluding poem appears to be consumed by the city, with the 'grey sky on ...[her] raincoat,' but as someone who is landless she is able to shrug off the coat and move on (2001, 48). In 'City Views,' her body becomes a map of experiences that creates a provisional and flexible concept of what a homeplace might look like for those whose work demands constant movement between urban spaces and who have no reserve to return to.

Mapping the In-Between

Linda McDowell notes at the conclusion of *Gender, Identity and Place* that 'the in-between is itself a process or dynamic, not just a stage on the way to a formal identity' (1999, 215), a claim that resonates with not only the poetry of Dumont but also the work of Joy Harjo, who employs cartographic alterna(rra)tives, turning her body into a map to reflect on the historical displacement of the Muskogee people and forge a meaningful homeplace. Bill Ashcroft elaborates on the traditional functions of cartography in *Post-colonial Transformation*, explaining that 'the map *itself* in which names, numerous in some places and sparse in others, inscribe a pattern of knowing by metonymizing the act of seeing, establishes the authority of European consciousness and European desire to enter the "unknown"' (2001, 131). IIe describes the white obsession with the spatial representation of land, in order to secure its possession, and notes that 'colonial discourse [typically] turns "empty" space into inhabited "place" through the discourse of naming and mapping' (132). The shift from space to place in this context, as noted earlier in the chapter, depends upon the belief that there are no present inhabitants worthy of mention; and, indeed, it is a shift in name only, because what is paradoxical about colonial mapping is that these maps do precisely the opposite of what might be expected: they disengage the 'links between place and space' by not attending to the strong connections among language, identity, and place already established by the local populations (152).

As Harjo outlines in a footnote to the 'Songline of Dawn' in *A Map to the Next World*, '*songline* refers to the Australian Aboriginal concept of enforcing relationship[s] to the land, to each other, [and] to ancestors via the mapping of meaning with songs and narratives' (2000a, 226), an extensive and important practice for Native communities worldwide which undermines the white western separation of space and place. Certainly such a concept is not new to Native North Americans, or particularly to the women writers in this chapter. For instance, Jeannette Armstrong stresses the importance of perceiving the land as a physical space and a homeplace, which comes from an Okanagan tradition of carrying stories about land and identity with the tribe as they migrate. Both Kimberly Blaeser and Marilyn Dumont use their poetry to explore the power of place from the perspective of those who live at a distance from the tribal communities. Harjo also is interested in the links between space and place, arguing that 'the poet cannot be separated from place. Even placelessness becomes place' (2002, xxiii). She feels compelled as a poet to record her 'journey on this earth' and chooses to do so by adapting and subverting colonial cartographic practices in her creative work (xxiii):

> I always wished for a map to show the way. When we come into this world, from the other side of death, we mark our existence with a cry ... I fought and struggled and nearly killed both my mother and me. 'Where is the map?' I asked. I want to see the map, first. The church people told me it was the Bible. The historians said, look back and then you can look forward. The ceremonial songs sing that it is all around you. The poets tell me it is in the heart, where poetry is born and the place it enters when it is finished. This is all true. (xxviii)

In her poetry, Joy Harjo recalls her tribal history to remind readers that the '"empty" space' claimed by European explorers for themselves was already 'inhabited,' and employs her own life-journey to reconnect space and place without imposing a singular definitive vision of the world (Ashcroft 2001, 132).

Poetry, as Craig Womack explains, allows a unique freedom of movement in a condensed and associative space. When examining the texts of Joy Harjo, Womack argues that 'the dense, extremely pared-down language of poetry allows for more of an overlap and simultaneity, rather than a mere rearranging; it makes possible movements across boundaries within the same line' (1999, 250), a claim that is also true of many of the other poets already discussed in this chapter. What is unique to Harjo is the way in which she creates her own topography of identity by collapsing, in Womack's words, the 'constructed boundaries that separate time ... [and] space,' along with myth and personal experience (226). While Harjo's work is strongly rooted in Muskogee traditions, as Womack so convincingly argues, she is also part of the emergence of an urban pan-tribalism that has resulted from the shift in Native populations to cities and the increasing numbers of Native people who may not have reservation lands to call 'home' but want their tribal sovereignty to be acknowledged. As an acclaimed writer, anthologist, teacher, and singer, her livelihood (as is the case for so many of the women in this chapter) necessitates movement, often to and from various cities, a pattern that may be chosen but also resonates with the forced migration of her ancestors:

> My journey on this earth in this life is marked by a path of red earth that leads from the mounds at Ocmulgee in what is now known as Georgia, to The Battle of Horsehoe Bend site at a curve in the Talapoosa River, in now-Alabama, to the Mvskoke Creek Nation in now-Oklahoma,to the grounds of Indian school in now-New Mexico, and since that collection has taken me to the red earth of O'ahu. It makes a distinct path.It is the color of blood ... of life, of breath. (Harjo 2002, xxiii)

Harjo's poetry can be said similarly to track both the movement of her predecessors from Georgia to Oklahoma, and her own journeying from her childhood in Tulsa, Oklahoma, to her early adulthood as a young parent in the American Southwest while attending the Institute of American Indian Arts of Santa Fe and the University of New Mexico, to her life as a writer, teacher, and musician working in cities such as Denver and Albuquerque, which has then taken her to readings and concerts all over the world; as well as, most recently, her decision to move to Hawai'i after being held up at gunpoint in Los Angeles, where she had relocated in order to teach at UCLA. In particular, this last move, much like the experience of her ancestors, may be understood as a forced migration at violent hands, one that can be traced through her poetry. Harjo's 'itinerary,' as Laura Coltelli describes it, not only 'bears a deep identification with the land, a geography of the remembered earth,' but also takes into account the importance of the contemporary American city, which is often a site of 'indifference, hostility, social, and psychological alienation' for Native Americans (1996a, 5). In some respects, Harjo's responses to urban landscapes can be read as paralleling those of Marilyn Dumont, whose Vancouver series emphasizes her disconnectedness to, yet absorption of, the city streets in which she lives. However, Harjo brings to her understandings of space and place a love of car travel, an enthusiasm for riding in and driving vehicles that dates back to her childhood: 'It was a family joke that at the rattle of keys I would be in the backseat ready to go' (Stever 1996, 75). Like Glancy, whose passionate series of prose poems in *The West Pole* about her 'War Horse,' a brown Buick station wagon, celebrates the liberty of the open road and ironically debunks the clichéd notion that all Natives are warriors on horseback, Harjo outlines the importance and privilege of having a car, which 'represented independence, certain freedom, ensured that I could move' (76). Driving has enabled Harjo to 'move into the landscape' and experience the passage through space and place differently, from inside a vehicle that she controls. And in contrast with Dumont, she does have an ancestral homeland in Oklahoma (albeit one that was chosen by the U.S. government), even though, as she notes, 'I've never felt Oklahoma as my only home' (75); rather, she explains, 'I've had to learn that my home is within me. I can take it everywhere,' and she does (76). To do this, Harjo creates a series of maps of her world that encompass not only her experience of various cities and rural locations but also the movement between different locational worlds, particularly in *A Map to the Next World*.

When asked to describe the landscape of her poetry, Harjo explains, 'It's between a woman and all the places I've ever been,' a comment that highlights the importance of the in-between to her writing about land, space, and place (Bruchac 1987, 99). Like Silko, Harjo positions herself in the landscape rather than looking at it from the outside, an act that recognizes her intimate and strongly ethical notion of land as something that 'took me in ... fed me so much and fed me well' (Coltelli 1996a, 3), and thus deserves in turn to be respected and nurtured as a source of life and knowledge. Land is also a compelling source of history and memory, providing Harjo with the means to explore the past, present, and future of Native Americans, especially those who live in cities and may feel disconnected from their Indian identity. Her poetic rendering of these spaces and places through the body[7] suggests an approach to cartography that is fundamentally flexible and ultimately oriented at both ensuring Native survival and providing possible models for Native self-creation and re-creation. The danger, of course, is that such an engagement with the history of American colonization of Native peoples, in particular, the subjects of dispossession and land loss, may be extremely psychologically debilitating. To counter this, Harjo employs what she calls 'the laughter of absolute sanity' (Carabi 1996, 142). In an interview with Angels Carabi, Harjo outlines the role of humour in her work: 'I think that Indian people have one of the most developed senses of humors I've ever heard ... the laughter becomes a release ... Maybe laughter is the voice of sense ... you cannot take everything too seriously because it will kill you' (141-2). Yet Harjo also insists that 'I have to be aware of everything that is happening,' and uses the idea that 'poetry is a bridge over the sea of paradox with the sea ... [as] the [mixed] blood' to convey the contradictions inherent in her work, an ironic twist that gives her humour its edge (142, 134). To illustrate what she means, and how these strategies function as part of a larger cartographic project, I want to turn to two earlier poems – 'Anchorage' and 'Santa Fe' – which portray the experiences of urban Natives, and then consider *A Map to the Next World*, which deals more explicitly with the process and products of mapping.

In the closing stanzas of 'Anchorage,' a poem dedicated to Audre Lorde, the black lesbian poet and activist, and published in 'Survivors,' the first section of *She Had Some Horses* (1983), Harjo's narrator relays the seemingly unbelievable and painfully humorous story of Henry, a Native-American man serving time in an Alaskan jail where Harjo once taught a writing workshop. Her speaker has already described the experience of walking through the streets of Anchorage, a city made 'of stone, blood, and fish,' which is framed by the 'Chugatch Mountains to the east / and whale and seal to the west,' elements of the natural world that invoke the historical presence of the Inuit in the region, especially because the mountains are named after the Inuit who have lived there for centuries (1983, 14). Harjo's narrator also has devoted considerable textual space to the development of the physical geography of the city through glacier movement – 'ice ghosts ... / [that] swim backwards in time' – and the action of volcanoes, or the 'cooking earth' (14), descriptions that pointedly remind readers that Anchorage is constantly changing shape. And the speaker alludes as well to the Muskogee concept of the Upper World when locating Anchorage geographically: 'It's quiet now, but underneath the concrete / is the ... earth, / and above that, air / which is another ocean, where spirits we can't see / are dancing joking getting full / on roasted caribou' (14). Although she attends to the physical and topographical characteristics of the city, Harjo's speaker is equally interested in the spiritual and mythological dimensions of place, which for the Muskogee have traditionally included the division of the cosmos into three primordial worlds: 'the Upper World, This World, and the Lower World' (Martin 1991, 24). Joel Martin outlines the rationale for this tripartite structure in Muskogee culture, stating that 'the division encouraged Muskogees to see reality as fundamentally dynamic. Reality was always being pulled simultaneously in opposite directions by contrary powers' (24). Hence, the poet's inclusion of the Upper World situates her exploration of place and space in both a Muskogee and a pan-tribal context.

The city in 'Anchorage' comes to represent the past, present, and future struggles of all Native Americans to survive in a world where

> ... someone's Athabascan
> grandmother, folded up, smelling like 200 years
> of blood and piss, her eyes closed against some
> unimagined darkness, where she is buried
> in an ache in which nothing makes sense. (1983, 14)

The speaker's feelings of inadequacy and distress, especially when faced with the image of this grandmother, who embodies a history of dispossession and exploitation and for whom little can be done 'except to speak of her home and claim her / as our own,' are countered by Henry's narrative, which, despite its violent nature, is surprisingly funny (14). Henry recalls 'being shot at / eight times outside a liquor store in L.A., but when / the car sped away he was surprised that he was alive' (14). When Henry tries to find his wounds, he discovers that there are 'no bullet holes' in his body; instead, 'eight cartridges [are] strewn on the sidewalk / all around him' (15). Here, Henry is ironically framed and contained by the cartridges that barely missed him, creating a space of sanctity in a lucky coincidence that enables him to walk away without a scratch. By recounting the story of Henry's miraculous escape, Harjo challenges the formulaic expectations of those who assume that Henry must have been shot and wounded, and illustrates the ability of those who have been dispossessed to survive even in urban spaces – despite historically having been in the wrong place at the wrong time.

Harjo also examines in 'Anchorage' the controversial issue of Native alcohol abuse, a legacy of the colonial quest for land, with a pun that offers one alterna(rra)tive to an otherwise grim reality. In *American Indians: Stereotypes and Realities*, Devon Mihesuah deconstructs the pervasive (and incorrect) myth of what she calls the 'drunken Indian,' noting that liquor was not widely used by Native peoples until it became recognized as a 'profitable trade item' by Europeans (1996, 97). Mihesuah ties Natives' increased consumption of liquor historically to the loss of 'family, friends, land, and culture, as well as to mitigate the social isolation and homesickness they felt' (97). In an interview with Joseph Bruchac, Harjo includes a detailed description of Henry, while narrating his story, stating, 'You know he was real dry when he was talking about ... all those bullet holes' (1987, 21). Here the word 'dry' playfully makes a pun of the process of detoxification, which Henry may have undergone after the shooting, and describes Henry's own sense of humour as well, a dry wit that ensures his survival against all odds. Rather than ignoring the subject of alcoholism altogether, in 'Anchorage' Harjo incorporates and refashions the stereotype of the 'drunken Indian' to illustrate and celebrate the fusion of irony and humour as strategies that continue to sustain a population that has been pushed towards self-destruction due to the loss of their homelands. In other words, what is so commonly seen as 'tragic' by social scientists, as Gerald Vizenor reminds us, becomes 'comic' through the assertion of a vitality of spirit and a presence that defies the odds (1987, 295).

In the last stanza of the poem, the claiming of space through survival is explored once again through irony and humour, as Harjo employs line-breaks and wordplay to juxtapose moments of suspense with a sense of relief, while those who are reading her poem struggle to make sense of this unlikely outcome. Here Harjo pays tribute to and ironically reformulates the last stanza of Audre Lorde's 'A Litany for Survival,' a poem that calls on African Americans (especially black women) to speak rather than remain silent. In her poem, Lorde examines how fear disempowers individuals and communities; she argues 'it is better to speak / remembering / we were never meant to survive' than to not speak at all (1978, 32). At the end of 'Anchorage,' Harjo presents her own version of Lorde's line:

> Everyone laughed at the impossibility of it,
> but also the truth. Because who would believe
> the fantastic and terrible story of all of our survival
> those who were never meant
> to survive? (1983, 15)

By placing words like 'impossibility' in the same sentence as 'truth,' and concluding the poem with an ironic turn in the form of a question, Harjo mocks a lengthy history of enforced tribal genocide that has failed, like Henry's shooter, to eradicate the existence of Native Americans. Moreover, her poetic 'I' questions the presumption that certain versions of the truth are more valuable than others through ironic repetition and the alteration of the word 'survival,' which becomes the verb 'to survive' in the last line of the poem. Instead of assuming that 'we were never meant to survive,' Harjo interrogates the basis of this belief linguistically on the page by dividing Lorde's phrase and adding a question mark, which suggests that such viewpoints need to be contested even more explicitly. The inclusion of Henry's story in the collection not only locates Anchorage and Los Angeles on Harjo's map of Native experiences as urban spaces of continued significance – because of their Native populations – but also, by example, clears textual space for the narratives of other dispossessed Native voices whose survival challenges the presumption that Native peoples are a dying race.

In Joseph Bruchac's interview with Harjo, she describes the reactions of fellow inmates to Henry's story and her own motivation for relaying this narrative:

> He thought for sure he'd been killed but he was alive and telling the story and everybody laughed because they thought he was bullshitting. And it's like a big joke that any of us are here because they tried so hard to make sure that we weren't, you know ... kill our spirits, move us from one place to another. (1987, 91)

By locating the shooting in Los Angeles and his incarceration in Anchorage within a poem dedicated to Lorde, Harjo adds several layers of irony to this story of survival. Harjo updates and complicates the legacies of racism and violence in urban America by depicting a scene of gun warfare in which visible minorities may become victims of a crime simply because of their skin colour. Henry's shooting specifically invokes the police brutality and gang violence associated with Los Angeles, a city where the high cost of living widens the gulf between rich and poor. In choosing the LA setting and writing the poem for Lorde, Harjo cuts across the borders that separate African Americans, Native Americans, and other groups vulnerable to racial, ethnic, and gender-based oppression; she shows how Henry's story epitomizes the histories of many different segments of the American population. At the same time that Harjo conveys the specificity of Henry's own Native heritage, a legacy of assimilation, removal, and genocide that is both particular to the individual and to the tribal community, she ensures that the poem is overtly pan-tribal in its concerns, as epitomized by its location in Anchorage and the presence of the Athabascan grandmother, who has also undergone dispossession.

Sacred Places

While 'Anchorage' employs irony and humour to reclaim urban spaces around the United States for their Native-American residents, 'Santa Fe' more overtly collapses what Womack calls the 'constructed boundaries that separate time, space, myth, and personal experience' (1999, 226) by foregrounding the provisionality and flexibility of these elements for Harjo's poetic speaker. The fundamental uncertainty that shapes 'Santa Fe' may seem, at first, to undermine Harjo's efforts to map her experiences, both nationally and globally, in a fashion that works towards the reclamation of a homeland individually and collectively for Native peoples. Harjo attended the Institute of American Indian Arts of Santa Fe as a young adult, where she studied fine art and wrote her first poems; thus the city holds a special place in her heart. Harjo also believes, as she outlines in the 'Notes' section of *How We Became Human: New and Selected Poems*, that 'Santa Fe' is one of those 'sacred places on this earth, places that generate power, hold and even protect power' (2002, 220). Harjo describes the power Catholics associate with Saint Francis, who is 'the patron saint of animals,' and recalls her early encounters with the statue of Saint Francis in Santa Fe while attending school there. She explains that his legacy of 'love and respect for all life' has proved helpful in understanding what power – and the power of place – can do when connections between 'all life, including the plants and animals,' are cultivated and supported (220). In 'Santa Fe,' which was first published in *In Mad Love and War*, Harjo's speaker offers a twist on this inclusive vision of the world by undercutting the narrator's reliability from the outset and focusing on the movement between spaces and places over time:

> The wind blows lilacs out of the east. And it isn't lilac season. And I am walking the streets in front of St Francis Cathedral in Santa Fe. Oh, and it's a few years earlier and more. That is how you tell real time. It is here, it is there. The lilacs have taken over everything: the sky, the narrow streets, my shoulders, my lips. I talk lilac. And there is nothing else until a woman the size of a fox, breaks through the bushes, breaks the purple web. She is tall and black and gorgeous … [she] lies to me now from a room in the DeVargas Hotel, where she has eaten her lover [cocaine], white powder on her lips.

That is true now; it is not true anymore. Eventually space curves, walks over
and taps me on the shoulder. (1990, 42)

Like much of her poetry, 'Santa Fe' contains overlapping images that
move rapidly between and among worlds: 'the world of dreams to the
world of waking, subconsciousness to consciousness, myth to concrete
experience, past to present, spiritual to physical' (Womack 1999, 224).
Craig Womack argues that 'in fact, [Harjo's] ... poetry demonstrates the
ways physical and spiritual realities are constantly rubbing up against
each other' (224), a means of resistance and recovery that may come
about, in John Scarry's words, 'at the most unlikely time and in the most
unpromising place' (1992, 290). In this prose poem, Harjo offers a playfully seductive and highly impressionistic portrait of Santa Fe that rejects
singular descriptions of place in favour of a series of ironic turns that
bring space and time to life, at least figuratively. By juxtaposing descriptive phrases, such as 'The wind blows lilacs out of the east' and 'I am
walking the streets in front of St Francis Cathedral' with lines that challenge the 'reality' being put forth, and by personifying space as someone
that 'walks over and taps me on the shoulder,' Harjo demands that her
readers look again at the story being told about Santa Fe, as well as at her
speaker's interactions with this particular place.

The poem shifts focus again in the second half, when Harjo's narrator
makes another effort to situate herself and to clarify her story, offering a
series of dramatic revelations that effectively dismantle the foundations
of her story in order to create an alterna(rra)tive that more accurately
reflects the complexities of space and place for this 'Indian' who is constantly in motion:

On the sidewalk I stand near St Francis; he has been bronzed, a perpetual
tan, with birds on his hand, his shoulder, deer at his feet. I am Indian and
in this town I will never be a saint. I am seventeen and shy and wild. I have
been up until three at a party, but there is no woman in the DeVargas Ho-
tel, for that story hasn't yet been invented. A man whose face I will never
remember, and never did, drives up on a Harley-Davidson. There are lilacs
on his arm; they spill out from the spokes of his wheels. He wants me on his
arm, on the back of the lilac bike touring the flower kingdom of San Francisco. And for a piece of time the size of a nickel, I think, maybe. But maybe
is a vapor, has no anchor here in the sun beneath St Francis Cathedral. And
space is as solid as the bronze statue of St Francis, the fox breaking through
the lilacs, my invention of this story, the wind blowing. (42)

Harjo's narrator begins by admiring the statue of St Francis, who is now of a bronze hue, frozen forever with deer and birds by his side, and contrasts her situation with that of the saint, noting that as an 'Indian ... in this town I will never be a saint' (42). Historically, Santa Fe was founded by Spanish colonizers in the early seventeenth century, who came ostensibly with the intent of pacifying and converting the local Native Americans, but were primarily interested in finding and exploiting natural resources for wealth; the site had previously been a pueblo. With the Pueblo Revolt of 1680, local tribes regained control of the city and held onto it until 1692, when Diego de Vargas led a reconquest. In the centuries that followed, Santa Fe grew as a capital city and part of a vital trading route called the Santa Fe Trail, which functioned as a commercial highway. Control of the city shifted with Mexico's independence from Spain in 1821, but with the Treaty of Guadalupe (1848), New Mexico was formally ceded to the United States, and by 1912 it became a U.S. state with Santa Fe as its capital.

This long history of conquest and revolt under various colonial governments makes the city an important site for Harjo, especially given her personal knowledge of the place and the changes it has undergone over time. By declaring the impossibility of her sainthood in Santa Fe, Harjo's speaker positions herself as both an insider (familiar with the statue of Saint Francis) and an outlaw who is paradoxically 'shy and wild' (1990, 42). In a final ironic turn, Harjo concludes 'Santa Fe' by contesting the solidity of space and of her own narrative, stating that 'space is as solid as the bronze statue of St Francis, the fox breaking through the lilacs, my invention of this story, the wind blowing' (42). The statue may be bronze, a hardy alloy that ensures its survival; however, the notion that 'space is ... solid' is mocked in this instance by the contents of the poem, which are themselves provisional and shifting in keeping with the narrator's own journey of self-discovery and self-creation within and beyond the poem. Like Massey, Harjo presents an idea of space that is dependent upon interactions between and among those who are present at a particular place and a specific time; in other words, space and place are by definition 'multiple, [and] shifting' (Massey 1994, 7).

For Harjo, the reclamation of Native lands and the recognition of Native sovereignty is an important project, as reflected in a wide range of poems, including 'New Orleans,' which recalls the forced removal of the Muskogee by steamboats up the Mississippi River, and 'Crossing the Border,' which describes a late-night encounter with customs officials when travelling by car from the United States to Canada, a border that Harjo explains 'doesn't exist' from 'an indigenous point of view' and yet remains 'hazardous for Indians' because they 'are singled out and searched, detained and questioned' (2002, 205). But Harjo also uses her poetry to explore a different understanding of space and place that accords with bell hooks's idea, mentioned at the beginning of the chapter, that 'spaces can tell stories and unfold histories. Spaces can be interrupted, appropriated, and transformed through artistic literary practices' (1990, 152). Of course, hooks is concerned with the possibilities made available by claiming the margin and embracing this homeplace as sacred and protected. Although Harjo does see her homelands as central to her identity, she does not believe she has to live there or even return there physically. As she explains in 'Oklahoma: The Prairie of Words,' 'Even if they move away they always return ... And some return only in their hearts and voices, singing, again and again – to Oklahoma red earth ... – to creeks and rivers that crossed over and through the land. No one has ever left' (1990, 3). It is this sense of the distant centrality of home, her confidence in that undeniable link, that enables Harjo to undertake what she calls the search for 'grace,' a specifically non-Christian concept that refers to 'those moments of vision when boundaries collapse between mythical spaces, personal spaces, the invisible world, and the physical world,' thereby enabling access to other dimensions (Womack 1999, 258). The search for grace through exploration of differently located worlds is evident in the title poem of her aptly named collection *A Map to the Next World*, which is dedicated to her third granddaughter, Desiray.

'A Map to the Next World' ironically reconfigures conventional cartographic principles – that the world can be measured and that reliable models of that reality can be rendered visually while effectively communicating the appropriate spatial data – through poetry, which foregrounds the process and limits of representing three dimensions on the page. The poem begins with Harjo's poetic 'I' outlining the purpose of her poem: 'In the last days of the fourth world I wished to make a map for those who would climb through the hole in the sky' (2000a, 19). For her speaker, the poem is intended to function as a guide for those wishing to go from what the Muskogee people traditionally called This World, where humans, animals, and plants live, to the Upper World, traditionally regarded as a place of 'order, [and] stability' (Hudson 1976, 128), rather than the Under World with its 'inversions, madness, ... [and] disorder' (128). Yet this is unlike any other map; here, the speaker explains, 'My only tools were the desires of humans as they emerged from the killing fields, from the bedrooms and the kitchens' (Harjo 2000a, 19). The use of precise measurements to create a map is displaced by the tangibility and power of human passions, especially when used for selfish gain. Harjo's speaker catalogues the state of decay in This World in no uncertain terms, and argues that 'forgetfulness' and capitalistic greed are the reasons for this growing ignorance about and disconnection from nature:

Take note of the proliferation of supermarkets and malls, the altars of money.
They best describe the detour from grace.

Keep track of the errors of our forgetfulness; the fog steals our children while we sleep....

Trees of ashes wave good-bye to good-bye and the map appears to disappear.

We no longer know the names of the birds here, how to speak to them by their personal names.

Once we knew everything in this lush promise.

What I am telling you is real and is printed in a warning on the map. Our forgetfulness stalks us, walks the earth behind us, leaving a trail of paper diapers, needles and wasted blood. (19)

Unlike a typical map, which focuses on physical features in an effort to convey a three-dimensional space in a two-dimensional form, Harjo's map is a series of poetic traces of a world and a population that have lost touch with their guiding values, what her narrator calls 'the detour from grace' (19). Harjo's speaker suggests that without memory, the map of past traditions and values – such as the equitable treatment of animals and birds – will 'disappear' (19). The vivid images of waste and destruction that litter the poem and the page – 'paper diapers, needles and wasted blood' – form a topographical guide to This World's surface that is intended to evoke shock and horror, and to motivate a change in behaviour (19).

Instead of simply feeling defeated, the narrator of 'A Map to the Next World' tells the child to whom the poem is dedicated that 'an imperfect map will have to do, little one,' and proceeds to describe the baby's birth into the world and the steps she will have to take to journey onward, while reaching back into the past for sources of strength and knowledge (2000a, 20). Paradoxically, however, it soon becomes clear that there is no single or correct map that can be used to guide young Desiray. The reality is that once a child is born – 'the place of entry is the sea of your mother's blood' – 'there is no exit,' and so she must make her own way, drawing on the knowledge and experiences of prior generations from the Upper World, here manifested in the form of 'relatives ... [making] a feast of fresh deer meat and corn soup, in the Milky Way' (20). The markings and coordinates found on conventional maps to guide travellers and provide route ideas are lacking. On this map, however, the visual is displaced by the aural, as the poetic 'I' urges her listener to 'to navigate by your mother's voice, renew the song she is singing,' an action that will garner results: 'Fresh courage glimmers from the planets. / And lights the map printed with the blood of history, a map you will have to / know by your intention, by the language of suns' (20). Much like Armstrong, Harjo's narrator insists on the importance of listening to the natural world and giving it the attention it deserves, and in doing so, finding a new path marked by the 'monster slayers' who came to 'the cities of artificial light and killed what was killing us' (20).

By turning away from what is constructed and manufactured and pollutes the cities, the poetic 'I' conceives of a way out of 'the destruction,' heralded by the presence of a 'white deer' (2000a, 20), a symbol central to the Creek people because deer were historically a crucial part of the tribe's 'food supplies before contact, then important to the Creek economy through trade with the English' (Womack 1999, 229). Womack notes that deer, for the Muskogee, are representative of 'adaptability, survival in the face of change, shifting worlds, and [have] the power to transcend boundaries' (229); in this case, this ability to adapt becomes crucial to ensuring the granddaughter's survival. But even the celebratory aspects of the 'last human climbing from the destruction' are undercut by Harjo, as her narrator proceeds on the next page to remind readers that 'we were never perfect,' only to counter this critique with the knowledge that every journey, even that of 'this earth who was once a star / and made the same mistakes as humans,' has its faults (2000a, 21). The concluding lines of the poem reinforce this message of provisionality, emphasizing the links between humans and earth to suggest the need for a change in attitude regarding the treatment of the spaces that they inhabit, and the real possibility that such mistakes 'might' be made again. Nonetheless, what emerges from the poem-as-map is that there is no single right journey: 'Crucial to finding your way is this: there is no beginning or end. / You must make your own map' (21). Cartography becomes an act of self-creation, for which one must take responsibility no matter how helpful a grandmother's directions may try to be.

In *Space, Place, and Gender*, Doreen Massey outlines the key challenge urban women, whose movement in cities is often regarded as threatening to an established 'patriarchal order,' face: 'The challenge is to … [keep moving] whilst at the same time recognizing one's necessary locatedness and embeddedness/embodiedness and taking responsibility for it,' and to accomplish this without being relegated to the realm of the 'local' (1994, 11). As Massey later notes, race and gender fundamentally shape the experience of mobility; moving is not always a choice, as Harjo reminds readers throughout much of her poetry. Yet Harjo tries to find a balance between the constant compulsion to move and travel, a migratory inheritance that she explains in relation to her ancestors – 'We are part of an old story and involved in it are migrations of winds, ocean currents, of seeds, songs and generations of nations' (2000a, 14) – and the need to establish an identity in a specific place, often an urban space, which has too readily relegated Native peoples to silence on the margins. Harjo describes the struggles with urban living for Native peoples such as herself in 'the psychology of earth and sky,' a prose poem in *A Map to the Next World*, stating, 'All of us lived in the back of somewhere in that city where we were defined by what it meant to be an Indian in a system of massive colonization. It was a standing joke. A backdoor joke' (14). But she counters this Muskogee history of genocide and forced migration from the southeastern United States to Oklahoma, and then into urban areas for the purposes of employment, with the assertion that 'my family survived, even continues to thrive, which works against the myth of Indian defeat and disappearance' (15). If maps, in a colonial context, are intended to be tools to divide space from place, physical land from the social relations that occur on it, then Harjo's maps do precisely the reverse, putting the experience of her poetic bodies and their relation to their environments at the centre of her texts, while refusing to dictate the terms of this experience for other people. Thus, the poem 'A Map to the Next World' is an elaborate joke with an important message; despite the promise conveyed by the collection title to provide a life map for Harjo's granddaughter, everyone 'must make … [their] own map' (21). Moreover, by exploring sacred topography through depicting the movement from one world to the next, Harjo playfully subverts what James Clifford has argued is a traditional assumption in cultural anthropology – that the 'traveling native' is less authentic than those Indigenous peoples who dwell consistently in a single location (1988, 338). Instead, bodies become maps that belie the need to be static in order to be deemed 'authentic,' and home, as Harjo has asserted, can be carried within those bodies through memory and the power of remembering.

In 'Returning from the Enemy,' a poem for her father, Harjo describes the impact of colonization, and particularly Christianity, on him and asserts her own right to be a map-maker and a Native woman who believes in the sacred as well as her own autonomy:

> The law of the gods I claim state:
> *When entering another country do not claim ownership.*
> *It is important to address the souls there kindly, with respect.*
> *And ask permission.*
> I am asking you to leave the country of my body, my mind, if you have any-
> thing other than honorable intentions. (2000a, 77)

Not only does she blur the boundaries between country and body in a manner that challenges the Eurocentric tendency to treat the New World as an empty (female) space ripe for exploitation, but she also establishes a new set of rules for engaging with these already populated places based on mutual respect and dignity. Moreover, in another poem in *The Map to the Next World*, Harjo debunks the notion that 'North America was settled by a relatively late migration of peoples from Asia,' a theory that her speaker in the wittily titled 'there is no such thing as a one-way land bridge' readily mocks: 'This / translated that prior rights of occupation…[were] tentative, and made land claims / of the indigenous peoples hold less weight, for if we were recent immigrants, / too, then who are we to make claims?' (38). For Harjo's poetic 'I,' however, 'the logic of that notion is so faulty as to be preposterous' because, as she explains, 'people, creatures and other life will naturally travel back and forth. Just as we will naturally intermarry, travel up and down rivers, cross oceans, fly from Los Angeles to Oklahoma for a powwow' (38). With this, Harjo articulates a global vision of her speaker's Native identity that accounts for the movement in-between and among places, between communities, and across bridges; this motion cannot be expressed through maps where there are no bodies, nor any recognition of the ongoing, complex, and individually nuanced interactions between places and people. And by employing irony and humour in her poetic efforts to rethink space, place, and the meanings of home, Harjo ensures that both the imaginative and pragmatic dimensions of these ideas are conveyed in a manner that is compelling, subversive, and entertaining, but also fundamentally open to revision as the map of her own life continues to unfold.

Conclusion: Intertextual Conversations

In *Absentee Indians & Other Poems*, Kimberly Blaeser includes a selection of poems titled 'From One Half Mad Writer to Another,' in which she overtly pays tribute to several of those writers who have played a significant role in the development of her work, creating an intertextual homage which celebrates the power of 'influence in Native literature' (Andrews 2007b, 4). Blaeser pointedly embraces this intertextuality:

> I don't want to pretend or to set myself up as if I were some individual creator, because I know so well that I'm not. So I feel that having a conversation that moves from this book to that book – that cuts across years and different voices – is more enriching for readers and also for me as a writer. I think it's important to notice that things that Indian authors like Gary Hobson ... or Joy Harjo, or whomever might have written have echoes and that those echoes will appear, for example, in my book. In some places I borrow from specific texts ... But in other places it might be an allusion or a gesture to something that someone else has said or written. (4)

What Blaeser describes reflects the sense of community contribution and collaboration that characterizes so much of contemporary Native writing: the dialogic relationship extends upon multiple lines, incorporating not only fellow writers but family members, ancestors, and the natural world. In 'The Voices We Carry,' Blaeser differentiates Harold Bloom's now famous idea of the 'anxiety of influence' from 'the poetries of American Indian nations,' which she contends are 'celebrations of influence,' an inversion and rejection of the solitary white male author so prominent in Bloom's formulation (2001, 1). Citing the example of a colleague who taught poetry-writing to a group of Lakota grade school students in South Dakota and was surprised to discover that they not only borrowed each other's finest lines but ended up submitting a single communal poem as a final project, Blaeser argues for the need to recognize and understand the centrality of such connections to Native art. As she notes, 'The experiences of my life have seldom seemed individual, isolated. They have been informed and sometimes determined by the strands of connection to people, place, and history. The meaning I build or extract is referential' (10).

To illustrate this point, the concluding poem of Blaeser's *Absentee Indians* incorporates selected well-known lines from the works of male and female Native North American poets, including Linda Hogan, Gerald Vizenor, Simon Ortiz, and Leslie Marmon Silko, in her own text, wittily titled 'Y2K Indian.' Published in 2002, two years after the millennium – a date nicknamed 'Y2K' in reference to the fear that because some early computer programs were thought to be unable to manage date-and-time functions as of 1 January 2000, there could be worldwide chaos – the poem attests to the ongoing survival of Native peoples, even after the threat of this global technological disaster, a disaster that turned out to be very minor. Blaeser's title can be read as mocking the energy and money devoted to the Y2K problem, in contrast with the unacknowledged disaster that is colonization, a legacy of Native genocide and marginalization for which there has been no adequate compensation. By putting the words 'Y2K' and 'Indian' side by side, the title also challenges the presumed stasis of Native cultures, which have been stereotypically perceived as anti-progressive and anti-technological, and thus threatened with extinction.

Blaeser's speaker tempers the layered ironies of the poem's title by examining the individual impact of Native removal and assimilation in a contemporary context. Her narrator reflects on the situation of the Y2K urban Indian who wakes up at 4:00 a.m. from a dream about the White Earth Reservation, the much longed-for homeplace, and must wrestle with that loneliness from the distance of the city. As 'another absentee Indian,' the speaker struggles with a sense of fundamental loss: 'Do I begin with the songs / whose words I've lost / forgotten / or shoved into drawers / of my past / like so many green stamps?' (2002, 129–30). This strategy of burying objects and memories in drawers, however, cannot get rid of what fellow Anishinaabe poet Maurice Kenny calls '*the wound beneath the flesh* / that might be all that remains' (130). Instead, Blaeser's speaker begins 'shucking / layers of easy Indian-ness' and '*smell[s] the wind for my ancestors*' (130), in the words of Laguna writer Leslie Marmon

Silko, finding ghostly evidence of the past reflected in the urban spaces where s/he lives:

> I follow the pine scent of their passing
> Find their images
> Reflected in the car mirror
> The splattered window glass. (130)

As with the poets in chapter 3, Blaeser's narrator embraces these spectres and their ability to move seamlessly between an array of different spaces and places, from 'the university and the pow-wow circuit / [to] the church pew and the cedar smoke circle' (131). The flexibility of these ghosts provide a model for living with 'the story of doubleness' (131), a way to negotiate the multiple and often conflicting identities that make up the experiences of the poets explored in this book.

The concluding lines of Blaeser's poem include a final intertextual invocation that suggests the power of contemporary Native women's writing:

> Another Y2K Indian
> *writing the circle*
> of return. (2002, 131)

Here, Blaeser alludes to *Writing the Circle: An Anthology: Native Women of Western Canada*, a groundbreaking collection of writings by fifty First Nations women, including early poems by Louise Halfe and Marilyn Dumont, that reflects the need to provide places 'for Native women to speak' (Perreault and Vance 1990, xi). The anthology contains a lively and provocative preface by Métis writer and scholar Emma LaRocque, who describes the 'power politics in literature ... evident in the decisions of publishers and audience reception' (1990, xvi). Recalling her own experiences as a young poet, LaRocque argues that traditionally most Native writings in Canada which did not replicate colonial expectations of what it is to be Indian went unpublished; she sees *Writing the Circle* as a important step in ending that silence. Though publication is still not easy for Native writers, particularly Native women whose work may not accord with 'conventional standards of literary excellence' (Perreault and Vance 1990, xi), Blaeser's poem, appearing at the end of her second published collection, is further evidence of the potential for change.

The final lines of 'Y2K Indian' invoke the legacy of *Writing the Circle* to demonstrate the possibility of return, fulfilling the speaker's longing to reconnect with a homeplace and to find ways to cope with living a life of border-crossing that is challenging and yet ultimately fulfilling. It is through the conversations between and among women writers that such a 'return' to wholeness is possible. Humour and irony are conduits for this journey, strategies of survival and sustenance that enable the women who are the subjects of this book to explore a whole range of topics from their unique perspectives, yet still find common ground. Harjo's vision of Native people as being 'in the belly of a laughing god' (Carabi 1996, 141) provides a crucial framework for understanding the poetry of these eight women. And, as Blaeser's poem illustrates, the intertextual conversations between and among Native North American women poets, with their ironic and humorous dimensions, create a rich and complex set of palimpsests that demand much more scholarly attention. With the '… Y2K Indian / *writing the circle* / of return' (2002, 131) in post-millennial North America, Blaeser suggests that Native women's poetry is not only alive and well – it is thriving.

Notes

Introduction

1 Terminology is always a challenge, and therefore I have tried to be inclusive and respectful in the language I use to describe Native populations. See Veronica Strong-Boag and Carol Gerson's *Paddling Her Own Canoe: The Times and Texts of E. Pauline Johnson (Tekahionwake)*, where they point out that 'usage varies among individual authors, scholars, and disciplines, and from one nation to another. What is acceptable in one time or place may well turn out to be deeply prejudicial in another' (2000, 8). To try to avoid cultivating an 'us-them' dichotomy, I have used the adjectival term – rather than the noun – 'Native' throughout this book. In addition, I have decided to limit the number of terms used for the sake of clarity and generalization.

2 See Shari M. Huhndorf's *Mapping the Americas: The Transnational Politics of Contemporary Native Culture* for a similarly transnational approach to Native Canadian and American texts.

3 Elvira Pulitano's *Toward a Native American Critical Theory* has been strongly critiqued by American Indian literary nationalists as prescriptive and divisive; see Jace Weaver et al., *American Indian Literary Nationalism* for the specifics of this debate from the perspective of several Native scholars who reject Pulitano's valuation of 'hybridity, high theory and postcolonial discourse' (2006, 19) in favour of a nationalist Native-centred approach.

4 See Thomas King's 'Introduction' in *All My Relations*, where he suggests caution when trying to define what constitutes a Native writer: 'And, when we talk about Native writers, we talk as if we have a process for determining who is a Native writer and who is not, when, in fact, we don't' (1990a, xi).

5 See also Terry Goldie's *Fear and Temptation: The Image of the Indigene in Canadian, Australian, and New Zealand Literatures*. He explores the indigene as

a semiotic field in Canadian, Australian, and New Zealand literatures, and argues that 'the shape and extent of the cultural conditioning in Canada, Australia, and New Zealand that consistently reifies the indigene, whether as an object of fear or ... of desire, must be universally recognized if the action necessary to oppose it is to be taken' (1989, 221).

6 See Joyce Green, ed., *Making Space for Indigenous Feminism* for a detailed assessment of the impact of the Indian Act on Native women in Canada and its relationship to Native concepts of feminism in Canada.

7 My thanks to Priscilla Walton, who originally coined this term when we co-authored *Border Crossings: Thomas King's Cultural Inversions* and has generously allowed me to use it here.

8 See Dean Rader and Janice Gould, eds, *Speak to Me Words: Essays on Contemporary American Indian Poetry*. This collection contains a wonderful selection of essays on Native North American women poets living on both sides of the forty-ninth parallel.

9 See Dean Rader's 'The Epic Lyric: Genre and Contemporary American Indian Poetry,' where he states, 'I am baffled by the preponderance of studies of American Indian fiction and the relative dearth of studies of American Indian poetry, particularly at a time in which some of the best literary critics in America – Helen Vendler, Marjorie Perloff, Albert Gelpi, Harold Bloom, Geoffrey Hartmann, James Longenbach, Alan Filreis, James Breslin, and Sharon Cameron – are working in the field of poetry and when perhaps the most interesting Native writing is being done in poetry' (2003, 125).

10 See also Agnes Grant's 'Traditional Native Poetry.'

11 See, for example, Jeannette Armstrong and Lally Grauer, eds, *Native Poetry in Canada: A Contemporary Anthology*; similar anthologies focusing on Aboriginal women's poetry have been published in the United States, including Joy Harjo and Gloria Bird, eds, *Reinventing the Enemy's Language: Contemporary Native Women's Writings of North America*, and Carolyn Dunn and Carol Comfort, eds, *Through the Eyes of the Deer: An Anthology of Native American Women Writers*.

12 See especially pp. 3–31.

Chapter 1: Spiritual Transformations

1 See *Oxford English Dictionary, Oxford Reference Online*, s.v. 'transformation,' http://www.oxfordreference.com.proxy.hil.unb.ca/views/SEARCH_RESULTS.html?q=transformation&category=s7&ssid=692963318&scope=subject&time=0.660031710193138 (accessed 18 May 2007).

2 See Jo-Ann Episkenew's *Taking Back Our Spirits: Indigenous Literature, Public Policy, and Healing* for a complementary analysis of the 'transformative functions' of contemporary Indigenous literature (15).

3 See the interview with Dumont in which she specifically describes the significance of 'Lac Ste. Anne' for her Métis community, stating, 'It was excusable if you missed Easter Mass, Easter Sunday, but it was not excusable if you missed [the yearly pilgrimage to] Lac Ste. Anne' (Andrews 2004b, 149). Dumont describes the singing of 'Cree hymns' at the pilgrimage, and the way in which Catholic doctrine was combined with traditional Native beliefs in her own family home while growing up, resulting in a sometimes uneasy cross-cultural synthesis of two religions and two languages (149).

4 See Sheila Hassell Hughes, 'Falls of Desire / Leaps of Faith: Religious Syncretism in Louise Erdrich's and Joy Harjo's "Mixed-Blood" Poetry,' for a useful discussion of the relationship between Christian and Native beliefs. She argues that 'the blurring of borders – between inside and outside, sacred and secular, human and nature, self and other – triggers a "fall" into a state of mutual need' (2001, 60). See also Kimberly Blaeser, 'Pagans Rewriting the Bible: Heterodoxy and the Representation of Spirituality in Native American Literature,' for a detailed exploration of the 'spiritual vision embedded' (1994a, 12) in a variety of Native-American prose works.

5 See *Troubling Tricksters: Revisioning Critical Conversations*, edited by Deanna Reder and Linda M. Morra, for a timely reconsideration of the significance of the trickster in Native literature and theory, especially in relation to the writings of Gerald Vizenor.

6 See Sam McKegney, *Magic Weapons: Aboriginal Writers Remaking Community after Residential School*, for an extended discussion of how residential schooling impacted the literary voices of survivors, particularly because this experience was usually characterized by 'denial and [the] loss' of 'language, culture ... and ... spiritual values' (2007, 48).

7 See Neil McLeod, 'Cree Poetic Discourse,' for a similar reading of *The Crooked Good*.

8 See Halfe's 'Keynote Address,' in which she reiterates this notion: 'The Elders teach that "All life is related"' (2006, 69).

9 See Maggie Siggins, *Bitter Embrace: White Society's Assault on the Woodland Cree*, 105–8, and David Young et al., *Cry of the Eagle: Encounters with a Cree Healer*, 27, for discussions of the significance of dreaming for the Cree.

10 See *Online Cree Dictionary*, s.v. 'kwêskî,' http://www.creedictionary.com/search/?q=kw%C3%AAsk%C3%AE&scope=2&x=36&y=20 (accessed 18 January 2009).

11 See Kristina Fagan's 'Code-Switching Humour in Aboriginal Literature' for a complementary reading of code-switching and its relationship to humour in Native texts.

12 See also Siggins, *Bitter Embrace*, 150–68, for a detailed account of the Catholic residential schooling practices used on Cree children in Saskatchewan and Manitoba.

13 See *Oxford English Dictionary, Oxford Reference Online*, s.v. 'crooked,' http://www.oxfordreference.com.proxy.hil.unb.ca/views/SEARCH_RESULTS.html?y=1&q=crooked&authstatuscode=200&category=s7&x=28&ssid=451745526&scope=global&time=0.264513591855014 (accessed 28 January 2009).

14 See *Oxford English Dictionary, Oxford Reference Online*, s.v. 'good,' http://www.oxfordreference.com.proxy.hil.unb.ca/views/SEARCH_RESULTS.html?y=11&q=good&category=s7&x=22&ssid=826032466&scope=subject&time=0.8504363446625 (accessed 30 January 2009).

15 See chapter 5 of this book for a detailed discussion of Native circularity and the way that some women poets, most prominently Marilyn Dumont, resist this stereotypical association.

16 See, for example, Peter Nabokov, *Indian Running*, where he argues that 'in practically every tribe's oral history, running folklore instructed and entertained. Mythic races helped to order the world … providing a model and mandate for the activity which human beings would perpetuate. Racing contests decided the first temperaments and physical characteristics, and played a part in allocating their territories and status in the emerging world' (1981, 23).

17 See 'Welcome to the Leader in Lieder Mit Midi Melodies,' which provides a complete lyrics sheet for the nursery rhyme 'Simple Simon' (http://ingeb.org/songs/simplesi.html; accessed 30 January 2009).

18 See Thomas King, 'Godzilla vs. Post-Colonial,' 11–13, where he makes a very convincing case for the need to avoid marking the chronological starting point for discussions of Native literature as being 'the advent of Europeans in North America' (1990b, 11).

19 See *Oxford English Dictionary, Oxford Reference Online*, s.v. 'om,' http://www.oxfordreference.com.proxy.hil.unb.ca/views/SEARCH_RESULTS.html?y=12&q=om&category=s7&x=21&ssid=1023500337&scope=subject&time=0.0995546856397311 (accessed 30 January 2009).

20 See *The Concise Oxford Dictionary of Music, Oxford Reference Online*, s.v. 'drum roll,' http://www.oxfordreference.com.proxy.hil.unb.ca/views/SEARCH_RESULTS.html?q=drum%20roll&ssid=453292690&time=0.0654218476472685 (accessed 20 January 2009).

Chapter 2: Generic Transformations

1 See Sheila Hassell Hughes, 'Falls of Desire / Leaps of Faith: Religious Syncretism in Louise Erdrich's and Joy Harjo's "Mixed-Blood" Poetry,' 59-83,
   for a very different reading of transformation in Harjo's texts.
2 I attended two readings by Harjo, on 13 November 1998 in Tucson, Arizona,
   and 2 April 2003 in Los Angeles, California. The first was billed as part of a set
   of three nights of poetry readings, sponsored by the University of Arizona's
   Extended University Writing Works Center, which incorporated student readings into the evening's events. Designed to highlight the Indigenous linguistic knowledge of the local population, each night's feature poet was asked to
   select poems for translation into Spanish, Yoeme, and O'odham. Harjo read
   on the first night of the series, bringing her saxophone to play as she sang the
   poems and created a lively and fun atmosphere in the high-school audito-
   rium where the event was held. The second reading was part of a series organized by the UCLA Friends of English, where Harjo teaches. Described as 'An
   Evening of Contemporary Poetry,' four writers read from their work. Harjo
   explicitly differentiated her performance from the others by playing her
   saxophone and bringing along her accompanist, guitarist Michael Sena, who
   also provided back-up vocals. Harjo sang two poems ('The Woman Hanging
   from the Thirteenth Floor' and 'Grace') and read one new work, 'No.'
3 See Jeannette Armstrong, 'Aboriginal Literatures,' 180-6, for a related
   discussion about the need to recognize Aboriginal literatures as forming a
   'distinctive genre within Canadian literature' (2005, 180). She argues for
   using the term 'literature' to refer to 'all artistry in words,' whether written
   or spoken (181).
4 Blaeser is currently working on a collection of poetry that will include photographs, family letters, and family memorabilia, and she is undertaking a
   collaborative book of photographs and texts about the White Earth Reservation. In addition, she notes, 'I want to produce a CD of my poetry some with
   music and maybe if I can get to work with someone who's in film put together
   a poetry video' (Andrews 2002a, 24). Marilyn Dumont was trained in film
   production and is engaged in two video projects, one involving footage of her
   mother and the other creating a collection of interviews about Métis history
   with those – including herself – who are descendants of Gabriel Dumont
   (Andrews 2004b, 154). Glancy has written texts that span a wide variety of
   genres and often challenge generic boundaries; her creative non-fiction
   and poem-essays are good examples of this resistance of generic categorization, and she also incorporates photographs in some of her texts. Halfe is

primarily a poet but uses visual collage in her volumes (see especially *Blue Marrow*) to explore questions of family history; see chapter 4 in this book. Finally, Marie Annharte Baker is an accomplished essayist, activist, performance artist, and dramatist; she constantly challenges generic boundaries and audience expectations through her creative work.

5 The three 'Bonus Trax with Music' on the *She Had Some Horses* album are 'She Had Some Horses' from *Letter from the End of the Twentieth Century*, and 'The Woman Hanging from the Thirteenth Floor Window' and 'Fear Song,' both taken from *Native Joy for Real.*

6 See *Oxford English Dictionary, Oxford Reference Online*, s.v. 'oratory,' http://www.oxfordreference.com.proxy.hil.unb.ca/views/SEARCH_RESULTS .html?q=oratory&category=t140&ssid=340772862&scope=book&ti me=0.855583556207481 (accessed 19 January 2009).

7 See, for example, Craig Womack, *Red on Red: Native American Literary Separatism*; Womack links Harjo's transformative poetry (e.g., 'Deer Dancer') with a larger aim of 'making the lure to other worlds the imaging of life without colonialism' (1999, 230).

8 See, for example, Stephen Morton, 'First Nations Women's Writing and Anti-racist Work in Institutional Locations: A Feminist Reading of Lee Maracle and Jeannette Armstrong,' 27–30; Morton repeatedly describes Armstrong's poetry as 'transformative' in its exploration of the potential of the English language, despite its colonial roots, and her poems as depicting the possibility of both the individual metamorphosis of readers and the experience of a shared transformation through 'collective participation' in 'her textual community' (1999, 28–9).

9 A notable exception in the case of Jeannette Armstrong is Karin Beeler's interview with Armstrong, which probes the intersections between text, language, sound, and visual art over the course of her career.

10 See Karin Beeler, 'Image, Music, Text: An Interview with Jeannette Armstrong,' 148–9.

11 See Laura Groening, *Listening to Old Woman Speak: Natives and alterNatives in Canadian Literature* for a discussion of the term 'alterNative' (2004, xiv).

12 See Olive Dickason, *Canada's First Nations*, 319-23, 334–5, for a detailed account of the Oka Crisis and the Canadian government's sustained refusal to recognize the Mohawks as having legitimate claim to their tribal land as an independent nation.

13 See Maxens Berre, 'Steel Pans: A Brief History' for a discussion of the origins of the steel pan and its subsequent banning by the British government 'since the British feared that the passing of secret messages by means of

drumming might become the impetus for social unity and revolt among the Blacks' (http://www.lafi.org/magazine/articles/steel.html).

14 See *Oxford English Dictionary, Oxford Reference Online*, s.v. 'rip into,' http://www.oxfordreference.com.proxy.hil.unb.ca/views/ENTRY.html?entry=t140.e66315&srn=12&ssid=857244676#FIRSTHIT (accessed 19 January 2009).

15 See *Oxford Essential Dictionary of Foreign Terms in English, Oxford Reference Online*, s.v. 'ripieno,' http://www.oxfordreference.com.proxy.hil. unb.ca/views/ENTRY.html?subview=Main&entry=t33.e6048 (accessed 25 January 2009).

16 Harjo makes large numbers of public appearances, both solo and with her new band; her schedule of readings and performances is posted on-line at http://www.joyharjo.com.

17 A guiro is a light percussion instrument, used primarily in South and Central America, which is made of a hollowed-out gourd with carved ridges on the outside. Rhythm is created by rubbing a stick against the ridges; the instrument is held in place by a thumb hole.

Chapter 3: Histories, Memories, and the Nation

1 See, for example, Mark Dockstator, 'Aboriginal Representations of History and the Royal Commission on Aboriginal Peoples,' 113; and Olive Patricia Dickason, *Canada's First Nations: A History of Founding Peoples from Earliest Times*, xi–62.

2 See Pauline Butling and Susan Rudy, *Poets Talk*, where Butling notes that 'Annharte [Baker] grew up in Winnipeg but often spent summer holidays with her Anishinabe grandparents on the reserve in the Interlake Region of Manitoba' (2005, 89).

3 See Makere Stewart-Harawira, 'Practicing Indigenous Feminism: Resistance to Imperialism,' for a useful exploration of why strategic essentialism is so critical to Native women.

4 See Stephen J. Summerhill and John Alexander Williams, *Sinking Columbus: Contested History, Cultural Politics, and Mythmaking during the Quincentenary*, 34–62.

5 Ibid., 116–19.

6 See Roger Simon, *The Touch of the Past: Remembrance, Learning, and Ethics*, 14–31, for another perspective on the counter-commemoration of the Columbus Quincentenary.

7 See Gerald Vizenor, *Manifest Manners: Narratives on Postindian Survivance*, who also links these massacres together: 'The Vietnam War, and the horrors

of racialism recounted in the literature of survivance, aroused the nation to remember the inseparable massacres at My Lai, Sand Creek, and Wounded Knee' (1994, 149).

8   See Carol Hunter, 'A MELUS Interview: Wendy Rose,' 82–3, for more details of the decline of the Miwok tribe.

9   See, for example, Renate Eigenbrod, *Travelling Knowledges: Positioning the Im/Migrant Reader of Aboriginal Literatures in Canada*, 85–91; and Jeanne Perreault, 'Memory Alive: An Inquiry into the Uses of Memory in Marilyn Dumont, Jeannette Armstrong, Louise Halfe, and Joy Harjo,' 259-61.

10 See Fagan, 'Code-Switching Humour,' 37–40, for a similar reading of this Baker poem.

11 See Fagan, 'Code-Switching Humour,' 33, for a brief but complementary reading of this poem.

Chapter 4: Haunting Photographs, Revisioning Families

1   Both Joy Harjo and Jeannette Armstrong have provided the written commentary for books of photographs. Armstrong paired with renowned Métis architect Douglas Cardinal to author *The Native Creative Process: A Collaborative Process*, which is structured around the photographs of Greg Young-Ing (Cree); and Harjo collaborated with astronomer, teacher, and photographer Stephen Strom to produce a powerful collection of images and words about the landscape of the Southwestern United States, titled *Secrets from the Center of the World*. But, as neither text focuses directly on issues of family or ghosts, they are not discussed in this chapter. Wendy Rose does include family photographs in her latest collection, *Itch like Crazy*. See Jennifer Andrews, 'Ghost Spaces, Living Histories: Memory and Photography in Contemporary Native North American Women's Poetry,' in *Nation in Imagination: Essays on Nationalism, Sub-Nationalisms and Narration*, for a discussion of Rose's use of photography in *Itch like Crazy*.

2   Phelan wryly argues, 'If representational visibility equals power, then almost-naked young white women should be running Western culture' (1993, 10).

3   For example, when I visited the Acoma Pueblo and the Taos Pueblo in New Mexico in 2000, I was given the option of purchasing camera permits for still photography ($10 at Acoma and $5 at Taos). However, each pueblo has its own distinct set of rules and regulations about visitors and visual images; at Acoma, no videotaping, drawing and sketching, or digital photography is permitted. At Taos, a movie or video camera fee of $5 is charged,

but again there are explicit rules laid out for visitors, who must ask before photographing tribe members and are not allowed to take pictures of the pueblo's church or ceremonies; professional photographers and commercial artists are required to apply for permission in advance, and fees vary for their entry to the pueblo. And there are many Native communities that still ban visitors from carrying cameras altogether; at the Hopi Mesas in Arizona, a large sign is posted at the entrance stating that no cameras, sketchbooks, or tape or video recorders are allowed, and these rules are strictly enforced to avoid having images of sacred Hopi dances or ceremonies exploited for profit.

4 Here Glancy is referring to her maternal grandparents' farm.

5 See King's photographic essay 'Shooting the Lone Ranger,' 36–7, for a detailed discussion of this portrait series of Native North American writers and artists, all of whom creatively posed for King wearing a signature Lone Ranger mask.

Chapter 5: Space, Place, Land, and the Meaning(s) of Home

1 See Helen May Dennis, *Native American Literature: Towards a Spatialized Reading* for a different approach to space, landscape, and home in recent Native-American fiction.

2 See *Oxford English Dictionary, Oxford Reference Online,* s.v. 'place,' http://www.oxfordreference.com.proxy.hil.unb.ca/views/SEARCH_RESULTS .html?q=place&category=s7&ssid=114292757&scope=subject&time= 0.45921827921703 (accessed 28 January 2009).

3 See *Oxford English Dictionary, Oxford Reference Online,* s.v. 'space,' http://www.oxfordreference.com.proxy.hil.unb.ca/views/SEARCH_RESULTS .html?q=space&category=s7&ssid=219324921&scope=subject&time= 0.274883885440556 (accessed 28 January 2009).

4 See, for example, the eviction notices circulated by the Lil'wat in March 1998 to guests staying in the resort town of Whistler, British Columbia, protesting the illegal exploitation of their tribal lands by timber companies and resort developers, at http://sisis.nativeweb.org/lilwat/mar2398sis.html (accessed 3 November 2009).

5 See Claudia Clark, *Radium Girls: Women and Industrial Health Reform, 1910–1935* for a compelling account of the history of the 'Radium Girls' in the United States.

6 See Carol Miller, 'Telling the Indian Urban: Representations in American Indian Fiction,' 29, where she notes the popularity of big cities for Native

Americans because they offer the promise of employment and economic
growth.
7 See Robert Warrior, 'Your Skin Is the Map,' for a fascinating examination of
the erotic in Harjo's poetry.

Bibliography

Alarcón, Norma, Caren Kaplan, and Minoo Moallem. 1999. 'Introduction: Between Women and Nation.' *Between Woman and Nation: Nationalisms, Transnational Feminisms, and the State.* Ed. Caren Kaplan, Norma Alarcón, and Minoo Moallem. Durham, NC: Duke University Press. 1–16.

Allen, Chadwick. 2002. *Blood Narrative: Indigenous Identity in American Indian and Maori Literary and Activist Texts.* Durham, NC: Duke University Press.

Anderson, Benedict. 1991. *Imagined Communities: Reflections on the Rise and Spread of Nationalism.* London: Verso.

Anderson, Eric Gary. 2003. 'Situating American Indian Poetry: Place, Community, and the Question of Genre.' *Speak to Me Words: Essays on Contemporary American Indian Poetry.* Ed. Dean Rader and Janice Gould. Tucson: University of Arizona Press. 34–55.

Anderson, Kim. 1997. 'Reclaiming Native Space in Literature / Breaking New Ground: An Interview with Jeannette Armstrong.' *West Coast Line* 31.2: 49–65.

– 2000. *A Recognition of Being: Reconstructing Native Womanhood.* Toronto: Second Story Press.

Andrews, Jennifer. 2000. 'In the Belly of a Laughing God: Reading Humor and Irony in the Poetry of Joy Harjo.' *American Indian Quarterly* 24.2: 200–18.

– 2002a. 'Interview with Kimberly Blaeser.' Unpublished tape transcription. 24 pages.

– 2002b. 'A Conversation with Diane Glancy.' *American Indian Quarterly* 26.4: 645–58.

– 2004a. 'Interview with Louise Halfe.' Unpublished tape transcription. 15 pages.

– 2004b. '"Among the Word Animals:" A Conversation with Marilyn Dumont.' *Studies in Canadian Literature* 29.1: 146–60.

– 2007a. 'Ghost Spaces, Living Histories: Memory and Photography in Contemporary Native North American Women's Poetry.' *Nation in Imagination: Essays on Nationalism, Sub-Nationalisms and Narration.* Ed. C. Vijayasree, Meenakshi Mukherjee, Harish Trivedi, and T. Vijay Kumar. Hyderabad: Orient Longmans. 192–9.

– 2007b. 'Living History: A Conversation with Kimberly Blaeser.' *SAIL* 19.2: 1–21.

Andrews, Jennifer, Arnold E. Davidson, and Priscilla L. Walton. 2003. *Border Crossings: Thomas King's Cultural Inversions.* Toronto: University of Toronto Press.

Apte, Mahadev. 1985. *Humor and Laughter: An Anthropological Approach.* Ithaca, NY: Cornell University Press.

Armstrong, Jeannette C. 1990. 'Words.' *Telling It: Women and Language across Cultures.* Ed. Telling It Book Collective. Vancouver: Press Gang. 23–9.

– 1991. *Breath Tracks.* Stratford, ON: Williams-Wallace / Theytus,

– 1992. 'Trickster Time.' *Voices: Being Native in Canada.* Ed. Linda Jaine and Drew Hayden Taylor. Saskatoon: University of Saskatchewan Press. 1–5.

– 1998. 'Land Speaking.' *Speaking for the Generations: Native Writers on Writing.* Ed. Simon Ortiz. Tucson: University of Arizona Press. 175–94.

– 2005. 'Aboriginal Literatures: A Distinctive Genre within Canadian Literature.' *Hidden in Plain Sight: Contributions of Aboriginal People to Canadian Identity and Culture.* Ed. David R. Newhouse, Cora J. Voyageur, and Dan Bevon. Toronto: University of Toronto Press. 180–6.

– 2007. 'Literature of the Land: An Ethos for These Times.' Keynote Address. The Association for Commonwealth Literature and Language Studies. University of British Columbia, Vancouver. 18 August.

Armstrong, Jeannette C., and Douglas Cardinal. 1991. *The Native Creative Process: A Collaborative Discourse between Douglas Cardinal and Jeannette Armstrong with Photographs by Greg Young-Ing.* Penticton, BC: Theytus,

Armstrong, Jeannette C., Delphine Derickson, Lee Maracle, and Greg Young-Ing, eds. 1993/94. *We Get Our Living like Milk from the Land.* Penticton, BC: Okanagan Rights Committee and Okanagan Indian Education Resource Society.

Armstrong, Jeannette C., and Lally Grauer, eds. 2001. *Native Poetry in Canada: A Contemporary Anthology.* Peterborough, ON: Broadview.

Ashcroft, Bill. 2001. *Post-colonial Transformation.* London: Routledge.

Aull, Bill, James McGowan, Bruce Morgan, Fay Rouseff-Baker, and Cai Fitzgerald. 1996. 'The Spectrum of Other Languages.' *Joy Harjo: The Spiral of Memory: Interviews.* Ed. Laura Coltelli. Ann Arbor: University of Michigan Press. 99–110.

Babcock, Barbara. 1984. 'Arrange Me into Disorder: Fragments and Reflections on Ritual Clowning.' *Rite, Drama, Festival, Spectacle*. Ed. John J. MacAloon. Philadelphia: ISHI. 102–28.

Baker, Marie Annharte. 1990. *Being on the Moon*. Winlaw, BC: Polestar.

– 1993. 'Borrowing Enemy Language: A First Nation Woman Use of English.' *West Coast Line* 27.1: 59–66.

– 1994a. 'Medicine Lines: The Doctoring of Story and Self.' *Canadian Woman Studies* 14.2: 114–18.

– 1994b. *Coyote Columbus Cafe*. Winnipeg: Moonprint Press.

– 2003. *Exercises in Lip Pointing*. Vancouver: New Star.

Baker, Marie Annharte, and Lally Grauer. 2006. '"A Weasel Pops In and Out of Old Tunes": Marie Annharte Baker as Scavenger Poet.' *Studies in Canadian Literature* 31.1: 116–27.

Basso, Keith H. 1979. *Portraits of 'The Whiteman': Linguistic Play and Cultural Symbols among the Western Apache*. Cambridge: Cambridge University Press.

Bauman, Richard. 1977. *Verbal Art as Performance*. Prospect Heights, IL: Waveland.

– 1990. *Story, Performance, Event: Contextual Studies of Oral Narrative*. Bloomington: Indiana University Press.

Beeler, Karin. 1996. 'Image, Music, Text: An Interview with Jeannette Armstrong.' *Studies in Canadian Literature* 21.2: 142–54.

Bennett, Tony. 1999. 'The Exhibitionary Complex.' *Representing the Nation: A Reader: Histories, Heritage, and Museums*. London: Routledge. 332–62.

Bergland, Renée L. 2000. *The National Uncanny: Indian Ghosts and American Subjects*. Hanover: University Press of New England.

Berre, Maxens. 2009. 'Steel Pans: A Brief History.' *Latin American Folk Institute*. http://www.lafi.org/magazine/articles/steel.html (accessed 14 January).

Berton, Pierre. 1958. *Klondike*. Toronto: McClelland & Stewart.

Bhabha, Homi. 2004. *The Location of Culture*. London: Routledge.

Bird, Gloria, and Joy Harjo. 1997. 'Introduction.' *Reinventing the Enemy's Language: Contemporary Native Women's Writing of North America*. Ed. Joy Harjo and Gloria Bird. New York: W.W. Norton. 19–31.

Blaeser, Kimberly M. 1992. 'The New "Frontier" of Native American Literature: Dis-Arming History with Tribal Humor.' *Genre* 25: 351–64.

– 1993. 'Native Literature: Seeking a Critical Center.' *Listening to the Words of Our People: First Nations Analysis of Literature*. Ed. Jeannette Armstrong. Penticton, BC: Theytus. 51–61.

– 1994a. 'Pagans Rewriting the Bible: Heterodoxy and the Representation of Spirituality in Native American Literature.' *ARIEL* 25.1: 12–31.

– 1994b. *Trailing You: Poems*. Greenfield, NY: Greenfield Review Press.

– 1996. *Gerald Vizenor: Writing in the Oral Tradition.* Norman: University of
   Oklahoma Press.
– 2001. 'The Voices We Carry.' Working paper, University of Wisconsin,
   Milwaukee, 2001. Later published in *After Confession: Poetry as Autobiography.*
   Ed. Kate Sontag and David Graham. Saint Paul, MN: Greywolf Press. 269–80.
– 2002. *Absentee Indians & Other Poems.* East Lansing: Michigan State University
   Press.
– 2006. 'Canons and Canonization: American Indian Poetries through Au-
   tonomy, Colonization, Nationalism, and Decolonization.' *The Columbia Guide
   to American Indian Literatures of the United States since 1945.* Ed. Eric Cheyfitz.
   New York: Columbia University Press. 183–287.
– 2007. *Apprenticed to Justice.* Cambridge: Salt.
Board, Christopher. 1967. 'Maps as Models.' *Models in Geography.* Ed. Richard J.
   Chorley and Peter Haggett. London: Metheun. 671–725.
Bondi, Liz. 1993. 'Locating Identity Politics.' *Place and the Politics of Identity.* Ed.
   Michael Keith and Steve Pile. London: Routledge. 84–101.
Brant, Beth. 1994. *Writing as Witness: Essay and Talk.* Toronto: Women's Press.
Bruchac, Joseph. 1987. *Survival This Way: Interviews with American Indian Poets.*
   Tucson: University of Arizona Press.
Butling, Pauline, and Susan Rudy. 2005. *Poets Talk.* Edmonton: University of
   Alberta Press.
Cagle, Amanda. 2006. '"Pushing from Their Hearts a New Song": The (Re)con-
   struction of the Feminine in American Indian Women's Poetry.' PhD diss.,
   University of Connecticut.
Carabi, Angels. 1996. 'A Laughter of Absolute Sanity.' *Joy Harjo: The Spiral of
   Memory: Interviews.* Ed. Laura Coltelli. Ann Arbor: University of Michigan
   Press. 133–42.
Carstens, Peter. 1991. *The Queen's People: A Study of Hegemony, Coercion, and Ac-
   commodation among the Okanagan of Canada.* Toronto: University of Toronto
   Press.
Chamberlain, J. Edward. 2004. *If This Is Your Land, Where Are Your Stories? Finding
   Common Ground.* Toronto: Vintage.
Chatterjee, Partha. 1993. *The Nation and Its Fragments.* Princeton: Princeton Uni-
   versity Press.
Churchill, Ward. 1997. *A Little Matter of Genocide: Holocaust and Denial in the
   Americas 1492 to the Present.* San Francisco: City Light Books.
– 1999. *Struggle for the Land: Native North American Resistance to Genocide, Ecocide
   and Colonization.* Winnipeg: Arbeiter Ring.
Clark, Claudia. 1997. *Radium Girls: Women and Industrial Health Reform, 1910–
   1935.* Chapel Hill: University of North Carolina Press.

Clifford, James. 1988. *The Predicament of Culture*. Boston: Harvard University Press.

Coltelli, Laura. 1990. *Winged Words: American Indian Writers Speak*. Lincoln: University of Nebraska Press.

– 1996a. 'Introduction: The Transforming Power of Joy Harjo's Poetry.' *Joy Harjo: The Spiral of Memory: Interviews*. Ed. Laura Coltelli. Ann Arbor: University of Michigan Press. 1–13.

– 1996b. 'The Circular Dream.' *Joy Harjo: The Spiral of Memory: Interviews*. Ed. Laura Coltelli. Ann Arbor: University of Michigan Press. 60–74.

Cook, Méira. 2000. 'Bone Memory: Transcribing Voice in Louise Bernice Halfe's *Blue Marrow*.' *Canadian Literature* 166: 85–110.

Cornell, Drucilla. 1993. *Transformations: Recollective Imagination and Sexual Difference*. New York: Routledge.

Cuthand, Beth. 1992. *Voices in the Waterfall*. New edn. Penticton, BC: Theytus.

David, Gabrielle. 1998. 'Joy Harjo / The Music of Her Poetry.' *Phati'tude Literary Magazine*. http://members.aol.com/phatlitmag/harjo2.html (accessed 5 December; site now discontinued).

de Certeau, Michel. 1986. *Heterologies: Discourse on the Other*. Trans. Brian Massumi. Minneapolis: University of Minnesota Press.

DeHaan, Cara. 2009. '"Exorcising a Lot of Shame": Transformation and Affective Experience in Marilyn Dumont's *green girl dreams Mountains*.' *Studies in Canadian Literature* 34.1: 227–47.

Deloria, Philip J. 1998. *Playing Indian*. New Haven: Yale University Historical Publications.

Deloria, Vine, Jr. 1969. *Custer Died for Your Sins: An Indian Manifesto*. New York: Macmillan.

– 1985. 'Foreword.' *New and Old Voices of Wah'kon-tah*. Ed. Robert K. Dodge and Joseph B. McCullough. New York: International. ix–x.

– 1994. *God Is Red: A Native View of Religion*. Golden, CO: Fulcrum.

Deloria, Vine, Jr, and Clifford M. Lytle. 1984. *The Nations Within: The Past and Future of American Indian Sovereignty*. New York: Pantheon.

Dennis, Helen May. 2007. *Native American Literature: Towards a Spatialized Reading*. London: Routledge.

Derrida, Jacques. 1994. *Specters of Marx: The State of the Debt, the Work of Mourning, and the New International*. Trans. Peggy Kamuf. New York: Routledge.

Dickason, Olive Patricia. 1997. *Canada's First Nations: A History of Founding Peoples from Earliest Times*. 2nd edn. Toronto: Oxford.

Dockstator, Mark. 2005. 'Aboriginal Representations of History and the Royal Commission on Aboriginal Peoples.' *Walking on a Tightrope: Aboriginal People and Their Representations*. Ed. Ute Lischke and David T. McNab. Waterloo, ON: Wilfrid Laurier University Press. 99–115.

Donovan, Kathleen. 1998. *Feminist Readings of Native American Literature: Coming to Voice.* Tucson: University of Arizona Press.

Dumont, Marilyn. 1993. 'Popular Images of Nativeness.' *Looking at the Words of Our People: First Nations Analysis of Literature.* Ed. Jeannette Armstrong. Penticton, BC: Theytus. 45–9.

– 1996. *A Really Good Brown Girl.* London: Brick.

– 2001. *green girl dreams Mountains.* Lantzville: Oolichan.

– 2007. *That Tongued Belonging.* Neyaashiinigmiing: Kegedonce.

Dunn, Carolyn, and Carol Comfort, eds. 1999. *Through the Eyes of a Deer: An Anthology of Native American Women Writers.* San Francisco: Aunt Lute.

Edwards, Jonathan. 2005. *Gothic Canada: Reading the Spectre of a National Literature.* Edmonton: University of Alberta Press.

Eigenbrod, Renate. 2005. *Travelling Knowledges: Positioning the Im/Migrant Reader of Aboriginal Literatures in Canada.* Winnipeg: University of Manitoba Press.

Emberley, Julia V. 2007. *Defamiliarizing the Aboriginal: Cultural Practices and Decolonization in Canada.* Toronto: University of Toronto Press.

Episkenew, Jo-Ann. 2009. *Taking Back Our Spirits: Indigenous Literature, Public Policy, and Healing.* Winnipeg: University of Manitoba Press.

Evans, Jessica. 1999. 'Introduction to Part Three.' *Representing the Nation: A Reader: Histories, Heritage, and Museums.* London: Routledge. 235–9.

Fagan, Kristina. 2002. 'Laughing to Survive: Humour in Contemporary Canadian Native Literature.' PhD diss., University of Toronto.

– 2005. 'Teasing, Tolerating, Teaching: Laughter and Community in Native Literature.' *Me Funny.* Ed. Drew Hayden Taylor. Vancouver: Douglas & McIntyre. 23–46.

– 2010. 'Code-Switching Humour in Aboriginal Literature.' *Across Cultures / Across Borders: Canadian Aboriginal and Native American Literatures.* Ed. Paul De Pasquale, Renate Eigenbrod, and Emma LaRocque. Peterborough, ON: Broadview Press. 25–42.

Fagan, Kristina, and Sam McKegney. 2008. 'Circling the Question of Nationalism in Native Canadian Literature and Its Study.' *Review: Literature and Arts of the Americas* 41.1: 31–42.

Fast, Robin Riley. 1999. *The Heart as a Drum: Continuance and Resistance in American Indian Poetry.* Ann Arbor: University of Michigan Press.

Fee, Margery. 1987. 'Romantic Nationalism and the Image of Native People in Contemporary English-Canadian Literature.' *The Native in Literature: Canadian and Comparative Perspectives.* Ed. Thomas King, Helen Hoy, and Cheryl Calver. Toronto: ECW. 15–33.

Fischer, Michael J. 1986. 'Ethnicity and the Post-Modern Arts of Memory.' *Writing Culture: The Poetics and Politics of Ethnography.* Ed. James Clifford and George E. Marcus. Berkeley: University of California Press. 194–233.

Fixico, Donald L. 2000. *The Urban Indian Experience in America.* Albuquerque:
University of New Mexico Press.

Foley, John Miles. 2002. *How to Read an Oral Poem.* Urbana: University of Illinois
Press.

Foucault, Michel. 1980. *Power/Knowledge: Selected Interviews and Other Writings,
1972–1977.* Ed. Colin Gordon. New York: Pantheon.

Francesconi, Robert. 1986. 'Free Jazz and Black Nationalism: A Rhetoric of
Musical Style.' *Critical Studies in Mass Communications* 31.1: 36–49.

Francis, Daniel. 1992. *The Imaginary Indian: The Image of the Indian in Canadian
Culture.* Vancouver: Arsenal.

– 1997. *National Dreams: Myth, Memory, and Canadian History.* Vancouver: Arsenal.

Freud, Sigmund. 1905 [1960]. *Jokes and Their Relation to the Unconscious.* Vol. 8
of *The Standard Edition of the Complete Psychological Works of Sigmund Freud.*
Trans. James Strachey. London: Hogarth.

– 1927 [1960]. 'Humour.' *The Future of an Illusion, Civilization and Its Discontents
and Other Works.* Vol. 21 of *The Standard Edition of the Complete Psychological
Works of Sigmund Freud.* Trans. James Strachey. London. Hogarth. 159–66.

Gingell, Susan. 1998. 'When X Equals Zero: The Politics of Voice in First
Peoples Poetry by *Women.' English Studies in Canada* 24.4: 447–66.

Giuliani, John B. 2001. 'John Giuliani.' John B. Giuliani Gallery. http://
udayton.edu/mary/gallery/johngallcry.html (accessed 15 December;
site now discontinued).

Glancy, Diane. 1992. *Claiming Breath.* Lincoln: University of Nebraska Press.

– 1997. *The West Pole.* Minneapolis: University of Minnesota Press.

– 1998 'A Fieldbook of Textual Migrations.' *Chain* 5: 79–84.

– 1999a. 'Give Me Land Lots of Land.' *Modern Fiction Studies* 45.1: 114–19.

– 1999b. *(Ado)ration.* Tucson: Chax.

– 1999c. *The Closets of Heaven.* Tucson: Chax.

– 2000. *The Relief of America.* Chicago: Tia Chucha.

– 2004. *Primer of the Obsolete.* Amherst: University of Massachusetts Press.

– 2005a. *In-Between Places.* Tucson: University of Arizona Press.

– 2005b. *Rooms: New and Selected Poems.* Cambridge: Salt.

Glenn, Cheryl. 2004. *Unspoken: A Rhetoric of Silence.* Carbondale: Southern
Illinois University Press.

Goldie, Terry. 1989. *Fear and Temptation: The Image of the Indigene in Canadian,
Australian, and New Zealand Literatures.* Kingston, ON: McGill-Queen's University Press.

Goodleaf, Donna. 1995. *Entering the War Zone: A Mohawk Perspective on Resisting
Invasions.* Penticton, BC: Theytus.

Gould, Janice. 2000. 'An Interview with Joy Harjo.' *Western American Literature*
35.2: 131–42.

Grant, Agnes. 1985. 'Traditional Native Poetry.' *Canadian Journal of Native Studies* 5.1: 75–91.

Gray, Lynn. 1985. 'The Power of Words: An Interview with Poet/Artist/Teacher Wendy Rose.' *Akwesasne Notes* 17: 14–15.

Green, Joyce, ed. 2007. *Making Space for Indigenous Feminism.* Winnipeg/London: Fernwood / Zed.

Groening, Laura. 2004. *Listening to Old Woman Speak: Natives and alterNatives in Canadian Literature.* Montreal: McGill-Queen's University Press,

Gross, Harvey, and Robert McDowell. 1996. *Sound and Form in Modern Poetry.* Ann Arbor: University of Michigan Press.

Grosz, Elizabeth. 1992. 'Bodies-Cities.' *Sexuality and Space.* Ed. Beatriz Colomina. New York: Princeton Architectural Press. 241–53.

Gruber, Eva. 2008. *Humor in Contemporary Native North American Literature: Reimaging Nativeness.* Rochester: Camden House.

Gunn Allen, Paula. 1986. 'Answering the Deer: Genocide and Continuance in the Poetry of American Indian Women.' *The Sacred Hoop: Recovering the Feminine in American Indian Traditions.* Boston: Beacon. 155–64.

– 1998. *Off the Reservation: Reflections on Boundary Busting, Border Crossing, Loose Canons.* Boston: Beacon.

Halfe, Louise. 1994. *Bear Bones & Feathers.* Regina: Coteau.

– 1998. *Blue Marrow.* 1st edn. Toronto: McClelland & Stewart.

– 2004. *Blue Marrow.* Rev. edn. Regina: Coteau.

– 2006. 'Keynote Address: The Rolling Head's "Grave" Yard.' *Studies in Canadian Literature* 31.1: 65–74.

– 2007. *The Crooked Good.* Regina: Coteau,

Halfe, Louise, and Linda Jaine. 1989. 'Traditional Cree Philosophy: Death, Bereavement, and Healing.' *Saskatchewan Indian* (March): 11.

Harjo, Joy. 1983. *She Had Some Horses.* New York: Thunder Mouth's Press.

– 1990. *In Mad Love and War.* Hanover: Wesleyan University Press.

– 1994. *The Woman Who Fell from the Sky.* New York: W.W. Norton.

– 1999. 'Finding the Groove.' *Sleeping with One Eye Open: Women Writers and the Art of Survival.* Ed. Marilyn Kallet and Judith Ortiz Cofer. Athens: University of Georgia Press. 151–2.

– 2000a. *A Map to the Next World: Poems and Tales.* New York: W.W. Norton.

– 2000b. 'Oklahoma: The Prairie of Words.' *Western American Literature* 35.2: 125–8.

– 2002. *How We Became Human: New and Selected Poems: 1975–2001.* New York: W.W. Norton.

Harjo, Joy, and Gloria Bird, eds. 1997. *Reinventing the Enemy's Language: Contemporary Native Women's Writings of North America.* New York: W.W. Norton.

Harjo, Joy, and Stephen Strom. 1989. *Secrets from the Center of the World.* Tucson:
    University of Arizona Press.
Holland, Sharon P. 2000. *Raising the Dead: Readings of Death and (Black) Subjec-*
    tivity. Durham, NC: Duke University Press.
hooks, bell. 1990. *Yearning: Race, Gender, and Cultural Politics.* Boston: South End.
Hoy, Helen. 2001. *How Should I Read These? Native Women Writers in Canada.*
    Toronto: University of Toronto Press.
Hudson, Charles. 1976. *The Southeastern Indians.* Knoxville: University of
    Tennessee Press.
Hughes, Sheila Hassell. 2001. 'Falls of Desire / Leaps of Faith: Religious Syncre-
    tism in Louise Erdrich's and Joy Harjo's "Mixed-Blood" Poetry.' *Religion and*
    Literature 33.2: 59–83.
Huhndorf, Shari M. 2001. *Going Native: Indians in the American Cultural Imagina-*
    tion. Ithaca, NY: Cornell University Press.
– 2009. *Mapping the Americas: The Transnational Politics of Contemporary Native*
    Culture. Ithaca, NY: Cornell University Press. Hunter, Carol. 1983. 'A MELUS
    Interview: Wendy Rose.' *MELUS* 10.3: 67–87.
Hutcheon, Linda. 1994. *Irony's Edge: The Theory and Politics of Irony.* London:
    Routledge.
Huyssen, Andreas. 2003. *Present Pasts: Urban Palimpsests and the Politics of Memory.*
    Stanford: Stanford University Press.
Hynes, William J., and Thomas J. Steele, S.J. 1993. 'Saint Peter: Apostle Trans-
    formed into Trickster.' *Mythical Trickster Figures: Contours, Contexts, and Criti-*
    cisms. Tuscaloosa: University of Alabama Press. 159–73.
j. poet. 2007. 'J. Poet.' Rock's Backpages. http://www.rocksbackpages.com/
    writer.html?WriterID=poet (accessed 10 December).
Justice, Daniel Heath. 2006. *Our Fire Survives the Storm: A Cherokee Literary History.*
    Minneapolis: University of Minnesota Press.
Kallet, Marilyn. 1996. 'In Love and War and Music.' *Joy Harjo: The Spiral of*
    Memory: Interviews. Ed. Laura Coltelli. Ann Arbor: University of Michigan
    Press. 111–23.
Kaplan, Caren, Norma Alarcón, and Minoo Moallem. 1999. 'Introduction:
    Between Woman and Nation.' *Between Woman and Nation: Nationalisms, Trans-*
    national Feminisms, and the State. Ed. Caren Kaplan, Norma Alarcón, and
    Minoo Moallem. Durham: Duke University Press. 1–16.
Katakis, Michael, ed. 1998. *Excavating Voices: Listening to Photographs of Native*
    Americans. Philadelphia: University of Pennsylvania Press.
Keith, Michael, and Steve Pile. 1993. 'Conclusion: Towards New Radical
    Geographies.' *Place and the Politics of Identity.* Ed. Michael Keith and Steve
    Pile. London: Routledge. 220–6.

292 Bibliography

Kelly, Don. 2005. 'And Now, Ladies and Gentleman.' *Me Funny*. Ed. Drew Hayden Taylor. Vancouver: Douglas & McIntyre. 51–65.
Kelly, Jennifer. 1991. 'The Landscape of Grandmother: A Reading of Subjectivit(y)ies in Contemporary North American Native Women's Writing in English.' *World Literature Written in English* 31.2: 112–28.
Kertzer, Jonathan. 1998. *Worrying the Nation: Imagining a National Literature in English Canada*. Toronto: University of Toronto Press.
King, Thomas. 1990a. 'Introduction.' *All My Relations*. Ed. Thomas King. Toronto: McClelland & Stewart. ix–xvi.
– 1990b. 'Godzilla vs. Post-Colonial.' *World Literature Written in English* 30.2: 10–16.
– 1992. *A Coyote Columbus Story*. Toronto: Groundwood / Douglas & McIntyre.
– 1993. 'Borders.' *One Good Story, That One*. Toronto: HarperCollins. 133–47.
– 1995. 'Shooting the Lone Ranger.' *Hungry Mind Review* 34: 36–7.
– 2003. *The Truth about Stories: A Native Narrative*. Toronto: House of Anansi Press.
– 2005. 'Performing Native Humour: The Dead Dog Café Comedy Hour.' *Me Funny*. Ed. Drew Hayden Taylor. Vancouver: Douglas & McIntyre. 169–83.
Koestler, Arthur. 1964. *The Art of Creation*. London: Hutchinson.
Kolosov, Jacqueline. 2003. 'Poetries of Transformation: Joy Harjo and Li-Young Lee.' *Studies in American Indian Literatures* 15.2: 39–57.
LaDuke, Winona. 1999. *All Our Relations: Native Struggles for Land and Life*. Cambridge, MA: South End.
Lapatin, Kenneth. 2002. *Mysteries of the Snake Goddess*. Cambridge, MA: Da Capo Press.
LaRocque, Emma. 1984. 'Three Conventional Approaches to Native People in Society and Literature.' Mary Donaldson Memorial Lecture 1984. Saskatchewan Library Association, Saskatoon.
– 1990. '*Preface* or Here Are Our Voices – Who Will Hear?' *Writing the Circle: An Anthology: Native Women of Western Canada*. Ed. Jeanne Perreault and Sylvia Vance. Edmonton: NeWest. xv–xxx.
Leuthold, Steven. 1998. *Indigenous Aesthetics: Native Art, Media, and Identity*. Austin: University of Texas Press.
Lincoln, Kenneth. 1993. *Indi'n Humor: Bicultural Play in Native America*. New York: Oxford University Press.
Lippard, Lucy. 1992. 'Introduction.' *Partial Recall: With Essays on Photographs of North American Indians*. Ed. Lucy Lippard. New York: The New Press. 13–46.
– 1999. 'Independent Identities.' *Native American Art in the Twentieth Century*. London: Routledge. 134–48.
Lorde, Audre. 1978. *The Black Unicorn*. New York: W.W. Norton.

MacKay, James, ed. 2010. *The Salt Companion to Diane Glancy.* Cambridge: Salt Publishing.

Mankiller, Wilma, and Michael Wallis. 1993. *Mankiller: A Chief and Her People.* New York: St Martin's.

Maracle, Lee. 2000. 'Preface.' *My Home As I Remember.* Ed. Lee Maracle and Sandra Laronde. Toronto: Natural Heritage. i.

Martin, Calvin, ed. 1987. *The American Indian and the Problem of History.* New York: Oxford University Press.

Martin, Joel W. 1991. *Sacred Revolt: The Muskogees' Struggle for A New World.* Boston: Beacon.

Massey, Doreen. 1994. *Space, Place, and Gender.* Minneapolis: University of Minnesota Press.

McClintock, Anne. 1995. *Imperial Leather: Race, Gender and Sexuality in the Colonial Contest.* New York: Routledge.

McDowell, Linda. 1999. *Gender, Identity and Place: Understanding Feminist Geographies.* Minneapolis: University of Minnesota Press.

McGlennen, Molly. 2006. 'It Is Evidence of Faith to Create: Spirituality and Contemporary Native American Women's Poetics.' PhD diss., University of California, Davis.

McKegney, Sam. 2007. *Magic Weapons: Aboriginal Writers Remaking Community after Residential School.* Winnipeg: University of Manitoba Press.

McLeod, Neil. 2010. 'Cree Poetic Discourse.' *Across Cultures / Across Borders: Canadian Aboriginal and Native American Literatures.* Ed. Paul DePasquale, Renate Eigenbrod, and Emma LaRocque. Peterborough, ON: Broadview Press. 109–21.

McMaster, Gerald. 1995. 'Border Zones: The "Injun-uity" of Aesthetic Tricks.' *Cultural Studies* 9,1: 74–90.

The Metis Nation. Ottawa: Metis National Council, 1984. 1–6.

Meyer, Melissa L. 1994. *The White Earth Tragedy: Ethnicity and Dispossession at a Minnesota Anishinaabe Reservation, 1889–1920.* Lincoln: University of Nebraska Press.

Mihesuah, Devon A. 1996. *American Indians: Stereotypes and Realities.* Atlanta and Regina: Clarity.

Miller, Carol. 2001. 'Telling the Indian Urban: Representations in American Indian Fiction.' *American Indians and the Urban Experience.* Ed. Susan Lobo and Kurt Peters. Walnut Creek, CA: Altamira. 29–45.

Minh-ha, Trinh T. 1989. *Women, Native, Other: Writing Postcoloniality and Feminism.* Bloomington: Indiana University Press.

Mohanty, Chandra Talpade. 1991. 'Cartographies of Struggle: Third World Women and the Politics of Feminism.' *Third World Women and the Politics of*

Feminism. Ed. Chandra Mohanty, Ann Russo, and Lourdes Torres. Bloomington: Indiana University Press. 1–47.

Momaday, N. Scott. 1968. *House Made of Dawn*. New York: Harper & Row.

Moore, Marianne. 1951. *Collected Poems*. New York: Macmillan.

Morton, Stephen. 1999. 'First Nations Women's Writing and Anti-Racist Work
in Institutional Locations: A Feminist Reading of Lee Maracle and Jeannette
Armstrong.' *Thamyris* 6.1: 3–33.

Nabokov, Peter. 1981. *Indian Running*. Santa Barbara: Capra Press.

Online Cree Dictionary. 2009. 'kwêskî.' http://www.creedictionary.com (word)
(accessed 20 January).

Ortiz, Simon. 2003. 'Song/Poetry and Language—Expression and Perception.'
Speak to Me Words: Essays on Contemporary American Indian Poetry. Ed. Dean
Rader and Janice Gould. Tucson: University of Arizona Press. 235–46.

Owens, Louis. 1992. *Other Destinies: Understanding the American Indian Novel*.
Norman: University of Oklahoma Press.

Perreault, Jeanne. 1999. 'Memory Alive: An Inquiry into the Uses of Memory in
Marilyn Dumont, Jeannette Armstrong, Louise Halfe, and Joy Harjo.' *Native
North America: Critical and Cultural Perspectives*. Ed. Renée Hulan. Toronto:
ECW. 251–70.

Perreault, Jeanne, and Sylvia Vance, eds. 1990. *Writing the Circle: An Anthology:
Native Women of Western Canada*. Edmonton: NeWest.

Peterson, Jacqueline, and Jennifer S.H. Brown, eds. 1984. *The New Peoples: Being
and Becoming Métis in North America*. Winnipeg: University of Manitoba Press.

Pettipas, Katherine. 1994. *Severing the Ties That Bind: Government Repression of
Indigenous Religious Ceremonies on the Prairies*. Winnipeg: University of Manitoba Press.

Phelan, Peggy. 1993. *Unmarked: The Politics of Performance*. New York: Routledge.

Powell, Chris, and George E.C. Paton, eds. 1988. *Humour in Society: Resistance
and Control*. Basingstoke: Palgrave.

Pulitano, Elvira. 2003. *Toward a Native American Critical Theory*. Lincoln: University of Nebraska Press.

Purdie, Susan. 1993. *Comedy: The Mastery of Discourse*. Toronto: University of
Toronto Press.

Rader, Dean. 2003. 'The Epic Lyric: Genre and Contemporary American Indian
Poetry.' *Speak to Me Words: Essays on Contemporary American Indian Poetry*. Ed.
Dean Rader and Janice Gould. Tucson: University of Arizona Press. 123–42.

Rader, Dean, and Janice Gould, eds. 2003. *Speak to Me Words: Essays on Contemporary American Indian Poetry*. Tucson: University of Arizona Press.

Reder, Deanna, and Linda M. Morra, eds. 2010. *Troubling Tricksters: Revisioning
Critical Conversations*. Waterloo: Wilfrid Laurier University Press.

Rimstead, Roxanne. 2003. 'Introduction: Double Take: Uses of Cultural
  Memory.' *Essays on Canadian Writing* 80: 1–14.
Rochon, Glenn. 2002. 'Glancy's "Well You Push Your Mind along the Road."'
  Explicator 61.1: 59.
Rose, Wendy. 1976. *Long Division: A Tribal History.* New York: Strawberry.
– 1977. *Academic Squaw: Reports to the World From the Ivory Tower.* Marvin, SD:
  Blue Cloud.
– 1985. *The Halfbreed Chronicles and Other Poems.* Los Angeles: West End.
– 1992. 'The Great Pretenders: Further Reflections on Whiteshamanism.'
  The State of Native America: Genocide, Colonization and Resistance. Ed. Annette
  Jaimes. Boston: South End. 402–21.
– 1994a. *Now Poof She Is Gone.* Ithaca, NY: Firebrand.
– 1994b. *Bone Dance: New and Selected Poems, 1965–1993.* Tucson: University of
  Arizona Press.
– 2002. *Itch like Crazy.* Tucson: University of Arizona Press.
Ross, Val. 1992. 'Book Learning.' *Globe and Mail,* 18 April. C14.
Ruwe, Donelle R. 1996. 'Weaving Stories for Food.' *Joy Harjo: The Spiral of
  Memory. Interviews.* Ed. Laura Coltelli. Ann Arbor: University of Michigan
  Press. 124–32.
Ryan, Allan J. 1999. *The Trickster Shift: Humour and Irony in Contemporary Native
  Art.* Vancouver and Toronto: University of British Columbia Press.
Said, Edward. 1993. *Culture and Imperialism.* New York: Vintage.
Scarry, John. 1992. 'Representing Real Worlds: The Evolving Poetry of Joy
  Harjo.' *World Literature Today* 66.2: 286–91.
Scott, F.R. 1981. *The Collected Poems of F.R. Scott.* Toronto: McClelland & Stewart.
Siemerling, Winfried. 2005. *The New North American Studies: Culture, Writing, and
  the Politics of Recognition.* New York: Routledge.
Siggins, Maggie. 2005. *Bitter Embrace: White Society's Assault on the Woodland Cree.*
  Toronto: McClelland and Stewart.
Silko, Leslie Marmon. 1981. *Storyteller.* New York: Arcade.
– 1996. *Yellow Woman and a Beauty of the Spirit: Essays on Native American Life
  Today.* New York: Simon & Schuster.
Simon, Roger. 2005. *The Touch of the Past: Remembrance, Learning, and Ethics.*
  New York: Palgrave Macmillan.
Sladen, Douglas. 1895. *On the Cars and Off.* London: Ward, Lock and Bowden.
Smith, Jonathan. 1993. 'The Lie That Blinds: Destabilizing the Text of Land-
  scape.' *Place/Culture/Representation.* Ed. James Duncan and David Ley. Lon-
  don: Routledge. 78–92.
Sontag, Susan. 1989. *On Photography.* New York: Anchor.
St Denis, Verna. 2007. 'Feminism Is for Everybody: Aboriginal Women, Femi-

nism and Diversity.' *Making Space for Indigenous Feminisms.* Ed. Joyce Green.
Winnipeg and London: Fernwood/Zed. 33–52.

Stever, Sharyn. 1996. 'Landscape and the Place Inside.' *Joy Harjo: The Spiral of
Memory: Interviews.* Ed. Laura Coltelli. Ann Arbor: University of Michigan
Press. 75–87.

Stewart-Harawira, Makere. 2007. 'Practicing Indigenous Feminism: Resistance
to Imperialism.' *Making Space for Indigenous Feminisms.* Ed. Joyce Green. Winnipeg and London: Fernwood/Zed. 124–39.

Strong-Boag, Veronica, and Carol Gerson. 2000. *Paddling Her Own Canoe: The
Times and Texts of E. Pauline Johnson (Tekahionwake).* Toronto: University of
Toronto Press.

Summerhill, Stephen J., and John Alexander Williams. 2000. *Sinking Columbus:
Contested History, Cultural Politics, and Mythmaking during the Quincentenary.*
Gainesville: University of Florida Press.

Taylor, Drew Hayden. 2000. *alterNatives.* Burnaby: Talonbooks.

– ed. 2005. *Me Funny.* Vancouver: Douglas & McIntyre.

Thornton, Russell. 1990. *The Cherokees: A Population History.* Lincoln: University
of Nebraska Press.

Tuan, Yi-Fu. 1977. *Space and Place: The Perspective of Experience.* Minneapolis:
University of Minnesota Press.

Tuhiwai Smith, Linda. 1999. *Decolonizing Methodologies: Research and Indigenous
Peoples.* London: Otego.

Turner, Nancy J. 2005. *The Earth's Blanket: Traditional Teachings for Sustainable
Living.* Vancouver and Toronto: Douglas & McIntyre.

Valaskakis, Gail Guthrie. 2005. *Indian Country: Essays on Contemporary Native
Culture.* Waterloo, ON: Wilfrid Laurier University Press.

Vannote, Vance. 1999. *Women of White Earth.* Minneapolis: University of Minnesota Press.

Vizenor, Gerald. 1987. 'Follow the Track Routes: An Interview with Gerald
Vizenor.' By Joseph Bruchac. *Survival This Way: Interviews with American
Indian Poets.* Ed. Joseph Bruchac. Tucson: University of Arizona Press. 287–
310.

– 1990. *Darkness in Saint Louis Bearheart.* Minneapolis: University of Minnesota
Press.

– 1994. *Manifest Manners: Narratives on Postindian Survivance.* Lincoln: University of Nebraska Press.

– 2007. 'Edward Curtis: Pictorialist and Ethnographic Adventurist.' http://
memory.loc.gov/ ammem/awards98/ienhtml/essay3.html (accessed
1 August; site now discontinued).

Vizenor, Gerald, and A. Robert Lee. 1999. *Postindian Conversations*. Lincoln: University of Nebraska Press.

Walker, Nancy A. 1988. *A Very Serious Thing: Women's Humor and American Culture*. Minneapolis: University of Minnesota Press.

– 1990. *Feminist Alternatives: Irony and Fantasy in the Contemporary Novel by Women*. Jacksonville: University of Mississippi Press.

Warrior, Robert. 2008. 'Your Skin Is the Map: The Theoretical Challenge of Joy Harjo's Erotic Poetics.' *Reasoning Together: The Native Critics Collective*. Ed. Craig S. Womack, Daniel Heath Justice, and Christopher B. Teuton. Norman: University of Oklahoma Press. 340–52.

Weaver, Jace. 1996. 'Introduction: Notes from a Miner's Canary.' *Defending Mother Earth: Native American Perspectives on Environmental Justice*. Ed. Jace Weaver. Maryknoll: Orbis. 1–28.

– 1997. *That the People Might Live: Native American Literatures and Native American Community*. New York: Oxford University Press.

Weaver, Jace, Craig S. Womack, and Robert Warrior. 2006. *American Indian Literary Nationalism*. Albuquerque: University of New Mexico Press.

White, Hayden. 1978. *Tropics of Discourse: Essays in Cultural Criticism*. Baltimore: Johns Hopkins University Press.

Wikipedia: The Free Encyclopedia. 2007. S.v. 'Don't Fence Me In.' http:// en.wikipedia.org/ wiki/Don't_Fence_Me_In_(song) (accessed 21 May).

Williams, Raymond. 1980. *Culture and Materialism: Selected Essays*. London: Verso.

Wilson, Alan. 2000. *Laughter: The Navajo Way*. Audio Forum.

Wilson, Norma C. 2001. *The Nature of Native American Poetry*. Albuquerque: University of New Mexico Press.

Womack, Craig S. 1999. *Red on Red: Native American Literary Separatism*. Minneapolis: University of Minnesota Press.

Young, David, Grant Ingram, and Lise Swartz. 1989. *Cry of the Eagle: Encounters with a Cree Healer*. Toronto: University of Toronto Press.

Yuval-Davis, Nira. 1997. *Gender and Nation*. London: Sage.

Yuval-Davis, Nira, and Floya Anthias, eds. 1989. *Woman-Nation-State*. Basingstoke: Palgrave Macmillan.

Zamora, Margarita. 1993. *Reading Columbus*. Berkeley: University of California Press.

Ziff, Larzer. 1991. *Writing in the New Nation: Prose, Print and Politics in the Early United States*. New Haven: Yale University Press.

Discography

Armstrong, Jeannette. 1992a. 'Threads of Old Memory.' *Till the Bars Break*.
    Cargo Records IMR-014 1S.
– 1992b. 'Threads of Old Memory Dub.' *Till the Bars Break*. Cargo Records
    IMR-014 1S.
Harjo, Joy. 2004. *Native Joy for Real*. Mekko C02990604.
– 2006. *She Had Some Horses*. Mekko MPK0452.
Harjo, Joy, and Poetic Justice. 1997. *Letter from the End of the Twentieth Century*.
    Silverwave Records SD91421685A 01.

Illustration Credits

Index

Stewart-Hawawira, Makere, 279n3
stories, 10, 17, 22, 25–6, 31, 37, 43,
    45–6, 48, 50, 69, 71, 77, 130–4, 138,
    140, 142, 150, 154–5, 171, 173, 175,
    181, 183, 202, 210, 212, 214, 222–3,
    225, 229, 239–40, 247, 254, 264
storying, 192, 204
Storyteller, 183
storytelling, 25, 69, 73, 101, 125, 138,
    157
strategic essentialism, 139, 167, 279n3
Strong-Boag, Veronica, 273n1
Summerhill, Stephen J., 279n4
sun-runners, 68–9
superiority, 18, 129
Supreme Court of Canada, 144
survival, 3–4, 8, 10, 12, 44, 46, 52, 56,
    67–8, 73, 93, 96, 100, 107, 110, 112,
    131, 149, 150, 171–2, 184, 192, 207,
    229–30, 232, 236, 256, 259–60, 263,
    266, 270, 272
survivance , 45, 111, 130, 279–80n7
Suspect Many, 103
Sweet, Denise, 37
syntax, 28, 171

*Taking Back Our Spirits: Indigenous
    Literature, Public Policy, and Healing*,
    275n2
'Talking Circle,' 68
Tapahanso, Luci, 37
Tasmania, 175–7
Tasmanian Museum, 176
Tasmanian tribe, 175
taxidermy, 175
Taylor, Drew Hayden, 8, 10, 16–17
teasing, 11, 20, 162
'Telling the Indian Urban: Represen-
    tations in American Indian Fiction,'
    281–2n6

'terminal creeds,' 45
textuality, 7, 19, 31–2, 48, 52, 80, 98–9,
    104, 108, 113–14, 121, 125, 183,
    198, 210, 217, 219, 225–6, 236, 245,
    247, 257, 260, 278n8
That the People Might Live, 220
That Tongued Belonging, 39
'Their Eyes Have Seen the Buffalo,'
    191
Thelma and Louise, 142–3
'There it is again, the circle, that god-
    damned circle, as if we thought,'
    244
'This poem is a letter to tell you that
    I have smelled the hatred you have
    tried to find me with; you would
    like to destroy me,' 91
This World, 258, 264–5
'Threads of Old Memory,' 9, 97,
    99–106, 154–5
'Threads of Old Memory Dub,' 102–3,
    106
Three Wise Men, 56
*Through the Eyes of the Deer: An Anthol-
    ogy of Native American Women Writers*,
    274n11
Till the Bars Break, 82, 97, 99, 102, 104
*Touch of the Past: Remembrance, Learn-
    ing, and Ethics, The*, 279n6
*Toward a Native American Critical The-
    ory*, 273n3
'Towards the Last Spike,' 171
tradition, 3, 5–6, 8, 10, 12, 17–19,
    21–2, 26, 30, 32–4, 40, 44–6, 49–50,
    53, 55–8, 66, 68, 72, 76–7, 81–3, 85,
    88–90, 94, 96–8, 101, 103–5, 107,
    113, 118–21, 124–6, 128–32, 135,
    138–41, 147–8, 154, 157, 159, 164,
    174, 177, 181, 183–4, 196–7, 204–5,
    209, 212–14, 220–1, 226, 233, 236,

248, 253–5, 257, 264–5, 267, 271, 274n10, 275n3

'Traditional Cree Philosophy,' 68, 213

'Traditional Native Poetry,' 274n10

Trail of Tears, 109, 144

Trailing You, 43, 123, 207–8, 212, 219, 237

transformation, 6, 20, 33, 38, 40–52, 55–9, 62, 64–6, 69, 73, 77, 79–80, 83–7, 91–122, 131, 253, 274n1, 277n1, 278n8; bodily, 49, 51, 64–5, 95; generic, 21, 35–6, 40, 78–80, 83–7, 91, 94, 98, 111, 114, 117–18, 120–2; personal, 48; psychological, 85; religious, 7, 21, 35–6, 40, 47, 49, 51–2, 55–7, 80, 122; spiritual, 38, 40, 42, 73, 77, 80, 93; textual, 48, 52, 59, 98, 121

'Transformation Band, The,' 53–5

'Transformations' (Gunn Allen), 46

'Transformations' (Harjo), 79, 84, 91–3, 95, 108

translation, 29, 66, 86–7, 115, 121, 212, 277n2

Travelling Knowledges: Positioning the Im/Migrant Reader of Aboriginal Literatures in Canada, 280n9

treaties, 33, 127, 129, 188, 263

Treaty of Guadalupe, 263

Tree of Knowledge of Good and Evil, 67

Tremblay, Gail, 37

tribal nationalism, 7

tribal nations, 129, 169, 181

tribal space, 242, 246

tribal status. *See* status

tribe, 6, 11, 15, 24–5, 33, 50, 52–3, 55, 68–9, 72, 81–2, 84–5, 93, 102, 105, 107, 118, 133, 137, 139, 144–5, 148–9, 160, 175, 184, 196, 223–6,

233, 238, 242, 251, 254, 263, 266, 276n16, 280n8, 280–1n3

trickster, 20, 45–6, 62, 130, 134, 137, 141, 149, 156–7, 161–3, 275n5

trickster discourse, 157

Trickster Shift: Humour and Irony in Contemporary Native Art, The, 20

Troubling Tricksters: Revisioning Critical Conversations, 275n5

'Truganinny,' 175–9

Truth about Stories, The, 131, 202

Tslei'wauthuth, 251

Tuan, Yi-Fu, 224

Tuhiwai Smith, Linda, 126, 128, 132, 134, 173

Turn-Around Woman, 65, 69, 73, 75

Turner, Nancy J., 227

'Twelve Steps to Ward Off Homesickness,' 233–4

UCLA, 24, 255, 277n2

Under World, 264

United Nations, 90

United Nations Working Group in Indigenous Populations, 169

United States of America, 3, 5–6, 15, 30, 35–7, 44, 53–4, 102, 124–5, 129–30, 133, 137, 140–2, 148, 181, 188, 203, 221–4, 232, 261, 263, 267, 274n11, 280n1, 281n5

University of California at Berkeley, 24

University of Iowa, 30

University of Massachusetts, 31

University of New Mexico, 90, 255

University of Regina, 26

University of Victoria, 89

University of Wisconsin at Milwaukee, 25

Unmarked: The Politics of Performance, 183